RESIDENTIAL FLATS

OF ALL CLASSES

ST JOHN'S PARK MANSIONS, TUFNELL PARK, LONDON.

(*Reproduced from a Drawing exhibited by the Author at the Royal Academy,* 1903.)

RESIDENTIAL FLATS

OF ALL CLASSES

INCLUDING ARTISANS' DWELLINGS

A PRACTICAL TREATISE ON THEIR
PLANNING AND ARRANGEMENT
TOGETHER WITH CHAPTERS ON THEIR
HISTORY, FINANCIAL MATTERS, ETC.
WITH NUMEROUS ILLUSTRATIONS

BY

SYDNEY PERKS

FELLOW OF THE ROYAL INSTITUTE OF BRITISH ARCHITECTS
PROFESSIONAL ASSOCIATE OF THE SURVEYORS' INSTITUTION
AUTHOR OF
"PARTY STRUCTURES, LONDON BUILDING ACT, 1894," "DILAPIDATIONS," &c.

WITH A LARGE NUMBER OF PLANS OF IMPORTANT
EXAMPLES BY LEADING ARCHITECTS IN ENGLAND,
THE CONTINENT, AND AMERICA; ALSO NUMEROUS
VIEWS FROM SPECIAL PHOTOGRAPHS

(JM)

CLASSIC EDITIONS

This edition digitally re-mastered and
published by JM Classic Editions © 2007
Original text © Sydney Perks 1905

ISBN 978-1-905217-76-2

TO

J. DOUGLASS MATHEWS, Esq., F.R.I.B.A., F.S.I., C.C.

MEMBER OF THE COUNCIL OF THE ROYAL INSTITUTE OF BRITISH
ARCHITECTS AND FOR SEVEN YEARS CHAIRMAN OF THE
PROFESSIONAL PRACTICE COMMITTEE OF THAT BODY

THIS BOOK IS RESPECTFULLY DEDICATED

PREFACE.

THE object of this book is to illustrate and describe all classes of Flats, from the poor man's tenement of one room to the most luxurious and expensive suite in London, Paris, or New York. Although several articles have appeared in journals, and papers have been read from time to time at various Architectural Societies, there is no book published in England upon this important subject.

Large numbers of blocks of Flats are being built every year, and there is a steady and constant demand for all classes of suites; it is therefore hoped that this volume may prove of value, not only to architects and builders, but also to those who are interested in the finance of the subject.

A large amount of work was involved in collecting the drawings from America and abroad, and much difficulty experienced in selecting those illustrated from several hundreds of plans placed at my disposal. In many cases the fundamental idea of the arrangement of the suites being similar, one plan only was chosen to show the system adopted by the architect. I wish to thank Mr W. J. Locke, the Secretary of the Royal Institute of British Architects, for his kind introduction to several eminent foreign members.

So far as I am aware, no history of "Flat" dwellings has hitherto been written, and my thanks are due to Mr George Washington Browne and Mr G. S. Aitken for their great assistance when I went to Edinburgh to examine the examples of these buildings erected there during the sixteenth and seventeenth centuries.

I have made a large number of the drawings for this book; and nearly all the photographs, both English and foreign, reproduced in its

PREFACE.

pages have been specially taken for it; indeed only a very few of the illustrations have been previously published.

I desire to thank Professor Max Freiherr von Ferstel, Dr P. J. H. Cuypers, Senhor L. C. Pedro d'Avila, Señor E. M. Repulles y Vargas, Professor Alois von Hauszmann, and the many other architects whose works are illustrated, and whose names are in all cases given on their plans; also Mr F. Treacher Terry for the use of some drawings from his large collection.

What literature there is upon the subject is scattered through many volumes of papers and journals, both English and foreign, and I am much indebted to Mr E. Wyndham Hulme, Librarian of the Patent Office, and to Mr Rudolf Dircks, Librarian of the Royal Institute of British Architects, for their kind assistance in my search for interesting matter.

SYDNEY PERKS.

Falcon Court, 32 Fleet Street, E.C.
April 1905.

CONTENTS.

CONTENTS.

LIST OF ARCHITECTS, SURVEYORS, &c., WHOSE BUILDINGS ARE ILLUSTRATED.

ENGLISH FLATS.

BALFOUR & TURNER. Figs. 154A, 155, 156, 157, 158.

CITY SURVEYOR, Birmingham. Fig. 67.

HIPPOLYTE J. BLANC, Edinburgh. Figs. 76, 77, 135.

THOS. H. BLASHILL, London County Council. Figs. 40, 41, 42, 43.

BOEHMER & GIBBS. Figs. 96, 97, 98, 117, 118, 119, 120, 143, 144. See also E. RUNTZ.

R. A. BRIGGS. Figs. 124A, 125, 126A, 127, 134, 134A.

DURWARD BROWN. Fig. 110.

JOHN D. CLARKE AND SEPTIMUS WARWICK. Figs. 129A, 130.

T. E. COLLCUTT AND STANLEY HAMP. Figs. 160, 160A, 161.

DAVIS & EMANUEL. Figs. 49, 50, 52.

T. E. EALES. Fig. 128.

BURGH ENGINEER, Edinburgh. Figs. 73, 74, 75, 78.

AMOS F. FAULKNER. Fig. 112.

ERNEST GEORGE & PETO. Figs. 92, 149A, 150.

ERNEST GEORGE & YEATES. Fig. 149.

E. T. HALL. Fig. 83.

ARTHUR HARRISON. Fig. 66.

HART & WATERHOUSE. Fig. 133.

HIPKISS & STEPHENS. Fig. 65.

PAUL HOFFMANN. Figs. 85, 88, 93A, 94, 99, 137, 138.

F. H. HOLFORD, Newcastle. Figs. 70, 71, 72.

J. A. J. KEYNES. Fig. 89.

H. S. & H. A. LEGGE. Fig. 90.

CITY SURVEYOR, Liverpool. Figs. 62, 63, 64.

J. DOUGLASS MATHEWS. Fig. 58A.

A. B. M'DONALD, City Surveyor, Glasgow. Figs. 79, 80.

T. DE COURCEY MEADE, City Surveyor, Manchester. Figs. 60, 61.

A. MOORE, Architect of the Waterlow Trust. Fig. 54.

REGINALD MORPHEW. Figs. 153, 153A.

E. W. MOUNTFORD. Fig. 112A.

H. M. NEWLYN. Fig. 57.

PALGRAVE & CO. Figs. 93, 122, 123, 124, 126.

PERKS, SYDNEY.

PERRY & REED. Fig. 95.

BERESFORD PITE. Figs. 56, 140, 140A, 140B, 147, 148.

ROWLAND PLUMBE & HARVEY. Fig. 51.

E. KEYNES PURCHASE. Figs. 121, 136, 154.

READ & MACDONALD. Figs. 100, 113, 113A.

JOHN W. RHODES. Figs. 141, 142, 146.

ARCHITECTS OF BUILDINGS ILLUSTRATED.

W. E. Riley, Chief Architect, London County Council. Figs. 44, 45, 46, 47.
E. R. Robson. Fig. 159.
E. Runtz, Boehmer & Gibbs. Figs. 114, 115.
Edwin Sadgrove. Fig. 84.
W. A. Scrymgour. Fig. 129.
Basil Slade. Figs. 86, 87.
Lewis Solomon and E. Carrington Arnold. Fig. 91.
R. Norman Shaw, R.A. Figs. 107, 108, 108a, 108b, 109.
Spalding & Cross. Figs. 48, 59.
E. J. Stubbs. Figs. 102, 103, 104, 116.
Turner & Withers. Fig. 131.
W. E. Wallis, Architect of the Peabody Trust. Fig. 53.
A. Waterhouse, R.A. Figs. 151, 151a, 152.
C. F. Wike, City Surveyor, Sheffield. Fig. 68.
Wm. Woodward. Figs. 105, 106.
R. J. Worley. Figs. 111, 111a.
Thos. Henry Yabbicomb, City Engineer, Bristol. Fig. 69.
Keith D. Young. Fig. 55.

FOREIGN FLATS.

Paris :—
    Victor Calliat. Figs. 16, 30, 31, 32, 33, 34, 35.
    F. Julien. Fig. 170.
    L. C. Lacau. Figs. 171, 172, 173.
    Gabriel Morice. Figs. 163, 164, 165, 166, 167, 168.
    M. Perronne. Figs. 178, 179.
    A. Pregnaud. Fig. 169.
    Gustave Rives. Figs. 174, 175, 176, 177, 181.
    Albert le Voisvenel. Fig. 180.
Vienna :—
    Professor von Ferstel. Figs. 185, 186.
    Krauss & Tölk. Figs. 183, 184.
    Julius Mayreder. Fig. 182.
Madrid :—
    E. Adaro. Figs. 187, 188, 189.
    Enrique M. Repulles y Vargas. Figs. 190, 191, 192.
Lisbon :—
    L. C. Pedro d'Avila. Figs. 193, 194.
Budapest :—
    Professor Alois Hauszmann. Fig. 196.
    Desiderius von Hültl. Fig. 195.
    Adorjan Gaál. Fig. 200.
    Korb & Giergl. Figs. 196a, 197, 198, 199.
Amsterdam :—
    Dr P. J. H. Cuypers. Fig. 201.
America :—
    Buchman & Fox. Fig. 206.
    Paul Emile Duboy. Figs. 202, 203.
    Israels & Harder. Figs. 204, 205.
    Janes & Leo. Fig. 207.
    Jennie & Mundie. Fig. 81.
    Kilham & Hopkins. Figs. 208, 209.

RESIDENTIAL FLATS
OF ALL CLASSES.

CHAPTER I.

MAINLY HISTORICAL.

A BLOCK of flats is usually considered a modern form of building. The average man has probably heard that there were flats in Scotland before they were built in London, and he knows there are similar buildings in Paris. He is little aware that there were flats in

ANCIENT ROME.

Mr J. Henry Middleton, writing in 1885, says: " Examples of private houses, in a good state of preservation, are comparatively rare, but the recent laying out of new quarters on the Esquiline, Viminal, and Quirinal Hills, and the formation of the river embankment, has brought to light a large number of houses, both the *domus* of the rich, and the crowded *insulæ* or blocks, which contained one or more families on each flat, as is the modern custom in Rome and other Italian cities."

Flats were built in Rome as early as 455 B.C. Dionysius relates that "the plebeians agreed to divide among themselves *bona fide* the building lots on the Aventine, each family selecting a space in proportion with the means at its disposal; but it happened also that families, not able to build independently, joined in groups of two, three, and more, and raised a house in common, one family occupying the ground floors, others the floors above."

Several references to these buildings are made by ancient writers. Plutarch, in his life of Sylla, states that "even after he was grown up he lived in hired lodgings. for which he paid but a small consideration." This may or may not have been part of a flat, but further on we read: "I am an old acquaintance; we lived long under the same roof, I hired the upper apartment at two thousand sesterces, and he that under me at three thousand," about £25; this is evidence of an upper floor.

Tenement houses at certain periods were very badly built, and frequently collapsed, and the remains are consequently few and throw but little light on the subject. It seems that about eighteen tenants lived in each house; usually one family occupied each floor. The height was limited by Augustus to 68 Roman feet, and by Trajan to 58 feet for the front portion of the house, and the back part was probably higher. An inscription was found in 1819 describing a tenement house as composed of ten shops and six floors above. These *insulæ* were not only inhabited by the poor, for Cœlius is said to have paid 30,000 sesterces, or £266, for a third-floor suite. It is much to be regretted that so little is known of these buildings. Remains only show a portion of the ground plan of a house, one complete floor has not yet been discovered, consequently it is only from the writings of ancient authors that interesting information has been obtained. Flats were unknown in provincial cities, such as Pompeii, Herculaneum, Valleia, &c.

SCOTLAND.

The word Flat or Flæt dates back to the twelfth century, and in the original form was used until the last century, but the suites were also known as "Houses." In the seventeenth century Lord Stair published his "Institutions of the Law of Scotland." He states (ii. 7, 6): "When divers owners have parts of the same tenement, it cannot be said to be a perfect division, because the roof remaineth roof to both, and the ground supporteth both; and therefore, by the nature of communion, there are mutual obligations upon both, viz., that the owner of the lower tenement must uphold his tenement as a foundation to the upper, and the owner of the upper tenement must uphold his tenement as a roof and cover to the lower, both which, though they have the resemblance of servitudes, and pass with the thing to singular successors, yet they are rather personal obligations, such as pass in communion even to the singular successors of either party."

Since that date many law cases have been reported dealing with disputes between the landlords and tenants of various flats.

In the flats in Scotland they had, and still have, an arrangement to hide the bed, which is placed in what is practically a large cupboard. This is known as a bed press or bed box. The bed is enclosed by doors, and is entirely hidden when they are closed. The bed press is a peculiar feature in Scotch planning, and several examples will be seen in the illustrations of both old and new Scotch flats (see Figs. 2, 4, 17, 18, 78, 79, and 80). The bed portion of these bed boxes was formed with wood battens about 2 inches apart; the under side was open, and often used for storing coals; the doors were frequently made to slide on runners, but many were hinged and hung folding in the ordinary way. A fine example of a bed box at Craigievar Castle is illustrated in vol. 8, Third Series of the "Architectural Association Sketch Book"; this, however, has boarding in place of laths. The cupboard was often left open for an ordinary bedstead. Under the present bye-laws bed boxes are not allowed to be enclosed by doors. The bed press is a very old arrangement. There is an account of an Englishman who visited Edinburgh in 1598. He says: "When at Edinburgh, I was at a knight's house. Their bedsteads were then like cupboards in the wall, with doors to be opened and shut at pleasure, so as we climbed up to our beds. They used but one sheet, open at the sides and top, but close at the feet, and so doubled. When passengers go to bed their custom was to present them with a sleeping cup of wine at parting." It is believed that this custom exists at the present day.

This recess for a bed shows a similarity between Scotch and French plans. If the reader will examine some French plans, he will often see a recess for the bed, sometimes very carefully planned, as in Figs. 30, 32, and 35. The old Scotch plans were similar, with the addition of the doors. When the doors open to the ceiling and the bed is an ordinary one, there is something to be said for the arrangement, for the room has a tidy appearance in the daytime, and is very suitable for workmen's single-room tenements. Modern French plans do not give many examples, and the bed recess seems out of favour with architects to-day.

The question of the height of buildings in Edinburgh received attention as long ago as the seventeenth century. An Act of Parliament, "Given at our Court at Kensington, the 4th day of April 1696," enacted as follows :—"The Parliament taking into Consideration the great Danger the Edinburghers were exposed to by the excessive height of their houses, both in respect to Fire and Falling; they enacted, That no building to be erected in the City thereafter, shall exceed Five Storys in Height, the Front-wall in the Ground-story to be Three Feet in Thickness, the second Two Feet nine Inches, the third Two Feet six, the fourth Two Feet three, and the fifth Two Feet." This is evidently one of the earliest attempts to prevent sky-scrapers. No doubt the buildings with walls of the thickness specified have stood well, especially as stone was at that time universally used. The thickness of the walls should be noted in Figs. 2, 3, and 4.

In old Edinburgh flats seem to have been popular and numerous. William Maitland, in his history of that city published in 1753, describes Netherbow Port in the following words :—

" The Buildings here, elsewhere called Houses, are denominated *Lands;* and the Apartments in other places named *Stories*, here called *Houses*, are so many Freeholds inhabited by different families, whereby the Houses are so excessively crowded with people, that the Inhabitants of this City may justly be presumed to be more numerous than those of some towns of triple its Dimensions. And the Ground Floors in *Edinburgh* are not only employed for Shops as in other places, but many of the Cellars, and the first, second, third and fourth Stories are used as such. Nor is it in this Town deemed mean to dwell or lodge in the highest Apartments ; for even Merchants and Bankers transact their affairs in the third and fourth Stories ; and many Persons of Distinction lodge higher. But by the great inconvenience of the several Floors or Stories being separate Properties, the Inhabitants are deprived of Cellars, which is attended with many Disadvantages. And the said Houses or Apartments being so many separate Dwellings, are ascended to by publick Stairs (like the Chambers of the Inns of Court at *London*, and the Houses in the City of *Paris*, in *France*. From the latter I am persuaded the Edinburghers learnt both their Method of building and Manner of Dwelling), those of ancient Construction being dark and wynding, but the modern are spaciously square with proper landing Places, and well lighted like those of London."

William Maitland also wrote a history of London, published in 1775, but unfortunately he does not describe the private houses with the detail he devoted to Edinburgh. This publication is in two large volumes, and is a general history with descriptions of public buildings, &c. But when he refers to London in his history of Edinburgh, he was no doubt well acquainted with the metropolis, and evidently knew Paris well. The influence of French architecture upon that of Scotland is well known, and this early reference to it is interesting.

In Green's " Encyclopædia of Scots Laws " he says : " The term 'common interest' is peculiarly applicable to the rights of proprietors of different flats, or dwelling-houses contained in a single building with possibly different entrances but under one roof and contained between the same gables and walls, over every part of the building other than the flats of which they are proprietors. Such buildings have long been technically known in Scotland as 'lands' or 'tenements of lands, and the use of the phrase 'common interest' now applies exclusively to the law of the tenements." The word "flat" does not seem to have been used in Scotland in the olden times.

In 1779 Hugo Arnot published his "History of Edinburgh." He also noticed the resemblance between Paris and Edinburgh, and observes: "From confinement in space, as well as imitation of their old allies the French (for the city of Paris seems to have been the model of Edinburgh), the houses were piled to an enormous height, some of them amounting to twelve stories: these were denominated *lands*. The access to the separate lodgings, in these high piles, was by a common stair, exposed to every inconvenience arising from filth, steepness, darkness, and danger from fire; and such, in a good measure, is the situation of the Old Town to this hour."

Maitland also refers to the great height of the blocks of flats. He writes: "Although Edinburgh consists of few Streets, and a number of Wynds, or Lanes, Courts, and Closes, yet the Houses are very magnificent Stonen Buildings, from one to twelve Stories in Height, both inclusive; the highest whereof fronts the Cowgate and Parliament Close. But the Houses in this Place, before the Conflagration in the Year 1690, are said to have been three Stories higher."

Old Edinburgh was no doubt crowded; in 1500 the population was about 8,000, and there were only 700 houses.

Apparently in olden times the plan varied very little from century to century. There are still a large number of buildings in existence dating from the end of the sixteenth century. The external walls, floors, and roofs remain, but unfortunately the internal divisions have been altered so much that in most cases it is impossible to trace the original plan. Flats formerly inhabited by people of the upper classes are now occupied by the very poor; they are let off in single rooms, often licensed for a fixed number of people. Nothing remains of the old plan except the staircase. This was usually circular with a solid newel or wall, and is still known as a "turnpike stair"; sometimes the staircase was oblong. When circular it was often about three parts detached from the building, and very similar in construction to the staircase to an upper part of a modern London theatre ; having no well hole and being all of stone it was the best form to resist fire. Where internal staircases are found they are often of wood and with a well hole. These turnpike stairs are very easy "going," even in the oldest buildings ; the rise of each step is about 6 in.

Over the external entrance to the staircase, which had no door, the date and a text are often found ; the following are a few examples :—

> Blissit be God for al his giftis   1609.
> Fear God in luif   1595.
> The feir of the lord is the begenen of wisdom   I. H.
> In the lord is my hope   1564.
> Be merciful to me o God   1574.
> Blissit be God of al his giftis   1596.
> Spes altera vitæ   1590.

Off this staircase there were usually two doors on each floor, each the entrance to a flat ; sometimes there was only one flat on a floor. These doors were fitted with a "tirling pin," which answered the same purpose as a modern bell. The main entrance door to the block of flats seems to have been introduced when the New Town houses were built.

According to Chambers, "after the first extension of the city between 1450 and the building of the Flodden wall scarcely a house arose beyond the second wall for 250 years, and if Edinburgh increased in any respect it was only by piling new flats upon the tenements of the ancient royalty, thereby adding to the height rather than to the extent of the city."

It is doubtful if any block of flats erected before the sixteenth century is still in existence, but it is presumed the plan was similar to those of a later date.   The external staircase was evidently a common feature, for in some stanzas written about 1500, we read, "Your foirstairs makis your housses mirk" ; or in other words, "Your outer stairs make your houses dark."

There were many buildings partly of wood in the sixteenth century, for we are informed by Maitland : " King James IV. having, by his Charter of 6th October anno 1508, impowered the Edinburghers to fet or lett in Fee-farm their common Lands called the Borough Moor, and their common Marsh denominated the Common Myre ; the Citizens were no sooner in Possession of this Grant, than they sat about clearing the Ground by cutting down a vast Number of large Trees ; whereby the Quantity of Wood in their Hands on that

Fig. 1.—Wardrop's Court, Edinburgh (Seventeenth Century).

Occasion was so very great, that they could not dispose of it : Wherefore, to encourage the Inhabitants to purchase the said Wood, the Town-Council enacted, That whoever should buy a Quantity thereof sufficient to newfront the Tenement he, she, or they dwelt in, should be allowed to extend the said new Front, the Space of seven Feet into the Street, whereby the High Street was reduced fourteen Feet in its Breadth, and the Buildings which before had Stonen Fronts, were now converted into Wood, and the Burgh into a wooden City."

Not only was wood partly used for the buildings, but the roof coverings were also very inflammable, for in 1621 it was "enacted that the Houses in this City, instead of Straw, Deals, or Boards, they should thenceforth be covered with Slates, Lead, Tyles, or Thackstones." Consequently when we read that the city was fired by the English in 1560, and burned for three days, we may fairly assume that it was entirely destroyed, and that the new city, as it is now, was principally built after the Reformation. A Roman Catholic city was destroyed, and a Protestant city was erected. These dates and particulars are important when we consider the plan of a flat built at the end of the sixteenth century, or at a later date. There are many small rooms in these flats, and the question is—Were they oratories or were they the sanitary closets, known as garde-robes, of the period?

The inhabitants of Edinburgh were staunch Roman Catholics up to the year 1560, the date of the Reformation; they were extremely devout, and no doubt small oratories were built, similar to those still in existence in old castles in various parts of Scotland.

The elevation of a block of these old flats is generally level and unbroken, bay windows were unknown. The windows were all of the same size, with the exception of those at the extremities of each floor, which were narrower and not so high as the others; these were the windows to each garde-robe, and the photograph (Fig. 1) is a typical example. Probably the closet had an external wall to facilitate emptying the pail or box into the street; this was done with the old cry of "Gardez l'eau," "Haud your hand," or "Get out o' the gait." *

---

* According to Jamieson's Scottish Dictionary, "Garde de l'eau" had been corrupted into "Jordeloo," which he defines as "a cry which servants in the higher stories in Edinburgh were wont to give after ten at night when they threw their dirty water, &c., from the windows; also used to denote the contents of the vessel." Smollett writes, "Gardy Loo; *French*, garde de l'eau." In "Humphry Clinker" Smollett wrote: "You are no stranger to their method of discharging all their impurities from their windows at a certain hour of the night as the custom is in Spain, Portugal, and some parts of France and Italy —a practice to which I can by no means be reconciled; for, notwithstanding all the care

A box somewhat similar to a modern earth-closet was used, water was also added. There may have been another reason for placing the closet against an external wall, which is mentioned later on. After careful consideration it seems probable that these small rooms were not oratories but the sanitary closets of the period (see page 14).

Three examples are here given of typical seventeenth and eighteenth century plans: Fig. 2 shows the plan of a flat, probably seventeenth century, in Wardrop's Court, Edinburgh: a building now carefully preserved, and occupied by students of the university. The names on the rooms indicate the probable use of the rooms when the

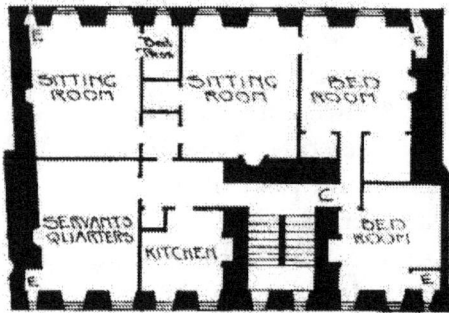

FIG. 2.

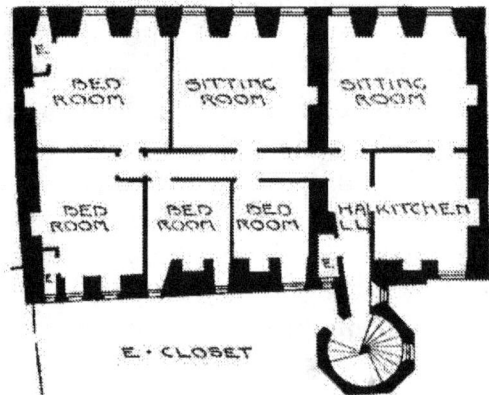

FIG. 3.

flats were first built. The line of the panelling dividing off two of the closets could not be accurately traced. It is doubtful if there was a door on each floor at c; the present openings appear to be modern. This example is interesting as it shows the "bed presses" or "bed boxes."

Fig. 3 is the plan of a flat in a building erected in 1726, and has a good example of the turnpike stair.

---

that is taken by their scavengers to remove this nuisance every morning by break of day, enough still remains to offend the eyes, as well as the other organs, of those whom use has not hardened against all delicacy of sensation." From other contemporary writers it would appear that little attempt was made to clear the streets, and they give particulars of the heaps of refuse.

The plan Fig. 4 is particularly interesting. Lady Stair's House is dated 1622, and this building no doubt was erected about the same time, the two rooms in the wing being built between the dates 1725-27. The building is several stories high, and this is the only floor with the partitions, doors, &c., in their original condition. In this block James Boswell lived and entertained Dr Johnson, fetching him from the White Horse Hostel in 1773. Boswell had what has been described as a somewhat extraordinary house for the time, as it consisted of two floors and an internal stair. The flat shown is the

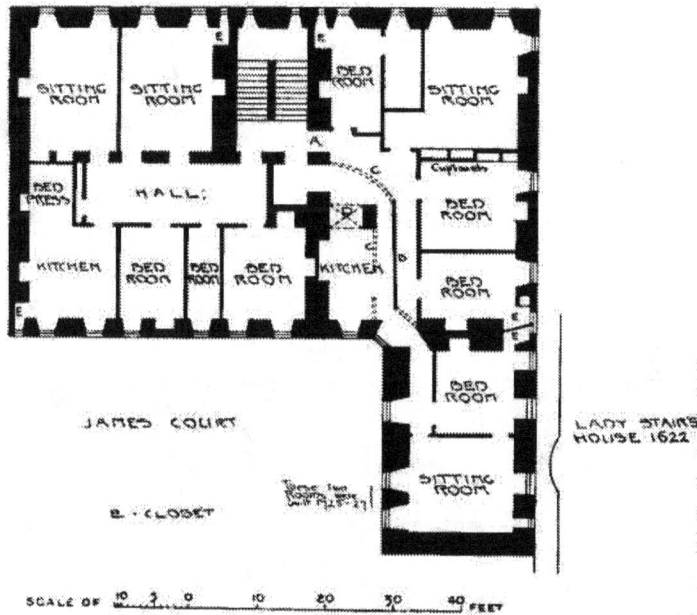

Fig. 4.

one immediately over it. In the seventeenth century the two rooms in the wing probably did not exist as the cross wall is so thick, and the doorway at A is probably a century later. The names of the rooms have been added indicating the original use. The partition B is the original one and those at C are later. It is possible that when the wing was erected there were three flats to the floor. At D there was a quaint arrangement: the space was divided into two parts by a shelf about half-way between the floor and the ceiling, the lower part was entered from the kitchen and used as a bed press for a maid servant, and the upper half was entered from the hall and used as a bed press for a man servant.

It is interesting to note that the partitions were generally framed, and still exist with the old mouldings on each side; quarter partitions

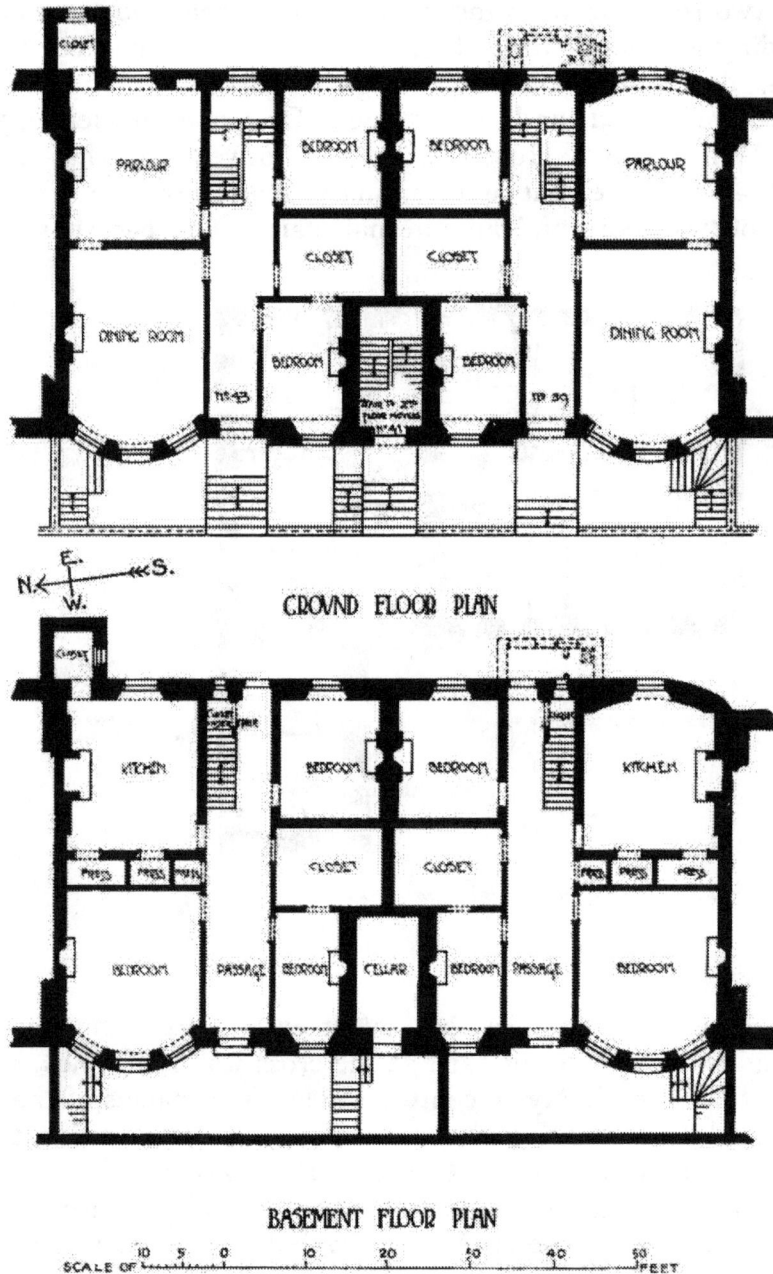

CROUND FLOOR PLAN

BASEMENT FLOOR PLAN

SCALE OF

FIG. 5.—NOS. 39, 41, AND 43 CASTLE STREET, EDINBURGH.

were not so common. One room was often entered from another; this feature shows the resemblance to early French plans.

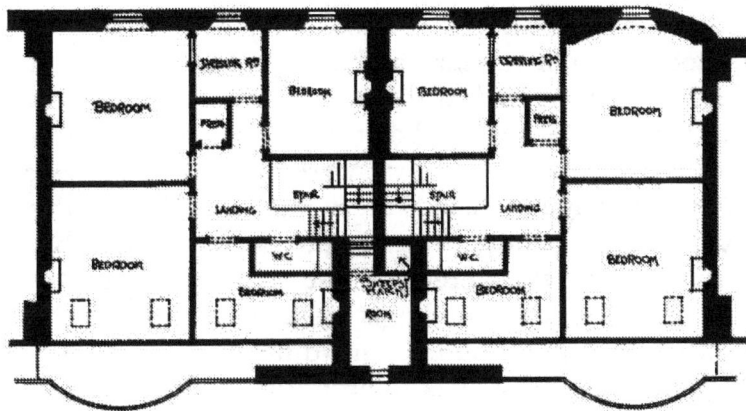

ATTIC FLOOR PLAN

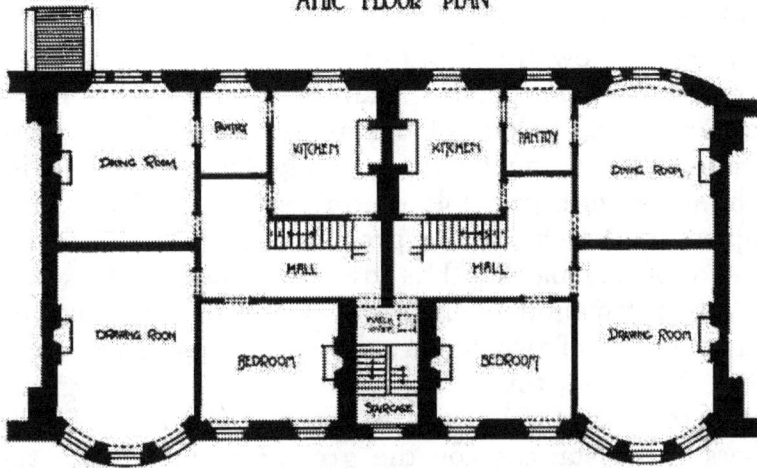

BEDROOM | STORK R⁰ | BEDROOM | BEDROOM | STORE R⁰ | BEDROOM
PANY | PANY
LANDING | STAIR | STAIR | LANDING
BEDROOM | WC | WC | BEDROOM
BEDROOM | OVERFLOW CISTERN ROOM | BEDROOM

SECOND FLOOR PLAN

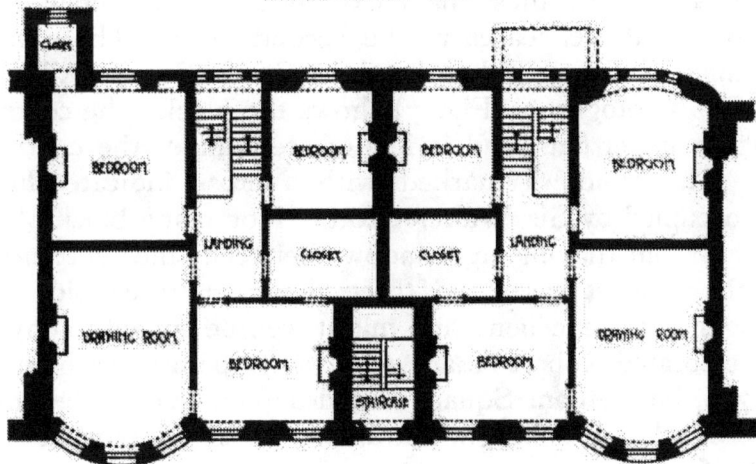

DINING ROOM | PANTRY | KITCHEN | KITCHEN | PANTRY | DINING ROOM
DRAWING ROOM | HALL | HALL | DRAWING ROOM
BEDROOM | WELL HOLE | BEDROOM
STAIRCASE

FIRST FLOOR PLAN

CLOSET
BEDROOM | BEDROOM | BEDROOM | BEDROOM
LANDING | CLOSET | CLOSET | LANDING
DRAWING ROOM | BEDROOM | STAIRCASE | BEDROOM | DRAWING ROOM

SCALE OF 10 5 0 10 20 30 40 50 FEET

FIG. 6.—NOS. 39, 41, AND 43 CASTLE STREET, EDINBURGH.

After the Act of Union in 1707 extensive building operations were carried on outside the city walls. There was no necessity to build high blocks of tenements, as the city could spread on all sides. The New Town was erected in the valley, and is bounded by Princes Street (not Prince's Street). To the north of this thoroughfare the houses of the eighteenth century were erected. The necessity for a flat dwelling no longer existed, there was no reason why separate houses should not be built. Many in fact were erected, but tradition is strong and so flats were erected, but they were not so universal as in the old city. These buildings exist to-day just as they were in the eighteenth century. There is no difficulty in tracing the plan. The buildings were peculiar, it is doubtful if anything like them exists in London, or any other city, and the plan is good, especially for a building without a passenger lift.

Figs. 5 and 6 show the floors of an eighteenth century block of flats, one of many similar buildings, and it is also interesting because Sir Walter Scott lived in one of the suites from 1798 to 1826. The general arrangement of the building should be noticed. It is an example of the maisonette principle on an extended scale. Sir Walter Scott occupied the basement, the ground floor, and the first floor of the south end of the block. His dwelling was what is known in Edinburgh as a "main-door house." Over his premises there is another flat tenement of two floors; the entrance was from a staircase entered from the street, this staircase commencing at the ground floor level (not basement) and going only to the second floor. There are no internal doors to this staircase on the ground or first floors, the upper flats are entered on the second floor, and each has an internal staircase to the top floor; these flats extend over the public staircase, which, as stated above, ceases at the second floor. There are many such buildings in the neighbourhood of Castle Street, Albyn Place, &c. &c. The photograph (Fig. 7) shows the block; the central door is that to the upper flats, and is immediately under the centre of the pediment. The windows marked with a cross indicate the rooms of the flat occupied by Sir Walter Scott. Not many blocks have the small sitting-room having a window between the entrance-doors, consequently in most cases the three doors are seen side by side. This arrangement is excellent, and might well be copied to-day.

The celebrated Robert Adam, who was appointed architect to the king in 1762, built Adam Square and designed many other domestic buildings erected in Edinburgh, but unfortunately no block of flats by him is to be found.

No doubt the people of Edinburgh had experienced the great inconvenience of the high blocks of flats in the old city, for the buildings of the eighteenth century are all of moderate height, and restrictions were evidently made limiting the front of the building to three stories above the ground, with one attic story. Scott's house is typical of many. The section of these flats is interesting, the front portion of the top floor is an attic story, but the back part is not—this has rooms of the ordinary shape; the ridge is nearer the back wall

FIG. 7.—NOS. 39, 41, AND 43 CASTLE STREET, EDINBURGH.

than the front wall, and sometimes the back portion of the roof has a lower pitch than the front portion. This arrangement is quite general for buildings of this date, which are all very similar. The attic windows are shown in the photograph (Fig. 7).

These streets in the New Town were frequently built entirely by one architect, and have the advantage of one scheme for the facade of an entire block of several buildings. Often the building at each end was a block of flats, and the buildings between were private houses;

there are many examples of this arrangement, such as Albyn Place, Randolph Crescent, &c.

It is interesting to note that although the plans of the sixteenth and seventeenth centuries were similar to one another, and no doubt were built on the lines of earlier buildings, when we come to the eighteenth century the plan is entirely different. This is no doubt partly due to the fact that high buildings were no longer necessary, but the development of sanitary ideas also had an influence upon the plan; this is referred to later on. It is also strange to note that the plans of the nineteenth century much more resemble those of the sixteenth than those of the eighteenth century. The plans shown on Figs. 2, 3, and 4, on pages 8 and 9, are in many respects very similar to modern blocks of flats.

Basements have always been general in Edinburgh ; in the old days the people in the flats above often kept pigs there. These were allowed to roam the streets in the day time, and were a sanitary precaution, in that they lived on the refuse thrown into the street. These pigs were often pets of the children, who rode them until they were thrown off. Even the children of the nobility are said to have done this.

From a sanitary point of view, the plan of a flat of the sixteenth century was much better than one of the latter part of the eighteenth or early nineteenth century, and many of the latter buildings are still used as when originally erected. In the former case the closet nearly always had a window opening into the external air. This may have been because it was more convenient for throwing the refuse into the street, or it may have been recognised that proper ventilation was desirable, and that these earth-closets ought not to be unventilated cupboards ; there was of course no drainage in those days. But when we come to the eighteenth century flats, there is an entire change of plan ; the W.C. is placed in the centre of the building, often under a staircase, or in any dark corner, and has no external ventilation. That is the usual arrangement of an eighteenth century building not only in Edinburgh, but also in London. Drainage in Edinburgh appears to have been first introduced in a systematic and general way at the date these flats were built. Was there any reason for this sudden change ? For centuries the closet had been ventilated, and then each one was placed in a most insanitary position. The reason, perhaps, was this : the old buildings had no drainage, but the new buildings were drained, and sewers were constructed at about the same time as the houses, and it is quite possible that the drainage was regarded as something very wonderful and new. All the refuse was taken away at once by pipes, and consequently it was thought that the closet would always have clean, pure, untainted air. It is quite likely that the builders and architects of that time imagined that to be so, and as sanitary science advanced, as it did with the introduction of drainage, so sanitary planning deteriorated, and it was not until a century later that the mistake was discovered and the old plan was again adopted, and the advantages of the two centuries were combined.

Figs. 5 and 6 must not be taken as typical examples to show the sanitary plan of an eighteenth century building, as alterations have been made. The W.C. usually ventilated on to the staircase, as in many London buildings of the same date.

Mr Henry Grey Graham, in his book "The Social Life of Scotland in the Eighteenth Century," writes: "In the flats of the lofty houses in wynds or facing the High Street, the populace dwelt, who reached their various lodgings by the steep and narrow 'scale' staircases which were really upright streets. In the same building lived families of all grades and classes, each in its flat in the same stair —a sweep and caddie in the cellars, poor mechanics in the garrets, while in the intermediate stories might live a noble, a lord-of-session, a doctor, a city minister, a dowager countess, or a writer. Higher up over their heads, lived shopkeepers, dancing-masters, or clerks."

The old flats in Paris were similar in this respect; the rich lived in the lower floors and the poor above. It was not until lifts came into use that the value of the upper part of the building increased so much that the poorer tenants were obliged to leave. The appearance of the lift made a great change in the history of flats, for afterwards people who lived in the same building were members of the same class, all paying about the same rent, and the poorer people had blocks in an inferior neighbourhood—in every way an improvement.

All the flats in old Edinburgh do not seem to have been very desirable residences, for we read of dark and dirty staircases, and an account about the year 1785 states: "At this period the inhabitants of Edinburgh were greatly incommodated for lodgings; people of quality and fashion were obliged to submit to small, dull, and unhealthy habitations."

In Scotland the whole building was, and is, known as a tenement or land. The freehold of a flat can still be bought, although the "feu" system is general; this may be shortly described as a lease in perpetuity; somewhat like a copyhold in England. A board out-

Freehold Flats.—There are many instances in olden times of one man owning one floor of a building, and another having the freehold of the floor below or the floor above. Certain sets of chambers in the Albany buildings are to-day owned in a similar manner. There is an old case as far back as Henry VII., which states the judges were agreed that "where I have an under room, and another has a room above (as people have here in London), I cannot abate my room to the destruction of the room above" (Anonymous Case, Keilway, *b*).

After the fire of London the remaining buildings became very crowded, and the following quotation is often given as a proof that flats had become general: "Then Mr Lee said that it might be of evil consequence, for now since the Great Fire every house hath many occupants." But it is clear that the rooms may have been let as furnished apartments.

The Albany is an example of the erection of flats built as far back as the commencement of the last century. The building was originally known as Piccadilly

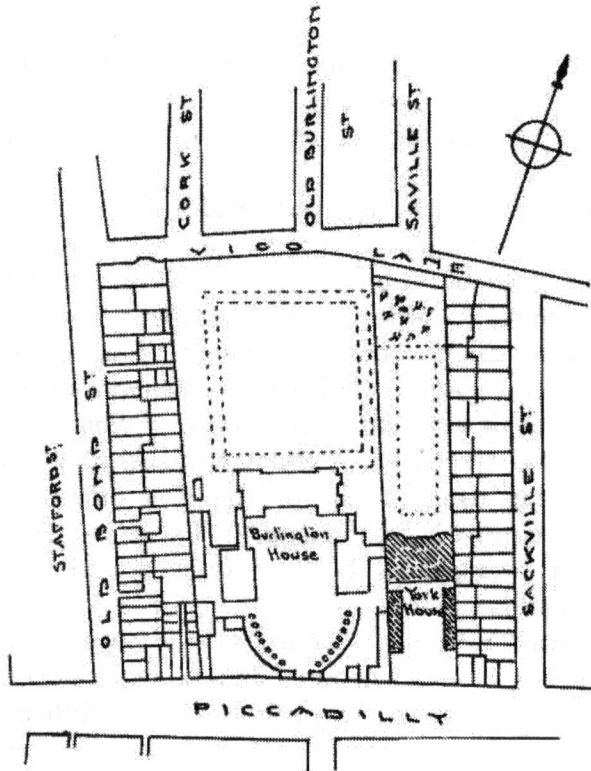

FIG. 8.—THE ALBANY, PICCADILLY (YORK HOUSE).

House; it was built for Stephen Fox, second Lord Holland. Sir William Chambers was the architect. At a later date it was known as York House, and Fig. 8 shows the house and garden. This plan is taken from Horwood's Survey of 1792. The long garden extended as far as Vigo Lane, now known as Vigo Street. In 1804 the house was converted into flats for bachelors, and the garden was partly built upon. The suites are known by letters. The main house is A, and the chambers are lettered up to L. The foregoing plans, Figs.

GROUND FLOOR PLANS

SCALE OF 10 5 0   10 20 30 40 50 FEET

GROUND FLOOR PLANS.

SCALE OF 10 5 0   10 20 30 40 50 FEET

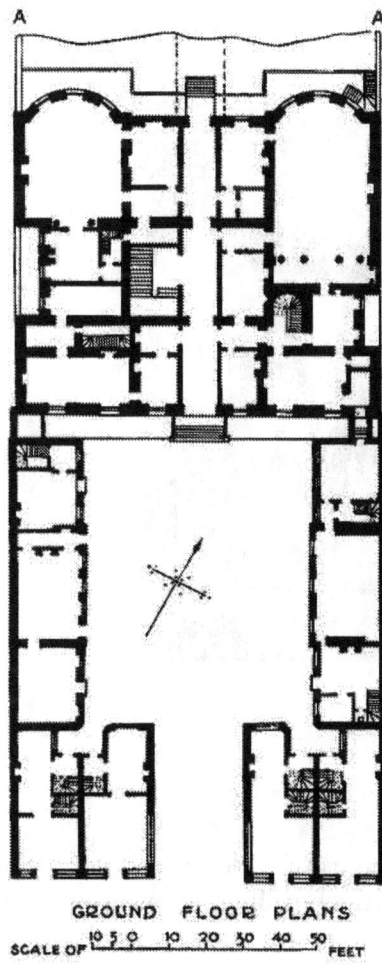

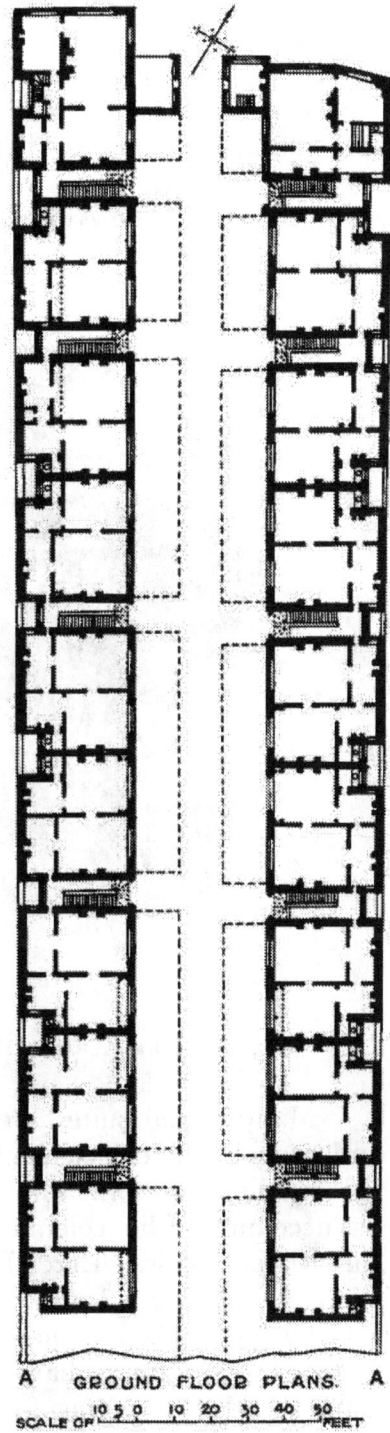

FIGS. 9, 9A.—THE ALBANY, PICCADILLY.

9 and 9A, show all the rooms on the ground floor. The suites facing
the garden are on the maisonette principle, the servants' rooms being
on another floor. Each suite has two large and lofty rooms in the
front, and a small room at the back, and a W.C. There is an
entrance hall to each set of chambers. The main house was altered
into suites, and some of them have charming rooms—the old reception
rooms of York House. When the alterations were made the buildings
were known as The Albany.

FIG. 11.—THE ALBANY, PICCADILLY. COVERED APPROACH TO SUITES.

Many of the suites are freehold; some rooms on an upper floor
and rooms in the basement, not underneath, but in a distant part of
the building, all form one freehold. The Albany is also interesting
on account of the celebrated men who have lived there, including
Sir Robert Smire, Lord Byron, Lord Clyde, Lord Macaulay, and
W. E. Gladstone. In one of his letters Lord Macaulay says :—
"I have taken a comfortable set of chambers in the Albany . . .
I have an entrance hall, two sitting-rooms, a bedroom, a kitchen,
cellars, and two rooms for servants, all for ninety guineas a year."
Figs. 10 and 11 are views of the building.

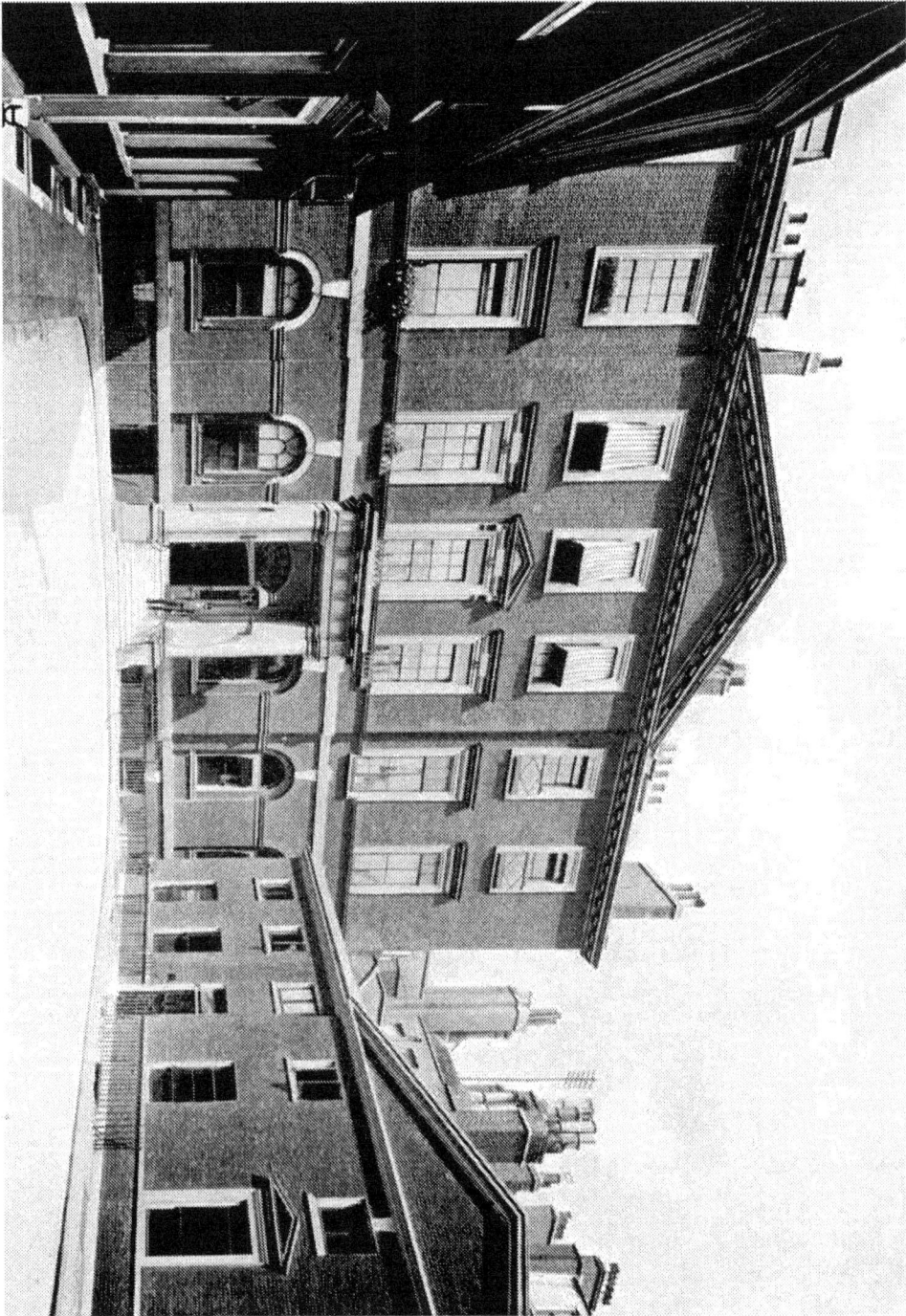

FIG. 10.—THE ALBANY, PICCADILLY.

After the instance just described in the year 1804, the flat movement does not seem to have progressed in London until early in the fifties. In the *Builder* of 3rd December 1853 there is a description of certain buildings near Victoria Station :—

"We must return to Victoria Street to mention the fine set of buildings erected there by Mr Mackenzie to supply what has long been a desideratum in London, namely, complete residences on flats as in Edinburgh and Paris. The accompanying plan of one floor will explain the arrangement. Each house, or rather collection of houses, has a frontage of about 117 feet by an average depth of 45 feet, and the height from the basement to the roof is 82 feet. Where several come together they form an imposing pile. The cost of each house has been £16,700. These buildings are fireproof, the floors are composed of iron girders and brick arches, and in cement between there are ceiling joists below, and joists and 1¼ in. floor battens above these, rendering them sound-proof. The roof is flat and is composed of girders and arches, with a covering of asphalte. All the water and gas pipes throughout the houses are of iron, proved to a pressure of 100 pounds to the inch, previous to fixing ; and every care appears to have been taken to make the building as substantial as possible, to avoid the necessity of repairs. Each house contains six shops. Three on either side of a fine staircase, with basement and entresol attached to each, and eight suites of apartments, the latter approached from a door outside, distinct from the shops. All the staircases are of stone. A porter resides on the premises, who performs all the duties usually performed by a hall porter in a private residence, and the hall and staircase are lighted at night at the expense of the proprietor and kept in a proper manner. There is a separate staircase for tradesmen, and a lift for raising heavy weights. The advantage of such residences to parties who remain only a portion of the year in London is obvious, as the porter in their absence takes charge of the apartments. The shops are priced at £150 per annum, exclusive of taxes, and the flats range from £200 to £80 per annum, the landlord paying all rates and taxes. It is Mackenzie's own speculation, and the idea, we believe, originated with him."

The description is interesting ; the architect was certain the floors were sound-proof, and yet we still want a sound-proof floor. On inquiry at the premises it seems that the rents have increased considerably since 1853; £150 per annum was the rent of each shop, now £500 is asked, and flats that let at £80 to £200, now let at £120 to £400. Most of the flats are, however, slightly larger, as additions have been made at the back of each block, and the sanitary arrangements, referred to below, have been re-modelled. The plan is given (Fig. 12):—

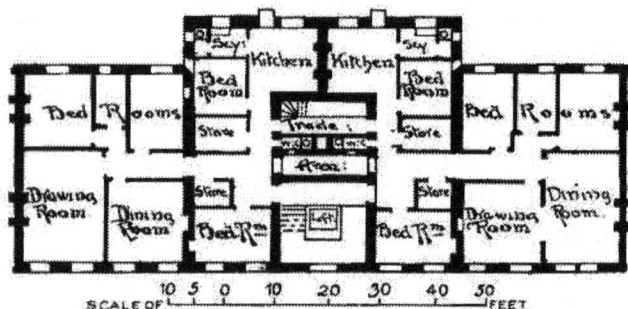

FIG. 12.—VICTORIA STREET, WESTMINSTER.

An examination will prove interesting, and it is needless to make comment; it may be noted in favour of the plan that the rooms are larger than those of most similar suites of to-day. It is doubtful if the architect ever saw a French plan.

It is clear from the above description in the *Builder* that flats had not been built in London, they were to supply what had "long been a desideratum." It is strange to find in the same number of the *Builder* a leading article describing some new "model dwellings for married soldiers, fifty-four dwellings having a common staircase of stone, 9 ft. wide," &c. These appear to have been very similar to modern artisans' dwellings.

In 1855 Messrs A. Ashpitel and J. Whichcord wrote a pamphlet entitled "Town Dwell-ings: an Essay on the Erection of Fireproof Houses in Flats, a modification of the Scottish and Conti-nental Systems." They were eminent archi-tects of their day, and the plans may fairly be considered as repre-

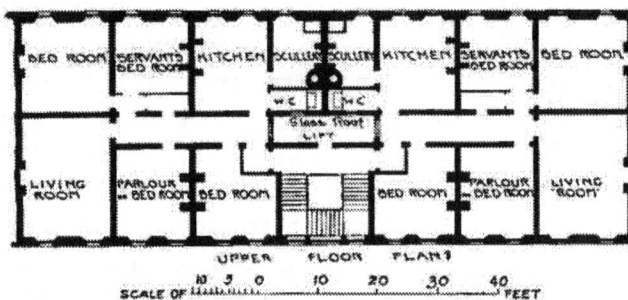

FIG. 13.

senting some of the best work of the time. Mr Whichcord had written upon sanitary matters, and his work would meet all the requirements of the period. The book was written partly with a view of showing the advantages of flats.

The plan Fig. 13 is one of the best; but according to modern ideas, it has little to recommend it. The W.C. is ventilated into a glass-covered air shaft, up which the provisions would be carried to each suite. Each hall would have been very dark. This

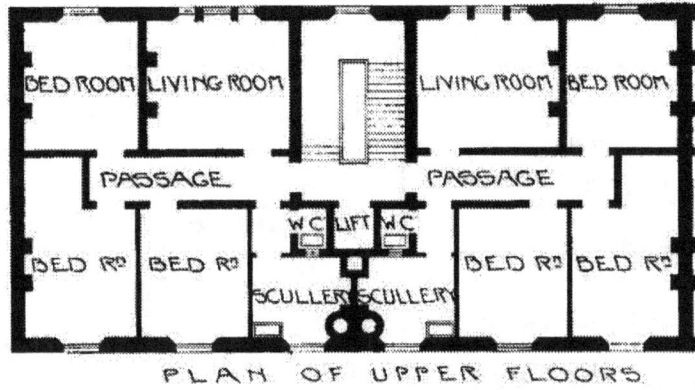

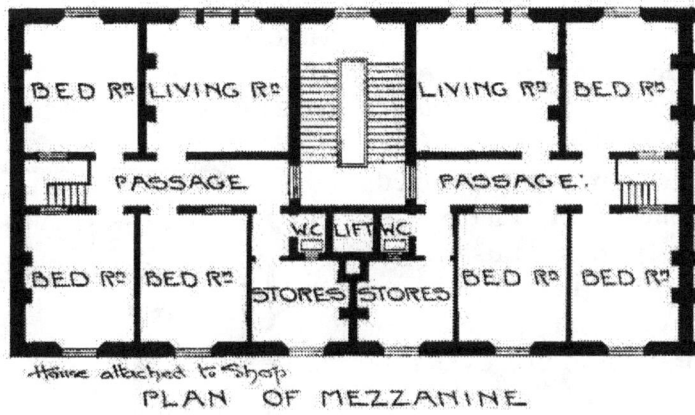

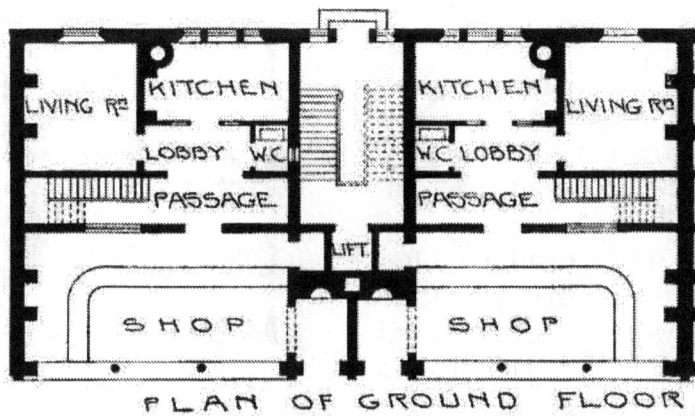

PLAN OF UPPER FLOORS

PLAN OF MEZZANINE

PLAN OF GROUND FLOOR

FIG. 14.

plan seems to be a modification of the Victoria Street buildings (Fig. 12).

PLAN ᴏꜰ UPPER FLOORS.

FIG. 15.

In Fig. 14 it will be seen that each W.C. has either no window, or else it ventilates into a room or staircase: the planning from a sanitary point of view is about as bad as it could be.

In Fig. 15 each W.C. is built against an external wall, but has no window; this is hardly a mistake, as there are two instances.

English architects have always considered that we have been more particular about sanitary matters than our friends on the Continent, but an examination of old plans hardly justifies that idea. Five years before the book by Messrs Ashpitel and Whichcord was published, the first volume of M. Victor Calliat's "Parallèle des Maisons de Paris construites depuis 1830 jusqu' à nos jours," was brought out. In the first volume there are over fifty plans and only five instances of unventilated W.C.'s; and in the second volume, of houses built between 1850 and 1864, there are over seventy plans and only two instances, and one doubtful case, of lack of ventilation.

The French plans at that date were very similar to those of to-day, and Fig. 16 is an example often given of a typical Paris flat. This was built between 1830 and 1850, and a reference to Calliat will show the excellence of French plans at an early date, and prove that as much care, if not more, was given to the arrangement of the rooms from a sanitary point of view, as in England.

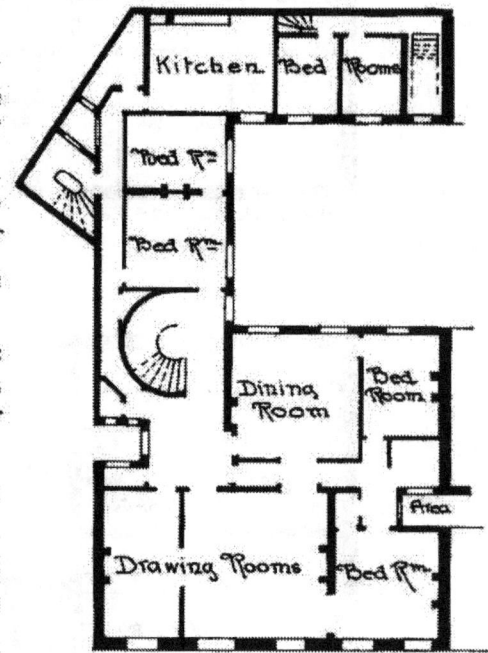

FIG. 16.

The following extract is from an article in the *Building News* of 1868, and refers back to 1838 or 1848 :—

"A movement began some twenty or thirty years ago to provide dwellings in flats, that is, complete houses fitted with every convenience upon each floor for the poorer artisans, and it has met with considerable success among them. The fact of its being a philanthropic movement, however, created some prejudice against it in the minds of the classes just above them, and we are aware of only one building in London divided into flats, and let to tolerably well-to-do occupants of the middle classes. (This is not far from the Walworth Road Station, and may be seen from the railway. Its privacy is, however, jealously guarded, and an application to inspect it, some time ago, was courteously declined.) Dwellings in flats, however, are no longer built exclusively for the lower classes. They are being adopted by the other extreme of society, and the success of those in Victoria Street has led to the building of others in the aristocratic Grosvenor Mansions at Pimlico."

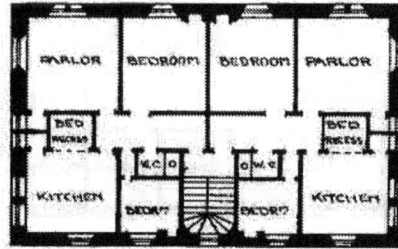

FIG. 17.—OLD GLASGOW PLAN.

With this article there are five plans. The first is Fig. 17; it is given as an example of a Scotch plan, and the unventilated W.C. caused no comment. A good example of the old bed recess is shown. Two plans were from Messrs Ashpitel and Whichcord's pamphlet, and are given above (Figs. 13 and 15). The fourth plan is that in Victoria Street (Fig. 12), and the remaining one is that of a French building.

In the *Building News* of 1867 a scheme was given with a plan for model dwellings on the balcony system. The rents were estimated to be as follows :—

Attics—10 single rooms at 2s.	-	-	-	£1	0	0
„ 2 dwellings at 5s.	-	-	-	0	10	0
„ 2 „ „ 4s.	-	-	-	0	8	0
First Floor—10 single rooms at 2s.	-	-	-	1	0	0
„ „ 6 dwellings at 5s. 6d.	-	-	-	1	13	0
Ground Floor—8 dwellings at 5s. 6d.	-	-	-	2	4	0
Basement—2 dwellings at 5s. 6d.	-	-	-	0	11	0
„ 7 „ or stores at 4s.	-	-	-	1	8	0
Total	-	-	-	£8	14	0

The rents and basement dwellings are interesting, and so are the allowances for outgoings, which are calculated at one-sixth the gross rents.

About the year 1875 a curious experiment was made in Hill Street, Berkeley Square. A building was erected on the maisonette principle throughout, each flat being on two floors; this was not unlike the "top and bottom" houses of Holland, except that the house was divided into three tenements. There were three doors, side by side; one door admitted to the ground floor and basement suite, one door to a staircase to the first and second floors, and one door to a staircase to the third and fourth floors. Each suite had a separate staircase, and these were built to intertwine in a skilful manner, but with no inter-communication, and each had an entrance from the street. Upon examination of the building, it was found to have been recently altered, and unfortunately the architects had no plans of the old building. There is an elevation in the office of Messrs Bywaters, but they have lost the plans. The appearance of the building is

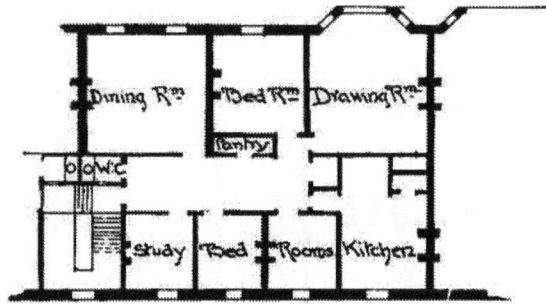

FIG. 18.—GLASGOW FLAT, 1876.

similar to many of the eighteenth century buildings in Scotland, three entrance doors adjoining, but the internal arrangement was quite different.

There are few plans published before 1880, but the above illustration (Fig. 18), from the *Builder* of 1876, is an example of a Glasgow flat. The plan is somewhat similar to Fig. 13; it has the same disadvantages. There is a reference in the *Morning Post* of 27th November 1861 to "the numerous family—in the fourth flat"; but it was not until about 1880 that the flat movement made any great progress.

In "Dickens' Dictionary of London," 1879, we read: "At present almost the only separate *étages* to be found in London are those in Queen Anne's Mansions, a good number of sets in Victoria Street, a few in Cromwell Road, and a single set in George Street, Edgware Road. Of all these, however, the last named, with a few sets in Victoria Street, are the only examples of the self-contained 'flat,' the inhabitant of which, whilst relieved of all the responsibility, and most of the troubles of an isolated house, yet enjoys to the full all the advantages of a separate establishment."

In the edition of 1885, the list is increased by "seven houses near Clarence Gate, Regent's Park, known as Cornwall Residences, the new buildings known as Oxford Mansions." These are still described as almost the only examples in London.

Cornwall Mansions are near Baker Street Station, and were built about 1872. There are several blocks with suites of various sizes; the rooms are large and lofty. This is noticeable in most of the early flats, the rooms are larger than those of to-day; but no attempt was made to build a good hall. Albany Buildings, Walworth Road, which are flats at low rentals, were built about 1878.

Few buildings in London have caused such public interest as the well-known Queen Anne's Mansions, often known as Hankey's Buildings. They were built in 1874, and 500 rooms were added in 1888. It is interesting to note that these buildings were among the first erected, and to-day they are certainly the largest blocks of catering flats in England. A plan of a portion of the buildings is given in Fig. 159.

Victoria Street, Westminster, was opened on 6th August 1851, and the oldest flats of the modern movement are to be found there. This street was not a success at first, and it was not until 1887 that all the buildings were erected, and the street may be said to have been completed.

In looking through old newspapers, it is interesting to see the objections then made to flats; one was the risk of illness from infectious diseases, another was the objection of servants to flats, and a third was, strange to say, the great risk of burglary. Time has shown, with regard to the second and third objections, that a flat has an advantage over an ordinary house, and also that there is no cause to fear infection.

During all the years that flats have been built, it has been said that the craze would suddenly cease and that the buildings would shortly be empty. Time again has proved the reverse to be the case, and it is interesting to read an article in the *Spectator* of 2nd April 1892, stating at that date the demand was greater than the supply.

It is to be regretted that English architects who built some of the early blocks of flats, did not refer to Continental plans. It was some few years before our plans showed any skill in the arrangement of the rooms. On the other hand the Continental plan was the result of the experience of many years. Not only in Paris, but in Rome, Madrid, Vienna, Budapest, and indeed in every large Continental city, flats had been built for generations. In St Petersburg, which has been described as the most modern of all European cities, practically all the houses are flats. The reason why these were so universal abroad, is no doubt due to the fact that each city was enclosed with walls, it could not grow larger by spreading, as London has done, and the houses had to be piled one over the other.

The flats in Paris seem always to have had a trade staircase; it is only during the last few years that trade staircases have become general in England, making the resemblance between English and French plans greater than it was a few years ago. The reason may be traced to the lift. Paris flats were built many years before lifts were used, and a trade staircase was necessary. We commenced to build when a trade lift was in constant use, and no staircase was then necessary; one has to be built now to comply with the regulations of the Building Act for escape in case of fire.

In America, as in England, the flat movement is of recent date. In New York flats were built for the poor people for many years before they were erected for the better classes. Only as recently as 1890, a writer in the *American Architect* said: "In the old country . . . rich and poor . . . 'live in flats.' In America people have not yet learned this lesson." The same mistake was made in America in the early days, as in London, an attempt to build suites with the frontage that was only suitable for a private house. An enormous number of buildings were erected in New York with a frontage of only 25 feet and a depth of 100 feet.

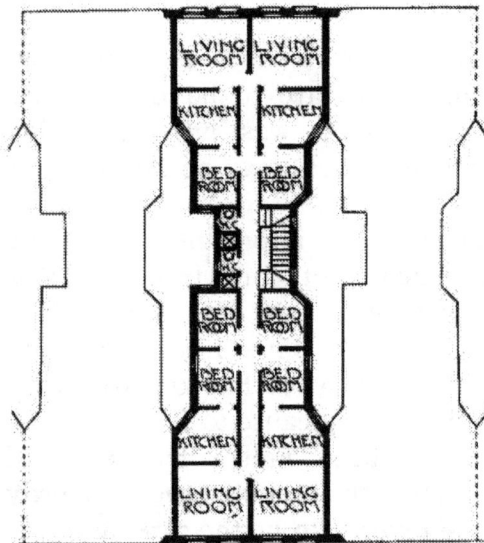

FIG. 19.—"HOUR GLASS" PLAN, NEW YORK.

The difficulty with such a site was to obtain enough light for the central rooms. The result was a plan now known as the "Double Decker," and also as the "Hour Glass" plan, an example of which is given in Fig. 19. Each house has four families to the floor, and only one room of each suite is well lighted. There is an enormous number

of these buildings in New York, but no more can be built as they
are not in accordance with the Tenement House Law of 1901. An
American writer has stated it is impracticable to get a courtyard if
plots of less than 40 feet frontage are built upon.

In America flats are known as "Apartment Houses," a title that
is often more correct than the one we use, especially when the
maisonette, or suite on two or more floors, is referred to as a "flat."

The following illustration shows the plans of New York buildings
built about 1870.

"All the rooms from front to rear were
required to open into each other. The
parlour, naturally, was put at the front of
the house, and the kitchen, where a certain
amount of light was desirable, at the back.
The dining-room adjoined the kitchen, and
to get from the parlour to the dining-room
it was necessary to pass through all the
bedrooms. The bathroom was in a dark
corner near the kitchen."

In some parts of America, small brick
shafts are still considered sufficient to ventilate a W.C., and a large residential hotel in
California has recently been erected with a

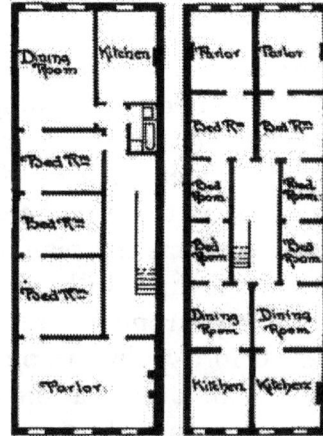

Fig. 20.

bath-room with W.C. apparatus and no other ventilation for it but this
small shaft.

According to an article in the *Architectural Record* of 1893,
American flats, as a rule, are badly built, and attention is called to the
superior construction of the French buildings. The maisonette system
was tried in New York, but was not a success.

The early American plans have been referred to in this chapter
upon the history of flats; they have been considered at the same time
as our own early and bad plans. Examples of the best recent
American buildings of to-day with several photographs are given on
page 206 *et seq*.

CHAPTER II.

THE PLAN.

IT is impossible to lay down any golden rule for the planning of flats. The special requirements of a certain class of tenants must be studied, the surrounding buildings influence the plan, there is the ever-present question of cost, and many other influences are brought to bear upon the architect, such as Acts of Parliament and Building Regulations, and, lastly, there is the question of the shape of the site, which in most cases governs the plan.

A layman will criticise a building without any hesitation, usually adopting strong expressions, but an architect requires further information before giving an opinion. What appears at first sight to be a defect in a plan or elevation is often found to have been unavoidable when the facts are known. If there is some remarkable feature in a building there is nearly always a good reason for it.

Light and Air.—Questions of light and air to neighbouring buildings must be carefully considered. It often happens that the back portion of a building must be lower than the remainder. In consequence of this one large block of flats has stairs inside each suite down to the servants' rooms, which are less in height than the other rooms; the higher the story the greater number of steps.

Speculation or Investment.—A block of flats is in certain respects quite different from any other domestic building. It is always built as a speculation or as an investment. A private house may also be built with the same object in view, but the most artistic residences are built by the owners for themselves. This, from the nature of the building, cannot happen to a block of flats, and the result is what we see in London to-day. It is possible that some day several people may club together and erect a building, each taking one suite. Then there may be a chance for an architect to carry out a design without considering the return upon the capital outlay, and having to consider the cost at every turn. A man who erects a house knows as a rule that it would not pay him to let it; he takes a pride in the building, and has thoughts above a return of so much per cent. upon his outlay.

Builders' Architecture.—The architecture of flats in London, speaking broadly and mildly, is not good, and people frequently remark, "How is it that when so many charming private houses are built, flats are so hideous?" One reason is that the outlay is cut down as much as possible, and there are other reasons. In most cases flats are built by speculating builders, who have their own ideas and carry them out. A builder's opinion upon a practical point and upon a plan is good, his experience is great, and he can detect a weak point at once, but he should trust his architect when the question of the elevation is to be considered.

One example may be given, the architect sent details for the windows thus :—(Fig. 21). The builder carried them out thus :—(Fig. 22). He explained that his modification was a saving, and also a great improvement upon the original. It was a case where the builder

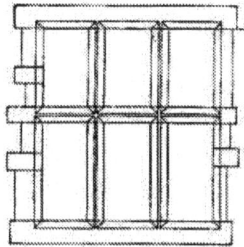 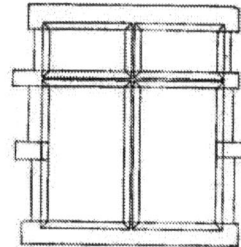

FIG. 21.   FIG. 22.

could do as he liked, and he did so. Fortunately that does not always happen, as flats are often erected under contract in the same manner as other buildings. With regard to builders' architecture the money is generally spent on useless ornament, hideous cornices, and plaster work that had far better be omitted. Flats taken as a whole are a modern development of street architecture that has done little to advance the art. Luckily there are a few exceptions, as some illustrations in this book may prove.

Passage Space.—To return to the plan, the amount of passage space is important, as it does not produce rent, either inside or outside the suite. Consequently the architect will strive to obtain a maximum of room area, and a minimum of passage area, and for every building optional plans should be made, and this floor area should be measured and compared.

Dark Passages.—Years ago a dark passage was considered a very bad, indeed unpardonable feature in a plan, but that idea has been modified since the introduction of electric light, for it may be cheaper to allow for a light to burn whenever wanted, rather than sacrifice valuable room space in order to continue a passage to an outer hall, and so obtain a window. This is worth considering when planning flats, for, apart from the question of artificial light, the position and use of the dark passage is of course important. What would be a defect

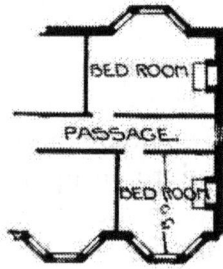 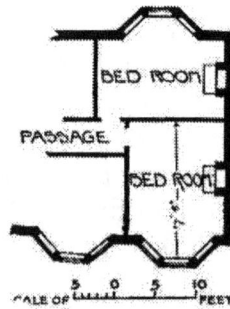

near the entrance to a suite, or approach to the servants' quarters, or indeed anywhere where the passage would be much used, would be of much less consequence at the end of a wing leading to two bedrooms. Borrowed light is ample in many such situations, it is not often that the occupant goes to the room during the day, and

FIG. 23.   FIG. 24.

electric light can always be turned on; but if some main position, a passage or a hall, is dark, then the gloomy, depressing effect of borrowed light is always being felt, and is a defect. It is not good to become a slave to a rule and apply it universally. The advantage of making the rooms large is shown above. Fig. 23 has the passage carried through to the outer wall, and Fig. 24 shows the great gain to one bedroom if the passage space is added to the room.

In some flats in London the only light to the hall of the suite is obtained from the staircase, which may be badly lighted; the halls are consequently dependent on artificial light.

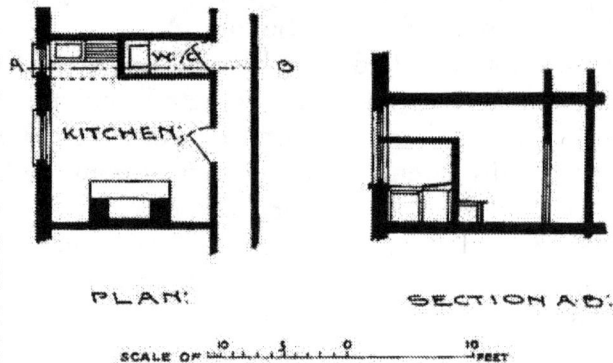

FIG. 25.

This seems carrying matters to an extreme, and is worthy of all blame if the hall is large and intended to be used as a room.

Borrowed Light.—This question has been tested in many flats. At Marlborough Chambers (Fig. 153) the upper part of all the doors opening on to each private hall is glazed with coloured glass, and the light of the hall is ample. It will be noted the hall is small and an unimportant feature.

Sometimes direct light can be introduced over a room, but this can only be done when the story is high, say not less than 11 or 12 ft. Then a room such as a bath-room can have a ceiling of match-boarding about 7 ft. high, and direct light may be obtained between the upper side and the main ceiling; but flats are not often 11 or 12 ft. from floor to ceiling. In one block of buildings a recess in the kitchen is formed for the sink, the W.C. is ventilated over this, the space being about 3 ft., as shown above, Fig. 25.

Plan of Site.—The site governs the plan, but if a large site is to be used for many blocks, each with a rectangular plan, it is a mistake to have a short side of a suite towards the street; a longer side should have the frontage. Some years ago several attempts were made to build flats on ordinary building plots, and with most

 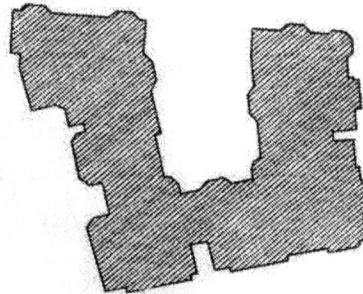

FIG. 26. FIG. 27.

unsatisfactory results. For flats, frontage is required rather than depth of plot. In America some years ago many attempts were made to build flats with narrow frontage; the result was the difficulty in obtaining light to the intermediate rooms, as mentioned in the last chapter. See Figs. 19 and 20.

In a plan with narrow frontage there are certain to be long passages, an outlay without any return of rent.

Areas and Recesses.—Areas should be avoided if possible, but so much depends on the shape of the site. It is better to have an irregular plan such as Figs. 26 and 27 than one containing even large areas. If areas must be introduced, it is of course better to have a large one such as Fig. 28 than several small ones, as is very general in America.

The London Building Act, 1894, section 45, contains regulations as to the size of areas with habitable rooms ventilated into them, and most large cities have their own rules; but as flats have not been built in many provincial towns there are no special regulations, and the first builders may obtain advantages that will be impossible later on.

When an area is necessary, arrange if possible to form an outlet, and so convert it into what is practically a recess. It involves the cost of an extra wall where the neck is, but it will be found an advantage. If this is done from the front wall the cost is increased, as cornices, &c., must be continued round the recess. See the Ansonia, New York (Fig. 203).

The avoidance of internal areas can be carried to excess, as a small area will light a hall, and ventilate a W.C., but the area that is practically only an air shaft must be avoided.

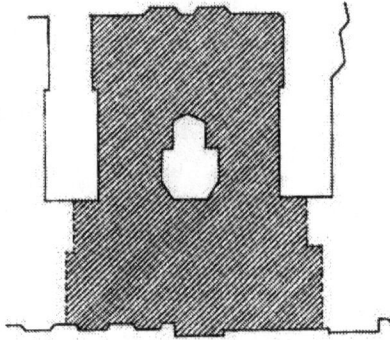   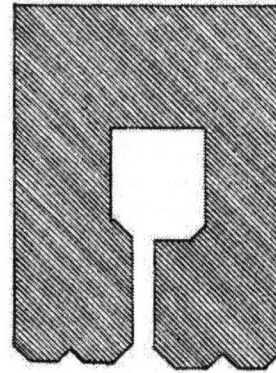

Fig. 28.   Fig. 29.

Shape and Size of a Room.—To the average English tenant the shape of a room is always of secondary importance to the size, but apparently that is not so abroad. In England the question of deciding if a house or a flat should be taken is usually settled by mamma and her daughter; the former is influenced by the size of the kitchen, and the latter by the size of the drawing-room—her sole standard of judgment is, "How many sets of lancers can be danced at the same time?" A room is usually praised if it is large, and condemned if it is small; proportion, plan, and architectural features are of no importance. The result is that architects dare not attempt to improve an irregular-shaped room by cutting off certain portions and making it symmetrical. When a site is at the corner of two streets not at right angles, the plan of one room at least is sure to be irregular. The English architect leaves the room as it is, uncomfortable and unsatisfactory, for what client would allow him to sacrifice floor space and make the room smaller?

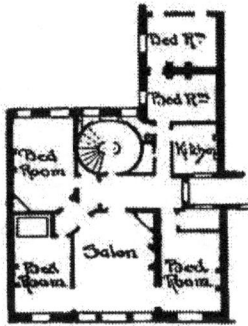

FIG. 30.

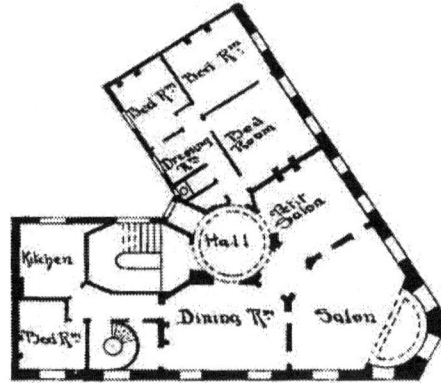

FIG. 31.

These things are managed better abroad, especially in France; but the entire praise must not be given to the architects. French people want, and will have, an artistic room, and the planning that is praised abroad would be condemned in England.

French Plans.—This careful consideration of the plan of a room is no result of the modern excellence of French architecture; the following examples are taken from Calliat's " Parallèle des Maisons de Paris, construites depuis 1830 jusqu'à nos jours," published in 1850 and 1864. Figs. 16, 30, 31, 32, and 33 are from flats built between 1830 and 1850, and Figs. 34 and 35 from flats built between 1850 and 1864, and show what was done even in those days to make a room symmetrical, when, from the force of circumstances, it was

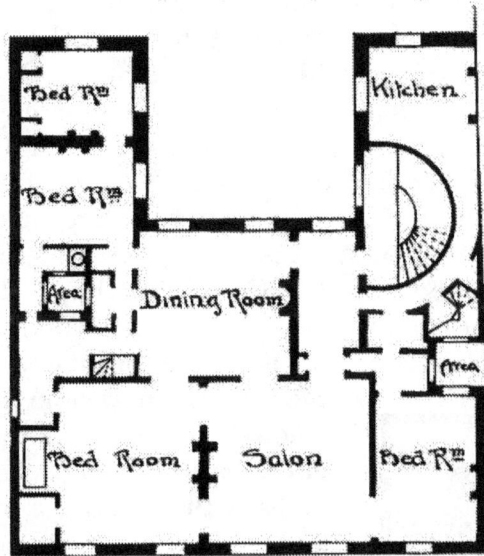

FIG. 32.

irregular. The original illustrations should be examined, as those given here are more or less in outline to indicate a principle, and many other examples can be seen in Calliat's volumes. In England not only are we content to accept the bad plan in consequence of the site, but we seem to aggravate the evil, for it frequently happens that when a room has a triangular shape at the corner of two streets, an

irregular-shaped bay is built at the angle, of a size out of all proportion to the room, which has finally practically eight irregular walls.   After examining the French plans of 1850 or earlier, they should be compared with the first flats in England, such as those in Victoria Street, of 1853 (Fig. 12), not only with reference to the shape of rooms, but also from a sanitary point of view.

FIG 33.

Two questions that usually arise when planning flats, are the desirability of having (1) shops and (2) basement suites.

Shops.—With reference to shops, it is nearly always a question of locality.   If the site is in a main street of shops, such as Bond Street or Oxford Street, no one would hesitate for a moment, because the rent of the shops would be considerable.   But often the solution is not so simple ; perhaps one part of the street has shops, and the remainder has none, as in Sloane Street ; or again, the scheme may be a large one, and it may be a question of creating a shop neighbourhood.   Certainly shops do not improve the value of the flats above, and the question is, Will they prove a detri-

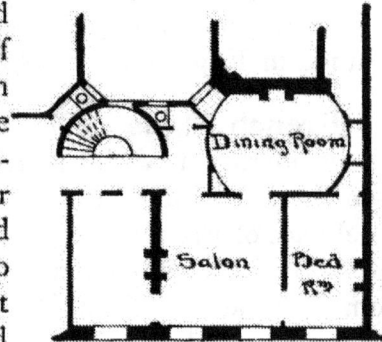

FIG. 34.

ment?   Some people do not care for a flat over a shop. Should it be decided to build shops, if possible the entrance to the suites should not be in the main street. Usually the site has a frontage to the main thoroughfare, and a return frontage to a side street, and it is there that the entrance should be arranged as in Figs: 85, 114. This has a double advantage ; all the valuable frontage is devoted to the shops, and the suites have a quiet entrance as far

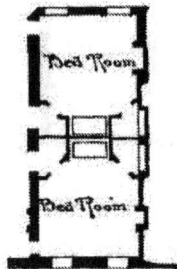

FIG. 35.

from them as possible.   As a rule, tenants do not care for ground-floor suites, especially if they are near the public way, and where people on foot or on omnibuses can see into the rooms. Frequently the ground-floor suites are the last to be let in a building.

If the main entrance must be in the same line of frontage as the shops, an attempt should be made to disconnect it from the general building line, to make a distinct feature of it, and as much as possible sever it from the shops. The shop windows should abut against the entrance to the suites, the shop entrances being as far as possible from the main door; the entrances should not adjoin. Examples of this arrangement are shown in Figs. 85, 101, and 137.

Basement Flats.—It does not pay to build basement or "lower ground-floor" suites except in a very good neighbourhood, and even then they are not always a success. They are bound to be dark, the front rooms are overlooked from the street, the coal places for all the tenants are frequently entered from the front area, and there are other objections to them. If a ground floor lets at, say, £175, a first floor at £200, a basement flat would probably let at about £120. There is a certain demand for these "lower ground-floor" suites: some people must live in a certain neighbourhood; they want the address, and if the rent is low, the suites may let well.

But if a basement is built there are other ways of using it beside devoting it to self-contained suites. The space may be utilised for store-rooms or extra-rooms for servants. There is a growing demand in high-class flats, say over £200 a year, for a room for a man-servant away from the suite; and these optional rooms are often the reason for tenants taking the expensive flats above. The number of bedrooms is not so limited, and one or two more can be obtained. This is a good idea where the area of the site is small, and it is only possible to plan a suite with a few bedrooms. Box-rooms and cellars in the basement let readily. Another method is to let a portion of the basement with the ground-floor suite, that is, the tenant has a "flat" on two floors; this is known as a "maisonette." There is a private staircase, the servants' rooms and offices are below, and sometimes a billiard-room is built. Examples are shown in Figs. 86, 96, 100, and 101.

Maisonettes.—With a little care the maisonette system (see page 49) can be used for part of the basement, and the remainder divided into extra-rooms for the suites above, or for rooms under shops, according to the locality. Sometimes a small self-contained suite is built in the basement for the servants of the flats above, the suite comprising two or three bedrooms, a bathroom, and a W.C. In a good district these will let at from £20 to £30 a room. Telephones or speaking-tubes connect the servants' quarters with flat above.

Flats in a Main Thoroughfare.— Some people have objected to flats on the first floor of a building in a main thoroughfare, as the people on tramcars and omnibuses can see into the rooms; blinds have had to be put up to prevent this nuisance.

Varying Number of Rooms.—It is a good arrangement to have suites in the same building with varying numbers of bedrooms, say from three up to six or seven. This is not easy to manage on account of the lift and staircase. Each flat is usually the same as the one above, with the exception of the ground floor, the space of at least one room above being devoted to the entrance hall. But in large suites the rooms need not be divided by partitions until the suite is let, and then they can be arranged to suit the requirements of the tenant. Sometimes a tenant wants a large drawing-room and few bedrooms, then one bedroom can be used as a dining-room, and the dining-room and drawing-room of the suite will form the large drawing-room, and no partition will be required, and the cornice, skirting, &c., can be made good at a small cost. Flat managers say that no two people want the same accommodation, and this omission of as many partitions as possible is becoming very general. In a new building one suite should be completed and decorated to show to applicants. The wall papers will soon be spoilt, but ladies like to see the effect of the rooms when finished.

Sizes of Rooms.—A careful analysis has been made to ascertain the average sizes of rooms of the various buildings illustrated in this book. In Class No. 1 ten examples were taken, and the result was as follows :—

Drawing-room	-	-	-	average area	341	sq. ft.
Dining-room	-	-	-	„	„ 329	„
Best bedroom	-	-	-	„	„ 262	„
Kitchen	-	-	-	„	„ 185	„

In Class No. 2 ten examples were also taken; the areas were as follows :—

Drawing-room	-	-	-	average area	242	sq. ft.
Dining-room	-	-	-	„	, 248	„
Best bedroom	-	-	-	„	„ 200	„
Kitchen	-	-	-	„	„ 160	„

In Class No. 3 eight examples were selected, and the result was as follows :—

Drawing-room	-	-	-	-	average area 157 sq. ft.
Dining-room	-	-	-	-	„ „ 165 „
Best bedroom	-	-	-	-	„ „ 153 „
Kitchen	-	-	-	-	„ „ 115 „

The average sizes of rooms in artisan dwellings are given in Chapter III.

Height of Rooms.—The average height of rooms is about 10 ft. to 10 ft. 6 in. ; for rooms about 14 ft. by 14 ft. the height should not be less than 9 ft. A good effect is obtained by making the passages lower. This is often done for the vestibule of a public building. At Marlborough Chambers (Fig. 153), the height from floor to floor is 10 ft. 6 in., and the halls and passages inside each suite are 2 ft. lower than the rooms, and the effect is excellent. The false ceiling is an additional expense, but it well repays for the outlay. This idea is not new ; it is used with excellent effect at the Pitti Palace, Florence.

Entrance Halls and Staircases.—It has been mentioned that in buildings with shops on the ground floor it is better to have the entrance to the suites in a side street. In artisans' dwellings and poor class flats the staircase is frequently placed in the front of the building, with windows over the entrance door. But as soon as a better class flat is contemplated it is found that the position is too valuable ; the space is wanted for a living room, and the position of the staircase is shifted to the back of the building. The advantage of having it in the front is, that the plan is a saving of space on the ground floor. In artisans' dwellings the entrance should be from a private court or playground.

The entrance to a block of flats abroad is considered of more importance than it is in England. A considerable amount is spent on the decoration, and the staircase becomes a central architectural feature of the whole building, as a reference to the plans of foreign flats will show. In England this is not so, even in the case of the most expensive buildings. We are satisfied with an approach to the lift, about 10 or 12 ft. wide, and a small fireplace. It is doubtful if the foreign idea should be adopted here. A large hall can only be planned at the expense of the remainder of the ground floor. An entrance hall should be wide enough to dispel the idea of a corridor or passage, and to allow tenants to pass one another without feeling the necessity to enter into conversation. It should be decorated in a quiet homely manner—wood in preference to marble—remembering it is the hall of a domestic building, and not the entrance to municipal offices. There should always be a large fireplace, and if the weather is at all dull or cold, a good fire should be lighted. In one block of small flats a strict rule is made that the entrance door is always to be kept locked. It is a good arrangement; a porter is nearly always ready to open it, and there is no chance for an objectionable character to gain admittance.

Flats abroad were of course built many years before lifts came into use. Before that time the staircase was used constantly by all the tenants, and was a more important part of the building than it is to-day. It takes a long while to alter a custom, and it may be that foreigners have overlooked the fact that the staircase is comparatively little used. With us it is different: the flat movement is more recent, and only a few of the earliest buildings were built without lifts. We have had no tradition to bind us, and have never made a distinctive feature of the staircase in the way that has been done on the Continent. It is not necessary to spend much money on the staircase, which is often wider than is required, considering how little it is used. Some architects advocate the idea of following the Continental custom of building large entrance halls, but there is no reason why money should be spent upon elaborate decoration of the staircase.

In England the usual plan of a staircase is rectangular, with a well-hole in the centre for the lift. We do not favour winders, one reason is that it is awkward to lay a carpet on them, and for the same reason the circular plan for staircases, so general on the Continent, is the exception in England; but Figs. 84 and 91 are examples of recent buildings with staircases circular on plan.

Ventilation of Staircase.—According to the London Building Act, 1894, section 69, the staircase of a block of flats must be ventilated upon every story by means of windows, or "otherwise adequately ventilated"; that means, generally, that there must be windows. This restriction is a great inconvenience and cause of heavy and unnecessary expense in planning flats. The legislature allows "Twopenny Tubes" to be built without ventilation for miles; these railways are used constantly by thousands of people, but it will not allow the staircase of a building occupied "by more than two families" to be without windows every few feet in the height, and that in cases where there is a lift, and the staircase is rarely used. Under the old Building Act a skylight at the top of the staircase was allowed. It is not as if a skylight did not ventilate properly, for the reports upon fires constantly refer to the draft created by the skylight making the staircase one large flue.

It is assumed the reason for the windows to each floor is that it is thought the building would be more healthy, but the authorities forget that the suites suffer in consequence. A building with a top-ventilated staircase is much cheaper than one with windows to each landing; this particularly applies to small flats such as are included under Class 3, Chapter IV. Many of these buildings are only slightly better than artisans' dwellings, and let at about £45 per annum. As pointed out elsewhere, they return a very small percentage on the outlay, competition is considerable, the utmost accommodation is given, and the increased cost of the staircase with an external wall is prejudicial to the rest of the suite. If the staircase had a top light these flats would have larger and healthier rooms.

Ventilation of Staircase in America.—This law has apparently come to us from America, and it is interesting to note that a strong protest has been made against it in New York. If it had been an insanitary arrangement to have a skylight and no external windows, such a plan would not have been carried out by eminent architects; certainly some buildings illustrated in this book could not have been built had they not been erected under the old Act of 1855.

Passages might with advantage be made wider. About three feet is the usual width, but often an additional six inches from the rooms on either side would not be missed, and a four feet passage would be a great improvement.

The Hall of the Suite.—In studying the history of the planning of flats, one important feature to notice is the development of the private hall of the suite. In the early buildings there was simply a passage, narrow and awkward, and usually badly lighted; and that often in a flat letting at a large rental. A hall is now absolutely necessary, and no architect would think of planning a first-class suite without one. The early examples of a good hall were in some cases virtues of necessity. In the plan (Fig. 101) of flats built in 1888, it was necessary to have the sitting rooms overlooking the park. A bedroom might have been built where the hall is shown with a passage to the outer wall for light; at best it would have been a poor arrangement, but it was decided to abandon the idea, and use the space as a hall or lounge, the entrances to the sitting-rooms opening off it and being well lighted. The result was that applicants were taken with the idea of a good hall, and did not realise it necessitated the loss of a bedroom. This is only one instance among many, where there has been some central space, some awkward difficulty in planning; the architect has made it into a hall, and it has been the most successful feature of the suite. Having found the advantage in the early days of flats of these "accidental" halls, architects have seen the benefit of them, and now they are a necessary feature of any good flat. In late years the demand for a good hall has increased in private houses; if we compare modern plans with those of houses built twenty or thirty years ago, we find this is one main difference. But if the idea is attractive in a house, it is still more so in a flat, because the hall of a flat is preferable to the hall of a private house, in consequence of the absence of draughts. It is impossible to prevent a draught in the hall of a house, the staircase opens off it, it is high, and there are many doors. That is not so in a flat. For similar reasons the hall of a private house is difficult to keep warm, and there again the hall of a flat has the advantage. Very few flats have three sitting-rooms, and the hall takes the place of a morning-room or study of a private house. It is rare to find a billiard-table in a flat, but if a hall is large enough, this would be a great attraction. There are many flats where the hall is sometimes used as a dining-room, and the larger it is the more the passage space is curtailed. A hall may be regarded as accumulated passage space.

Outer Hall.—In a private house it is usual to have an inner and an outer hall. This is in consequence of the draught when the outer door is opened. This outer hall is unnecessary for a suite. When built it often becomes nothing but a dark nuisance. If a hall is anything more than a passage it should have a fireplace, and a door should be built to shut off the passage to the bedrooms. This will keep the hall warm, and tend still further to make it into a room, which in fact it becomes.

Side Entrances from Street.—When suites are arranged on the ground floor, each should have a private entrance from the street, in the return frontage if possible (see Figs. 91, 97). If it can be arranged the suite can also have an entrance from the main hall (see Fig. 91).

Form of Suites.—The simplest form is one covering an entire floor; examples are shown on Figs. 83, 87, and 99. Then comes the usual plan of a staircase serving two suites on a floor, such as Figs. 84, 97, 98, 99, 101, 115, and 126. This is by far the most common plan, and it is economical in that there is no public passage way.

Lift Service to Suites.—A staircase and lift often serve more than two suites on a floor. Of course the public passage space is increased, but the cost of the lift for construction and working must be considered. Examples of one lift to three suites are shown in Figs. 88 and 102; of one lift to four suites in Figs. 114, 129, 131, 138; of one lift to five suites in Figs. 119 and 120; of one lift to six suites in Fig. 115. It is hard to make a rule, but it is rarely an economical arrangement to make a lift serve more than three suites on a floor.

Noise from other Suites.—One objection made to flats is the annoyance from noise in the flat above or below. As a rule the piano is the nuisance complained of. Years ago nearly every manufacturer of a patent fireproof floor claimed that it was sound-proof, and nearly every architect had some pet form of construction to prevent the trouble. Experience has shown that no floor is sound-proof; it is not so much a question of the construction of the floor as a question of the amount of sound. But the floor is not alone responsible; sound is conveyed by means of windows, out of one room and into the rooms above and below; it also travels by means of the flues. Ordinary sound can be prevented from being a nuisance, and the best floors have some hollow space in them. The steel or iron should not be brought in contact with the wood, and felt may be placed upon the concrete and under the bearers.

This question of noise is not so great a nuisance to the flat dweller as other people think it is. They imagine the horror of going to bed and hearing a cornet overhead and a clarionet below, each accompanied by a concert grand piano; but they forget that as a rule, each suite has a plan exactly similar to the others in the building, and that a bedroom is over a bedroom and a drawing-room is over a drawing-room, and that although there may be a great noise in the drawing-room of one flat, no sound will penetrate to the bedrooms of the neighbouring suites. As a rule the piano played in one flat is faintly heard in the room above or below, but if the piano is played in that room the other sound is not noticed and is no annoyance.

Infectious Diseases.—It has been said that flats are undesirable residences, because if a contagious disease broke out in one suite, it would rapidly spread throughout the remainder of the building. Experience has proved to the contrary. In one large block there was a case of smallpox and the tenant died, but no one else suffered. The flat was disinfected by the authorities, and the suite relet without any unpleasant result. The manager of the building was very careful; he would not allow the doctor to use the lift, and had all the stair carpets renewed. There has also been at least one other case of smallpox and also cases of typhoid and scarlet fever in flats, and the disease has not spread. Statistics show that artisans' dwellings are healthy, and better class flats may reasonably be supposed to have at least the same advantages.

Servants' Quarters.—One reason that was often quoted in favour of flats in the early days was, that the mistress would have more control over her servants than in a private house; in other words, there was no "back door." It was true then, but it is not so true now. All the large modern buildings are provided with fire escapes; these are generally iron external staircases approached through the servants' quarters and also used for trade purposes. Usually a staircase serves more than one suite on a floor, it is approached by a balcony; the result is that servants can visit each other or leave the building at any time, and the mistress has less control than in a private house. Complaints were made some time ago that servants would not live in flats, now many prefer them, perhaps in consequence of these fire escapes, so the owners get some compensation. These trade staircases have only recently become general in England, but they have been built on the Continent for many years. This feature makes our plans more similar to those abroad than they used to be. Sometimes these staircases are of stone or concrete and enclosed with walls; these are preferable to the external iron structures, but cost more. Many tenants strongly object to iron staircases.

In considering the planning of a suite the servants' offices should perhaps receive the first attention. The success or failure of a plan often depends on the solution of this difficulty. And a small flat is a harder problem than a large one.

Optional Plans.—In the case of a flat on a site with space only sufficient for two rooms to face the street, the reception rooms are naturally placed in the front of the building; if the kitchen and offices are to be near, it follows that the bedrooms must be at the rear of the building, the servants' offices being sandwiched in between. This is not a very satisfactory arrangement, the objections being that the servants' rooms must be passed in order to reach the bedrooms, and the noise and smell from cooking in the centre of the flat. Such an arrangement is shown in Fig. 36 (A).

The other alternative is to put the servants' quarters at the far end of the suite as in Fig. 36 (B). If this is done, dishes are carried the entire length of the flat, and become colder than in the other

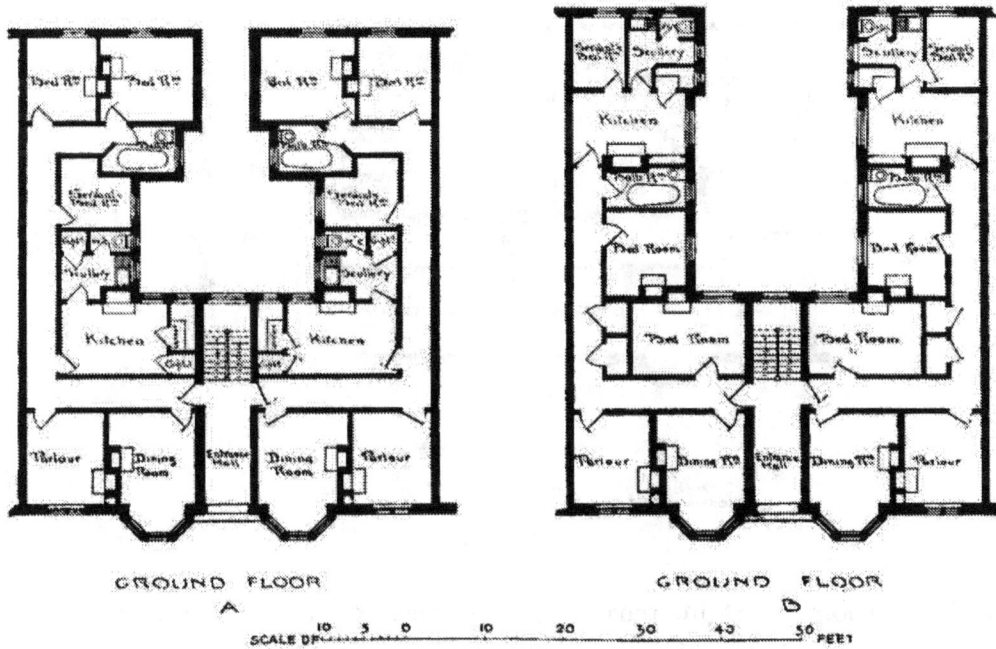

FIG. 36.

arrangement. The best bedrooms have a bad outlook, the best light and perhaps a good view being given to the kitchen and servants' bedroom. In the plan Fig. 36 (A), the cupboard off the scullery might be omitted, and access arranged off this lobby to the servants' room. Fig. 36 (B) is a more economical plan as there is less passage room, and is perhaps preferable, but it is impossible to get a good plan for an inexpensive flat with small frontage and six or seven rooms.

In Fig. 36 A the floor area is 2,136 sq. ft.
  "   B   "   "   2,125 "
  "   A   passage "   461   "
  "   B   "   "   364   "

The plans have practically the same area for each room.

In more expensive flats it is possible to make a more satisfactory plan. If the frontage allows for three rooms facing the street, the problem is also simpler (see Fig. 37) ; with larger frontage the passage space becomes smaller.

Servants' Rooms.—These should be well cut off from the other rooms and main passages or hall, and at the same time should be near the entrance and the reception rooms. That is an ideal arrangement, but double doors are often necessary to prevent sound from the kitchen being heard in the remainder of the flat. Should a kitchen be next

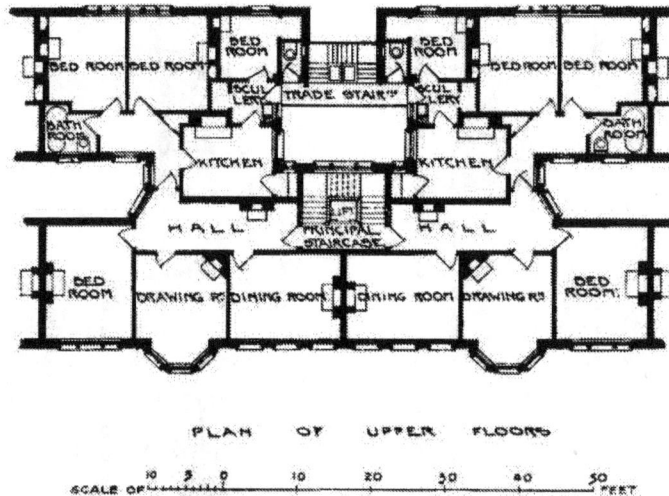

FIG. 37.

a sitting-room, a 4½ in. partition, or even a 9 in. brick wall, will not stop the annoyance, and it is impossible to prevent laughter and a certain amount of noise in a kitchen.

Kitchen.—It is better to have a kitchen next the dining-room, rather than the drawing-room. The former being used for meals there is usually a certain amount of noise in the room, but a drawing-room is often occupied by people reading, and the slightest sound would be heard. A dining-room, again, is in use for less time than a drawing-room. A wall between a kitchen and a reception room should never be less than 9 in. ; this is usual in good class flats, see Fig. 101.

If the windows of kitchens are facing one another the servants will shout across an area ; this is a nuisance, and if possible should be avoided. The kitchen should certainly be near the dining-room, if the

remainder of the plan do not suffer in consequence, for it is a mistake
to insist on any one such idea and in order to carry it out, spoil the
remainder of the plan. If a flat has three reception rooms, the dining-
room can be at the back or in the centre of the suite, near the kitchen.
This plan prevents the dishes being carried from one end of the flat to
the other, and the consequent smell of the cooking that seems to cling
to some flats. A good example is shown in the French plan, Fig. 171.

In planning a kitchen the same rule applies to a flat as to a
private house, the window should be in a position to light the
range, and consequently should not be at the side of it.

Serving Hatch.—In houses built some few years ago there was
often a serving hatch formed when the dining-room was next the kitchen.
These are hardly the advantage they seem to
be ; certainly meals are served hotter, but the
sound from the kitchen is an annoyance even
when the hatch is closed. A serving hatch
may be made with advantage from the kitchen
or dining-room into a passage or hall ; this is
convenient when the kitchen door is far from
the dining-room. Examples are shown in
Figs. 84 and 105. It is a good arrangement
to have two doors between the kitchen and hall
and a pantry opening off the space between ;
this shuts off sound. Crockery and glass can
be taken into or from the pantry without being
carried into the kitchen thus—(Fig. 38).

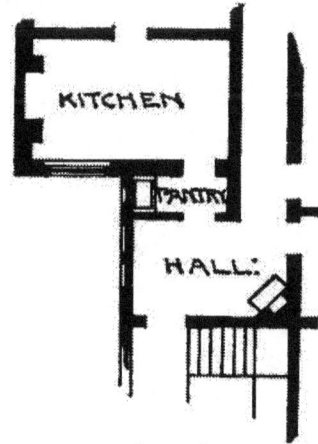

FIG. 38.

Servants' W.C.—It is a convenient plan to make the entrance
to the servants' W.C. from the scullery, which is a common arrangement, and one that has been used for many years in private houses as
well as flats. Some sanitary authorities object to it, they say a scullery
is a room used for the preparation of food, and that there should be a
passage or lobby to cut off the W.C. A scullery is rarely used for the
preparation of food, especially the small rooms usually found in flats,
they are only just large enough to contain a sink. This objection
is hardly necessary considering the sanitary arrangements of the
average modern W.C., and only a few authorities raise such objections.
Many modern flats planned by the best architects of to-day, who may
be trusted to properly consider the sanitary details of a building, have
this arrangement.

There is a tendency to make the entrance to the servants' W.C. from a balcony, which in some cases passes from one portion of the building to another, as in Fig. 119. From a sanitary point of view the plan is of course good, but care must be taken that this balcony or entrance to the W.C. is not seen from any important part of any flat, either above or below. Again, servants will probably object to such an arrangement, they will not like to leave the building in bad weather. Considering the excellence of modern plumbing, and the care taken for all sanitary fittings, disconnection, &c., is not this question of sanitary planning somewhat carried to excess? If we were dealing with pan closets and drainage of fifty years ago, it might be understood.

Servants' Bedroom.—The position of the servants' bedroom requires careful consideration. If it opens off the kitchen, the plan is simple and cheap, but there is this objection, the slops from the bedroom must be carried through the kitchen every morning. It is not a nice idea, but in poor class flats the arrangement is common, see Figs. 136, 138, 139, and 144.

But this arrangement is also found in good class flats (see figs. 84, 97, 114, and 122). If the plan is to be avoided, it is clear that the servants' W.C. must be placed so as to be accessible between the kitchen and the bedroom. Examples of this plan are shown in Figs. 91, 94, 95, and 101.

In France the servants usually sleep on the top floor, the advantage is that at least one bedroom is gained for the family residing in the flat. Some such arrangement may become general in England, and Fig. 90 is a plan of a building where this has been done. In most of our flats the top floor lets at practically the same rent as the floor below, some tenants like to go as high as possible, and if servants cease to sleep in the flat, the accommodation will doubtless be provided for them in the basement. Such an arrangement would be objected to by many ladies, it destroys the idea of the mistress exercising control over her maids; but this arrangement seems to be forced on by the trade staircases, and the free entrance and exit from the flat that a servant has at all times. If they can do that, they may as well have their rooms away from the suite, and this power to leave at any time must be recognised.

Cupboards.—Ample cupboard accommodation is being provided in the latest flats. A few years ago a first-class suite had few if any cupboards. A butler's pantry is also built in some of the best blocks (see Figs. 84, 86, 90, 94, 98, and 119). In America and France much more cupboard accommodation is given than in England (see Figs. 173 and 202).

Scullery.—Our kitchens, as a rule, are much larger than those in France, but our cooking is not better in consequence. A scullery is unknown abroad, though it is true a pantry or " office " is provided, but there is no reason why the scullery should not be abolished in England, especially in poor class flats. A sink in the kitchen is all that is required, and the combined floor area for one room is more useful than when it is divided. Examples of a kitchen with a sink and no scullery, are shown in Figs. 90, 93, 96, and 113.

It has been suggested that in first class flats the kitchens should be smaller, and the space added to the servants' bedroom, making it large enough to contain a table, so that the maids could use it as a sitting-room instead of the kitchen. It seems a doubtful advantage, for in cold weather they must be in the kitchen on account of the fire, and the extra space is of more use in the kitchen where work is done.

A balcony is a valuable addition to a plan, if not to an elevation. Sometimes it is possible to plan one about 8 ft. by 8 ft.; a square shape is more useful than the usual arrangement, about 3 ft. wide. A large balcony is a great luxury during the summer, and much appreciated by tenants.

Maisonettes.—In the early days of the flat movement, one suite was sometimes on two or more floors. The idea was to build very lofty reception rooms in the front of a building, and bedrooms or offices at the back, with less height, so that two floors of reception rooms would about equal the height of three floors of bedrooms or offices. The best example of this arrangement is the block of buildings known as Albert Hall Mansions, shown on illustrations 107, 108, and 108A. The letters on the plan indicate the suites. The ground floor suite comprises the back part of the basement and also the front part of the mezzanine floor. The second floor suite comprises also the back portion of the first floor. The second and third floors being lofty, each about 15 ft. high, three floors of bedrooms or offices are built, making up the height of the two floors, and so on. The arrangement is exceedingly ingenious, and a few other blocks of flats were built about the same date with a similar idea. But it would seem that when people want a flat they object to any stairs, and with the exception of the "maisonette" (ground floor and basement), the system has found little favour. Fig. 111 is, however, a modern instance, and the flats have let well. The maisonette seems an ideal arrangement for a flat, but some agents say that every ordinary flat in a building will be let before the maisonette.

Bath-room and W.C.—Some architects object to a W.C. in a bath-room. It is better to keep them separate if possible, but in most cases they are together as a matter of economy. In a flat of moderate size, if it is only possible to have one W.C., then the apparatus should not be in the bath-room. In a private house let at £100 a year, there are usually three W.C.'s, but this number is very rarely provided even in the best flats. Figs. 96, 97, and 98 show examples where it has been done. An additional W.C. apparatus occupies little space in a bath-room ; it is often of great convenience ; if the occupants of the flat object to the arrangement they need not use it. In any flat let at £75 or more, there should be at least two W.C.'s, one for the servants only. If there are two W.C.'s, it may be convenient and cheap to have them adjoining, but it is a bad arrangement; the servants' W.C. should not be near the other unless the doors are far apart, as in Fig. 95. A reference to the plans will show it is a common custom to put the W.C. in the bath-room in bachelor flats and also in American suites.

The plan of flats (Fig. 119) was made with a view to preventing a servant passing through the hall when going to the entrance door. This may seem an advantage to some people, but it is an unimportant point unless it can be arranged without spoiling the plan.

Bedrooms.—Many foreign flats have one bedroom opening out of another. This system has not been tried in England, but there are many cases where it might work well; two sons or two daughters could have adjoining rooms, a long length of passage could be saved, and larger rooms obtained.

Flats are rarely built with more than one servant's bedroom even in a good neighbourhood, but two servants' rooms are often required ; one should be in a convenient position for a man-servant.

It is an advantage to have a small room next the best bedroom ; this may be used either as a bedroom or dressing-room. A bedroom next to a bath-room can have a door between so that the bath-room could be used as a dressing-room. A dressing-room is rarely provided in the best flats ; it is a mistake not to do so.

In flats at low rents, such as Fig. 139, one sitting-room and three bedrooms are usually provided, but the demand for flats with so little accommodation is not great, and if they have one more room they let much more readily. Then two rooms can be used as sitting-rooms if required, but if there are only three bedrooms it is unlikely that the flat would be taken by any applicant who wanted two sitting-rooms ; there would only be the servant's room and one other bedroom remaining.

Storage-room.—This should be allowed for in the roof or basement ; a tenant wants some place for boxes and portmanteaus. Dark store-rooms in the basement let readily. The basement plan Fig. 96 shows many such rooms.

Coals.—Provision must be made for coals ; cellars are usually built under the street.

Bicycles.—A common-room is often built for bicycles and perambulators (see Fig. 96). Sometimes a separate cycle-house is built for each flat.

Larder.—Avoid placing the larder next a W.C., although if each is well ventilated it is not a serious detriment, provided the partition between them is properly constructed.

Gardens and Common-rooms.—Some flats are built around ornamental gardens, with tennis courts and croquet lawns for the tenants. These are kept up at the expense of the owners of the flats, but tenants usually pay a small contribution per annum. These gardens may attract tenants, but they occupy land that in many cases might have been built upon. They are a doubtful blessing ; many managers are strongly opposed to them. The tenants meet constantly, and there are numerous complaints, petty jealousies, and a thousand and one annoyances in consequence. The manager of the flats often has an unpleasant time during the summer. Ornamental gardens are a great expense, and if allowed to get into a bad condition, the appearance of the flats is affected. The same objections apply to common drawing-rooms but not to dining-rooms. It is far better that the tenants should remain strangers, and the ordinary flats where there is little chance of social intercourse are much easier to manage. In one block of buildings where the catering is all done for the tenants, there is the necessary large dining-room, but the manager said he was strongly opposed to a common drawing-room for the above reasons.

It has often been suggested that the roof of a block of flats should be laid out as a garden, the roof being a flat finished with asphalte or one of the many patent roof-coverings, that gravel paths and flower-beds should be made, so that the tenants would have the advantage of a garden in a town. This has been tried at Bexhill, and the plans Figs. 137 and 138 show the lower floors. The lifts were constructed to take the tenants on to the roof, which was laid out at great expense and summer-houses were constructed. The result has been a failure; the tenants never use the garden. Flat roofs have been constructed in London for artisans' dwellings, and these have also been a failure. The dirt and smuts of London make a roof garden impossible.

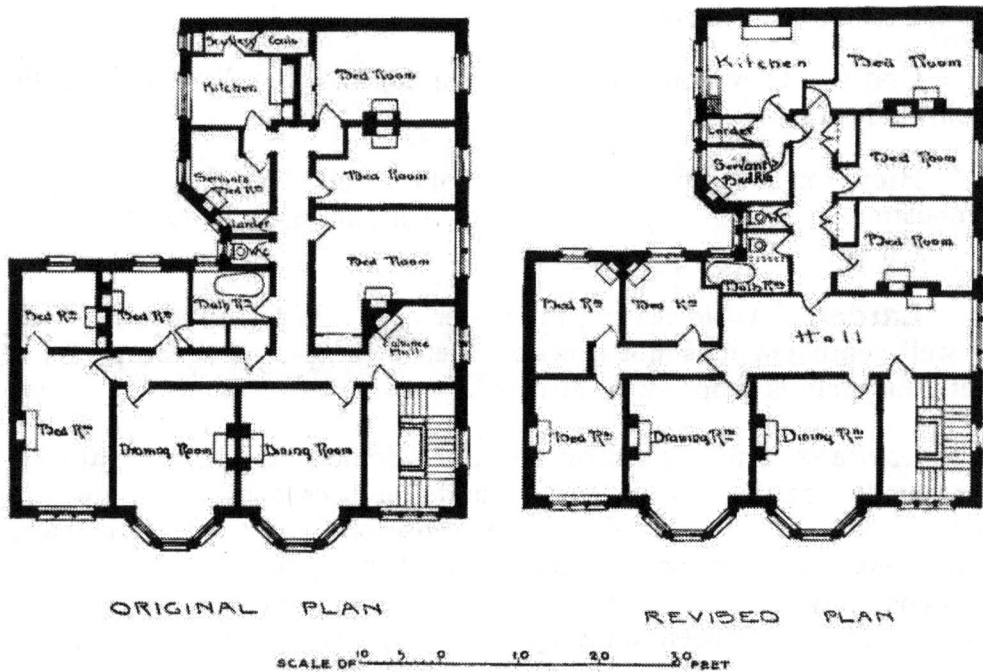

ORIGINAL PLAN   REVISED PLAN

SCALE OF

FIG. 39.

Bad Plans.—Some plans of flats are no doubt very bad, especially those of some early buildings. One plan of a recent building is given (Fig. 39). It will be noticed that the entrance hall is small, and that the passages are long and narrow; one bedroom opens out of another, when the passage space would not have been missed from the front room. The large bedroom has a bad shape, and is larger than is needed for a flat, and there is only one W.C. The revised plan beside it is an attempt to improve it. The main walls are practically the same, the only alteration being near the servants' bedroom. A large hall is obtained, an extra W.C. is provided, and if the bath-room is divided as shown by dotted lines, it can be separate from the W.C. The scullery and kitchen are in one, the larder is near the kitchen and away from the W.C.; each bedroom has a separate entrance, and the dark passages are much curtailed.

Many cupboards on a plan may appear an attraction, but their existence is often due to bad planning; awkward dark spaces are left, and that is the only way to make use of them.

Another example may be given of bad planning. Fig. 39A will be understood at once. At first it was thought that a connection between the two suites was contemplated, a door in the wall across the passage; that, however, was not so, there was no reason for the bad plan. One side of each of two rooms might have been saved, and larger rooms obtained by building the doors as shown by dotted lines.

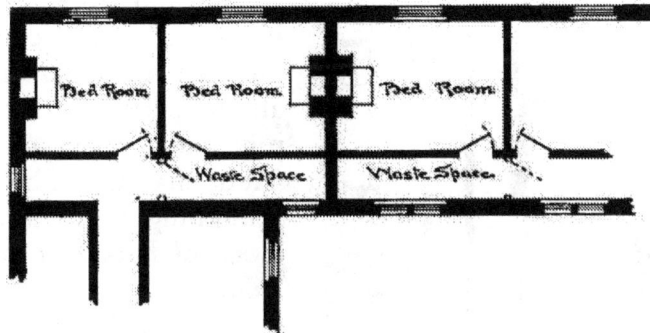

FIG. 39A.

Sometimes a W.C. is 12 or 14 ft. long. This is often the result of a bad plan, for the space is useless.

Fig. 37 is an illustration to show how much more simple a plan becomes if the frontage allows three rooms to be built facing the street. An area gives light only to the hall and bath-room of each suite; the kitchen is lighted by a recess, the servants' W.C. is entered from a balcony and not overlooked by any of the principal windows. Many plans are given with two rooms in the front of the building, and a comparison will show the advantage of a plan on the lines of Fig. 37. It will be noticed that there is very little passage space.

The ideal plan for a high-class suite has all the servants' rooms well cut off from the other part of the suite; they form in fact another suite inside the main suite, with an entrance door. Such an arrangement is shown in Figs. 84, 85, 87, 97, and 99. If possible the entrance to the servants' suite should be near the main entrance, as in Fig. 97.

Fig. 39B is a good arrangement for the servants' quarters; the kitchen, being the most noisy room, would be shut off by two doors. For first-class flats a pantry should be added.

Fig. 39C is a variation of the last plan; part of the suite is on each side of the servants' quarters, and a small inner passage is necessary to prevent direct entrance to these rooms from the main corridor.

Catering Flats.—The existence of these buildings is no doubt due to the difficulty of obtaining good servants. The family has a self-contained suite of almost any number of rooms and usually a pantry, but there are no servants' offices. There is a common dining-room, and sometimes in large blocks there are common drawing-rooms, billiard-rooms, &c.; all the service is included in the rent, meals are paid for at a fixed charge. The building is something between an ordinary block of flats and an hotel. In London they have not all been a success, in many cases the owners have obtained a license and turned the buildings into hotels.

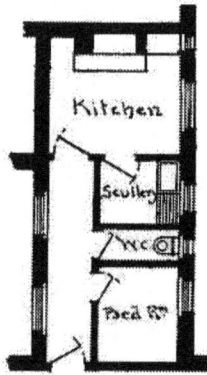

FIG. 39B.

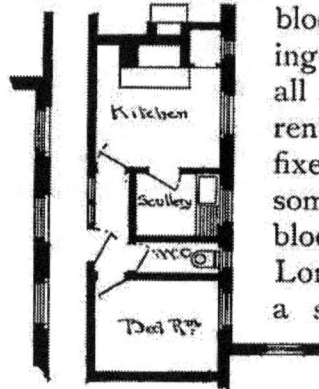

FIG. 39C.

These flats offer great advantages to people who are away frequently, and who are willing to pay for the conveniences they obtain. Success or failure depends far more upon the manager than upon the architect who designed the building, consequently the subject need not be dealt with in much detail here.

In one successful building in Kensington the rents obtained may be of interest. The building is a large one, and was a block of self-contained flats. When converted into catering flats the rent, of course, included service, but even allowing for that, the increase in amounts obtained is surprising, for it must be remembered that all meals are paid for at a similar rate to an hotel.

A suite on the sixth floor was originally let at £75 per annum, the kitchen was made into a bedroom, and the flat relet at £175 per annum. A flat at £120 was altered and relet for £375. One suite formerly let at £240 was converted into two suites, £400 was spent upon the work, but the flats relet at £175 and £285, a total of £460.

With a good manager these buildings are a success, but it all rests with him.

Bachelor Flats have been built for many years. In some cases all the catering is done, but often breakfast is the only meal served. As a rule there are no common-rooms.

The extension of the Savoy Hotel is somewhat of a new departure, small suites being combined with an hotel. Plans are given, Figs. 160, 161. Catering flats are more similar to an hotel than to a block of the ordinary suites: the tenants would obtain advantages that they could not get in other buildings, and if catering flats have cut into the business of the hotel the compliment is now being returned. Most large buildings of the catering flats class do an ordinary hotel business; you can obtain a room for one night.

The plan of these flats seldom varies; the accommodation includes a small hall, a sitting-room, and a bedroom, with a bath-room and W.C. between. Several plans are given, and are referred to in a subsequent chapter.

Seaside Flats.—Upon careful inquiry it is evident that flats at the seaside are not a success, they are not wanted. A few have been built, but considering the recent growth of most south coast watering-places, the proportion of flats is very small. This is speaking generally, some of course have been a success, but the time has not yet arrived for "a flat movement" anywhere out of London.

CHAPTER III.

ARTISANS' DWELLINGS.

FOR many years past the housing of certain classes has occupied the attention of charitable people and also municipal authorities. The result is that a very large number of dwellings, usually blocks of flats, have been erected in London and most of the large provincial cities. Housing schemes in connection with street improvements have been recently carried out in Manchester, Liverpool, Birmingham, &c.

"Associated" and "Self-contained" Suites.—These dwellings are either on the "associated" plan, *i.e.*, one that has certain rooms used by more than one tenant, or "self-contained," *i.e.*, where each tenant has a flat complete with all the accommodation he may require.

One-roomed Tenements.—The simplest form of dwelling is obviously the one-roomed tenement, which must be constructed on the associated plan. Examples of these buildings are shown in Figs. 65, 72, 78, 79.

The one-roomed dwelling is not in favour with the London County Council, which has built self-contained flats for artisans with as many as six rooms.

Position of Rooms.—In planning flats for the working classes, it is advisable to place the bedrooms in a quiet position; the back of a block is preferable to a room overlooking a main and usually noisy thoroughfare, which, again, is the position preferred by the tenants for a living room, so that they can obtain a good view of the street.

Bay Windows.—If economy in building must be studied, all bay windows and broken frontage lines must be avoided. This, it will be seen, has been done in almost all buildings, and is a rule to be strictly followed.

In flats of two or more rooms the W.C. and scullery should be within the entrance door to a suite and not across a public passage.

If it is impossible to avoid some such arrangement, the scullery should be cut off rather than the W.C. A mixture of the self-contained and associated systems is not a good arrangement, and has been found unsatisfactory.

Stairs and Public Passages.—On account of the children the stairs should be particularly easy going. About 6 ft. 6 in. should be the width allowed for a double flight. Handrails should have knobs at intervals to prevent children sliding down them. Blocks of these buildings sometimes have the staircase exposed, but tenants complain of the inconvenience and prefer a staircase protected from the weather. Ample ventilation should always be arranged by large windows and ventilators that cannot be closed. Where the balcony system is adopted, the staircase is always exposed. Public passages must be avoided as much as possible. As a rule two or three suites on each floor are served by one staircase. Examples of the former will be seen in Figs. 57, 61, 66, and of the latter in Figs. 47, 56.

Fig. 45 shows how four suites can be arranged; the passage room is inside the suite instead of outside. One way to save the cost of staircases is to build on the balcony principle. It will be seen that the balconies are practically long passages outside the buildings. Examples are given in Figs. 59, 64, 74, 78. At Manchester, the Oldham Road scheme is in the form of a square; the balconies are at the back of the buildings, and overlook a vacant space about an acre in extent, which is used as a recreation ground. A staircase is at each corner and serves a large number of tenements. It has been argued that these balconies stop the light to rooms, but the windows can be made larger than is usual so as to allow for this diminution. Tenants like the balconies, but they tend to destroy the privacy of the dwellings, for unless the glass is obscured, any one passing along can see into the rooms. Other examples of the balcony system are given—it is more popular for low buildings than for high blocks. The idea is not a modern one, and was advocated in 1855 by Messrs Ashpitel and Whichcord in their essay. On the Continent the balcony system has been much used, not only for artisans' dwellings, but also for better class flats, particularly at Budapest, and an example is given in Fig. 195.

Scullery.—If this is provided it should have a copper, but it is sometimes advisable to omit the scullery and throw the space into the living room, and provide a sink there. This arrangement is increasing in favour, but if the tenants are dirty people the sink is likely to become a nuisance.

W.C.—A difficulty often arises with reference to the W.C.; the most convenient plan is to enter it from the scullery. In some districts this is allowed but not in others, as it is contended that a scullery is a room used for the preparation of food. If the tenants are dirty people the W.C. will often get into a bad condition. This, as a rule, is not discovered until the drains have become blocked. If possible the W.C. should be accessible to the caretaker, who can inspect it without entering the flats. This is often done, see Fig. 55.

Baths.—A fitted bath is rarely provided, as there are usually public baths in the neighbourhood, but baths can be fitted at small cost in the scullery when specially made for these dwellings. Hot water is sometimes provided for the tenants by the owners; the fires are not always alight, hot water being obtainable at certain hours. This is no doubt a convenience, but the cost is heavy.

Playground.—It is usual in planning these dwellings to have the block backing on to a court or playground. The entrance to the suites should be from this private ground and not directly off the street. This system is preferable, as it keeps out loafers and other objectionable characters. The entrance is often through an archway, as at the St Pancras Buildings. The caretaker has rooms adjoining, and can at once stop trespassers. The system reminds one of the better class flats in Paris.

Laundry.—In the Oldham Road scheme the staircase at each corner of the square is continued up above the fourth story, and a laundry and drying rooms have been provided. Each drying room has a lantern light. This arrangement is general in Germany for better class flats. Wash-houses are often provided as separate buildings in the yard, and are a great convenience to tenants.

Through Ventilation.—Another point to be considered is the question of through ventilation; it is a fundamental principle, and will govern the plan. Some medical authorities are of opinion that in the same suite there should be communication between the front and back rooms, so that when the windows and doors are open there will be a through draught (see Figs. 55, 57, 67, 68). It will be seen by comparing the plan Fig. 53 and those providing for through ventilation, that the latter system necessitates a more expressive plan than one giving the same accommodation in other buildings of the "back to back" type. The question arises—Is it worth while increasing the outlay for an advantage that may be used, but probably never will be? The working man has a great dislike to ventilation; he will keep the windows closed, and stuff up ventilators with newspaper.

It is somewhat strange, this call for through ventilation for artisans' dwellings, when such a thing is never mentioned in connection with more expensive flats. It is very doubtful if the questionable advantage is worth the great additional cost.

Dust.—The removal of dust and refuse may be arranged in two ways. Dust shoots may be constructed with an entrance to the shaft outside each flat, and a receptacle on the ground floor or in the basement; or dust pails emptied by hand may be used. The first system is objected to by many architects, the cost of construction must be considered and the shoot gets foul after a time, dust from one floor may be a nuisance to the floors below, unless some special traps are fixed. The tenants will send anything down the shoot, and it is often impossible to discover the delinquent. If this system is adopted the shoot should be continued above the roof for ventilation, and should also have a ventilating flue carried up as an ordinary chimney. Examples are shown, Figs. 53 and 65. The architect to the Peabody Trust much prefers this system; he finds it is not a nuisance, and of course it is a great saving in labour. The plans (Fig. 53) are described further on.

The pail system is generally preferred, and is the only one known in better class flats; the pails should be emptied every morning into a common bin or receptacle, or placed upon the pavement. The pail, in small tenements, takes up a certain amount of space, and these pails are rarely kept clean.

A small balcony is much appreciated by a tenant even when only a few feet square, as shown in Figs. 48, 60, and 61.

Cupboards.—Good cupboard accommodation is always an inducement when letting a flat, but in the case of artisans' dwellings the architect need not consider the subject from that point of view. These dwellings always let well, and the low rate of interest upon the capital outlay shows that the poorer classes get better accommodation for the rent they pay than tenants in better class flats. Then the question of little luxuries is of much more importance for the owner to consider. It is sometimes suggested that cupboards should be provided in every room, but if the tenants have certain furniture they are not required; in the bedrooms the cupboard would take the place of a wardrobe, and in the living rooms the place of a sideboard, which a tenant often owns. Cupboards are of course necessary as food stores, and should be well ventilated. An angle cupboard is cheaper than any other as no sides are required, it should have no top as a receptacle for dust, but should be continued to the ceiling.

Construction of Floors.—The floor of each scullery, washhouse, and W.C. should not be of wood, but should be finished in cement or in some similar way.

In buildings of this class it is advisable to have cement skirtings, with the angle of junction with the floor rounded off. The tenants are sometimes very destructive, and iron balusters and handrails should always be fixed. Lead pipes should be avoided, iron being used; in short it is advisable to avoid any material that can be broken or stolen. It is true economy to spend a good price upon sanitary and plumbing fittings, and the stoves and ranges should be strong.

Wall Surfaces.—The tenants are often very dirty people, consequently a distempered wall is preferable to a wall paper. If wall paper is hung it should stop a few inches from the ceiling; if carried up, the angle is a favourite resort for vermin. For the same reason a picture rail should not be fixed close up to the ceiling. If one is fixed a short way down, a rule can be made that no nails for pictures are to be driven into the walls. The angles of a room should also be rounded off.

Paintwork.—The tenants like grained work, and it is the cheapest in the end, however strongly one may object to it for æsthetic reasons.

Windows.—Sashes should be divided into panes, the strength of the sash is increased, the appearance from without or within is improved, and if the glass is broken the cost of reglazing is less than when each sash has one sheet of glass.

Health.—Large blocks of buildings are healthy, and certainly more sanitary than most artisans' dwellings in the country. Dr Saunders, the Medical Officer of Health for the City of London, has given statistics of five blocks of buildings in Houndsditch, owned by the Corporation. The average death-rate during the five years 1894 to 1898 was 12 per 1,000, whilst for London during the same period it was 18 per 1,000. The death-rate in the Peabody Buildings for the year 1891 was 4 per 1,000 below the average for London.

Flat Roofs.—Many blocks of buildings have been erected with flat roofs and the staircase carried up for easy access. The idea was to use these roofs for drying clothes, but in large cities they have not been a success on account of the dirt and smoke. Tenants who live on the top floor also object to the roof being used as a playground, on account of the noise made by the children running about.

Rents as a rule do not vary on the different floors. A lower story may be more convenient, but an upper suite is quieter, lighter, and generally brighter.

Birmingham One-Room Tenements.—Single-room tenements at Birmingham are shown on Fig. 65. The architects have provided a sink with a food cupboard over it. The bed is in a recess, and there is a W.C. and coal store for each tenant. There is a scullery for each seven tenements. The plan is simple, and the width of the passages is a good feature. There are also several other examples of one-room dwellings in other cities.

Size of Rooms.—This question is important, and the following figures may be of interest :—

LONDON.

London County Council Boundary Street Estate. At first the areas were 144 sq. ft. for a living-room, and 96 sq. ft. for a bedroom ; these were afterwards increased to 160 and 110 sq. ft. respectively.

		Ft.	In.		Ft.	In.	
First Premiated Designs	Living-room -	16	3	by	9	9	Two-room tenement.
(not carried out) -	Bedroom -	12	3	„	8	8¼	„ „
	Living-room -	16	4½	„	10	2½	Three-room tenement.
	Bedroom -	12	5½	„	9	6	„ „
	„ -	10	2½	„	10	4½	„ „
Peabody Buildings -	Bedrooms about	13	6	„	9	9	
	Living-room -	14	6	„	12	6	Two-room tenement.
	„ -	13	6	„	11	9	Three-room tenement.
BIRMINGHAM.							
See plan, Fig. 65 -	Living room -	12	0	„	11	0	Single tenement.
	Bedroom -	12	0	„	10	0	„ „
	Living-room -	12	0	„	11	0	Double tenement.
	Bedroom -	12	0	„	7	0	„ „
	„ -	8	10	„	9	0	„ „
Milk Street Buildings -	Living-room -	13	0	„	14	0	Single tenement.
	Bedroom -	12	2	„	9	6	„ „
	Living-room -	13	4	„	14	0	Double tenement.
	Bedroom -	8	2	„	14	0	„ „
	„ -	9	0	„	9	0	„ „

		Ft.	In.		Ft.	In.	
BRISTOL - - -	Living-room -	14	0	,,	14	0	Double tenement.
	Bedroom -	14	0	,,	8	0	,, ,,
	,, -	12	0	,,	9	0	,, ,,
GLASGOW. See Fig. 80	Single - room dwelling -	13	0	,,	15	0	
	Living-room, with bed-recess -	11	0	,,	12	0	Single tenement.
	Bedroom, with bed-recess -	14	6	,,	11	0	,, ,,
LIVERPOOL.							
Juvenal Street (1890) -	Single - room dwelling -	14	3	,,	11	0	
	Living-room -	14	0	,,	11	0	Single tenement.
	Bedroom -	12	0	,,	11	0	,, ,,
	Living-room -	14	0	,,	12	3	Double tenement.
	Bedroom -	14	3	,,	14	0	,, ,,
	,, -	14	0	,,	9	9	,, ,,
Dryden Street (1901) -	Living room -	15	0	,,	10	6	Double tenement.
	Bedroom -	12	0	,,	10	9	,, ,,
	,, -	12	0	,,	9	6	,, ,,
	Living-room -	11	0	,,	11	0	Single tenement.
	Bedroom -	10	0	,,	8	6	,, ,,
Kempston Street (1902)	Living-room -	13	10	,,	12	6	Double tenement.
	Bedroom -	12	0	,,	10	4	,, ,,
	,, -	11	4	,,	9	0	,, ,,
	Living-room -	14	5	,,	12	9	Single tenement.
	Bedroom -	12	5	,,	9	2	,, ,,
Fontenoy Street (1902)	Living-room -	14	0	,,	12	3	Four-room tenement.
	Bedroom -	11	0	,,	9	0	,, ,,
	,, -	12	3	,,	7	9	,, ,,
	,, -	9	0	,,	7	9	,, ,,
	Living-room -	12	3	,,	11	6	Single tenement.
	Bedroom -	12	3	,,	9	9	,, ,,
Kew Street (1903)	Living-room -	13	6	,,	10	6	Double tenement.
	Bedroom -	13	0	,,	10	0	,, ,,
	,, -	13	6	,,	7	6	,, ,,
	Living-room -	14	6	,,	10	3	Single tenement.
	Bedroom -	10	3	,,	9	9	,, ,,
MANCHESTER - -	Single-room dwelling about 130 sq. ft.						
	Living-room about 174 sq. ft.						Single tenement
	Bedroom about - 108 ,,						,, ,,
	Scullery about - 45 ,,						,, ,,

The areas for different rooms recommended by the Local Government Board are as follows :—

Living-room -	-	-	200 sq. ft., height from 8 to 9 ft.
Scullery -	-	-	90 ,, ,, ,, ,,
Parents' Bedroom -	-	-	120 ,, ,, ,, ,,
Children's ,, -	-	-	80 ,, ,, ,, ,,

It will be noticed that in Liverpool the rooms are larger than those usually built in London. The height of rooms has gradually decreased in Liverpool, and it is interesting to note the variations :—

Corporation buildings erected in 1869, height of rooms 9 ft.

„	„	„	1885,	„	„	9 „
„	„	„	1890,	„	„	9 „ to 9 ft. 3 in.
„	„	„	1897,	„	„	8 „ 6 in.
„	„	„	1897,	„	„	8 „
„	„	„	1901,	„	„	8 „
„	„	„	1903,	„	„	8 „

In Manchester the height allowed is 9 ft. In Birmingham and in the Peabody Buildings the dimension is 8 ft. 6 in.

The cost of large blocks of tenements is heavy, and has increased enormously during the last twenty years. The following table gives some figures with reference to recent buildings :—

Locality.	Building.	Date.	Cost per Room.	Cost per Foot Cube.
London	County Council— Boundary St. Estate :—			
„	Cleeve Buildings -	—	£79 ⎫ These are the	—
„	Sonning „ -	—	£68 ⎪ cheapest buildings	—
„	Taplow „ -	—	£71 ⎬ erected for the	—
„	Marlow „ -	—	£67 ⎭ L.C.C.	—
„	Scheme generally -	1900	£91. 10s.	8¼d.
„	Peabody Buildings -	—	£86 to £110	8d.
Glasgow -	- - - - - -	—	£70 to £85	4¼d. to 6d.
Birming- ham	Milk Street Buildings -	1900	£62 (if sculleries are included, £45)	—
„	"Homes Limited" -	—	(3-room tenement) £48	—
„	„ „ -	—	(2-room „) £57	Smaller block 6d.
„	„ „ -	—	(1-room „) £96	
„	„ „ -	—	Large block, £52	5¾d.
Liverpool -	Arley Street - -	1897	£61. 5s. (floors not fire- proof)	4.81d.
„	Dryden Street - -	1901	£59. 6s. 8d.	7.07d.
„	Kempston Street - -	1902	£81. 8s. 6d.	6.27d.
Manchester	Oldham Road - -	1894	£116	—
„	Pollard Street - -	1894	£98	—
London	Shoreditch Vestry -	—	£91	—
„	Millbank Estate - -	—	£90 to £105	—
„	Cobham Buildings -	—	— —	10d.
„	E. End Dwellings Co. :—			
„	Winton Houses, Pen- tonville - -	1895	£80	8d.
„	Victoria Park, Gretton Houses - - -	1901	£90	9½d.
„	Old Ford Dwellings -	1904	£80	9d.

Housing "the Poor" or "Working Classes."—There is little doubt that the majority of people imagine that these large blocks of buildings are erected to house the poor. Years ago this was a great social question. To-day we hear little of it. The question now is—How to house the working classes? who, all things taken into consideration, are not badly off. Apparently the idea of housing the poor has been abandoned, or has become less attractive to candidates when canvassing for votes.

Mr John Honeyman, R.S.A., in his paper read at the Royal Institute of British Architects on 2nd April 1900, remarked : "It is a mistake to praise the London County Council and the corporations of other cities for erecting artisans' dwellings, while they do absolutely nothing towards providing suitable dwellings for the poorest classes."

It is quite clear that the very poor cannot afford more than one room ; these are the people who live in the slum areas, and the first idea was to rehouse them in the new buildings. But experience has proved that these poor people are not rehoused, and if they could only afford one room, it is clear that very little provision was made to rehouse them.

London.—The Boundary Street Estate was the largest scheme carried out by the London County Council. It was condemned as an insanitary district; 2,300 adults lived on the area, and when classified according to the various occupations of the tenants, the largest group consisted of labourers ; there were almost the same number of hawkers; there were no bricklayers, plumbers, or plasterers. It would be interesting to see a return of the occupations of the tenants to-day, for only eleven of the old inhabitants were recently living in the area.

On this estate, although there are no returns showing the number of rooms formerly occupied by the tenants, it is apparent from the returns of their occupations, and also from the fact that it was a slum district, that the majority of the people occupied only one room, and it is not to be wondered at that only eleven people were rehoused out of a total of 5,719, when one considers the accommodation supplied.

The following are particulars of the present buildings :—

        10 specially large tenements.
        103 suites of four rooms exclusive of scullery.
        400   „   three   „   „   „
        541   „   two   „   „   „
        15 single-room tenements.

A total of 1,069 suites, and only 15 tenements of one room. Naturally the houses are occupied by a superior class to those who were dispossessed.

The following figures from "The London Manual" of 1904 give some interesting totals :—

GENERAL SUMMARY OF THE WORK OF THE LONDON COUNTY COUNCIL UP TO 31ST MARCH 1903.

	Number of Persons Discharged or to be Displaced from Insanitary Areas.	Number of Tenements of						Total Number of Tenements.	Total Number of Persons Provided or to be Provided for.	Estimated Value of Land for Housing Purposes and Cost of Buildings.	Estimated Cost of Clearance.
		One Room.	Two Rooms.	Three Rooms.	Four Rooms.	Five Rooms.	Six Rooms.				
Buildings already completed and occupied - -	—	105	2,129	1,453	219	8	3	3,912	19,628	£ 1,261,000	£ —
Buildings in course of erection	—	35	478	581	56	11	—	1,161	6,851	381,000	—
Buildings for which working drawings are being prepared	—	26	399	852	255	133	—	1,665	10,133	540,000	—
Insanitary areas already dealt with - -	8,669	—	—	—	—	—	—	—	8,672*	—	360,924
Insanitary areas now being dealt with - -	7,886	—	—	—	—	—	—	—	{6,981* / 1,030}	—	749,500
Totals - -	16,555	166	3,006	2,886	530	152	3	6,738	57,642	2,182,000	1,131,900
Buildings for which plans are in course of preparation	—	28	744	4,813	2,201	1,047	—	8,833	60,466	2,671,000	—
Grand Totals - -	16,555	194	3,750	7,699	2,731	1,199	3	17,571	98,108	4,853,000	1,131,900

* These are included in other divisions of this summary, and are therefore not included in the total.

The above table shows that out of a total of 47,728 rooms built, only 194 have been constructed as single-room tenements—the only accommodation possible for the poor. This is remarkable when we are informed that 16,555 persons were displaced from the insanitary areas alone.

Bristol.—It is the same elsewhere. In Bristol, long before the new buildings could be erected, the former tenants became absorbed in the surrounding population, and the Corporation dwellings were tenanted by a superior class of artisan, instead of the labouring classes formerly dwelling on the site.

Liverpool.—The Report mentioned elsewhere shows that a few years ago the buildings erected for the poor were unsuitable, for we read: "After the erection of these buildings it was still felt that nothing had been done to provide for the actual persons who had been dispossessed, the rents charged in the new buildings being beyond the means of those who had been dispossessed." Since 1896 all dwellings erected by the Corporation have been reserved exclusively for tenants who have been dispossessed.

London.—It seems clear from the above figures that the County Council never intended to rehouse the poor. There are many difficulties to be overcome when building single rooms, with common W.C.'s, sculleries, &c. &c., and the policy has evidently been to pull down slum property and cater for a better class. That some people are strongly opposed to one-roomed tenements is clear. Dr J. F. Skyes speaking at the Architectural Association stated : "People sometimes said, 'You ought to build for the very poorest.' That could not be done, and he should be sorry to see the architectural profession trying to do so. To build down to the requirements of the lowest and poorest of a population was the very worst thing they could do" (*The Builder*, 17th May 1902). He was strongly opposed to one-roomed tenements. It is interesting to compare these words with those of the late Mr Thomas H. Blashill, formerly Architect to the London County Council: "As to rehousing, the County Council had never rehoused, and would never be likely to do so, upon the lines it was compelled to go. The Council had taken in another class, and some of the people who had been turned out had gone and overcrowded other localities" (*The Builder*, 17th February 1900); and again, "If the municipal authorities did not build for the very poorest, he did not know why they should build at all" (*R.I.B.A. Journal*, 7th April 1900).

The London County Council at present seems to favour the idea of building suburban cottages under Part 3 of the Amendment Act of 1900. Large estates are being developed at Tooting, Norbury, Tottenham, &c. In connection with this policy the extension of electric tramways and other cheap methods of travel are being developed.

The large town blocks of dwellings can hardly be said to have been a success. The expense has been considerable. In London, the cost of pulling down and clearing the site has been as much as £500 for each family displaced; then the cost of erection is very heavy, and the authorities have suffered from their own regulations. Two-story buildings cost less per foot cube, and the comparatively low value of suburban land is an important consideration.

Nottingham.—The city of Nottingham built a large block of dwellings twenty-five years ago; it has never been regarded as successful, and the Corporation is considering the question of erecting two-story flats.

Profit.—As these blocks of buildings have been erected either by charitable people or municipal authorities for the benefit of certain classes, the question of a good return for the money invested has not been the main consideration. It is generally admitted that they cannot yield a fair return on the capital outlay. The Peabody Trustees started with the idea of a 5 per cent. return, but that was altered to 3 per cent., which the scheme pays. The East End Dwellings Company pays 4 per cent. on Preference Share Capital, and 5 per cent. on Ordinary Share Capital, an exceptional result. Most of the buildings have been erected by local authorities, and the result is that private enterprise has practically ceased. In Glasgow, Mr John Honeyman informed the Royal Institute of British Architects in 1900: "During the last ten years not one single house of £6 and under has been erected; but, on the other hand, during the same period the number of such houses has been considerably reduced. During the same period the total number of houses at £6 and under erected by the Corporation was seventy-nine."

Mr Douglass Mathews's Scheme.—The debate at the Royal Institute of British Architects on 2nd April 1900 upon "Working Class Dwellings" has been referred to elsewhere. Mr Douglass Mathews expressed strong views against the erection of these buildings by public authorities, and his opinion was supported by other well-known architects. At the Conference on the Housing of the Working Classes held at the Sanitary Institute in 1900, Mr Mathews read an important paper, giving particulars of a novel scheme. The paper has since been published in pamphlet form. His idea is to exempt the owners of these buildings from such general rates as are intended for the very poor, such as poor, asylums, education, inhabited house duty, and other similar rates. Only purely local rates such as cleansing, lighting, watching, &c., to be paid. The buildings to be erected by private persons. The public authority to purchase the site and to let on building lease for sixty years, at a ground rent equal to that which would be given for working-class dwellings in the suburbs, say 5s. per foot frontage, at the rate of £5,000 per acre. The authorities to advance 75 per cent. of the cost of the building by instalments during progress, and this, the interest at 3 per cent. per annum, together with a proportion of the capital, to be refunded by equal quarterly payments during the whole term. The staircase of each block to be treated as a street, and cleansed, lighted, and watched by the public authority. Mr Mathews is opposed to buildings being erected except for the very poor. Fig. 58A gives two plans which are described later on. The plan B is taken as an example of the system, one cubicle opens out of the living room, and there would be twelve single tenements. The cost at 7s. per foot cube would amount to £2,300 for the block. The balance-sheet for one year would be as follows :—

12 suites of rooms at 4s. and 12 suites at 2s. 6d. per week—per annum - - - -				£202 16 0
Less outgoings—				
Ground rent - - -	£13 10 0			
Insurance - - - -	1 10 0			
Water rate - - - -	4 4 0			
Local rates (2s in £ on net rating at £105) - - - -	10 10 0			
Repairs, &c. - - -	40 0 0			
Loss of rent and collection -	29 10 0			
Repayment of principal and interest, £1,725 advanced - -	62 0 0			
			161 4 0	
			£41 12 0	

The advance by the authorities of 75 per cent. of the cost of the building would leave a balance of £575 to be provided by the owner, and £41. 12s. would be equal to 7 per cent. on that sum.

The local authority would be no loser, as the repayment of the principal and interest quarterly would increase the security, and the reversion to the rack rental at the end of sixty years, would be a valuable asset to the ratepayers within a reasonable period. The repayment would form a fund for future loans on similar property. One of the conditions for lending the money would be that the buildings were erected in accordance with approved drawings and in a substantial manner, and another that the rents would not be increased without consent. As landlords, the lessors would have power to insist on the property being kept in good condition, and as the sanitary authority, care would be taken that there was no over-crowding, and that the premises were kept clean and wholesome.

The scheme is original, and well worth serious consideration by public authorities, and all persons interested in this important question. Further details are given in the pamphlet; the above is only a short *résumé*, but it illustrates the fundamental principles of the proposal.

DESCRIPTIONS OF THE EXAMPLES ILLUSTRATED.

London County Council.—*Gainsborough Buildings* (Fig. 40) shows tenements of two and three rooms, each with scullery and W.C. The plan is economical, as each staircase serves four suites. The W.C. is entered from a small open space.

A Self-contained Block (Fig. 40).—A good plan; one staircase serves four suites on a floor, with two and three rooms each. Here again the W.C. is entered from a small open space; there is no public passage area.

Ann Street, Poplar (Fig. 40).—A London example of the balcony system; suites with two and three rooms, and a similar arrangement to the last plan for W.C. and scullery.

Taplow Buildings (Fig. 41) is an attempt to make a still cheaper plan; five tenements on each floor are served by one staircase. Only the extreme suites can be self-contained; the others have the W.C.'s and sculleries across the passage. One scullery serves three small suites, although each has a separate W.C.—an economical plan. The Council has not favoured the balcony system, which is so general in the provinces.

Sonning Buildings (Fig. 42).—One staircase serves four suites on each floor; on the associated plan; one common scullery, but each

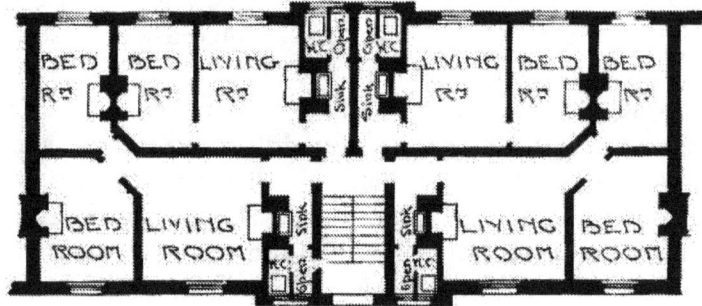

A·SELF-CONTAINED·BLOCK·

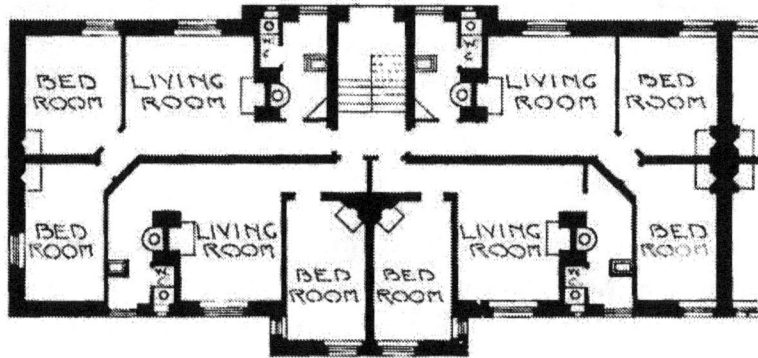

GAINSBOROUGH BUILDINGS

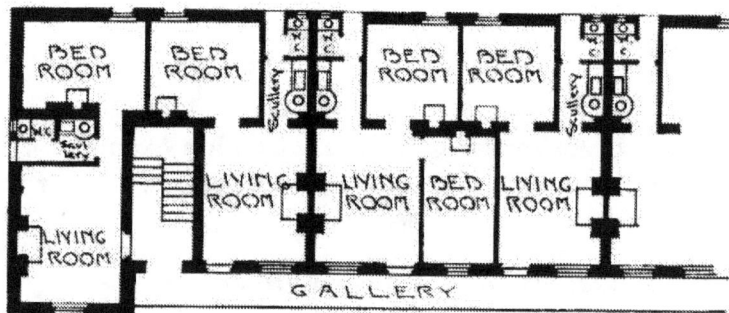

ANN STREET POPLAR

SCALE OF 0 5 0 10 20 30 40 FEET

FIG. 40.

London County Council.   Thos. H. Blashill, Architect.

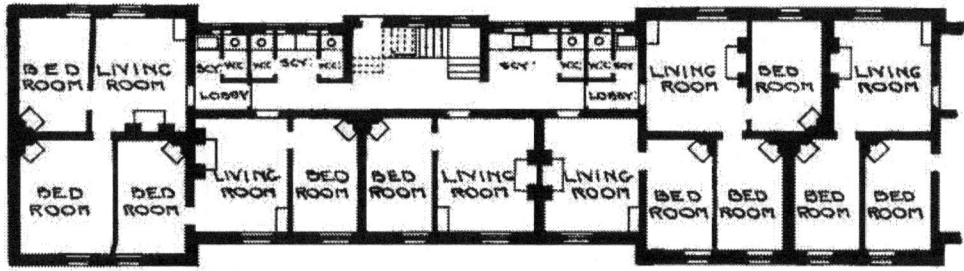

TAPLOW BUILDINGS:

SCALE OF 10 5 0 10 20 30 40 FEET

FIG. 41.

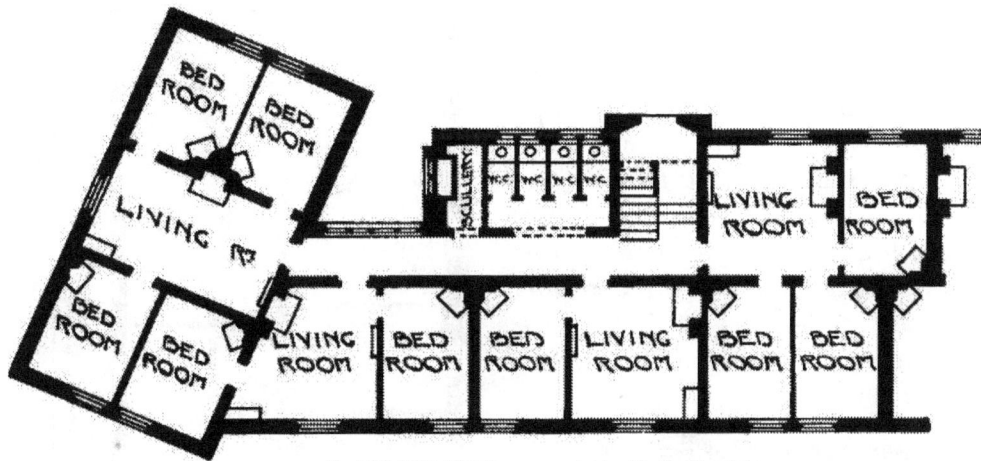

SONNING BUILDINGS

SCALE OF 10 5 0 10 20 30 FEET.

FIG. 42.

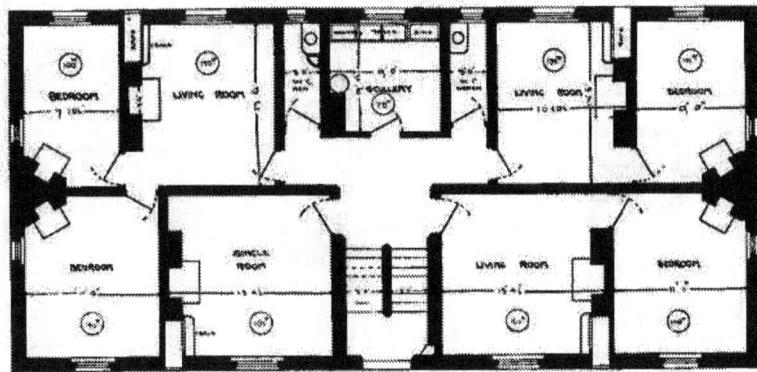

THIRD FLOOR

SCALE OF 10 5 0 10 20 30 40 FEET

FIG. 43.—AN ASSOCIATED BLOCK.

London County Council.   *Thos. H. Blashill, Architect.*

suite has a private W.C.   The suites contain two, three, and four
rooms.   A great advantage of this plan is that the scullery and each
W.C. can be inspected at any
time by the caretaker without the
knowledge of the tenants.

An Associated Block (Fig.
43).—One staircase serves four
suites on each floor; a single
room tenement is shown; common
scullery and W.C.'s.

*Seaford Buildings, Rother-
hithe* (Fig. 44).—A good example
of the balcony system applied to
a small block, and so avoiding an
internal public passage.   There
are four suites on each floor,
containing two and three rooms.
Each scullery is a good size,
and contains, as usual, a copper.

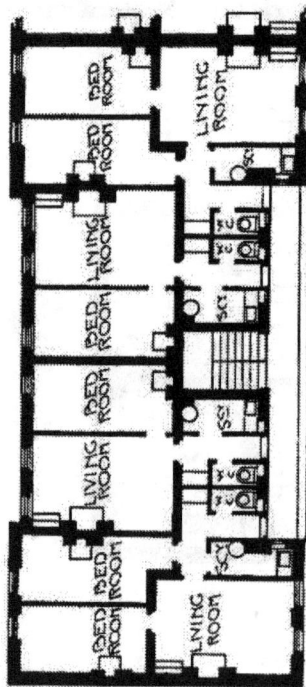

FIRST FLOOR PLAN:

FIG. 44.—SEAFORD BUILDINGS, ROTHERHITHE.

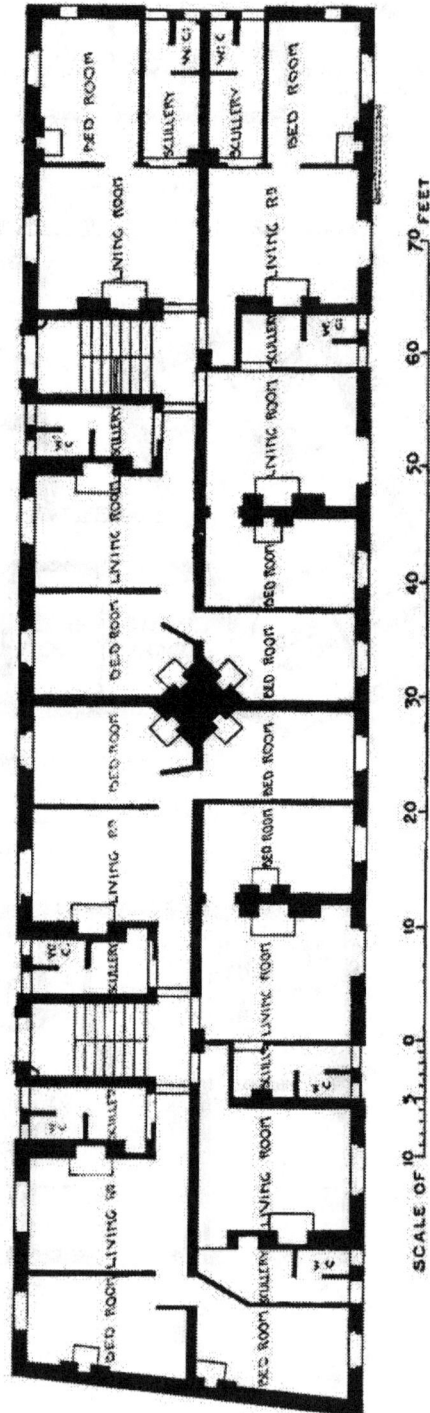

FIG. 45.—STIRLING BUILDINGS, DRURY LANE.

W. E. Riley, Superintending Architect.

London County Council.

RED ROOM

DED ROOM

DED ROOM

SCY

LIVING ROOM

LIVING ROOM

BED ROOM

SCY

W.C

LOBY

W.C

SCULLERY

WASH HOUSE

LIVING ROOM

W.C.

W.C.

W.C.

BED ROOM

SCULLERY

LIVING ROOM

LIVING ROOM

BED ROOM

SCY

BED ROOM

SCALE OF 10   5   0   10   20 FEET

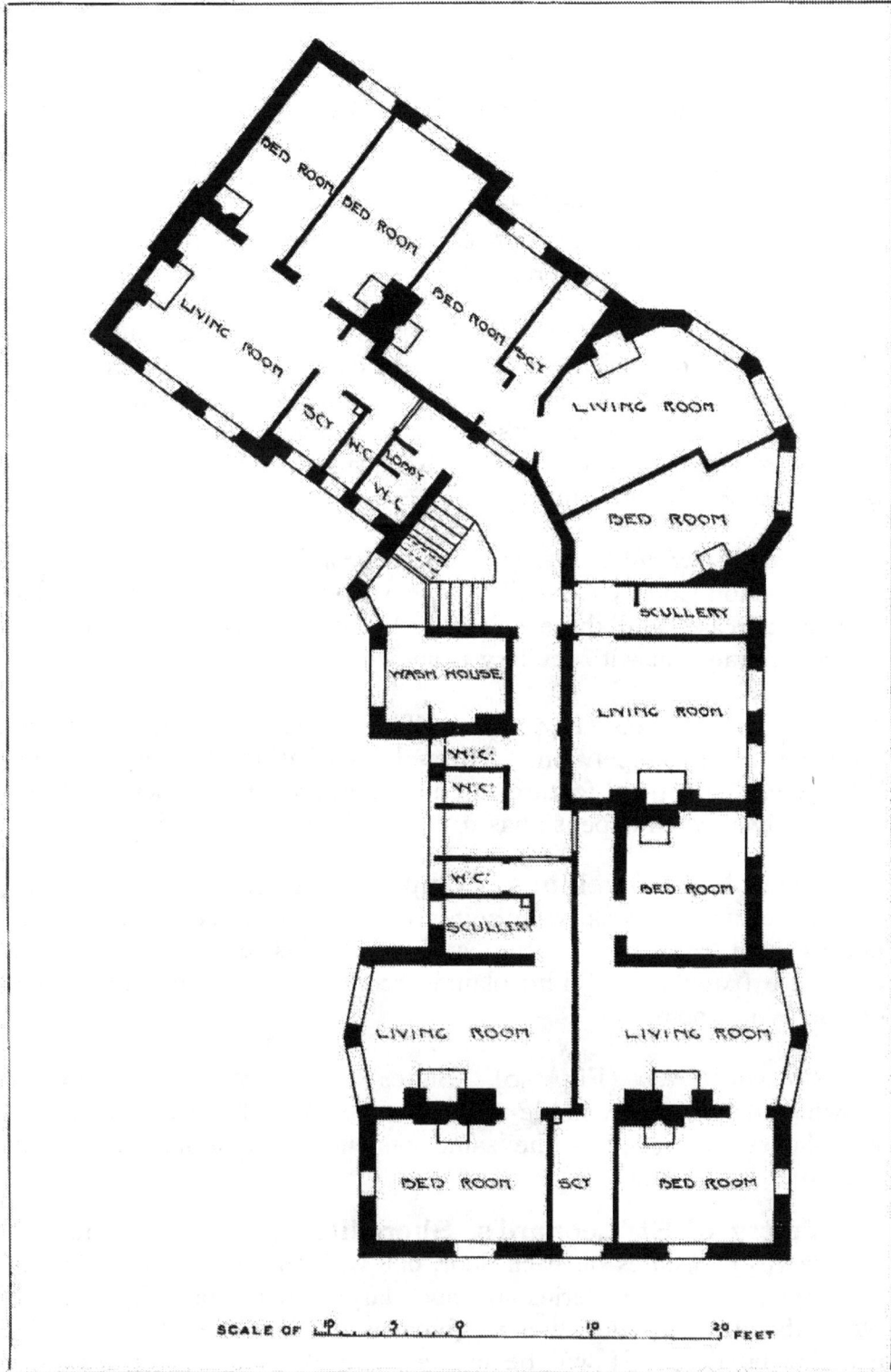

FIG. 46.—MILLBANK ESTATE, LEIGHTON AND MILLAIS BUILDINGS.

London County Council.   *W. E. Riley, Superintending Architect.*

Stirling Buildings, Drury Lane (Fig. 45).—A recent block erected by the London County Council. It has the usual four suites opening off the staircase on each floor, and no public passages, the necessary space being included in the suite, and made part of a room. The bedrooms do not communicate; the thick lines show partitions and not open doors.

Leighton and Millais Buildings, Millbank (Fig. 46). — Five suites on each floor. This necessitates a certain amount of public and private passage space. Only two of the suites are self-contained; the tenants of the others must cross a public passage to reach the W.C.; one is provided for each of the three suites. There is a common wash-house for the five suites.

Siddons Buildings, Drury Lane (Fig. 47).—Another recent plan of the London County Council. Five suites are served on each floor by one staircase, and three suites by the other, all self-contained. A one-room tenement with scullery is shown.

Millbank Estate (Fig. 48). — These plans obtained the first premium in the competition. Through ventilation is provided. The balcony yard is a good feature. The accommodation is better than is usually given when expense has to be carefully considered.

East End Dwellings Company: *King's Cross* (Fig. 49), shows a complete block, with suites of two and three rooms. Some figures with reference to the success of this company are given elsewhere (page 221). The plan is economical; the bedrooms open off the living-room.

Bethnal Green (Fig. 50).—Suites of two or three rooms are shown, and also some single-room tenements, and there are common wash-houses provided. The same system of communicating rooms is used.

Vestry of St Leonard's, Shoreditch (Fig. 51).—One staircase serves two suites on each floor, one with two rooms, and one with three rooms. The sculleries are much larger that those shown on the plans above. The elevation is given as an example of a cheap but effective building. It will be noticed that the staircase is enclosed,

London County Council.

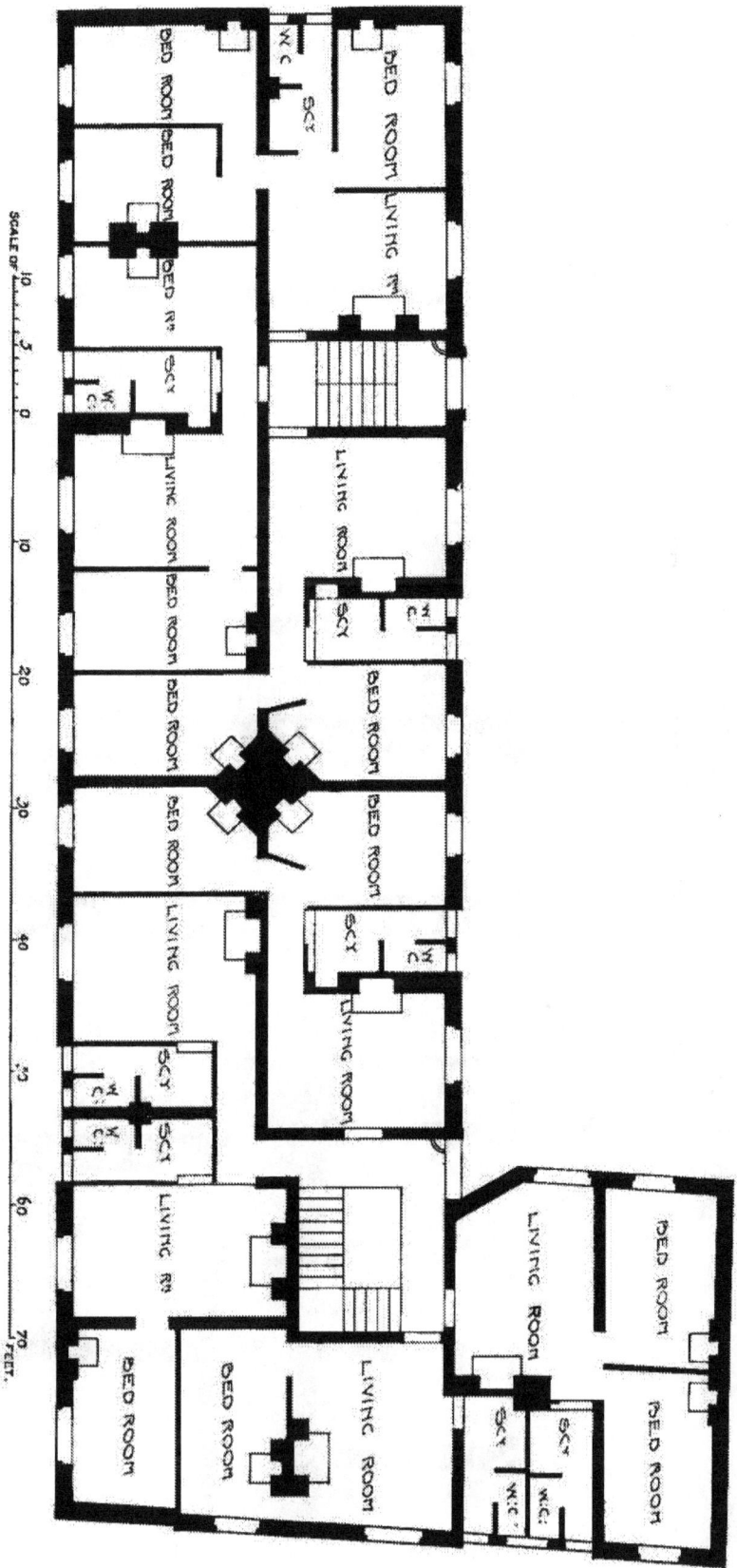

FIG. 47.—SIDDONS BUILDINGS, DRURY LANE.

W. E Riley, Superintending Architect.

SCALE OF
10   5   0   10   20   30   40   50   60   70
                                                              FEET.

BED ROOM

BED ROOM BED ROOM

BED Rᴰ

SCY
W C

LIVING ROOM BED ROOM

BED ROOM

BED ROOM LIVING ROOM

SCY
W C

LIVING ROOM

SCY
W C

W C

W C

SCY

SCY

LIVING RM

BED ROOM

LIVING ROOM

BED ROOM

LIVING ROOM

SCY

SCY

W C

W C

BED ROOM

BED ROOM

LIVING ROOM

BED ROOM

W C

SCY

SCY

LIVING ROOM

BED ROOM

BED ROOM

LIVING RM

BED ROOM

BED ROOM

SCY

W C

BED ROOM

London County Council.

Fig. 48.—PROPOSED DWELLINGS, MILLBANK ESTATE, WESTMINSTER.

Spalding & Cross, Architects.

THREE ROOM TENEMENTS
PLAN OF FOURTH FLOOR

DRESSER

LIVING ROOM
16' 4½" × 16' 2¾"
263 FEET SUPER.

BED ROOM
16' 4½" × 16' 2¾"
262 FEET SUPER.

BED ROOM
12' 9½" × 9' 9"
125 FEET SUPER.

SCULLERY

W C

LOBBY

BALCONY

LANDING

LANDING

BALCONY

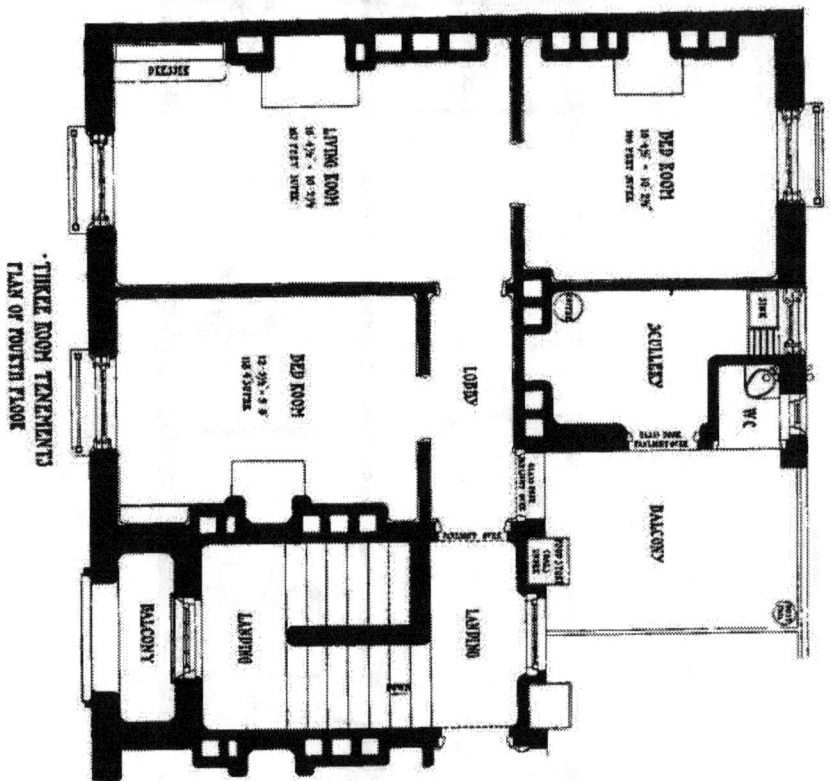

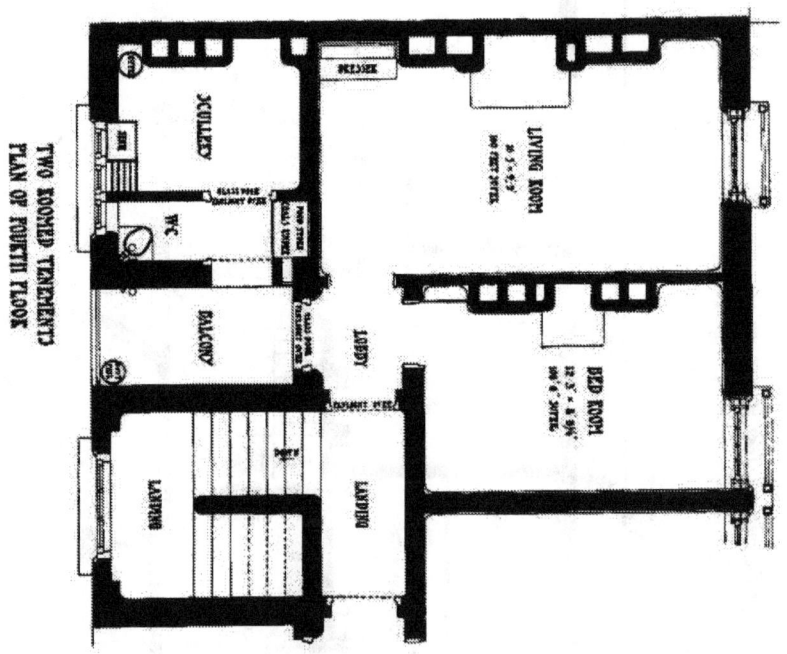

SCALE OF 0 1 2 3 4 5   10   20 FEET

TWO ROOMED TENEMENTS
PLAN OF FOURTH FLOOR

SCULLERY

W C

DRESSER

LIVING ROOM
16' 5" × 14' 4"
263 FEET SUPER.

BED ROOM
13' 3" × 11' 9½"
208 FEET SUPER.

BALCONY

LOBBY

LANDING

LANDING

YARD

YARD

YARD

YARD

BED ROOM

BED ROOM

BED ROOM

LIVING ROOM

LIVING ROOM

SCY

SCY

LIVING ROOM

LIVING ROOM

SCY

LIVING ROOM

SCY

Dust

Dust

SCY

SCY

LIVING ROOM

LIVING ROOM

BED ROOM

BED ROOM

BED ROOM

BED ROOM

SCALE OF 10 5 0 10 20 30 40 50 FEET

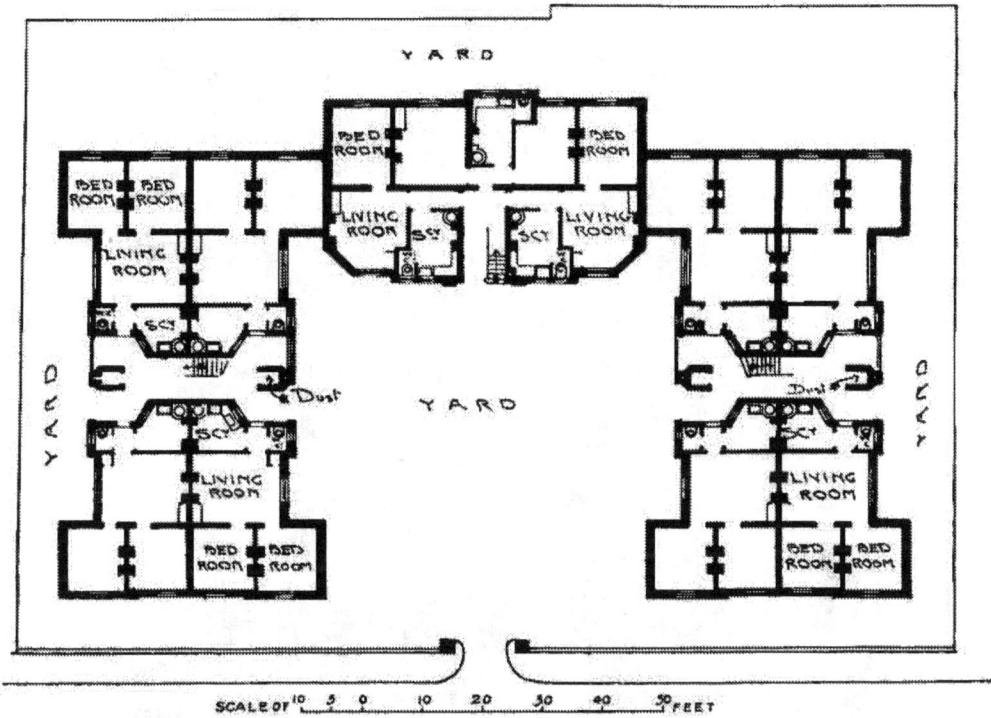

FIG. 49.—WINTON HOUSE, KING'S CROSS.

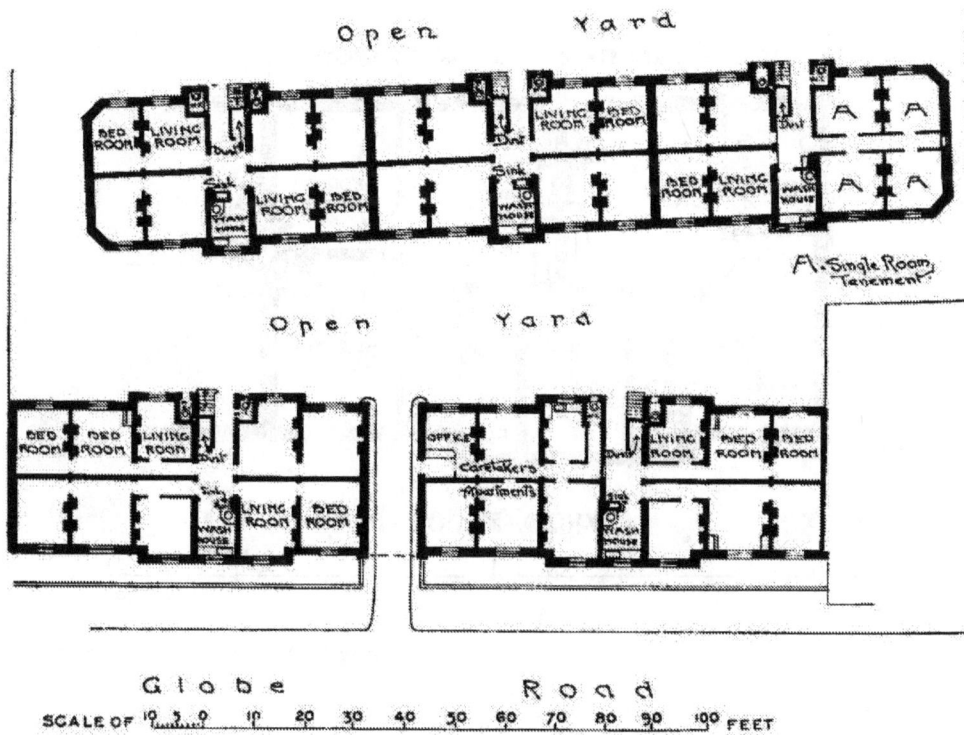

Open Yard

BED ROOM

LIVING ROOM

Dust

LIVING ROOM

BED ROOM

Dust

LIVING ROOM

BED ROOM

Dust

A

A

A

A

Sink

LIVING ROOM

BED ROOM

Sink

WASH HOUSE

BED ROOM

LIVING ROOM

WASH HOUSE

A. Single Room Tenement.

Open Yard

BED ROOM

BED ROOM

LIVING ROOM

Dust

OFFICE

Dust

LIVING ROOM

BED ROOM

BED ROOM

Caretakers Apartments

Sink

LIVING ROOM

BED ROOM

WASH HOUSE

LIVING ROOM

WASH HOUSE

Globe Road

SCALE OF 10 5 0 10 20 30 40 50 60 70 80 90 100 FEET

FIG. 50.—BETHNAL GREEN.

East End Dwellings Company.

Davis & Emanuel, Architects.

· COVRTYARD · ELEVATION ·

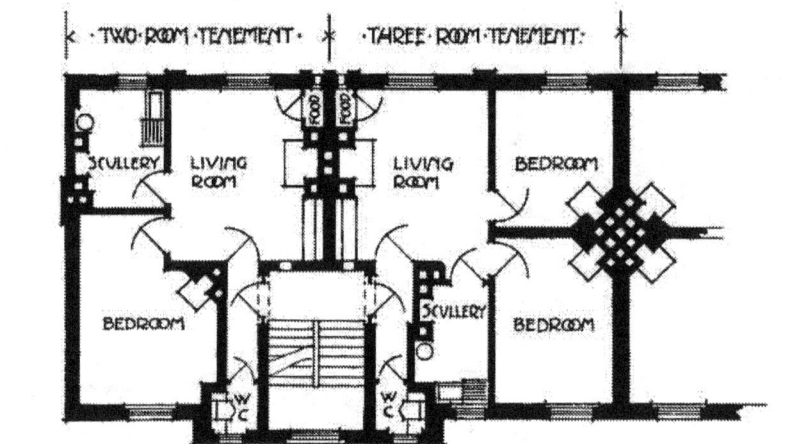

· THREE · ROOM · TENEMENT ·

· TWO · ROOM · TENEMENT ·

· THIRD · FLOOR · PLAN ·

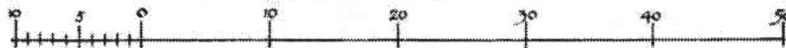

· SCALE · OF · FEET ·

FIG. 51.—WORKING CLASS DWELLINGS ERECTED FOR THE VESTRY OF
ST LEONARD'S, SHOREDITCH.

Rowland Plumbe & Harvey, Architects.

and ventilated by windows. Many tenants object to an open stair-case; it seems unnecessary when the ventilation can always be regulated by the caretaker.

Old Ford Road (Fig. 52).—Two and four suites on each floor served by one staircase. The large suites have a hall, and are a superior class of tenement to the ordinary artisans' dwelling. The other suites have two and three rooms. The living-room is made the central feature of the latter flats, and a certain amount of passage space is avoided; this should be done as much as possible. The living-room can be made a passage-room, and it will be kept clean, but passages are often allowed to get into a very dirty condition. The roof would be cheap, as the plan is simple.

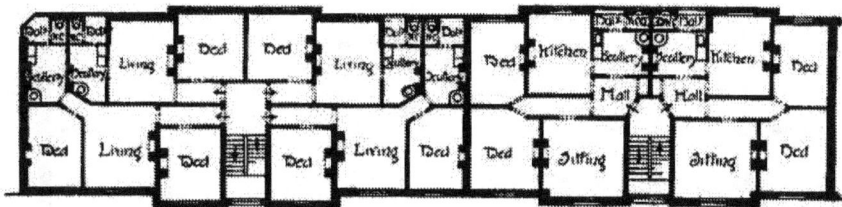

FIG. 52.—ARTISANS' DWELLINGS, OLD FORD ROAD, E.

Davis & Emanuel, Architects.

The Peabody Trust has carried out a large number of buildings in London. Up to the end of 1899 £1,300,000 had been spent. The schemes have been carefully considered and carried out on thorough business lines. The modern blocks pay from $3\frac{1}{4}$ to $3\frac{1}{2}$ per cent., the old buildings slightly less, but taking them together the return is over 3 per cent.

Fig. 53 shows the ground floor and upper floor plans of a typical block. The sizes of the rooms are large. Generally in these blocks the living-rooms are 13 ft. 6 in. by 11 ft. 9 in., and bedrooms 13 ft. 6 in. by 9 ft. 9 in. Height 8 ft. 6 in. The cost is about £86 per room. On the ground floor of the Herne Hill buildings a dust cellar is provided 7 ft. 6 in. by 5 ft. 6 in., for the architect is strongly in favour of dust shoots; it will be seen this cellar is quite bricked off from the remainder of the building. The shoot is 14 by 9 in. open at top and bottom, and a flue 9 by 9 in. is also built for ventila-tion. On the ground floor there are two suites of two rooms each and

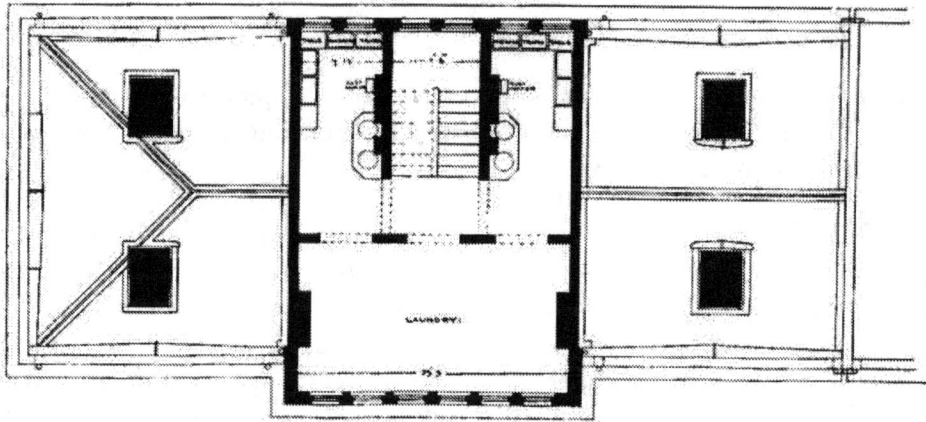

LAUNDRY PLAN

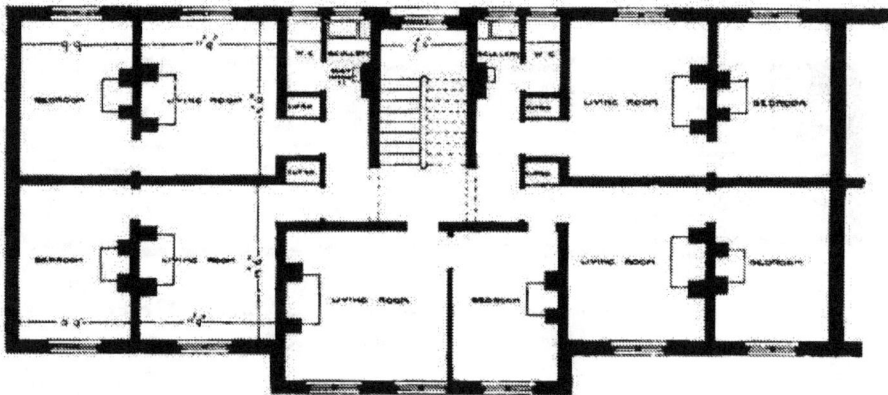

IST 2ND & 3RD FLOOR PLANS

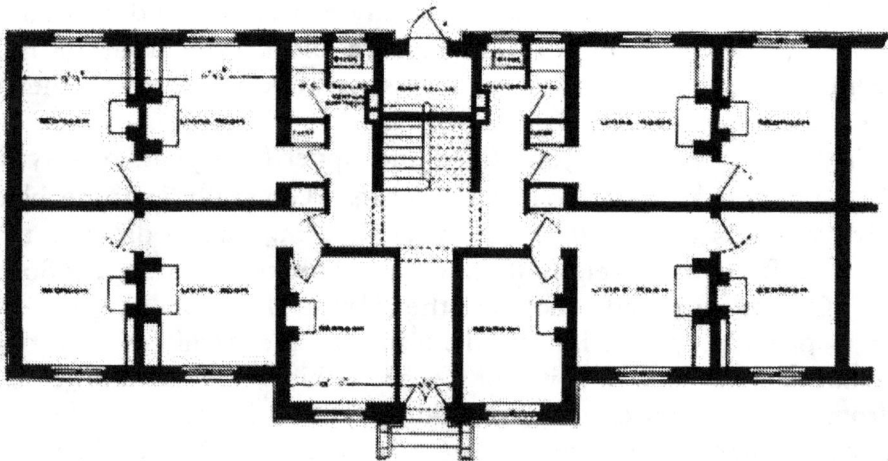

GROUND PLAN.

SCALE OF ⟨10 5 0 10 20 30 40 50⟩ FEET

FIG. 53.—PEABODY BUILDINGS, HERNE HILL.

The Peabody Trust.   *W. E. Wallis, Architect.*

two suites of three rooms each; one scullery and W.C. is provided for each two suites; there is also good cupboard accommodation.

On the first floor there are five suites of two rooms each, and two W.C.'s and sculleries in common. This associated plan is, no doubt, one of the reasons why the cost of the buildings is low, plumbing being a most expensive item in the cost of model dwellings. The staircase is not open to the air, but is ventilated by windows as in Fig. 51. The top floor contains a large laundry, washing trays, sinks, coppers, &c.

The net income returns about 3 per cent. upon the capital outlay.

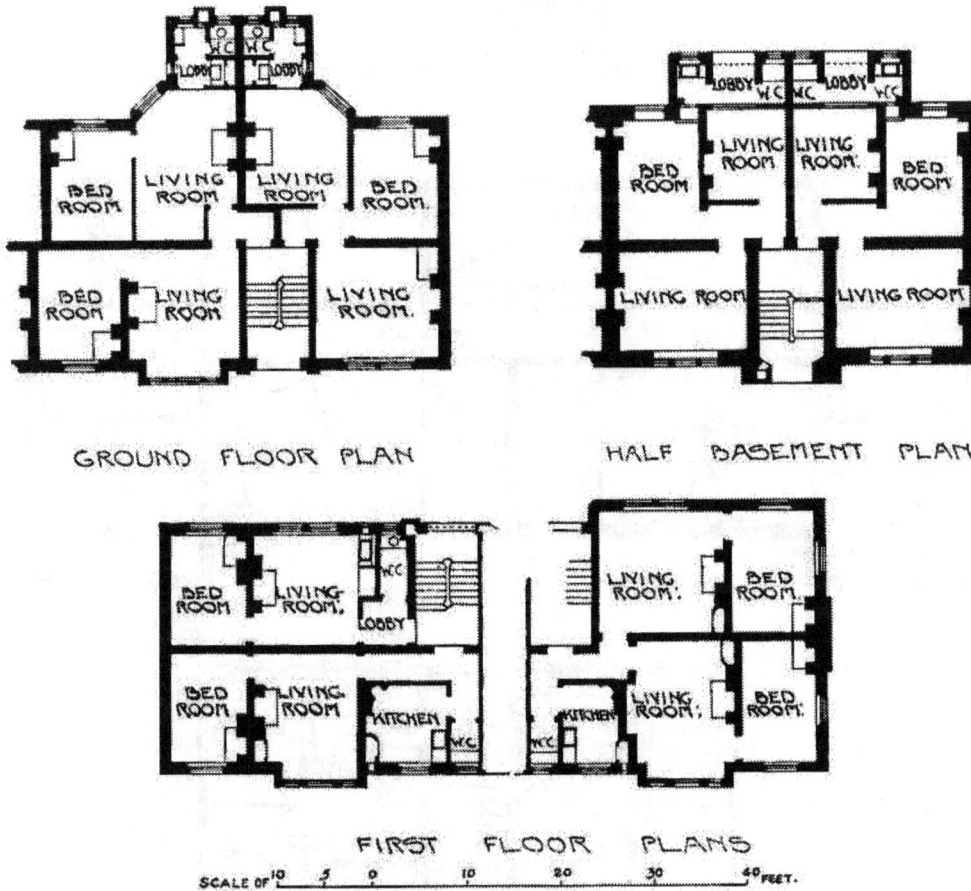

GROUND FLOOR PLAN   HALF BASEMENT PLAN

FIRST FLOOR PLANS

SCALE OF FEET

FIG. 54.—WATERLOW BUILDINGS.

Improved Industrial Dwellings Company.   *A. Moore, Secretary.*

The Improved Industrial Dwellings Company.—Fig. 54 shows three plans, having suites with two, three, and four rooms.

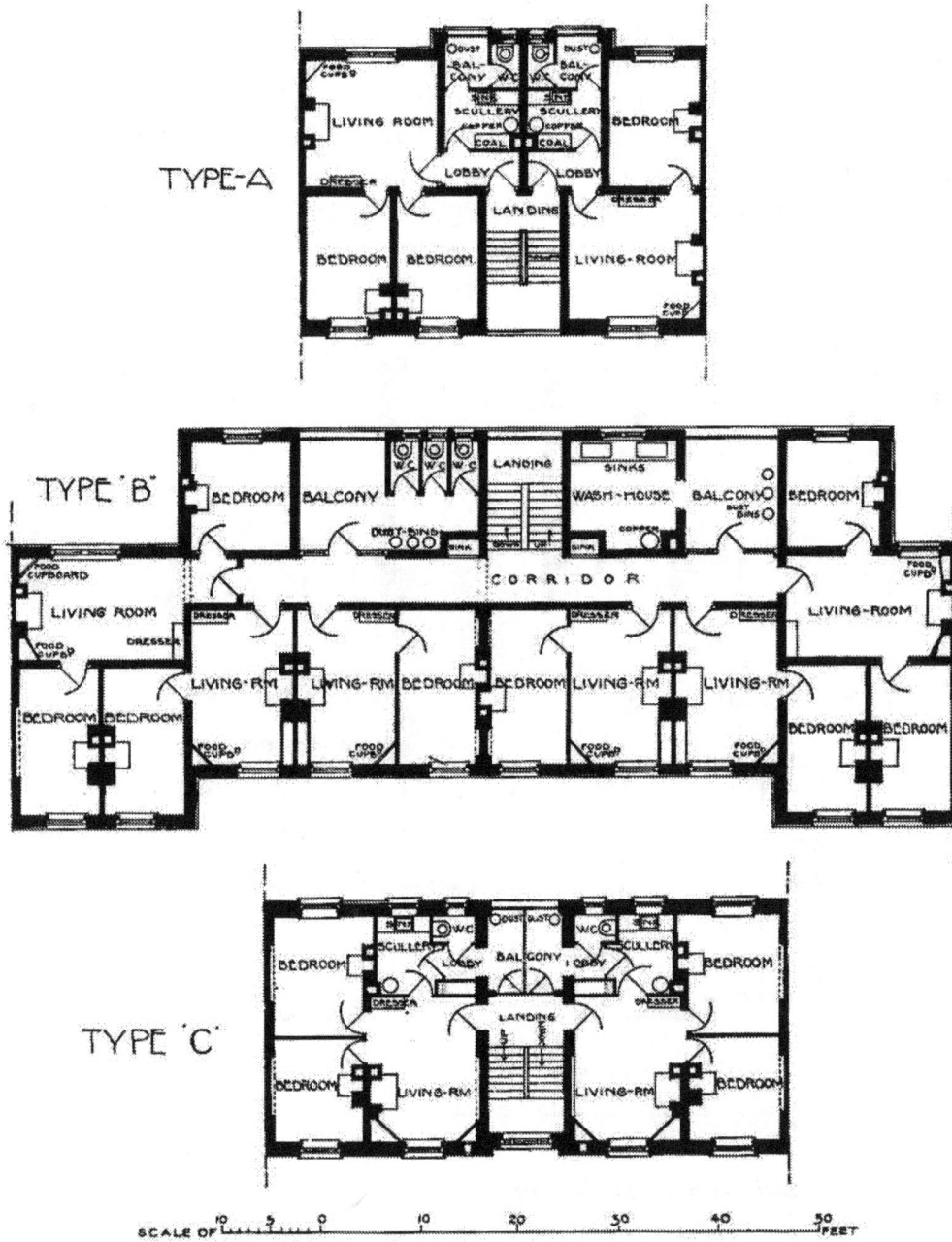

FIG. 55.—DWELLINGS DESIGNED FOR THE ST PANCRAS BOROUGH COUNCIL.

Keith D. Young, Architect.

Through ventilation has not been attempted, and planning is consequently simplified. In each example the staircase is enclosed. In some of the suites there is no scullery. Dust shoots were provided. These tenements are generally known as the Waterlow Buildings, and the earliest were erected in 1864, but comparatively few have been built in recent years. Marlborough Buildings were erected in 1890, and the last block was built in 1894. Waleran Buildings were erected 1881-1900, and Stalbridge Buildings in 1887. The total number of suites is 5,597, including 28 of one room, 381 of two rooms, and 2,991 of three rooms. The total expenditure has been £1,117,443. The cost per room has risen from £40 in 1863 to £75 in 1900. This is a good example of the enormous increase in the cost of building in London.

Saville Street, W.—Fig. 56 shows tenements of a similar character to artisans' dwellings, although the tenants are of a different class in consequence of the neighbourhood. The building has three suites to the floor. In every case there is a sink in the kitchen and no scullery.

St Pancras Borough Council. —Fig. 55 shows three varieties of plans, two being self-contained, and one on the associated system. Type A has a staircase open on one side, and the door allows for through ventilation. This has suites of two and three rooms with scullery, &c. Type C is somewhat similar, and has three rooms. The great advantage of the latter plan is that the caretaker is able to inspect the W.C. without entering any room or disturbing the tenant. The balcony is divided from the landing by a high iron railing with a gate; this also enables the tenant to see who a visitor may be without opening the door, as objectionable characters often

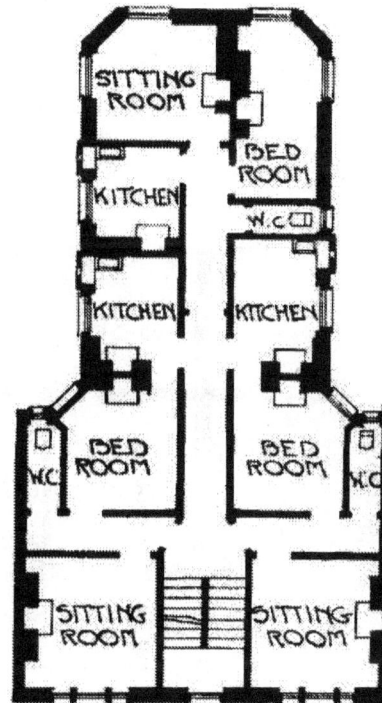

UPPER FLOOR PLAN.

SCALE OF ......FEET

FIG. 56.—Nos. 25 AND 26 SAVILLE STREET, W.

Professor Beresford Pite, Architect.

manage to enter these blocks of buildings. The gate is an excellent idea.

Type B is the plan of a building with suites of two rooms. The plan is much cheaper than type A ; one W.C. is provided for each two tenements, an ample provision, and there is one common wash-house with sinks for the six tenements. The saving in plumbing alone is considerable, and one staircase is sufficient. The corridor is well ventilated and not too long, and has sinks and draw off taps. The W.C.'s and wash-house are always open for inspection. The W.C. accommodation for artisans is usually on a much more liberal scale than is provided in the best class flats. It is quite unnecessary to have a W.C. to every tenement of two rooms ; often a highly rented flat of six or more rooms is only provided with one W.C., as a reference to the plans in this book will show.

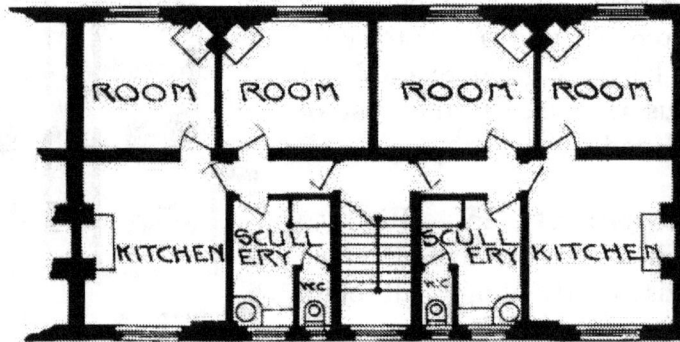

PLAN OF UPPER FLOORS

FIG. 57.—HIGH STREET, HAMMERSMITH.

H. M. Newlyn, Architect.

High Street, Hammersmith (Fig. 57).—In this case a strip of land, difficult to deal with, has resulted in a very successful enterprise. A private roadway 20 ft. wide was formed, with gates at the end. It was only after much opposition the scheme was carried out, and the arrangement has been satisfactory, and is an example of what might be done with similar sites. The tenements have the advantage of quiet dwellings in a crowded neighbourhood. The W.C. opens off the

Ground floor plan (Fig. 58):

13·1½"
Bed. Rm.
8'0"
W.C.
36'9"
Scullery
12'0"
Kitchen
11'0"
bath
Pantry
Coals
Bed Rm.
25·10"
up.
6'·6"
Sitting Rm.
7'·5"
15'6"

Ground Floor

First floor plan (Fig. 58):

Cement Flat
W.C.
Scullery
Pantry
Kitchen
bath
lav.
Bed. Rm
Bed Rm
Sitting Room
7'·6"
Cement Flat

SCALE OF 10 · · · · · · · · 0 10 20 FEET

First Floor

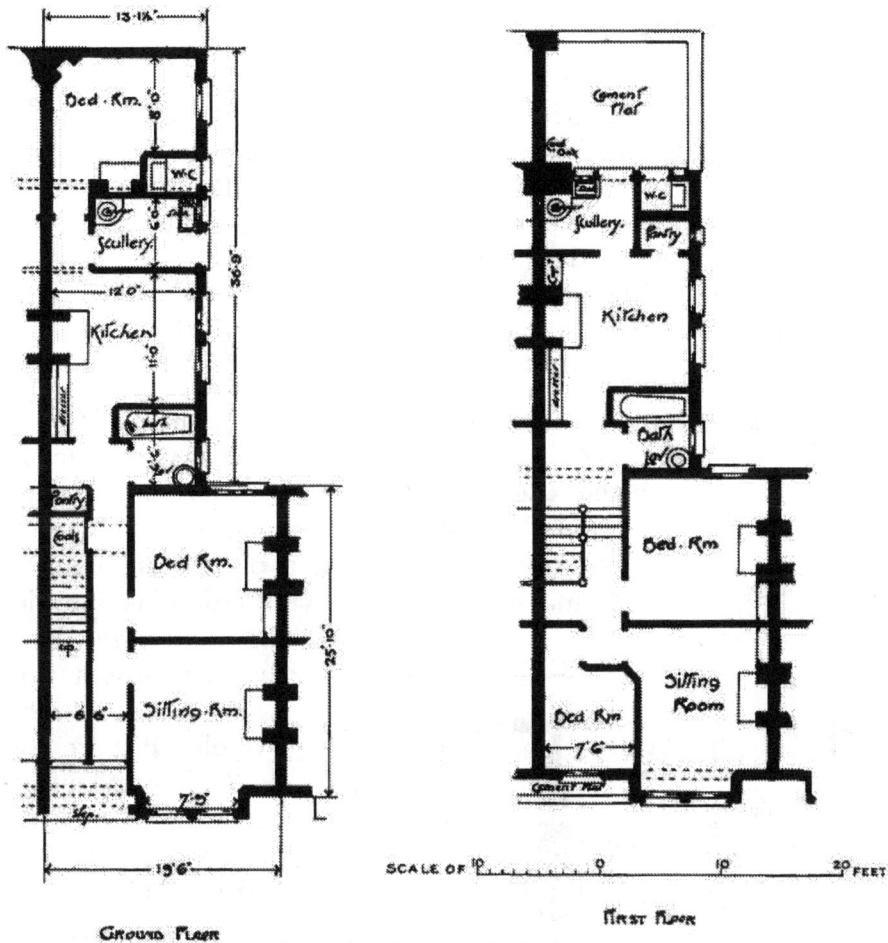

FIG. 58.—FLATS AT CLAPHAM.

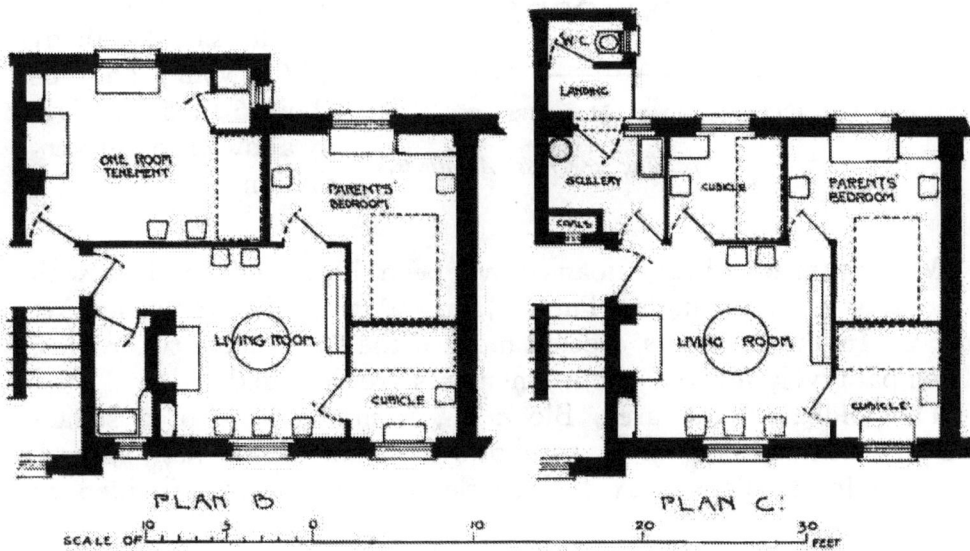

Plan B (Fig. 58a):

ONE ROOM TENEMENT
PARENTS' BEDROOM
LIVING ROOM
CUBICLE

PLAN B

Plan C (Fig. 58a):

W.C.
LANDING
SCULLERY
COALS
CUBICLE
PARENTS' BEDROOM
LIVING ROOM
CUBICLE

PLAN C.

SCALE OF 10 5 0 10 20 30 FEET

FIG. 58A.—PROPOSED SCHEME.

J. Douglass Mathews, Architect.

scullery, as stated above. The authorities in some neighbourhoods allow this arrangement, while others object to it.

In many suburban districts flats of two floors let well. The plan shown in Fig. 58 is a good example. It will be seen that the ground floor flat has a bedroom at the rear, this is covered by a lead flat, very useful for drying clothes, and pleasant in the summer for the tenant to use as a little garden. The tenant on the first floor obtains an additional small bedroom over the hall. The W.C. in each flat is approached from the open.

Proposed Scheme.—The chief features of these plans, Fig. 58A, already referred to (p. 67 *et seq.*), are the absence of passage space and the use of cubicles. The parents' bedroom would be enclosed from floor to ceiling, but the cubicles would have partitions about 6 ft. 6 in. high. Cross ventilation is provided for, and the fire in the living-room would warm the cubicles. For plan B there would be W.C.'s and a wash-house in the yard for the lower tenements, and similar accommodation on the top floor for the upper tenements. On plan C the divisional wall by W.C. would only be about 6 ft. 6 in. high, to allow through ventilation.

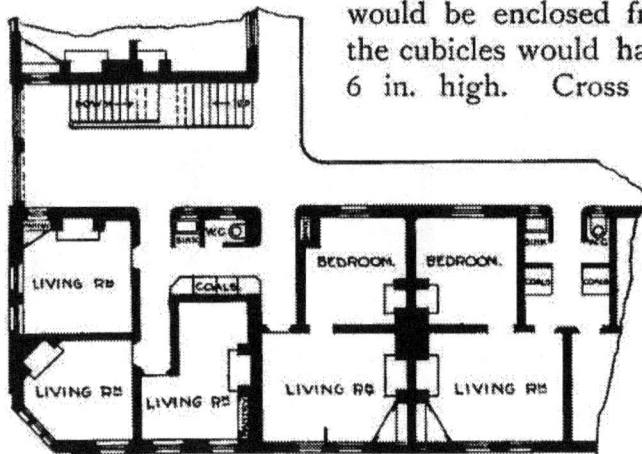

1ST, 2ND, 3RD, AND 4TH FLOORS

SCALE OF [10 5 0   10   20   30 FEET]

FIG. 59.—OLDHAM ROAD, MANCHESTER.

Spalding & Cross, Architects.

Manchester.—Large loans have been borrowed to deal with the housing problem, under Parts 1, 2, and 3 of the Housing Act of 1890. In the buildings erected most of the suites have two rooms, and comparatively few one-room tenements are provided.

The Oldham Road area, Block II., is in the form of a square about an acre in extent. Fig. 59 shows the plan of the first, second, third, and fourth floors. A few single tenements are provided at

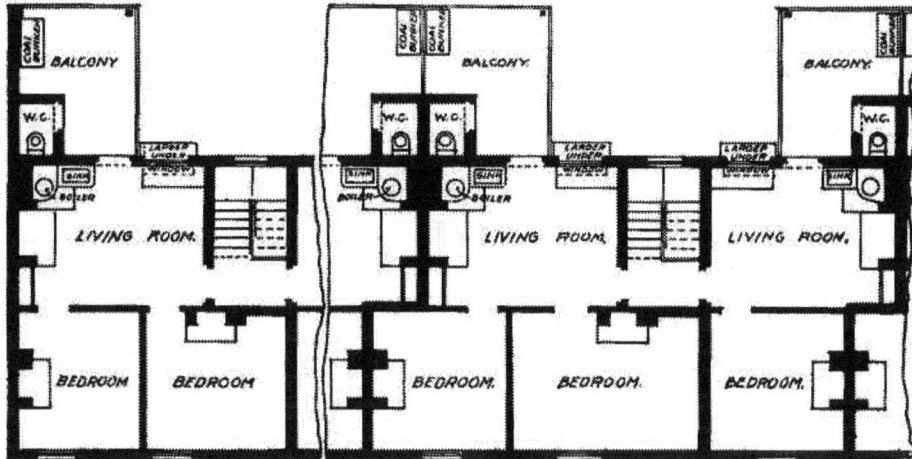

FIRST FLOOR PLAN.

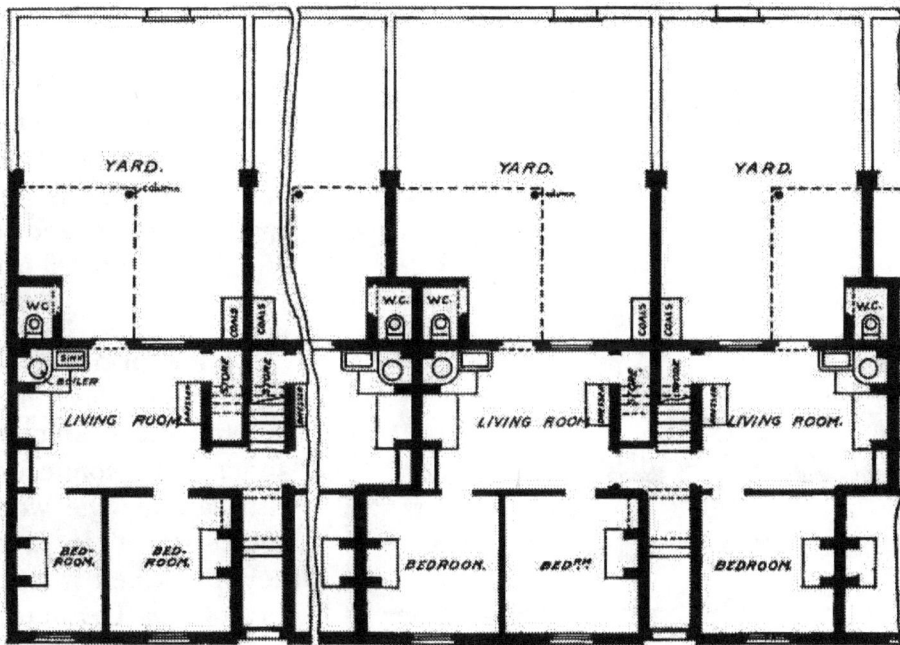

GROUND PLAN.

SCALE OF 10   5   0   10   20   30 FEET

FIG. 60.—CHESTER STREET, MANCHESTER.

T. de Courcey Meade, City Surveyor.

the four angles of the block. The balcony system is adopted, and it is said the balconies are, to a certain extent, protected from the weather, as the buildings are in a square. Dust shoots are provided.

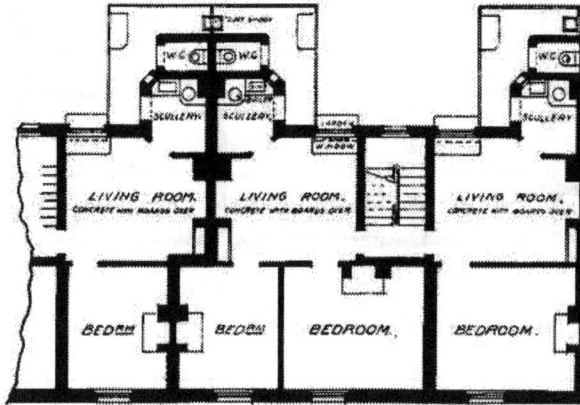

1ST. & 2ND FLOORS.

One peculiarity is that no sculleries are built. Each tenant has a sink in the lobby—an economical arrangement.

Chester Street area (Fig. 60) has buildings of a better class. One tenement of two rooms and one of three rooms are provided on each floor. Sinks are in the living-rooms.

The Pott Street area tenements (Fig. 61) have suites of two and three rooms and small sculleries, and the W.C.'s are entered from the open.

Liverpool. — The city authorities have devoted much time and labour in connection with flats for the working classes. In 1901 they published a "Report of the Deputation of the Housing Committee to Glasgow, Manchester, Salford, and London," and in 1903 the Housing Committee published a useful pamphlet which also contains plans.

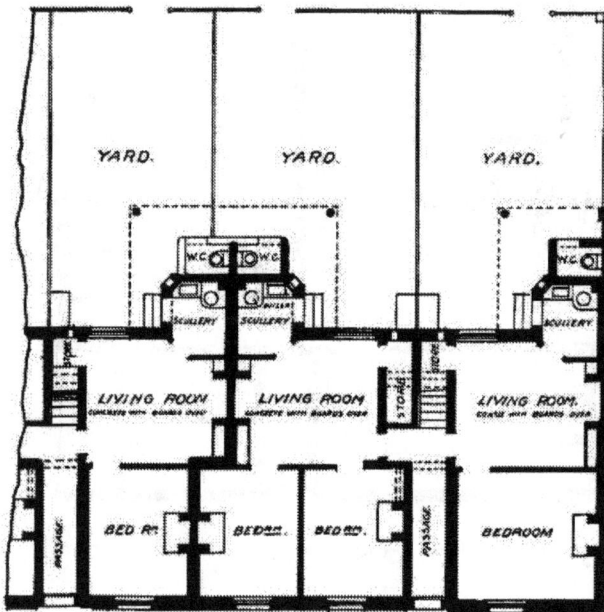

GROUND PLAN.

SCALE OF 10 5 0 10 20 30 FEET

FIG. 61.—POTT STREET, MANCHESTER.

T. de Courcey Meade, City Surveyor.

FRONT ELEVATION

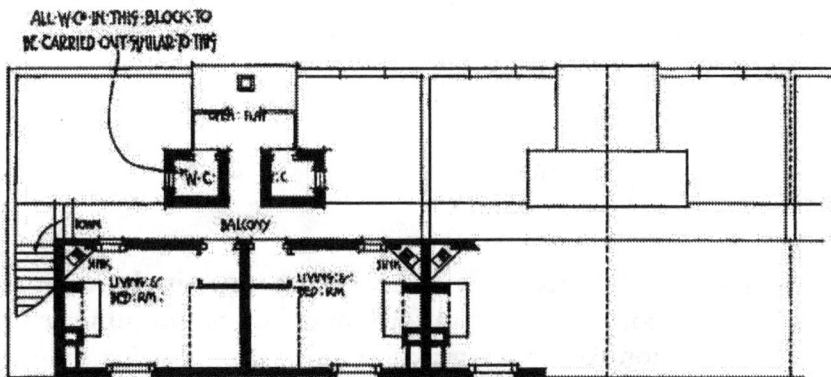

ALL W.C⁰ IN THIS BLOCK TO
BE CARRIED OUT SIMILAR TO THIS

FIRST FLOOR

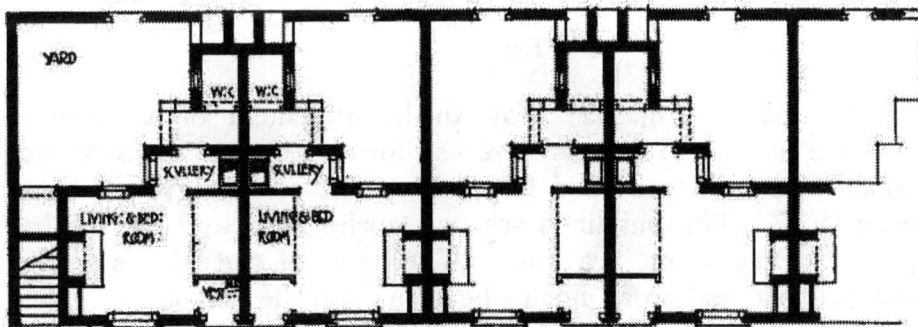

GROUND FLOOR

SCALE OF   10   5   0   10   20   30   40 FEET

FIG. 62.—LIVERPOOL LABOURERS' DWELLINGS, ADLINGTON STREET AREA.

Surveyor's Department, Municipal Offices.

The following table gives the percentage paid by some of the schemes carried out :—

St Martin's Cottages (opened in 1869), average for 10 years
    ending 1902, paid -   -   -   -   -   £1 18 11¾ per cent.
Victoria Square Dwellings (opened in 1885), average for
    10 years ending 1902, paid -   -   -   -   2 4 10   „
Juvenal Street (opened in 1890), average for 10 years
    ending 1902, paid -   -   -   -   -   3 1 1¾ „
Arley Street (opened in 1897), average for 5 years ending
    1902, paid -   -   -   -   -   -   4 4 3¾ „
Gildart's Gardens (opened in 1897), average for 5 years
    ending 1902, paid -   -   -   -   -   3 5 11¾ „

In this pamphlet some interesting statistics are given. Nine schemes had been carried out, and in only two of them was there single-room accommodation. The following are the totals :—

Number of tenements of one room -   -   -   66
  „   „   two rooms -   -   -   669
  „   „   three „ -   -   -   226
  „   „   four „ -   -   -   49

The total number of tenements is 1,010.

Apparently the authorities have seen that the single-room tenement is all that a poor man can afford, and out of the nine schemes in course of erection or contemplated, six provide for one-room dwellings. The following are the totals :—

Number of tenements of one room -   -   -   176
  „   „   two rooms -   -   -   260
  „   „   three „ -   -   -   637
  „   „   four „ -   -   -   106

The plans (Fig. 62) show the arrangement of a scheme with 48 single rooms. There is a recess for the bed, as in Scotland, and a small scullery is provided for each tenant on the ground floor, and also a W.C. The buildings are two stories high, and on the balcony system. Dust shoots are built. The doors of the W.C.'s on the first floor are planned so as not to be seen from the balconies. The first-floor tenants have a sink in the living-room; the little scullery is omitted. The elevations are a great improvement on the usual blocks of buildings.

Fig. 63 gives the plans of some flats with two rooms. On the ground floor each tenant has in addition a large scullery with food

FRONT ELEVATION

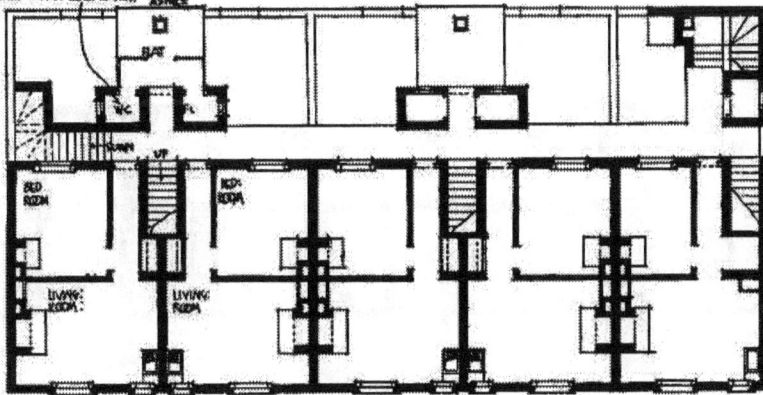

ALL W.C.ˢ IN THIS BLOCK TO
BE CARRIED OUT SIMILAR TO THIS.

FIRST FLOOR

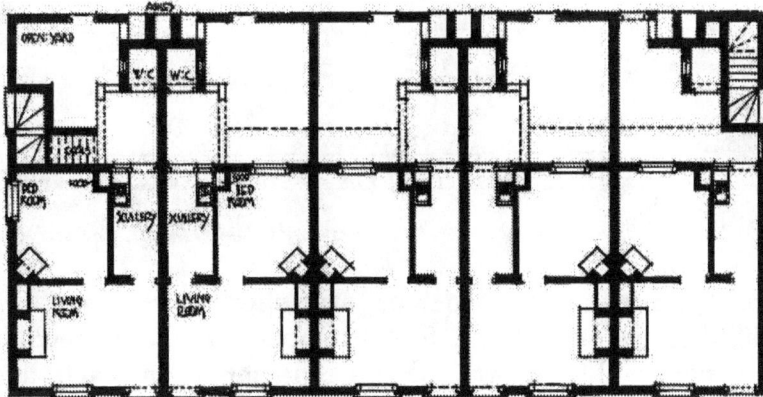

GROUND FLOOR

SCALE OF 10 5 0   10   20   30   40   50 FEET

FIG. 63.—CITY OF LIVERPOOL LABOURERS' DWELLINGS, ADLINGTON STREET AREA—
TWO-ROOMED DWELLINGS.

Surveyor's Department, Municipal Offices.

cupboard. On the first floor the scullery is omitted, and there is a sink in the living-room. The balcony plan is adopted, and generally the arrangement is similar to the single-tenement blocks.

There are also some three-room dwellings all very similar to those described above, but in this scheme a scullery is built for every first-floor suite. The dust shoots are kept well away from the living-rooms.

Fig. 64 gives the ground-floor plan for some dwellings on the Clive Street area, a recent scheme. These have three rooms and a scullery, the balcony system is adopted. and the plans generally are compact and economical.

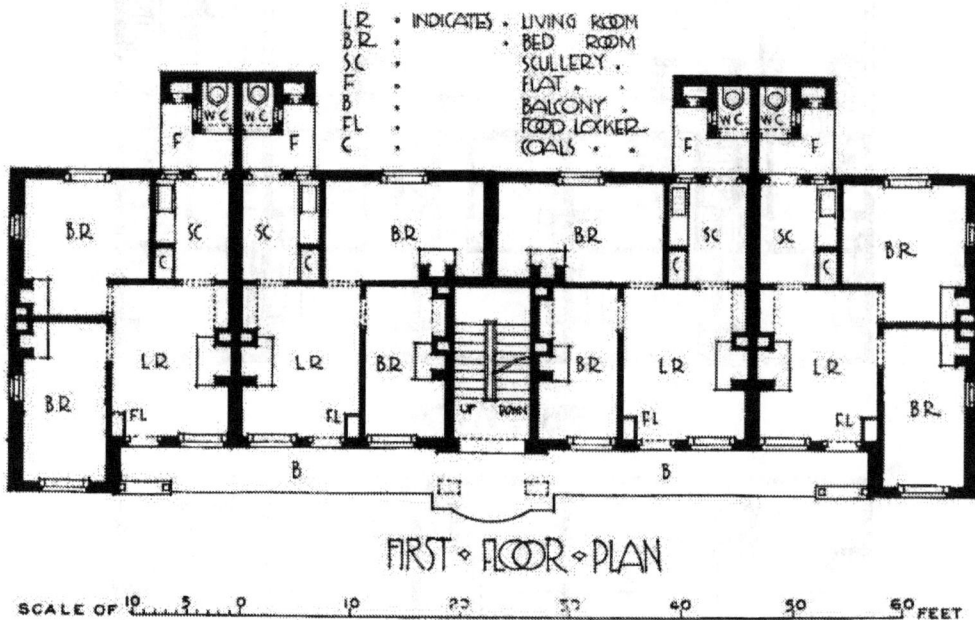

FIG. 64.—LABOURERS' DWELLINGS, CLIVE STREET AREA, LIVERPOOL.

Surveyor's Department, Municipal Offices.

Birmingham.—Two schemes are shown on Fig. 65. The smaller building is one of the few attempts that have been made to house the poor. There are seven tenements on each floor; the staircase is open to the air; the main corridor is 5 ft. wide and well lighted and ventilated. A scullery 12 ft. by 9 ft. is provided for the common use of the tenants, but each one has a separate W.C. approached from a balcony, and a sink in the living room. The block plan shows the entrance is from the playground and not directly off the street.

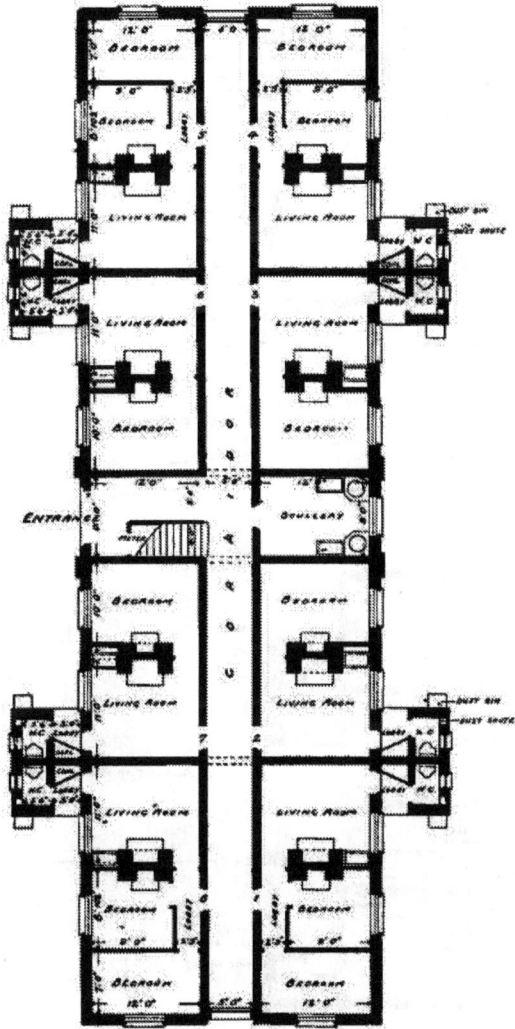

GROUND FLOOR PLAN

BLOCK PLAN

From Watery Lane

LITTLE BARR STREET

LITTLE BARR STREET.

From Great Barr Street

LITTLE EDWARD STREET

PALMER STREET

To Glover Street

TENEMENT 6

TENEMENT

TENEMENT 5

SCULLERY

CORRIDOR

ENTRANCE

TENEMENT 8

TENEMENT 4

DUST BIN

DUST SHUTE

TENEMENT 7

TENEMENT 1

DUST BIN

DUST SHUTE

SCALE OF 10 5 0   10   20   30   40   50 FEET (BLOCK PLAN)

SCALE OF 10 5 0   10   20   30   40 FEET (BUILDINGS)

GROUND PLAN.

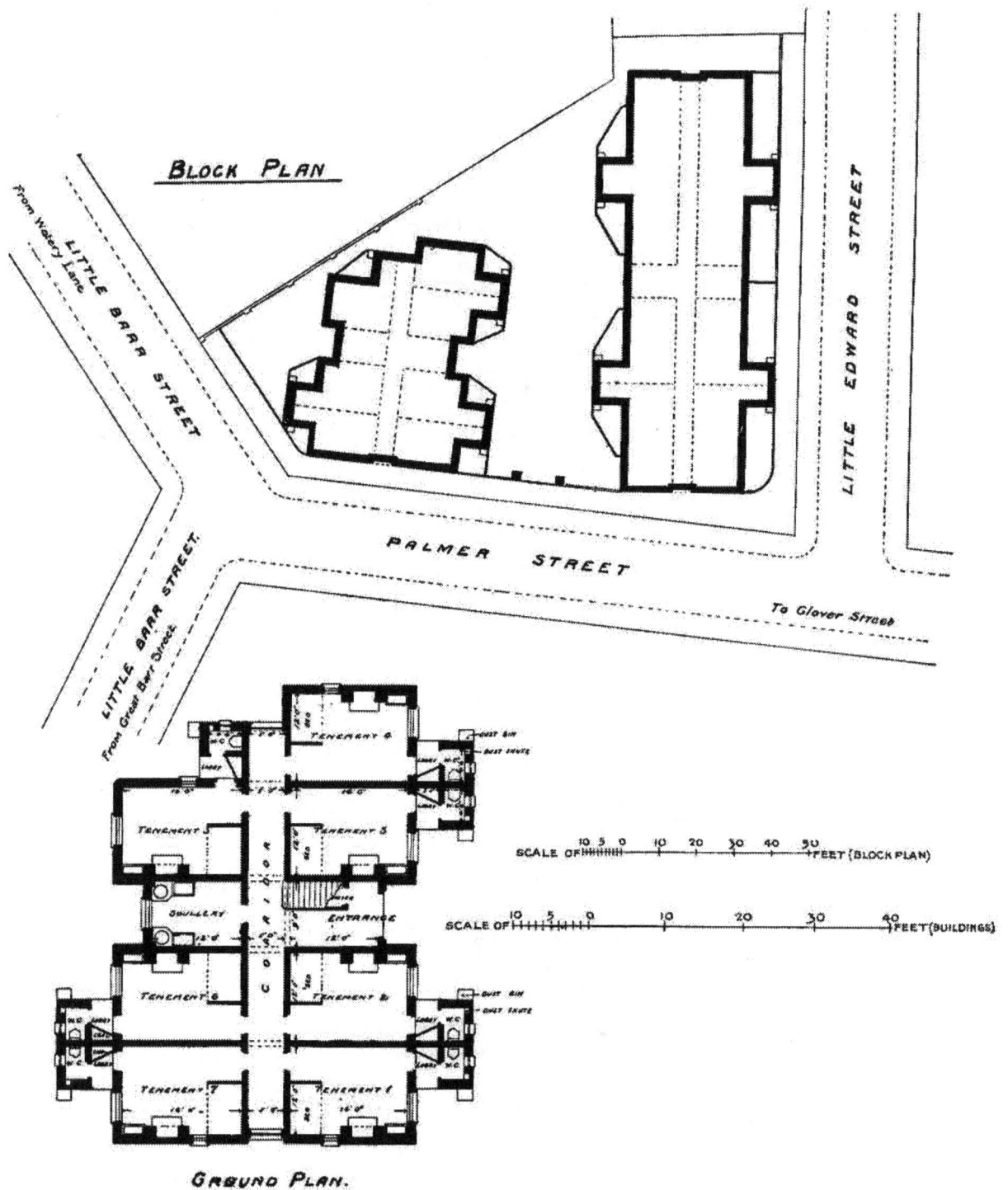

FIG. 65.—PALMER STREET, BIRMINGHAM.

Hipkiss & Stephens, Architects.

The building contains twenty-eight tenements; each one is provided with a dust shoot discharging into a dust bin in the open. The sizes of the rooms are given in the table above. It will be seen that a screen is made so that the bed fits into a recess, as in Scotland.

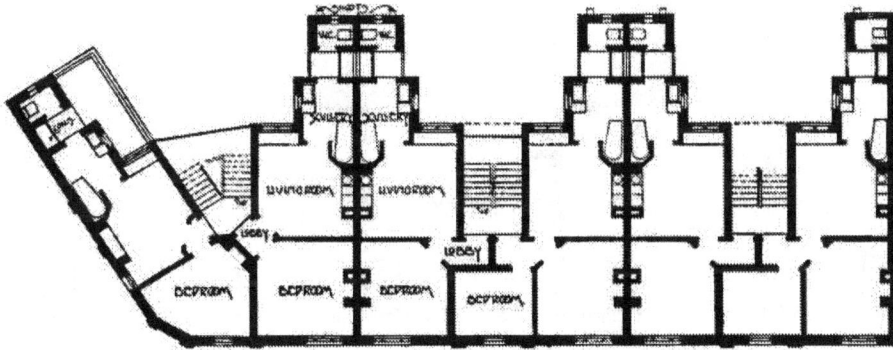

FIRST FLOOR PLAN. REPEAT SECOND AND THIRD FLOORS

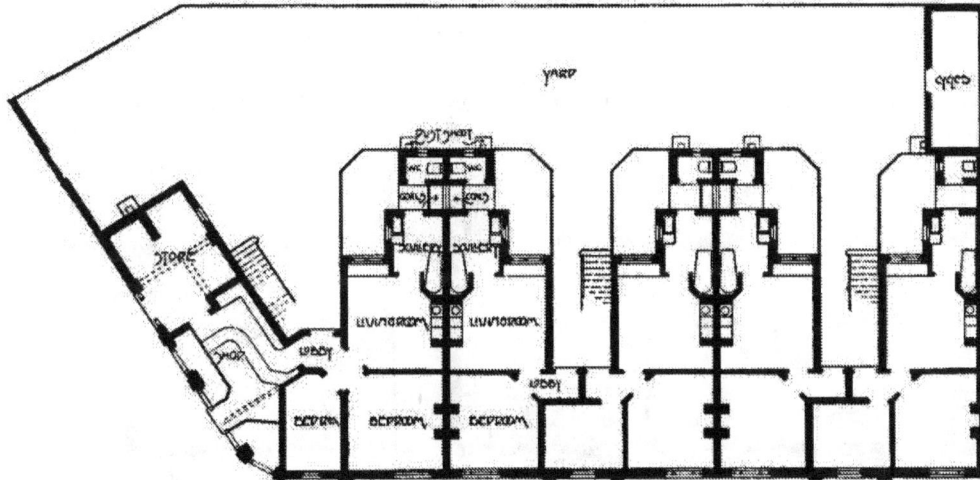

GROUND PLAN.

SCALE OF 5 0 5 10 15 20 25 FEET

Fig. 66.—Artisans' Dwellings, Hospital Street, Birmingham.

Arthur Harrison, Architect.

The larger building contains sixteen two-roomed tenements and sixteen three-roomed tenements, and the same corridor plan is adopted. There appears to be an unnecessary length of corridor, but the idea evidently was to obtain through ventilation, even at an extra outlay

upon the building.   These buildings are a private enterprise which is
calculated to pay 5 per cent.   The cost of the large block was 5¾d. per
foot cube, and of the smaller block 6d. per foot cube.

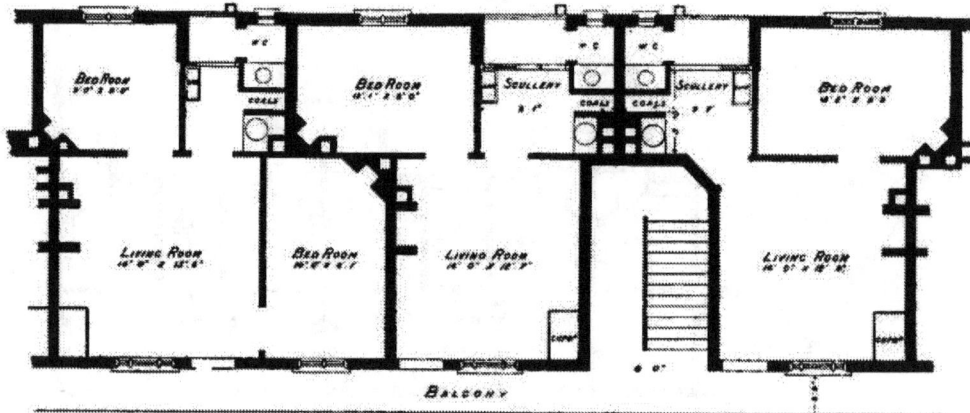

FIRST FLOOR PLAN.

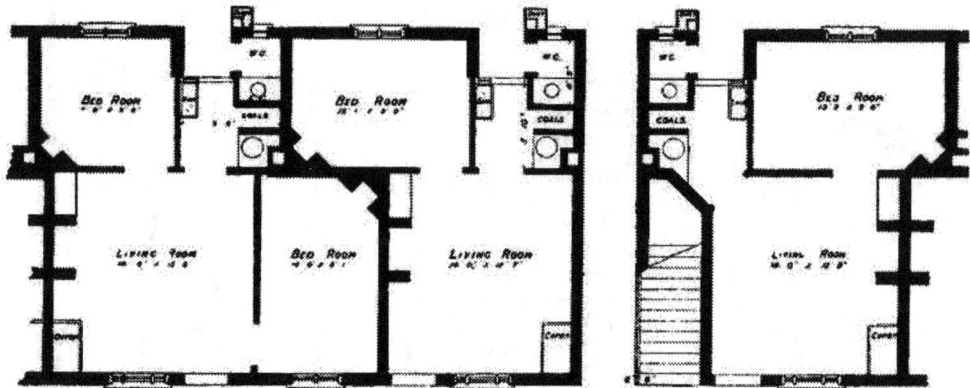

GROUND PLAN

SCALE OF 0   5   10   20   30   40   50 FEET

FIG. 67.—MILK STREET AREA, BIRMINGHAM.

Surveyor's Department.

The cost per tenement of three rooms is about £145, for two
rooms £115, and for one room about £96.   The cost per room in the
large blocks is about £52.

The Improvements Committee of the city have built a large number of two-story tenements on the balcony principle. Each suite contains two rooms and a scullery, W.C., and dust shoot.

The authorities of this city are now following the example of Miss Octavia Hill. They repair old houses, redrain them, provide new sanitary fittings, and make them healthy and desirable dwellings—a much cheaper method of reform than pulling down and entirely rebuilding large areas.

The Hospital Street buildings (Fig. 66) are for a better class of tenants. They are very compact, and arranged with the entrances from the yard. The buildings are four stories high, fifteen two-room and eight three-room tenements. The height of the rooms is 8 ft. 6 in. Each tenement is self-contained. The window in each living room is recessed, and the space thus formed contains a dresser, with a ventilated food cupboard. The exceptional feature is the bath in the scullery, heated from the living room. Dust shoots are provided.

The Milk Street site (Fig. 67) is an area upon which sixty-one labourers' dwellings have been erected; including sculleries the cost was £45 per room, excluding sculleries £62 per room. The balcony plan is adopted; each staircase is 4 ft. 6 in. wide. The tenements are of two and three rooms with a scullery and W.C. in each case. Dust shoots are provided. Gas is supplied on the penny-in-the-slot system. The following table is interesting :—

RECEIPTS AND EXPENDITURE IN RESPECT OF THE SIXTY-ONE LABOURERS'
DWELLINGS ERECTED IN MILK STREET IN 1900, FOR THE TWELVE
MONTHS ENDED 31ST MARCH 1903.

Dr.	£	S.	D.	Cr.	£	S.	D.
To Interest and Sinking Fund Charges on				By Rents received -	602	10	5
Loan - - -	441	15	8	(*Gross Rental, £663. 15s. 3d.*)			
„ Poor Rates -	70	0	6				
„ Improvement Rates	22	19	3				
„ Water Rents - -	28	8	6				
„ Insurance - -	3	15	9				
„ Repairs, Papering, &c.	32	8	1				
„ Gas to Lamps - -	5	4	2				
„ Commission on Collection of Rents -	15	1	3	Balance	17	2	9
	£619	13	2		£619	13	2

Sheffield.—The Crofts Improvement Scheme (Part I.) is a clearance of five acres; the plan Fig. 68 shows part of the scheme. Nearly all the buildings are tenements of two or three rooms with sculleries and W.C.'s. The plan of each block contains one tenement

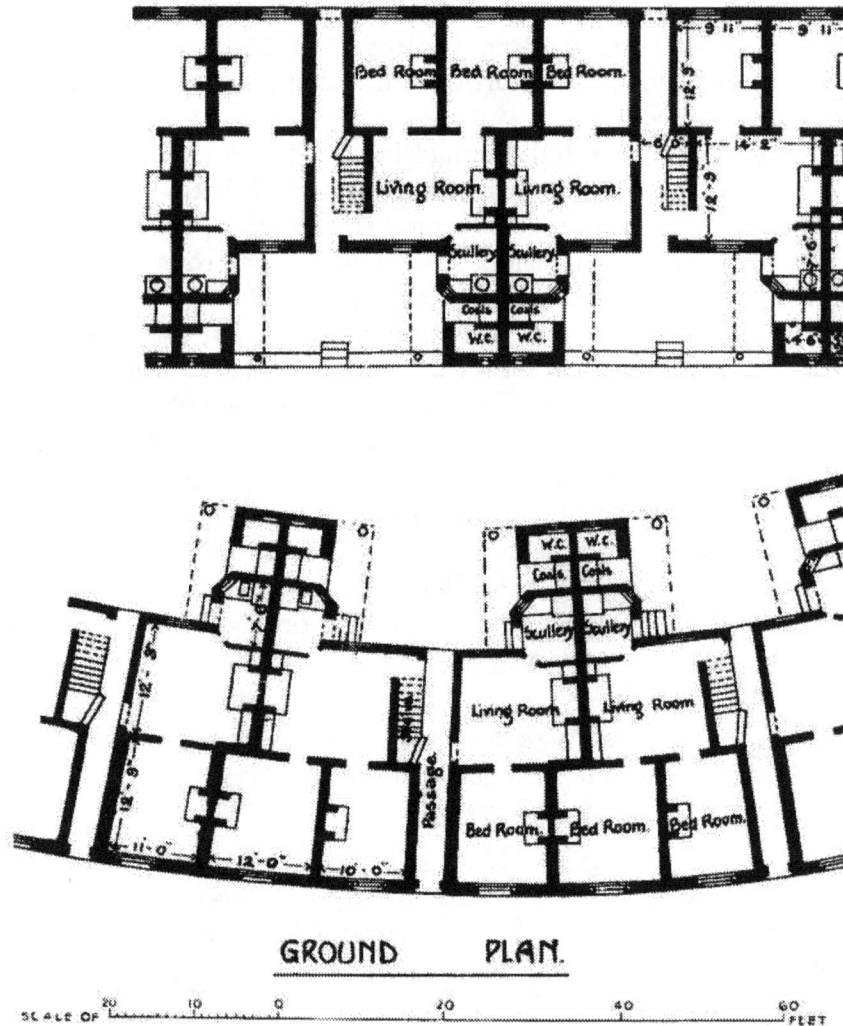

GROUND PLAN.

FIG. 68.—CITY OF SHEFFIELD CROFTS IMPROVEMENT SCHEME.

C. F. Wike, City Surveyor.

of each description. A few single-room tenements are provided; these are at the end of the rows of houses, and apparently provided as the space was not suitable for a larger dwelling. The authorities are contemplating blocks with a proportion of single tenements amounting to 30 per cent. of the whole.

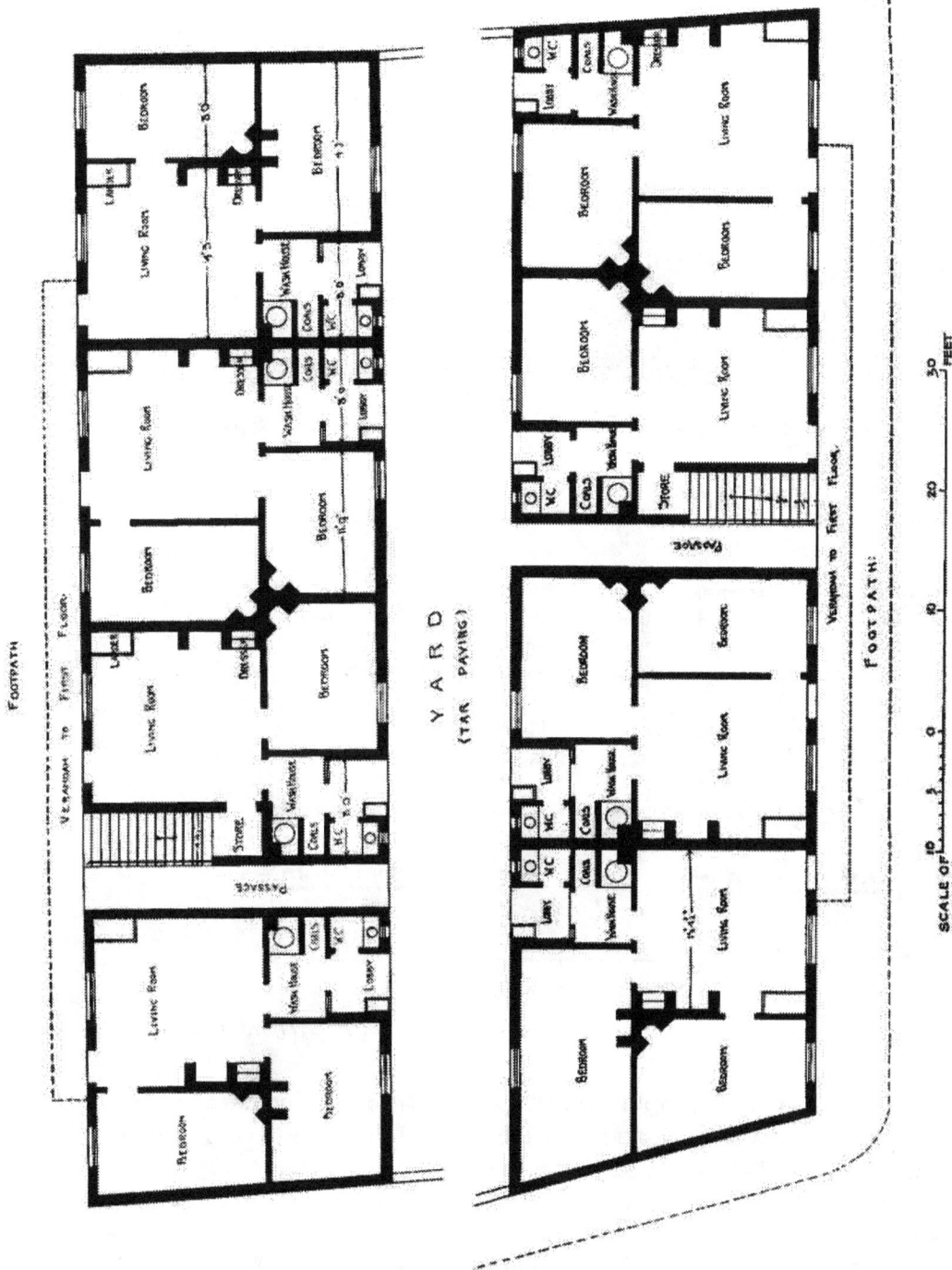

FIG. 69.—CITY OF BRISTOL.

Thos. Henry Yabbicom, City Engineer, Bristol.

Thos. Henry Yabbicom, City Engineer, Bristol.

Bristol.—The plans of a scheme are shown on Fig. 69. They are built on the balcony system. The steps to the first floor are of stone. Some tenements have two rooms and some three rooms ; each is complete with washhouse, coal cupboard, and W.C. The ash bins are in the centre of the yard. The three-room suites are intended for five persons, and the two-room suites for two people. The entire

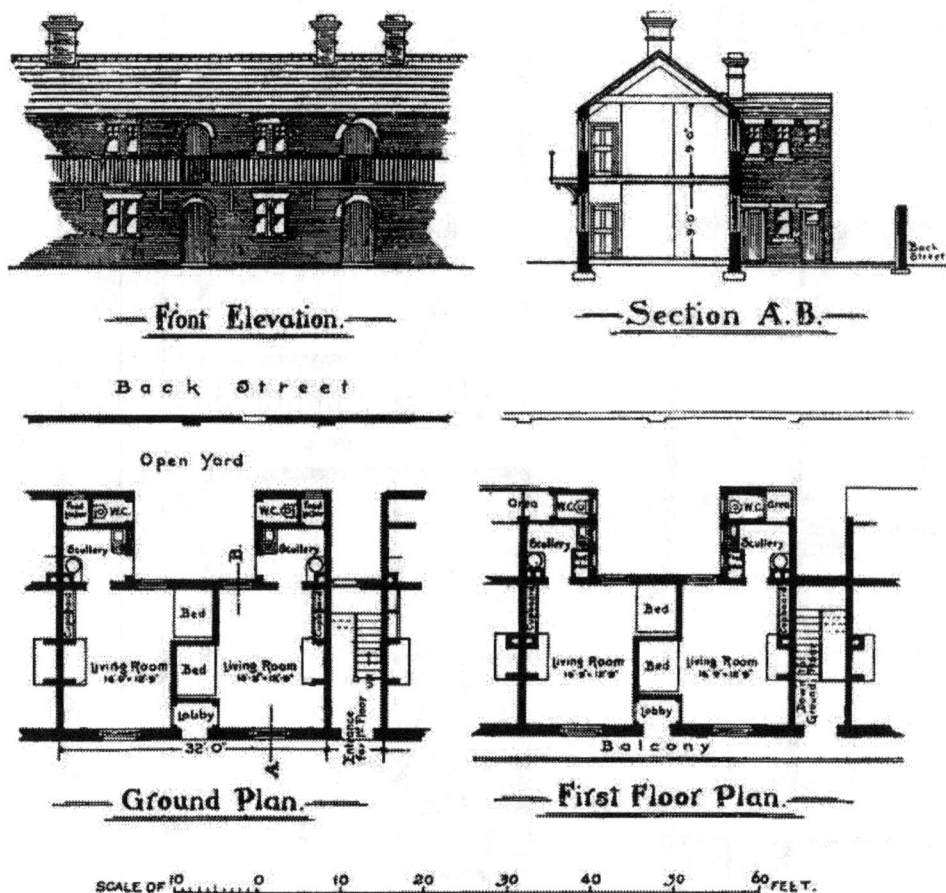

— Front Elevation. —   — Section A.B. —

— Ground Plan. —   — First Floor Plan. —

SCALE OF 10 0   10   20   30   40   50   60 FEET.

FIG. 70.—NEWCASTLE.

F. H. Holford, Architect.

scheme will house 340 people. Cost of construction including roads and sewers will amount to about £14,000. The weekly rents, when all suites are let, will amount to £838. 10s.

Newcastle.—Two-story buildings to an economical plan have been erected (see Fig. 70). The yard at rear is divided, and the W.C.'s are as far as possible from the main building. Fig. 71 shows a scheme for single-room tenements. Each has a scullery with copper, a food locker, and W.C.; they are two-story buildings on the balcony system.

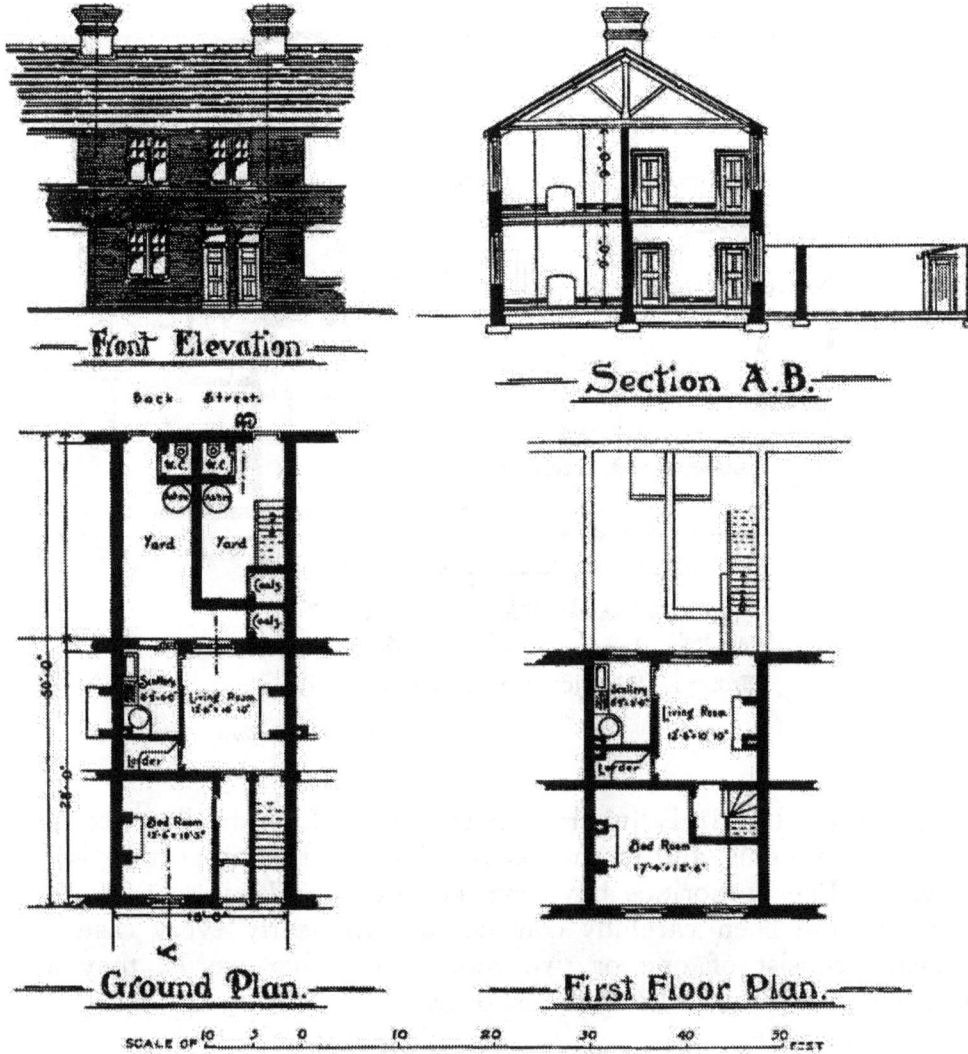

Front Elevation

Section A.B.

Ground Plan.

First Floor Plan.

SCALE OF

FIG. 71.—NEWCASTLE.

F. H. Holford, Architect.

The rooms are 9 ft. high, and as the main walls appear to be 14 in. on the first floor, an additional story might have been built at small cost.

Fig. 72 shows another scheme somewhat similar to Fig. 70. The yard at the rear of the end block is divided for the two tenements, second floor and first floor. The other tenements are single rooms, each with a scullery.   There is a common yard at the rear with an ash bin.

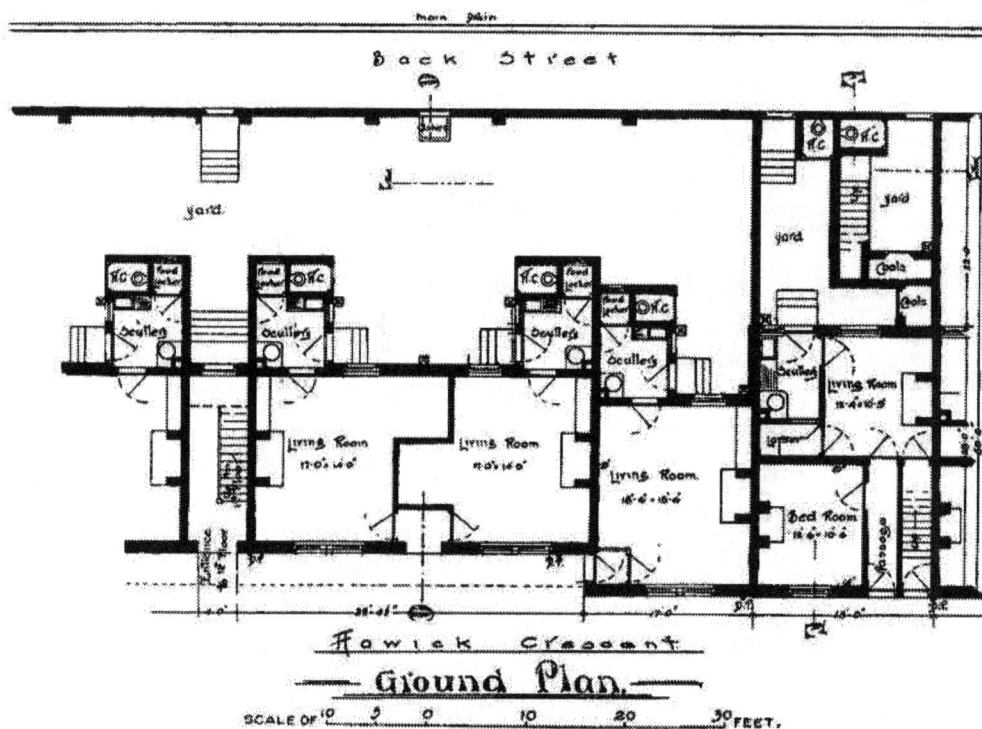

FIG. 72.—HAWICK CRESCENT, NEWCASTLE.

F. H. Holford, City Surveyor.

Edinburgh.—In Edinburgh, more than half the dwellings consist of one or two rooms, and in the poorer districts the proportion is 70 per cent.   The authorities have carried out many large schemes, and the poor have been carefully considered.   In nearly every case the tenements consist of one or two rooms; in other words, they are suitable for the people who were dishoused.

Potterrow block (Fig. 73) is three stories high, containing single and double apartment houses.   It is built on the balcony plan.   The single rooms have sinks and food cupboards, and one W.C. for each two rooms—an ample allowance.   A dust shoot is provided in the well of the staircase, a somewhat peculiar position, and a good one.   It seems a compromise between the pail and ordinary "shoot" principle. The dust shoots are usually 9 in. diameter and built with fireclay pipes,

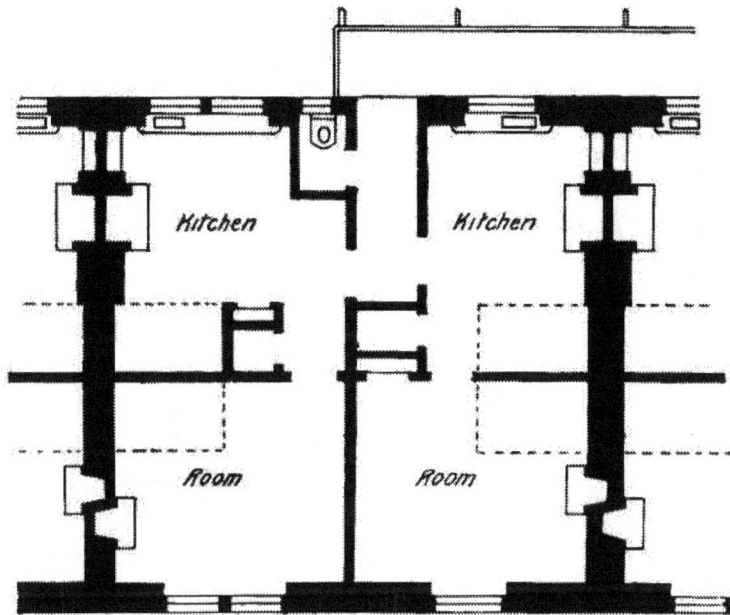

—1st FLOOR PLAN—

SCALE OF 10 ... 5 ... 0 .... 10 .... 20 FEET

FIG. 73.—POTTERROW, EDINBURGH.

Burgh Engineer's Office.

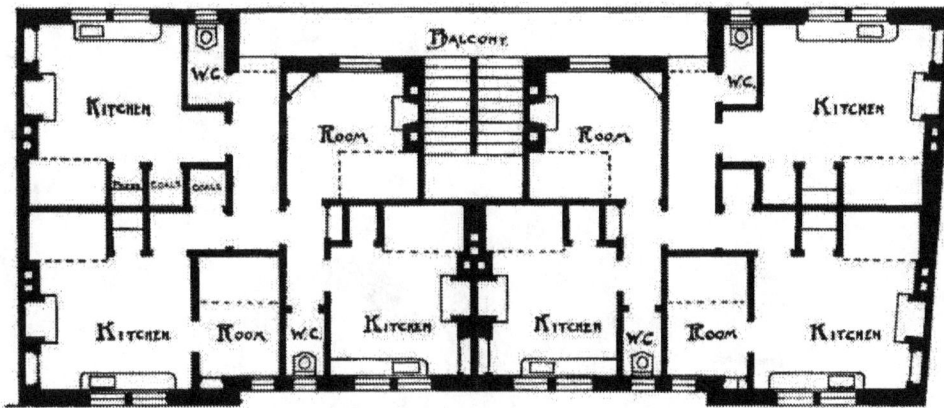

UPPER FLOORS PLAN·

SCALE OF 10 ... 5 ... 0 ... 10 ... 20 ... 30 ... 40 ... 50 ... 60 FEET

FIG. 74.—DEAN STREET, EDINBURGH.

Burgh Engineer's Office.

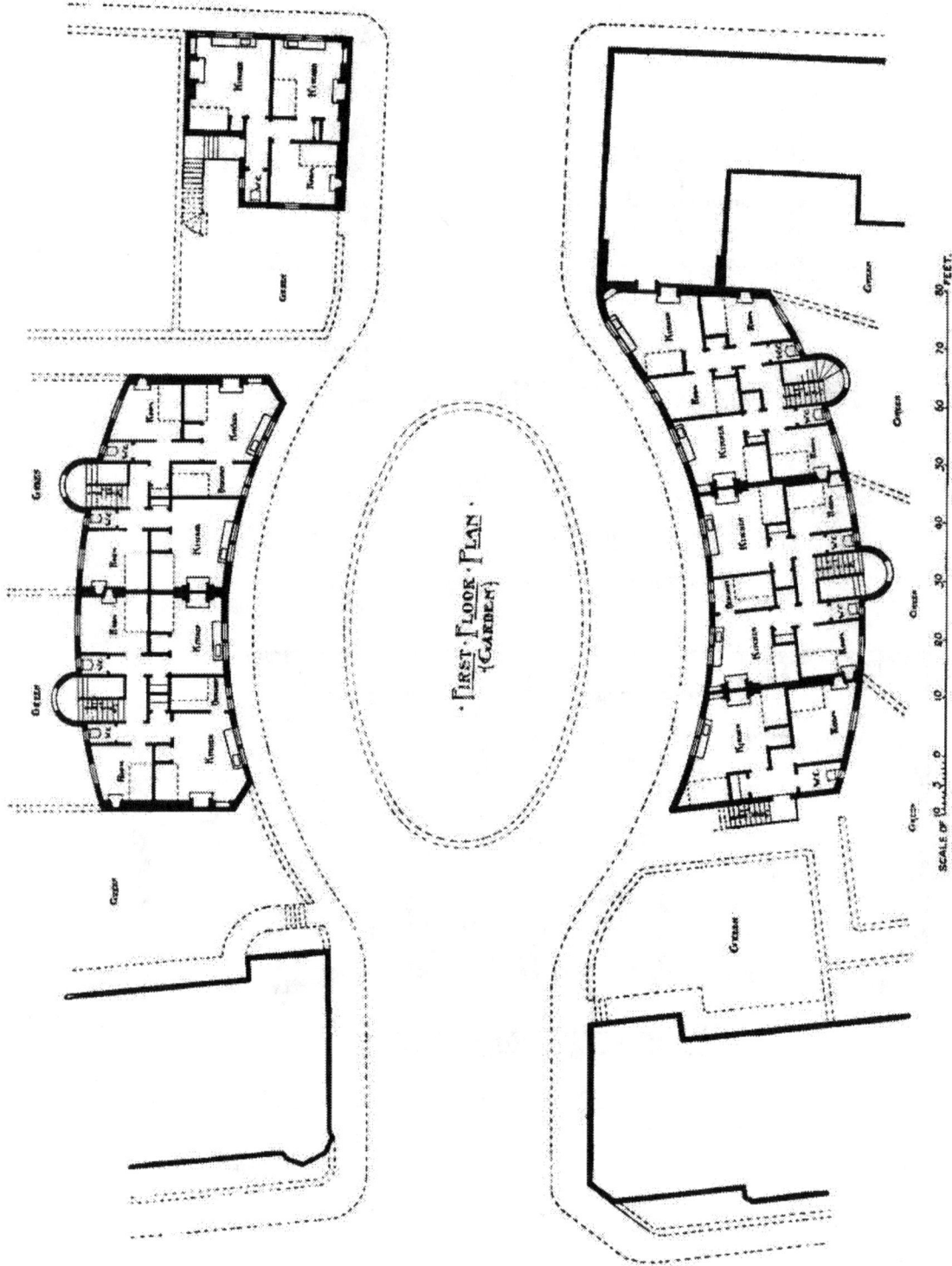

FIRST·FLOOR·PLAN.
(GARDEN)

SCALE OF

FIG. 75.—ALLAN STREET, STOCKBRIDGE, EDINBURGH.

Burgh Engineer's Office.

but they have not been a success, and in many cases have had to be closed.

Dean Street (Fig. 74) is also three stories high, with double and single tenements, and is part of a scheme of fifty-one dwellings. It is also constructed on the balcony system. Recesses are formed for the beds in some rooms. The tenements in Scotland are better provided with cupboards than is usual in England. The burgh engineer is ·in favour of the balcony system, as the public parts of the building are easily kept in a sanitary condition.

Flats of three rooms are often built by private enterprise; in these and also in many with only two rooms, a bath is provided with hot-water supply. In the Corporation schemes common baths and wash-houses are often built near the tenements.

Allan Street, Stockbridge (Fig. 75), has been laid out with the buildings facing an oval garden. Each suite has two rooms and a W.C. The bed recesses are again shown; a small bed-closet opens off the kitchen in

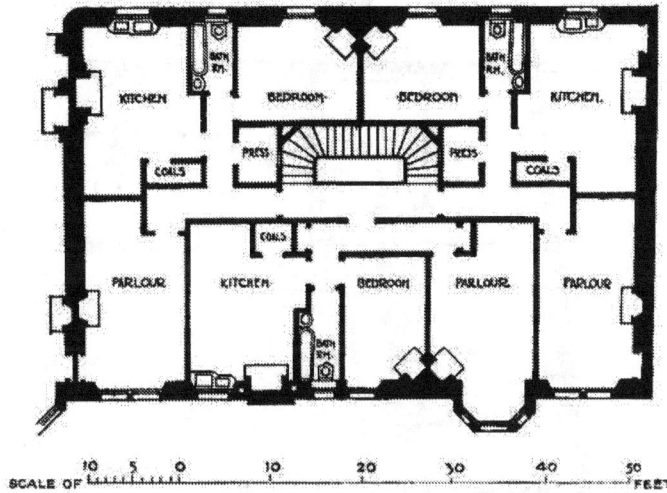

FIG. 76.—PIERSHILL PLACE, NEAR PORTOBELLO.

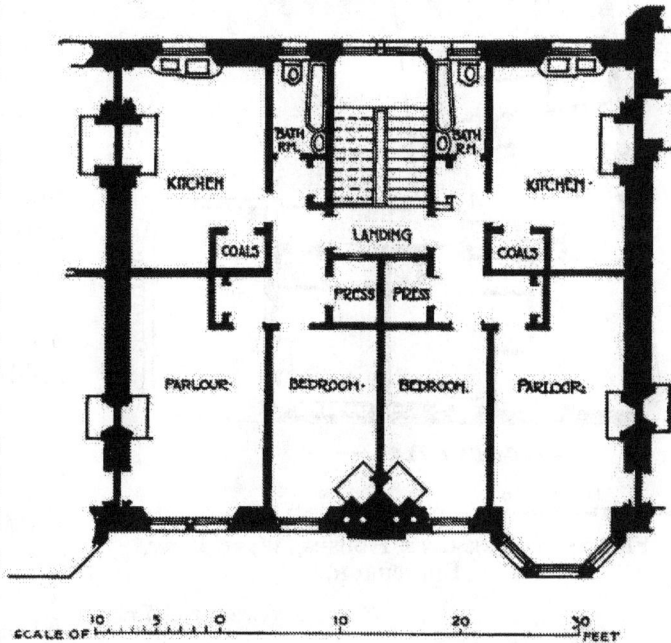

FIG. 77.—PIERSHILL PLACE, NEAR PORTOBELLO.

Hippolyte J. Blanc, Architect.

some cases, practically making the suite one of three rooms. The cupboard accommodation should be noted.

Tenements, Piershill Place (Fig. 76).—These plans illustrate a private enterprise. There are three rooms to each suite, and three suites on each floor with a staircase top-lighted. These are better than the ordinary artisans' dwellings, as each tenant has a bath-room, also a large press and a good coal cupboard. When the staircase has a central position and is top lighted, the plan at once becomes cheaper. Fig. 77 shows the same accommodation, but there are only two suites on each floor.

The absence of a scullery should be noted; a good sink is fixed in each kitchen. The rooms are large when compared with English tenements.

Fig. 78 shows a portion of a large block built upon the balcony system. There are single-room tenements, usually with one W.C. for each two holdings.

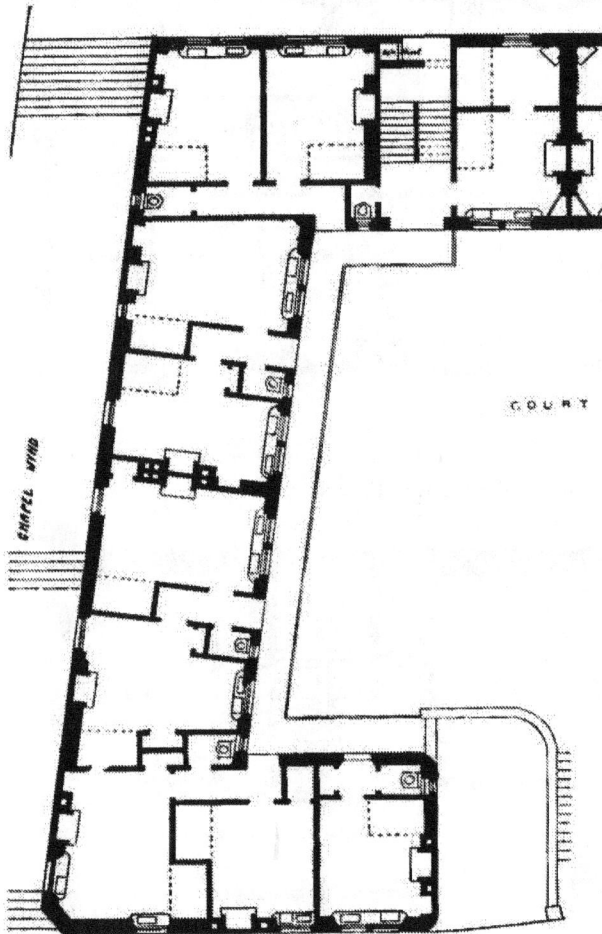

— GROUND PLAN —

SCALE OF 10 5 0 10 20 FEET

FIG. 78.—WORKMEN'S HOUSES, WEST PORT, EDINBURGH.

Burgh Engineer's Office.

Glasgow.—Including the year 1902 the Public Works Department has erected as many as 1,515 tenements. About one-third are built specially for the poorest classes, and the proportion of one-room dwellings is large. The total of 1,515 comprises 431 one-room dwellings, 921 two-room tenements, 152 three-room tenements, and only eleven suites of over three rooms; also 187 shops.

The plans of labourers' dwellings, St James Road (Fig. 79), show single-room tenements with provision for a crib for a child. The balcony system is adopted, but the staircase is built in so that the tenants would get protection from the weather until they had to pass along the balcony. There is a wash-house and a W.C. for each two tenements. Had the W.C. been placed next the wash-house it would perhaps have been an improvement. Through ventilation is provided for the room. Fig. 80 shows an arrangement for one single and two two-roomed tenements on each floor. The Scotch arrangement for a recess for the bed is provided. The cloak-rooms and lobbies seem unnecessary for this class of building.

In 1901 there were 36,000 single tenements in Glasgow, and 70,000 dwellings of two rooms; the total number of occupied dwellings was 156,000, consequently, it is only natural that the authorities have devoted so much time and thought to the difficult subject of housing the poor. The cost of building has been carefully cut down as far as possible. Mr A. B. M'Donald, the City Engineer, described the construction in 1901 as follows:—

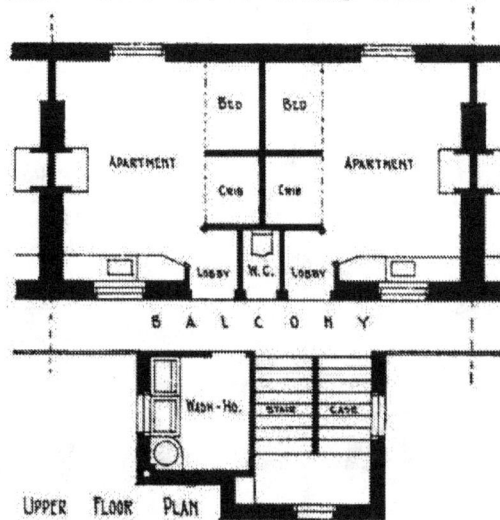

FIG. 79.—ST JAMES ROAD, GLASGOW.

A. B. M'Donald, Office of Public Works.

" The method adopted is balcony access, with a central stair. There are ten apartments on each floor, or thirty in each tenement, as it is not suggested to carry the building higher than three stories. Every single-room house will possess 1,200 cub. ft. of space, without measuring the bed recess. The outside walls are intended to be built of common brick. The partition walls are also of plain brickwork. All lintels, sills, kitchen jambs, and stair steps will be formed of concrete. The exterior and interior wall surfaces are not to be plastered. The joiner and carpenter work are to be of the plainest description. Batten doors for presses and passages. Outside doors cross-lined. No jamb linings, soffit linings, or window facings. No skirting. Door facing, 3 in. by ½ in., plain. Double-hung windows. Only outer doors to have locks. Latches for the other doors. No

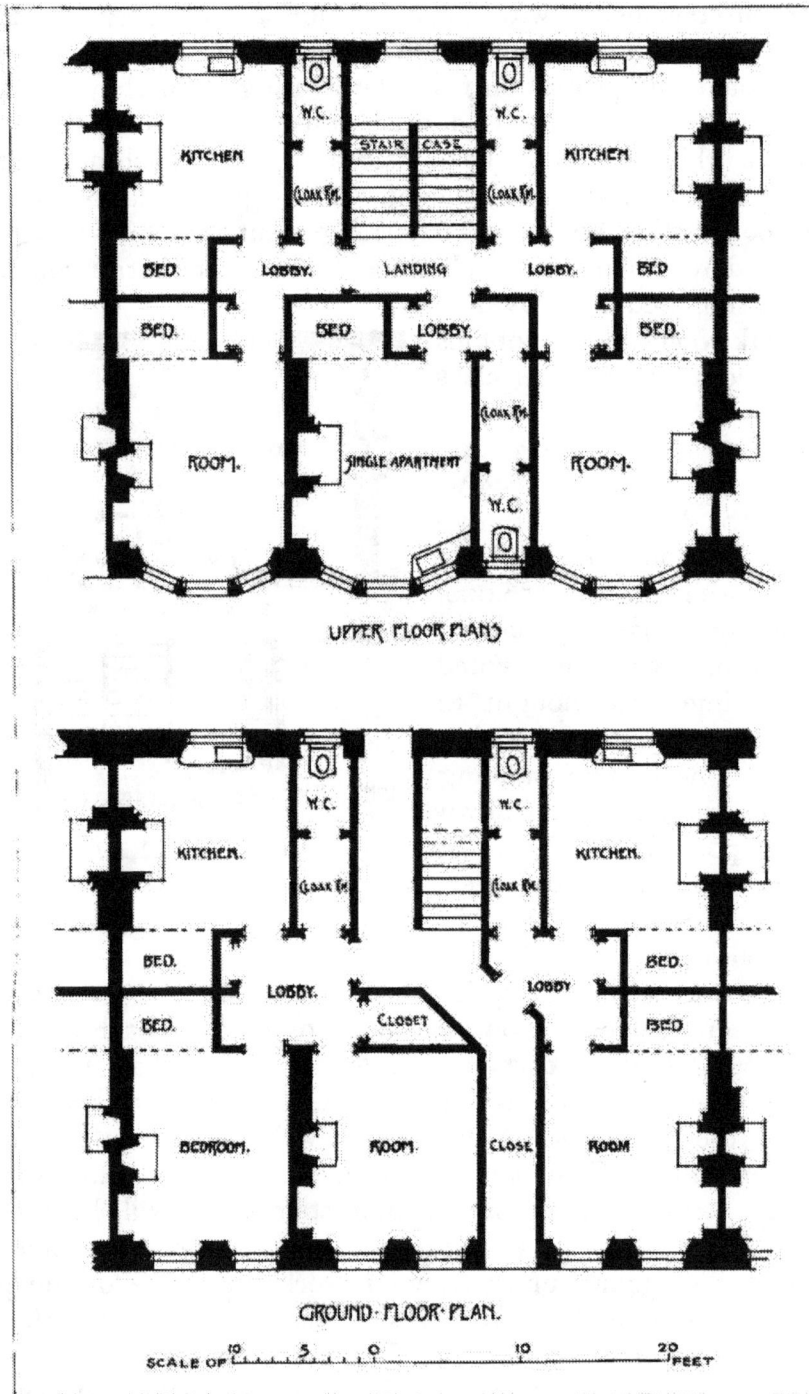

UPPER FLOOR PLANS

GROUND·FLOOR·PLAN.

SCALE OF | 10 | 5 | 0 | 10 | 20 FEET

FIG. 80.—GLASGOW.

City Improvement Trust, Glasgow.   *A. B. McDonald, Office of Public Works.*

plaster work except in bedding window cases. The ceiling of each room to consist of the under side of the flooring boards of the room above, or of slabs fastened to the roof timbers. All exposed woodwork to be saturated with vermin-proof fluid. Kitchen sinks of cast-iron, and the W.C.'s of the strongest pattern of wash-down design. No tile work. Paint to be used on woodwork only."

The cost of building is about 4½d. to 5¼d. per foot cube, much less than in London (see table above). In Liverpool the cost has been as high as 8½d. The reason why the cost of erection in Glasgow is small, is because the building regulations are not so absolutely strict as in Liverpool and London. In Scotland the dwellings are erected without any plaster work inside, so that a hose can be turned into the room when a tenant has left, and the whole well scoured out.

In London the cost of clearance alone has been as high as £100 for each man, woman, and child.

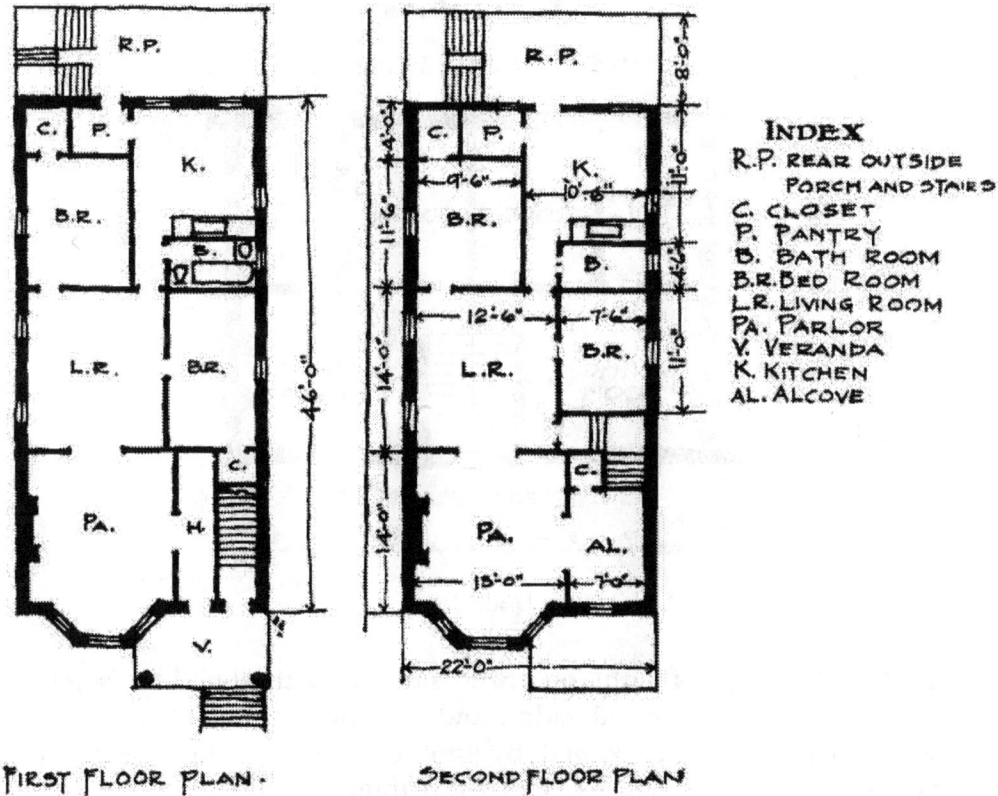

INDEX

R.P. REAR OUTSIDE PORCH AND STAIRS
C. CLOSET
P. PANTRY
B. BATH ROOM
B.R. BED ROOM
L.R. LIVING ROOM
PA. PARLOR
V. VERANDA
K. KITCHEN
AL. ALCOVE

FIRST FLOOR PLAN.   SECOND FLOOR PLAN

FIG. 81.—CHICAGO.

Jennie & Mundie, Architects.

America.—The artisan in America has better accommodation than in England. Fig. 81 is a typical plan of a block; there are thousands of these in the larger cities. The illustration is well worth careful consideration. With the addition of a servant's bedroom, it would be similar to a flat in England let at £50 to £60. The site

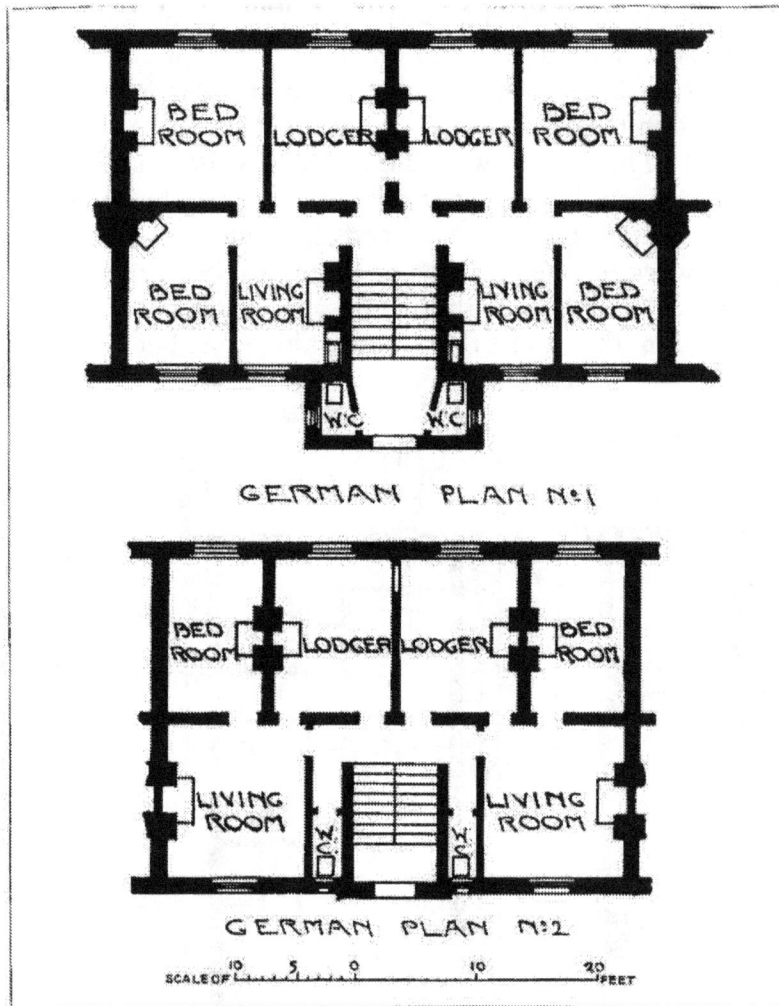

FIG. 82.

has the advantage of light on three sides, and the building is set back so as to get windows on all sides, and one must assume that the living-room would not be darkened by another building three feet off. If that is so, then the plan has many advantages. Except for a few feet outside the bathroom (containing a W.C.), there is an entire absence of passage. It will be noticed that all the slops must be taken through the living-room, but not through the kitchen. The living-room is what we should call a hall. Note that the parlour in front with the alcove is over 20 ft. long. Each flat has a bath-room, and apparently a fitted lavatory.

Germany.—Fig. 82 gives examples of two German plans. The lodger has a separate entrance off the main staircase, and there is also a connection with the remainder of the tenements. The lodger is not considered in England, and the plans are interesting. The W.C. is frequently entered off the staircase in Germany and France, but rarely in England. The idea has advantages; it is far away from the living-rooms, and the caretaker would also be able to inspect it without entering the tenements.

CHAPTER IV.

DIFFERENT CLASSES OF FLATS—COMPARISON OF PLANS.

THE best way to study the planning of flats is to compare the plans of different buildings. The examples given are nearly all of recent date; indeed, a few of the blocks have not yet been commenced. The selection has been made in order to give as many varieties as possible without repetition, and many possible buildings have been omitted, because their general scheme is on the lines of another selected for illustration.

Class No. 1.—The drawings have been divided into four groups or classes. In this class will be found plans of flats that are let at very high rentals, including small flats in the expensive neighbourhoods.

Class No. 2.—These are plans of flats let at lower rents, several of them being some little way from the most fashionable centres, and others quite out of London.

Class No. 3.—Consists of plans of flats at still lower rents, some of them only slightly better than artisans' dwellings.

Class No. 4.—This class comprises plans of bachelor flats and catering flats.

Generally.—The division into Classes Nos. 1, 2, and 3 has been more or less roughly made in order to group the plans for the purpose of comparison; no strict line is drawn between one and the other, and the exact amount of rent has not been considered.

A few remarks are made on each plan to call attention to some point of interest.

The Mansions, Sloane Gardens (Fig. 83).—This is an
example of a suite occupying the entire area of one floor, an advantage

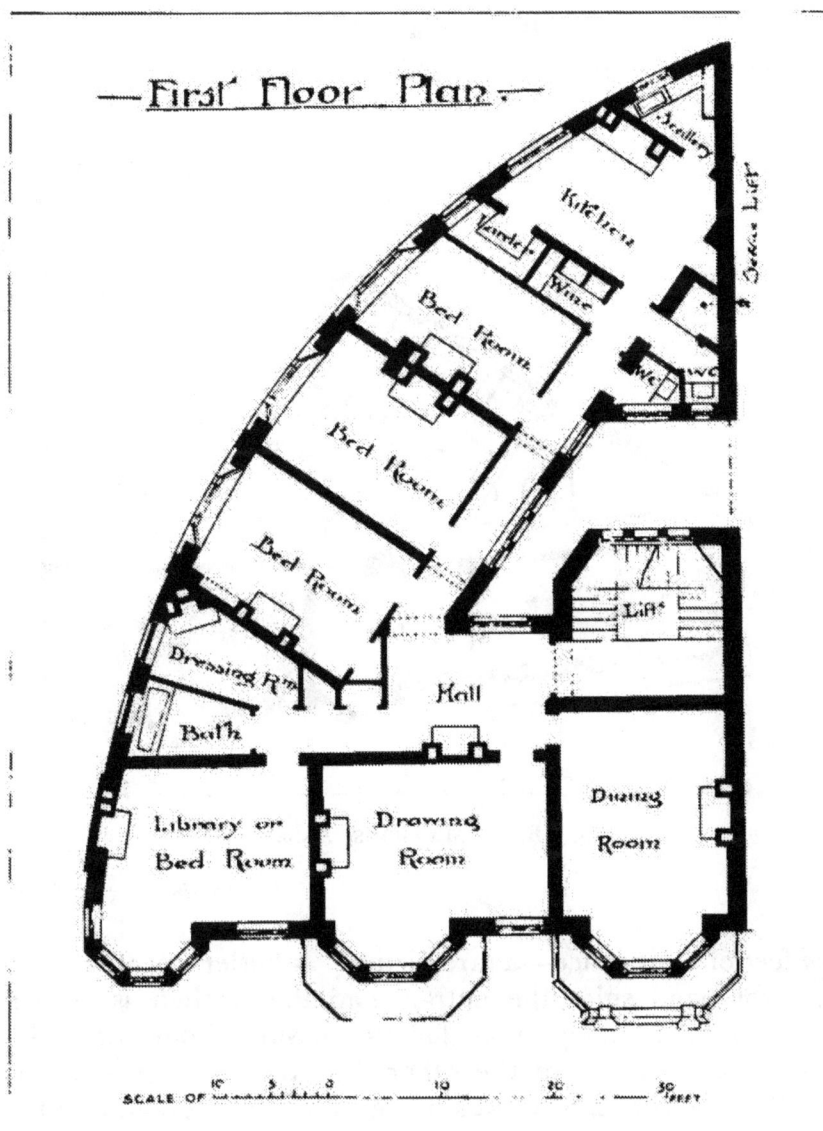

FIG. 83.—THE MANSIONS, SLOANE GARDENS.

Edwin T. Hall, Architect.

obtained in a flat on a small site.   The servants' W.C. is not entered
from the scullery, and the door by the other W.C. cuts off the servants'

offices.   There is a good larder and wine store.   The hall is large, and
had it been possible to include part of the area at the side of the staircase, it might have been much larger.

Basil Mansions, Albert Gate (Fig. 84).—This plan shows the
effect of French influence.   The staircase is circular, and the architect
has attempted to make one drawing-room symmetrical at the expense

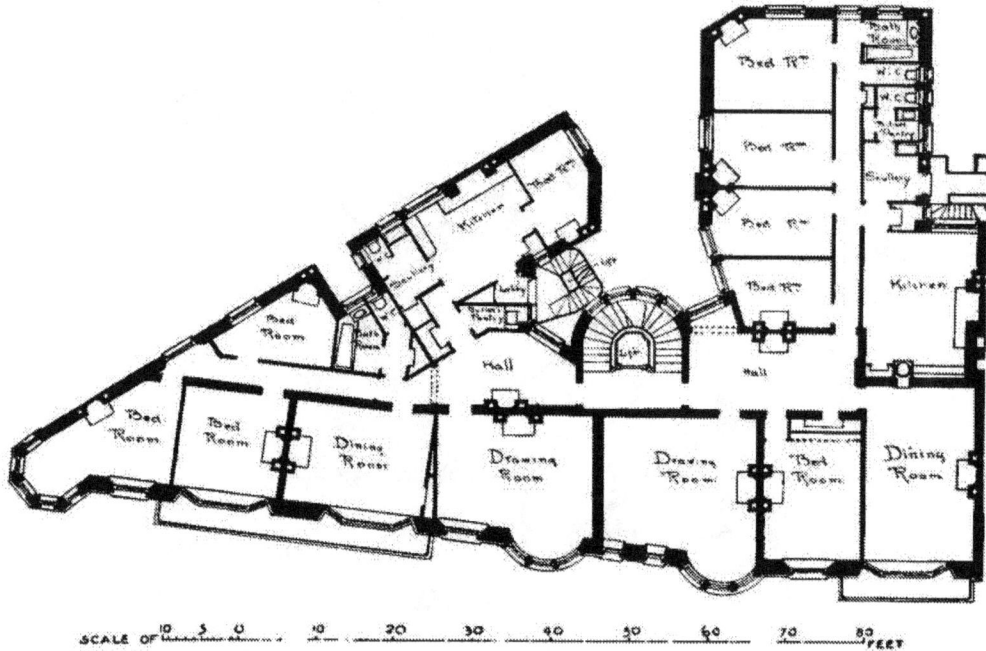

FIG. 84.—BASIL MANSIONS, ALBERT GATE.

Edwin Sadgrove, Architect.

of a few feet of floor space—a rare virtue.   A butler's pantry is provided.
In the right hand suite the entrance to the kitchen is through the
larder, in order to keep it as far as possible from the hall.   The
servants' W.C. is close to the other, but the entrances are entirely
separated.   The servants' offices are exceptionally good, and there are
no areas ; where necessary, recesses have been formed.

Hanover Square (Fig. 85).—The ground floor is principally
occupied by shops, and is an example of the best way to arrange the
entrance to the flats by breaking the line of frontage.   The doors of
shops Nos. 6 and 7 are as far as possible from the main entrance.

FIRST FLOOR PLAN

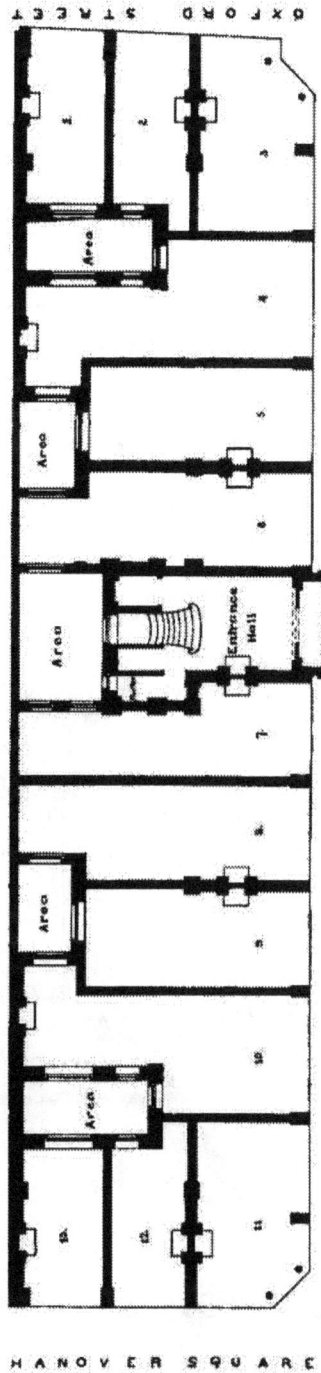

PLAN OF GROUND FLOOR SHOPS.

SCALE OF FEET

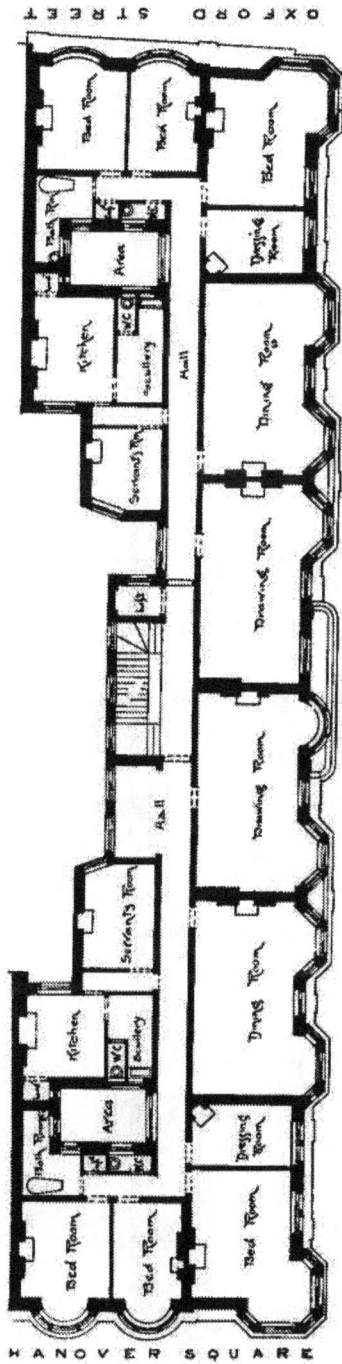

FIG. 85.—14 HANOVER SQUARE, W.

Paul Hoffmann, Architect.

GROUND FLOOR PLAN

Dressing Room

Bed Room

Bed Room

Bath Room

W C

Bed Room

Hall

Lobby

Drawing Room

Dining Room

Study

BASEMENT PLAN

Larder

Coals

Scullery

Kitchen

Servants Bed Room

Pantry

Caretaker's Room

W C

Lift

Billiard Room

Cellar

Cellar

Cellar

SCALE OF 10 5 0 10 20 30 40 50 FEET

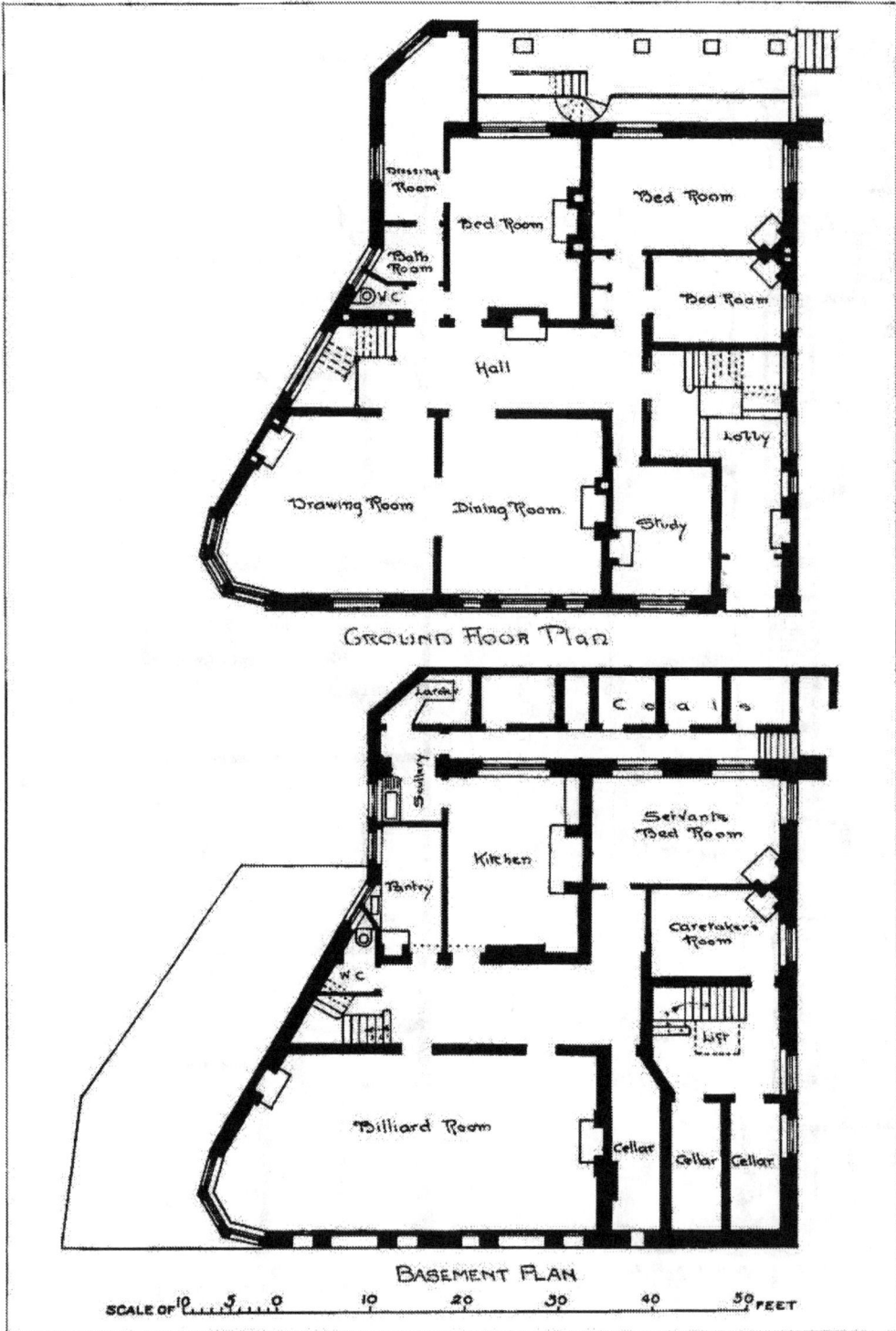

FIG. 86.—NOS. 1 AND 2 GRAFTON STREET, W.

Basil Slade, Architect.

One hall on the first floor is good, and the architect was evidently
prevented from making the other larger than it is. This is a rare
example of an English plan having the lift divided from the main
staircase—which is often done on the Continent.

Grafton Street (Figs. 86 and 87).—These suites are exceptionally well planned. The one on the ground floor has all the
servants' rooms and also a billiard-room in the basement. The first

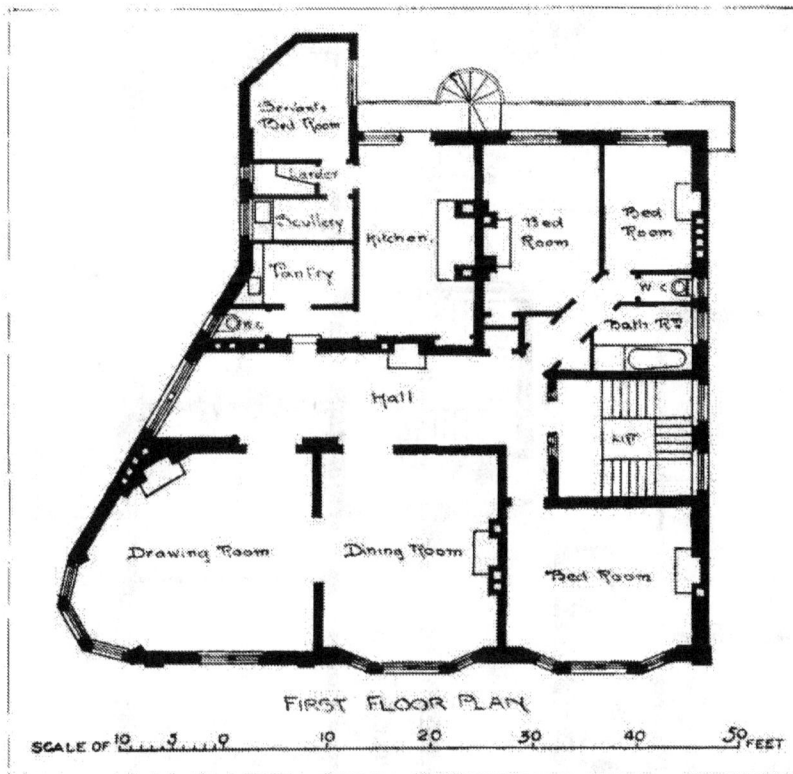

FIG. 87.—NOS. 1 AND 2 GRAFTON STREET, W.

Basil Slade, Architect.

floor suite has a large hall, and the servants' offices form a self-contained
suite, cut off by one door. These rooms occupy about a quarter of the
total area of the flat. The number of bedrooms is small. The building
has the advantage of light on all sides, consequently there are no
areas or recesses.

Burton Court (Fig. 88).—A compact plan showing three suites
opening off one staircase. The hall of each suite is entered without

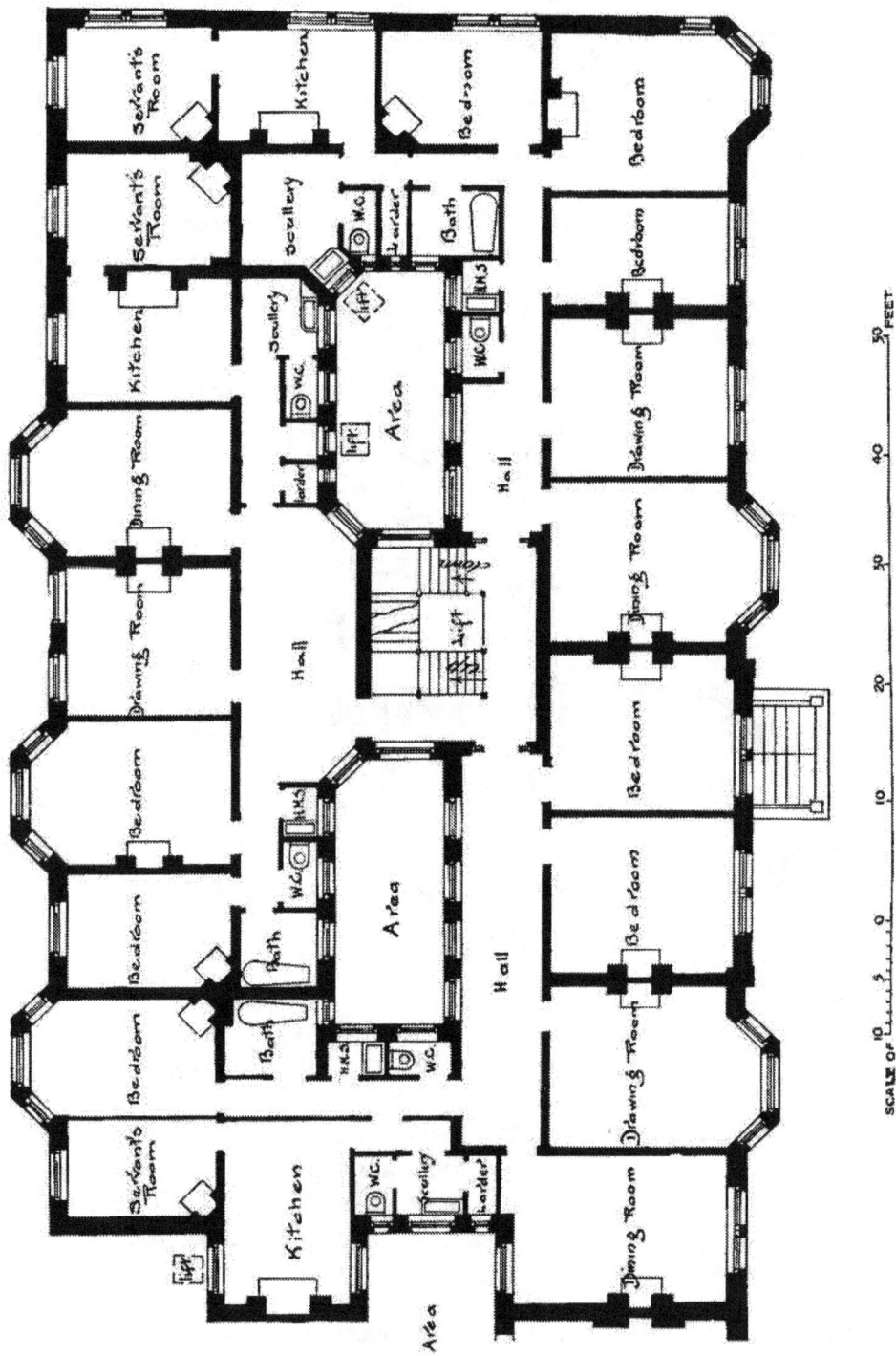

FIG. 88.—1 TO 20 BURTON COURT.

Paul Hoffmann, Architect.

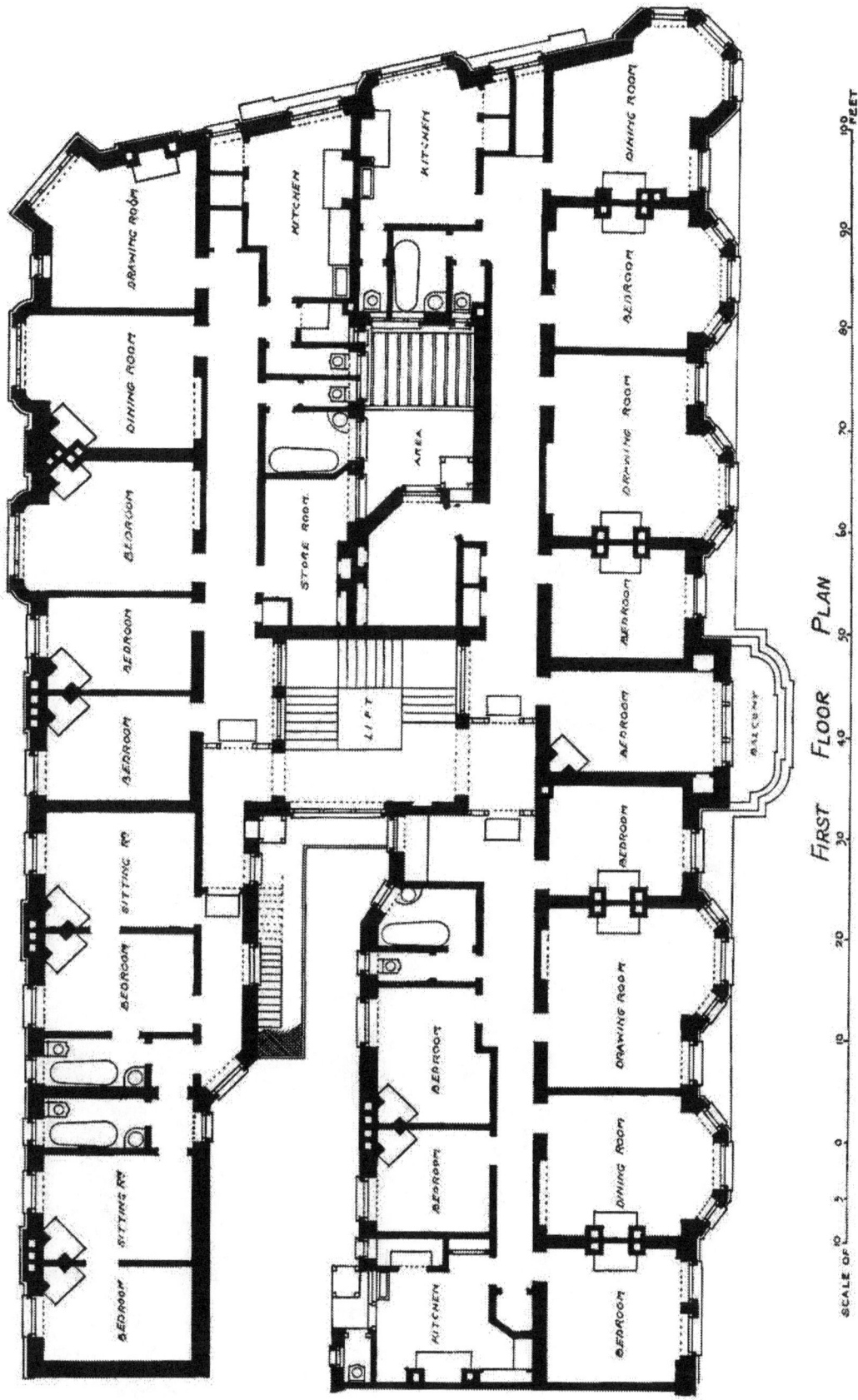

FIG. 89.—RESIDENTIAL MANSIONS, EARL'S COURT SQUARE.

FIRST FLOOR PLAN

SCALE OF FEET

J. A. J. Keynes, Architect.

any public passage and waste of space.   If it is necessary to have such a passage it is better to include it with the suite, placing the door at the staircase end.   Ten-ants can always make some use of a passage; they will hang pictures and furnish it, and in many flats it becomes quite a good feature: it should be at least four feet wide.   No living-rooms are lighted by the areas.

Earl's Court Square (Fig. 89).—This is the plan of the ground floor of a successful building in Kensington.   Some bachelor suites are pro-vided, and there is good kitchen and bedroom ac-commodation in the base-ment for the caterer.   A billiard-room and a read-ing-room were provided in the basement, but have been used for other pur-poses.   These common rooms are often a source of trouble to the manager, and as a rule should not be built (see Chapter II.).

Green Street, Park Lane, W. (Fig. 90).— On the ground floor the site is occupied by busi-

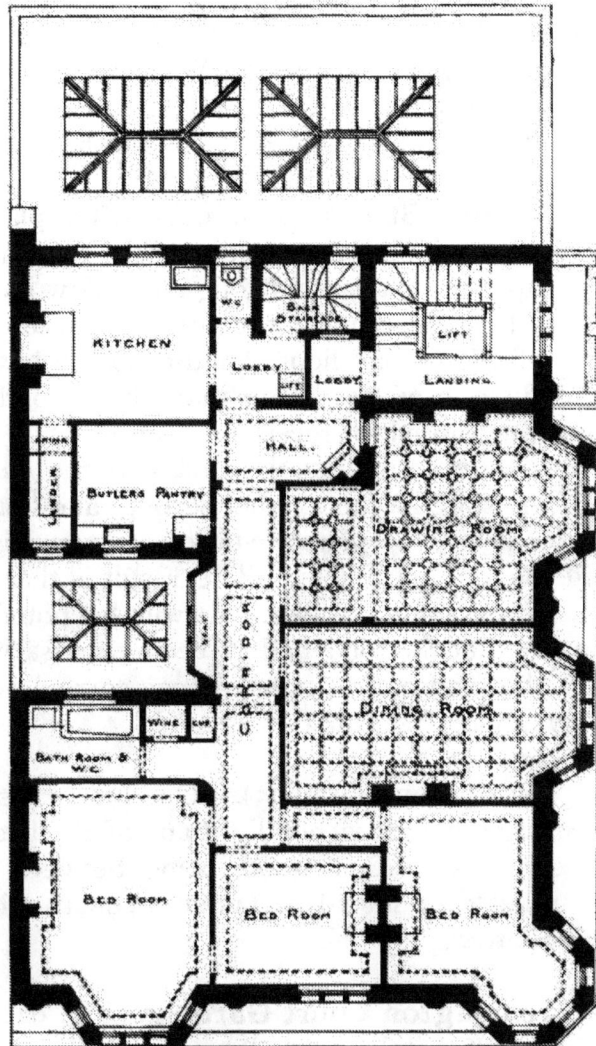

NOTE EACH FLAT HAS TWO SERVANTS BEDROOMS ON TOP FLOOR.

—— UPPER FLOORS ——

SCALE OF

FIG. 90.—FLATS, GREEN STREET, PARK LANE, W.

H. S. & H. A. Legge, Architects

ness premises, the entrance to the suite is kept well away from the other external doors.   This building is erected on the French principle;

each suite has two bedrooms on the top floor. There is no scullery, a sink is fixed in the kitchen, and a large butler's pantry is provided. The reception rooms are exceptionally large. The principal W.C. is in the bath-room.

Cavendish Square (Fig. 91).—This is an example of a circular staircase. One suite is particularly large, having seven bedrooms; two are for servants, and the W.C. is between them and the kitchen— an excellent position. There is a private entrance to one suite on the ground floor in addition to the one from the main hall.

Mount Street (Fig. 92).—The plan of these flats is very ingenious, and shows an arrangement not unlike that of Dutch houses. The site was not large enough to allow one flat to each floor, and if one suite had occupied the first and second floors, the rooms in the front of the second floor would probably have been bedrooms, and the third floor is of less value than the second, consequently the second floor was wanted for reception rooms. The problem has been solved by one suite occupying the first and the back part of the third floor; another suite occupies the second and fourth floor. They do not communicate, the private staircases intertwine. There is a bachelors' suite on the third floor. The result is that there are reception rooms in the front of each floor. It will be noted that the staircase is only ventilated at the top; had it been necessary to put windows on each floor, this plan could not have been carried out. A view of the exterior is given (see Fig. 149A).

Hampstead (Fig. 93).—One lift serves four suites. The area is very large, but does not light any of the best rooms. The position of the servants' W.C. is good, being between the kitchen and the bed- room, but care should be taken in construction when the W.C. is next to the larder.

Kensington Court Gardens (Fig. 94).—This plan is suggestive of the Continental arrangement, two suites on each floor, and a large area in the centre. The halls are large, and the lower flat has the servants' rooms well planned; they form a suite entered by one door. A very large pantry is provided.

Kensington Court Mansions (Fig. 95).—The plan given is that of a small portion of a very large block of flats. The servants'

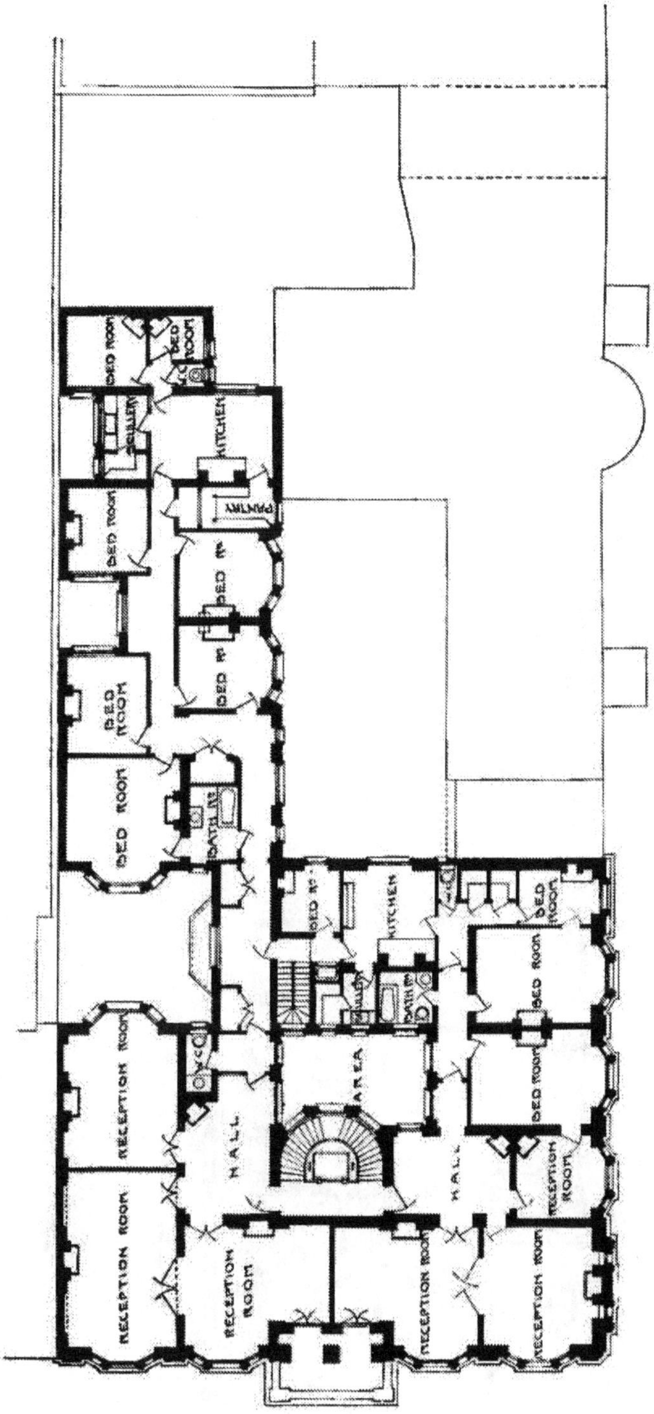
BED ROOM
BED ROOM
W.C.
SCULLERY
KITCHEN
PANTRY
BED ROOM
BED RM
BED RM
BED ROOM
BED ROOM
BATH RM
BED RM
KITCHEN
W.C.
BED ROOM
BATH RM
BED ROOM
BED ROOM
W.C.
RECEPTION ROOM
AREA
HALL
HALL
RECEPTION ROOM
RECEPTION ROOM
RECEPTION ROOM
RECEPTION ROOM
RECEPTION ROOM

PLAN OF UPPER FLOORS

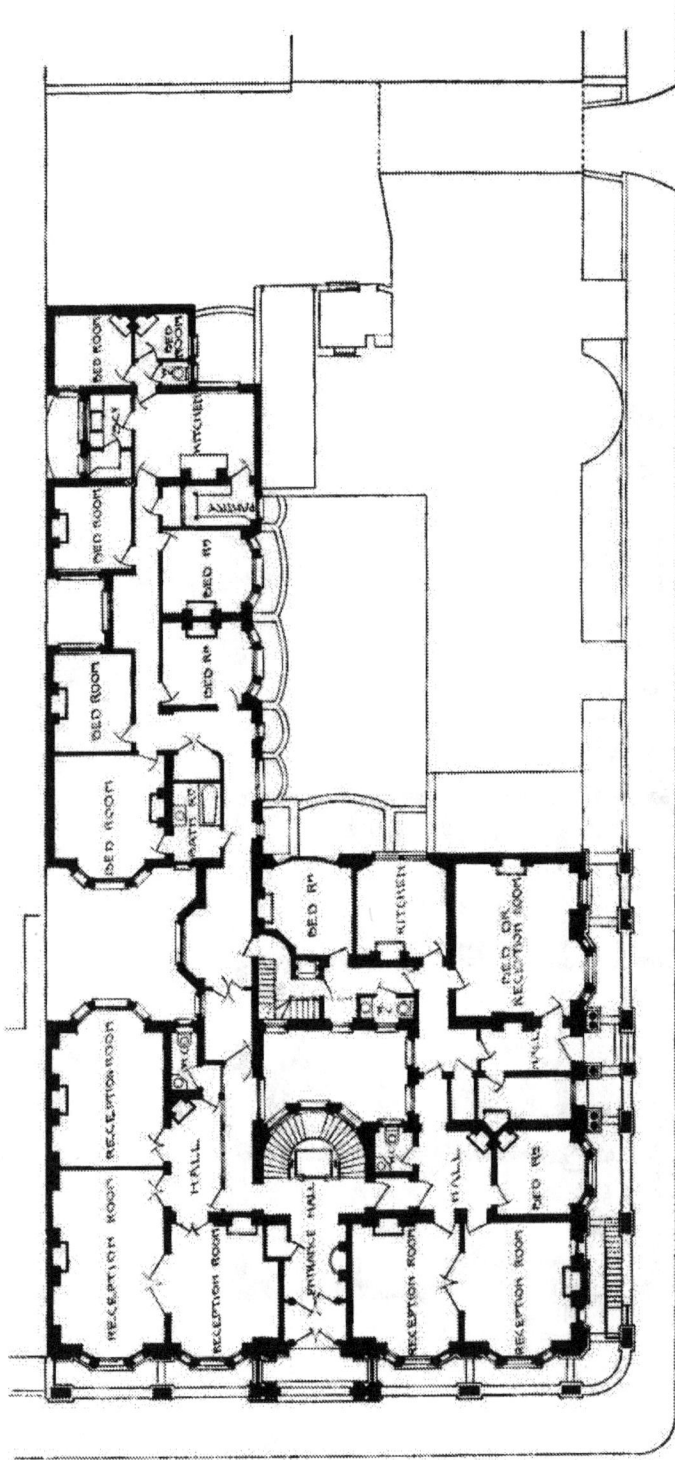

RECEPTION ROOM

RECEPTION ROOM

HALL

BED ROOM

BED ROOM

BED ROOM

BED ROOM

BED ROOM

BATH RM

BED RM

BED RM

PANTRY

KITCHEN

CLOSET

BED ROOM

BED ROOM

ENTRANCE HALL

RECEPTION ROOM

RECEPTION ROOM

HALL

BED RM

BED RM

BED RA

KITCHEN

W.C.

BED OR RECEPTION ROOM

PLAN OF GROUND FLOOR

SCALE OF FEET
10 5 0   10   20   30   40   50   60   70   80   90   100
FEET

FIG. 91.—MANSIONS, CAVENDISH SQUARE, W.

Lewis Solomon, } Joint.
E. Carrington Arnold, } Architects.

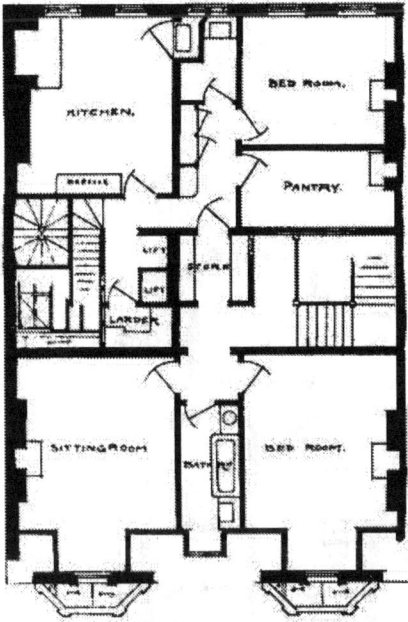

THIRD FLOOR PLAN.

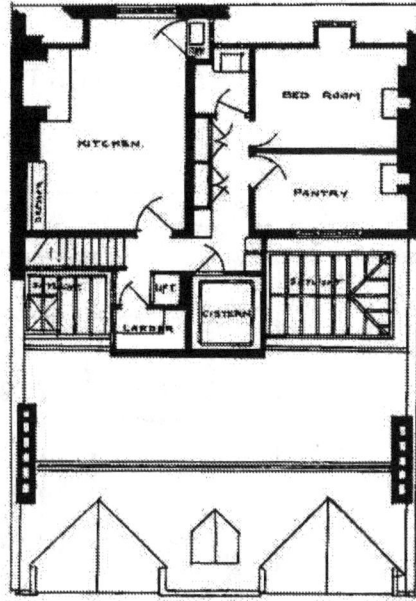

FOURTH FLOOR PLAN.

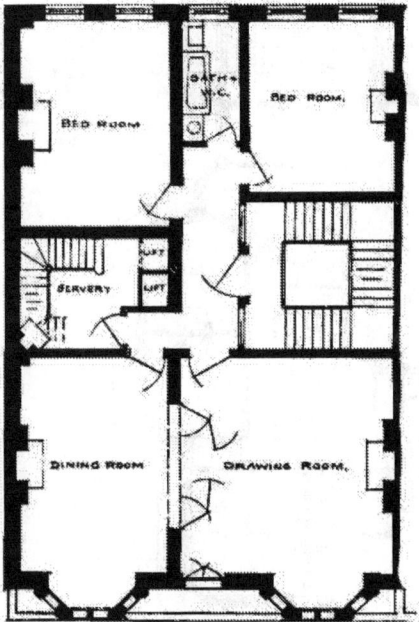

FIRST FLOOR PLAN

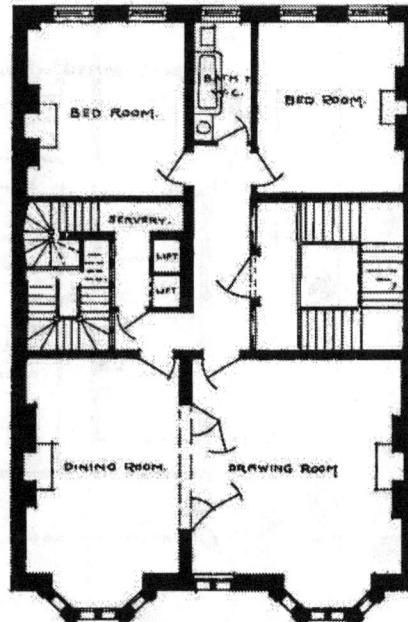

SECOND FLOOR PLAN

SCALE OF ⊢⊢⊢⊢⊢⊢⊢⊢⊢⊢ FEET

FIG. 92.—MOUNT STREET W

Ernest George & Peto, Architects.

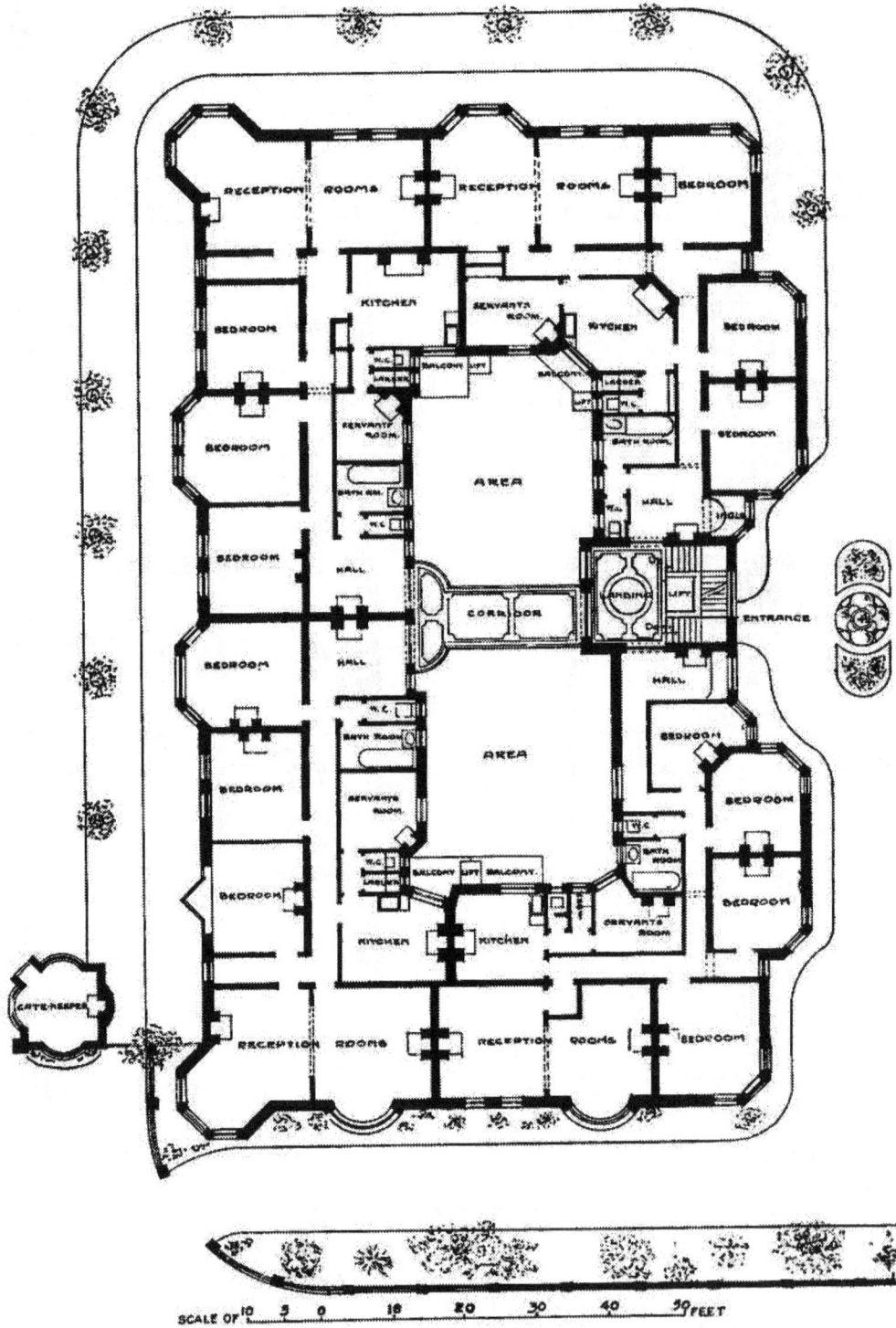

FIG. 93.—FROGNAL, HAMPSTEAD.

Palgrave & Co., Architects.

FIG. 93A.—ST ALBAN'S MANSIONS, KENSINGTON COURT GARDENS.

Paul Hoffmann, Architect.

quarters are so isolated from the other rooms that they could be let as a separate suite. The plan is excellent, and has already been mentioned. A servant going to open the entrance door would not pass through

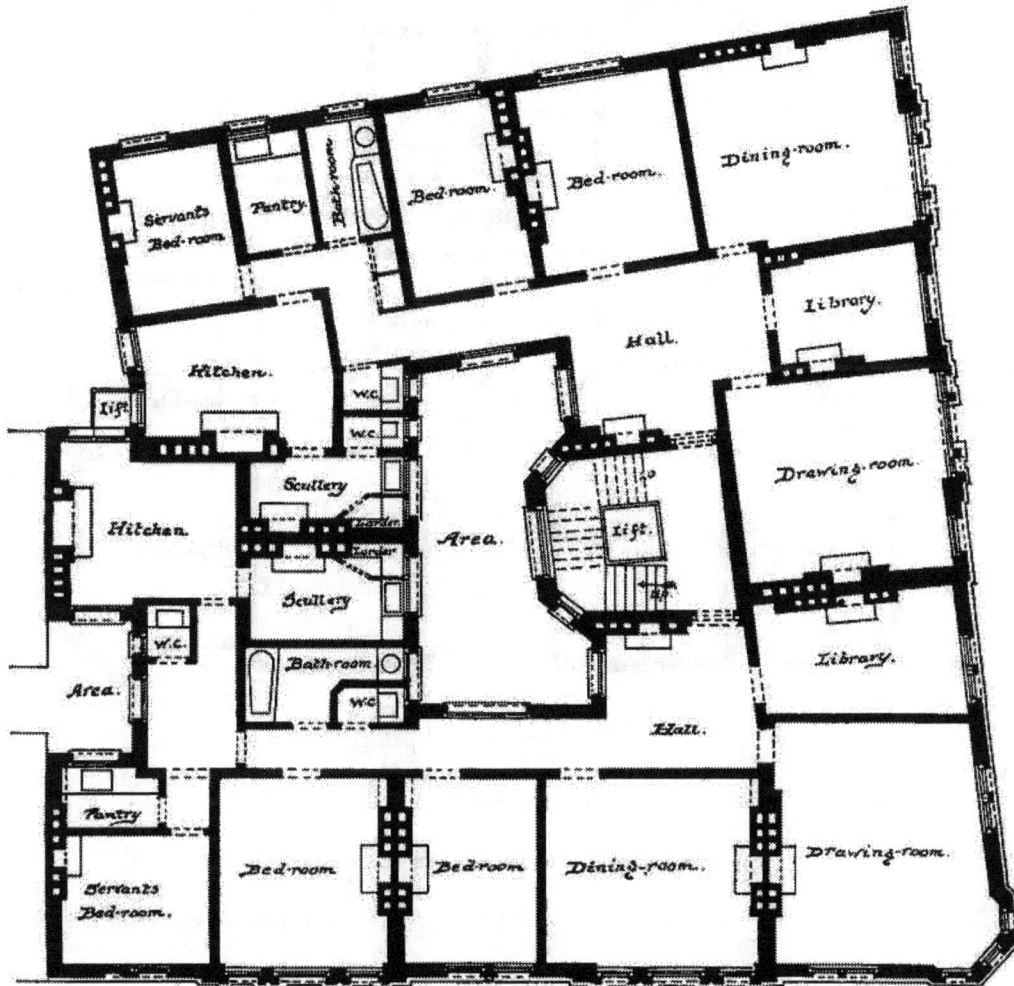

Plan of Fourth Floor.

SCALE OF [10 5 0   10   20   30   40   50 FEET]

FIG. 94.—ST ALBAN'S MANSIONS, KENSINGTON COURT GARDENS.

Paul Hoffmann, Architect.

the entrance hall. Slops from the servants' room would not be taken through the kitchen, and all sound or smell of cooking is cut off by two doors. The arrangement of the W.C.'s is economical, they are adjoining, although the doors are far apart. It is a mistake to have the door of the servants' W.C. next to that of the other closet. The lift is not in the well hole of the staircase.

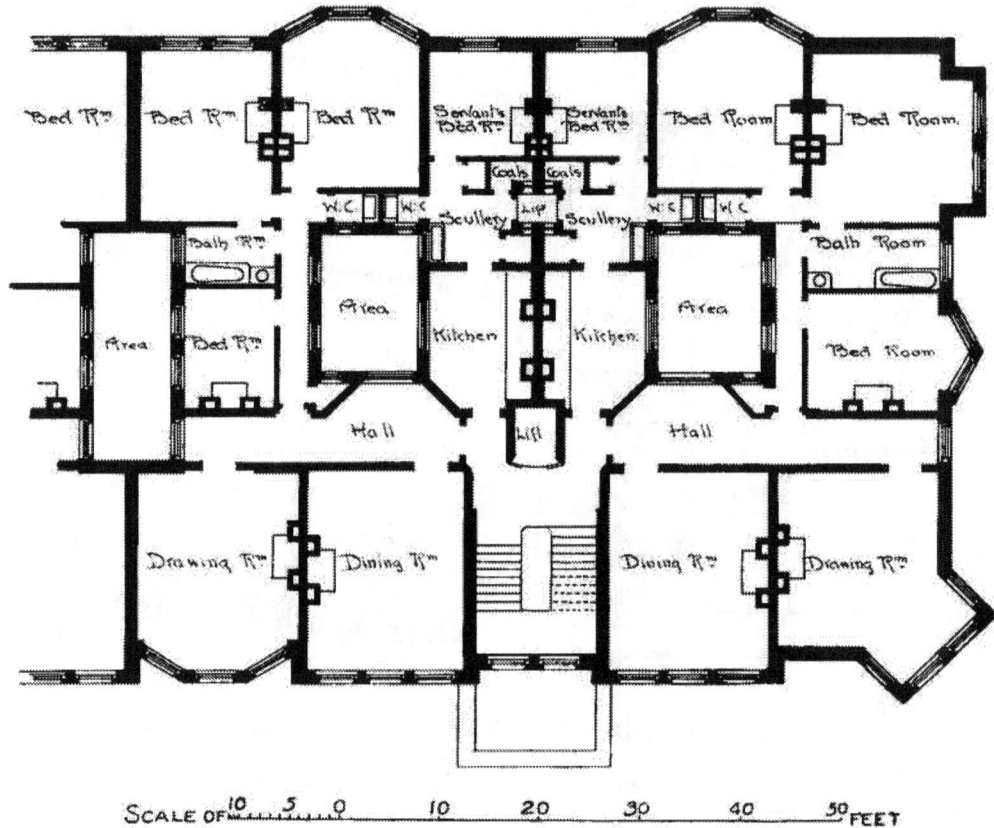

FIG. 95.—KENSINGTON COURT MANSIONS.

Perry & Reed, Architects.

Harley House, Regent's Park (Figs. 96, 97, and 98).—These are plans of one of the most successful of recent buildings. The basement has some self-contained suites, and the maisonette principle is adopted for some others. There are a large number of box-rooms and some spare bedrooms in the basement. These all let easily, and are a great advantage to the owner of a block of flats who may fail to secure a tenant because he wanted one or two more rooms. On the ground floor one suite has a private entrance. The plan of the upper floors is interesting, the kitchen is next to the dining-room, but

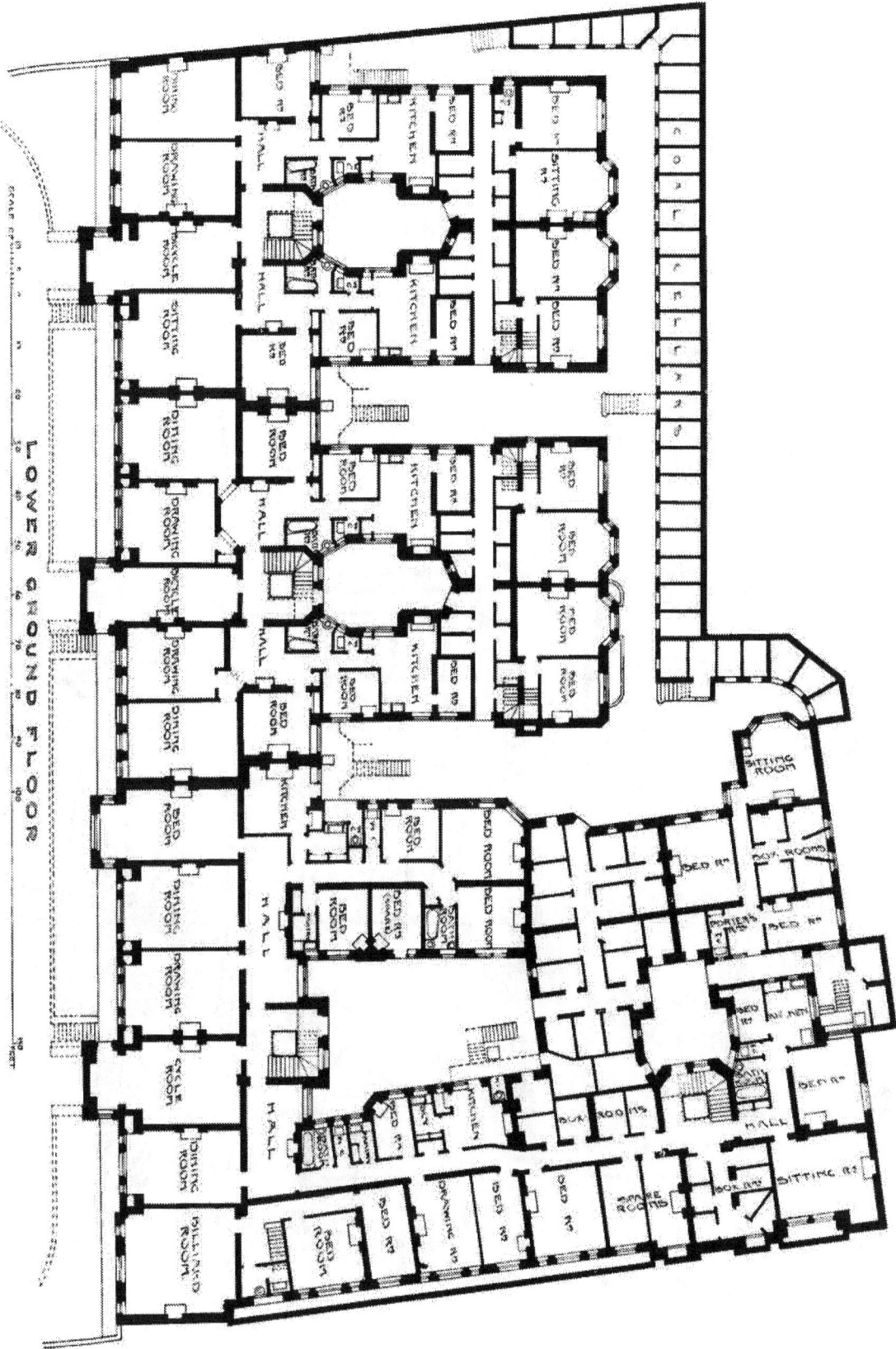

FIG. 96.—HARLEY HOUSE, REGENT'S PARK.

LOWER GROUND FLOOR

Beshane & Gibbs, Architects.

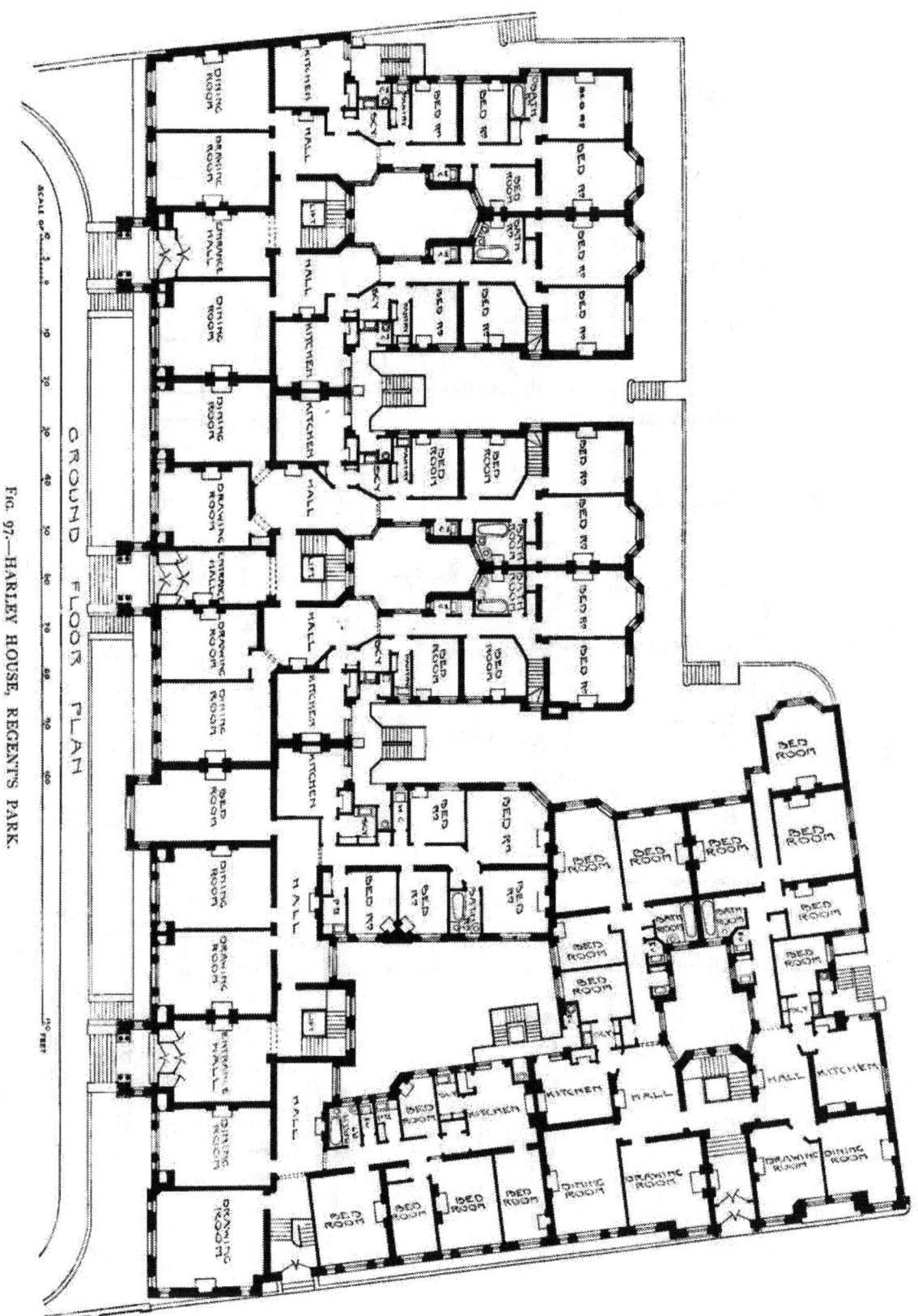

FIG. 97.—HARLEY HOUSE, REGENT'S PARK.

Boehmer & Gibbs, Architects.

GROUND FLOOR PLAN

SCALE OF

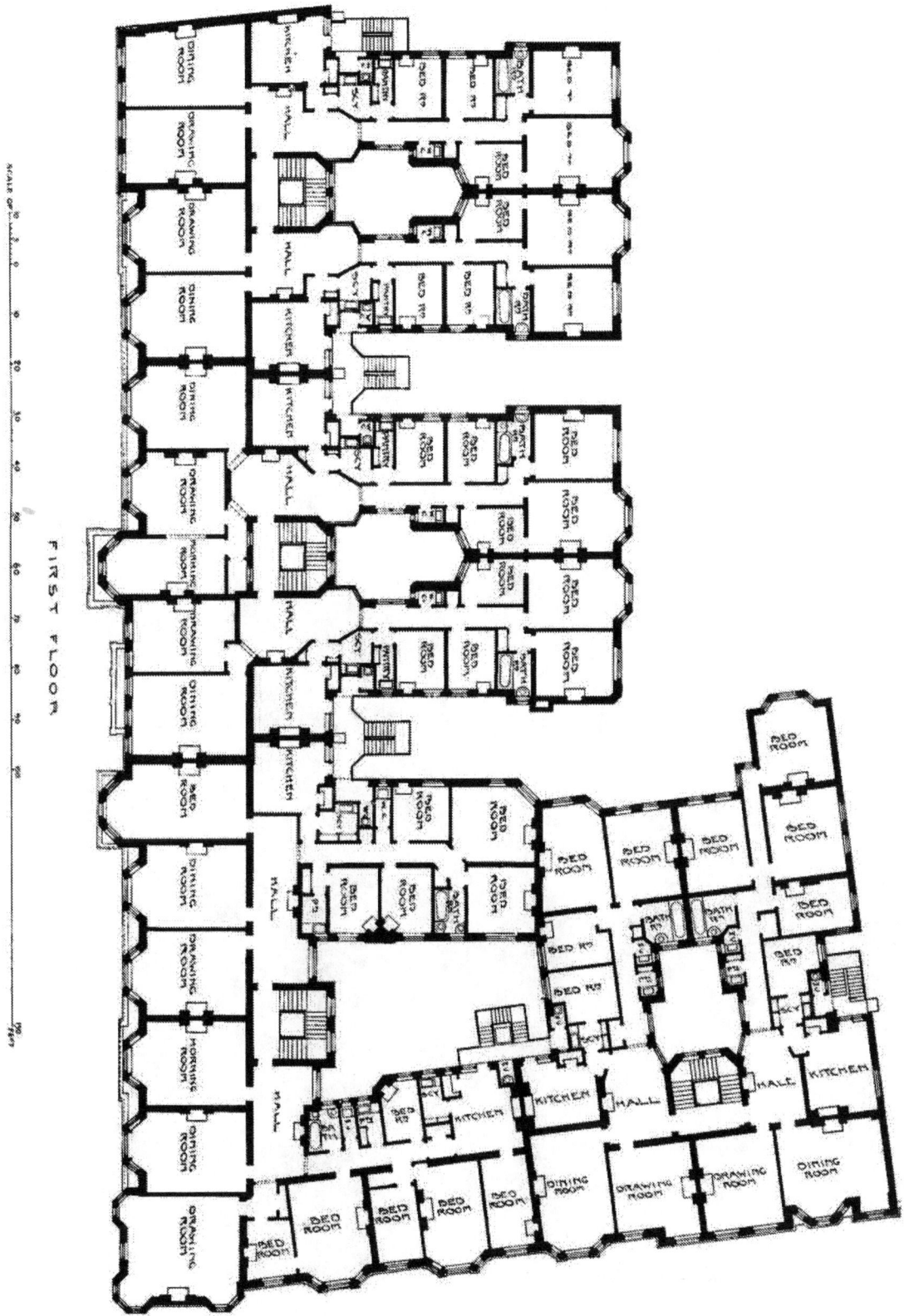

FIRST FLOOR

FIG. 98—HARLEY HOUSE, REGENT'S PARK.

Boehmer & Gibbs, Architects.

divided from it by a 14 in. wall. The scullery and kitchen are each cut off from the hall by two doors, which are quite necessary. What is practically a second passage is formed through the scullery to the servants' room, consequently the hall has a peculiar shape; this arrangement is to be noticed in most of the suites. The servants' W.C. is entered from the balcony, and is in a well-sheltered position, and there is the unavoidable communication between the suites in consequence of the fire-escape staircase. The hall to each flat on the return frontage is large and symmetrical. There are good larders, pantries, sculleries, &c. This building has only two front rooms to most of the suites; this, as stated elsewhere, increases the difficulties of planning, a suite with three front rooms being a much simpler problem.

Alexandra Court, Queen's Gate (Fig. 99).—This is built on the best system for a large block of flats; it has a courtyard as a central feature. There are two suites on each floor of the wings, and one suite in the main back portion. This has the least passage room, as the rooms are grouped round the lift. The hall is large, but dependent upon borrowed light. The other suites have the servants' rooms well planned. The flats facing the courtyard are preferable to the others, as the servants' bedroom is well away from the kitchen, and the W.C. is placed between them. These suites have also much less passage space than the others.

Cliveden Place, Sloane Square (Fig. 100).—This is another example of a plan without an enclosed area. The main entrance is at the side of the building, consequently no frontage valuable for a room is lost on the main street. Part of the building has self-contained suites, and part bachelors' suites. The maisonette principle has been adopted for the best flats on the ground floor. Each has a large basement containing a billiard-room entered without passing through the servants' quarters. There is a second lift and staircase approached by a glazed corridor. There are three suites on each floor except the basement, where there is good accommodation for the caretaker and caterer. The private staircases are exceptionally spacious, and each suite on the maisonette principle has three W.C.'s. One suite has a large servants' hall.

45 Albert Gate (Fig. 101).—No. 45 Albert Gate has a long narrow site, but it is lighted on all sides. The wide end has a frontage

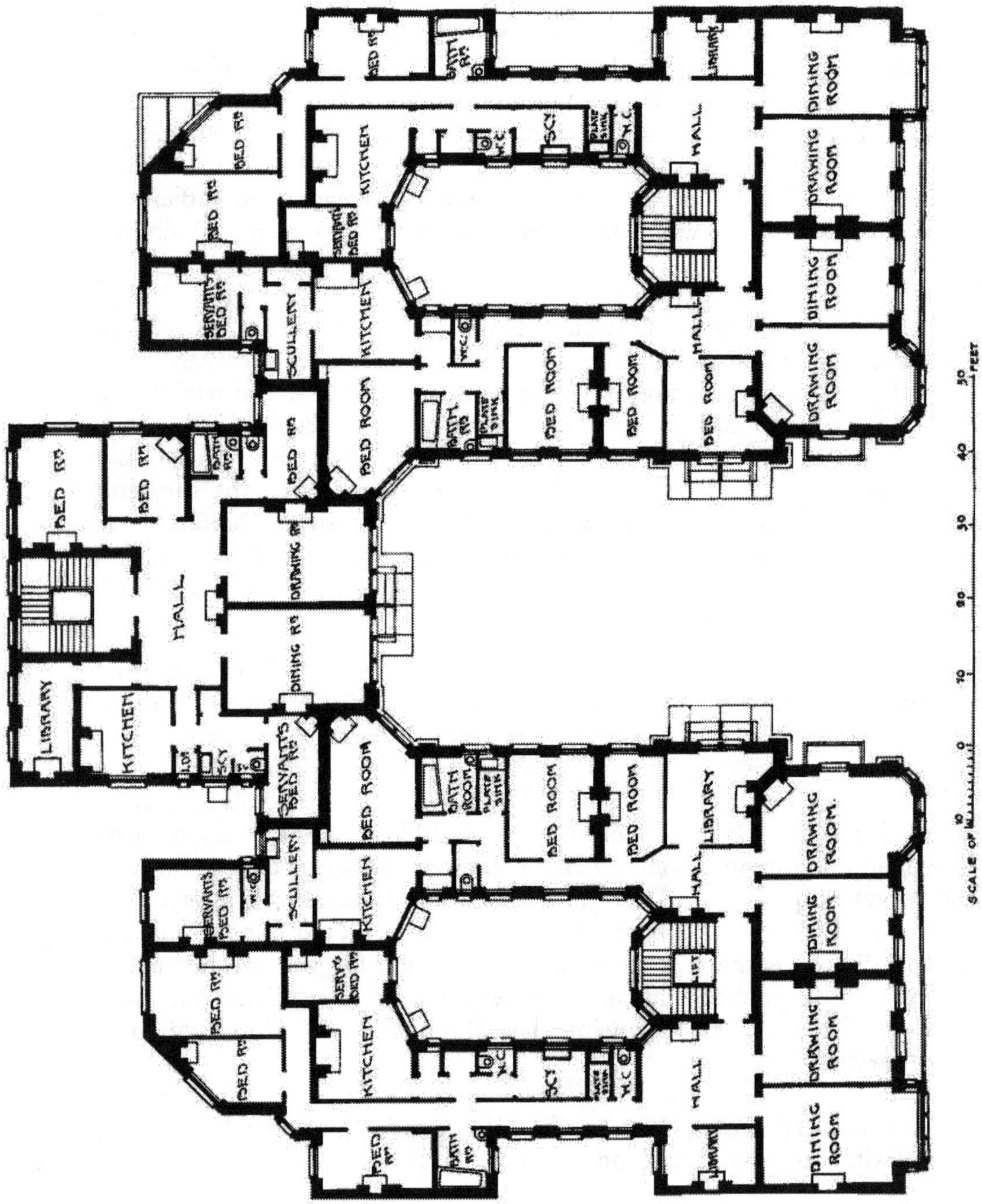

FIG. 99.—ALEXANDRA COURT, QUEEN'S GATE, S.W.

Paul Hoffmann, Architect.

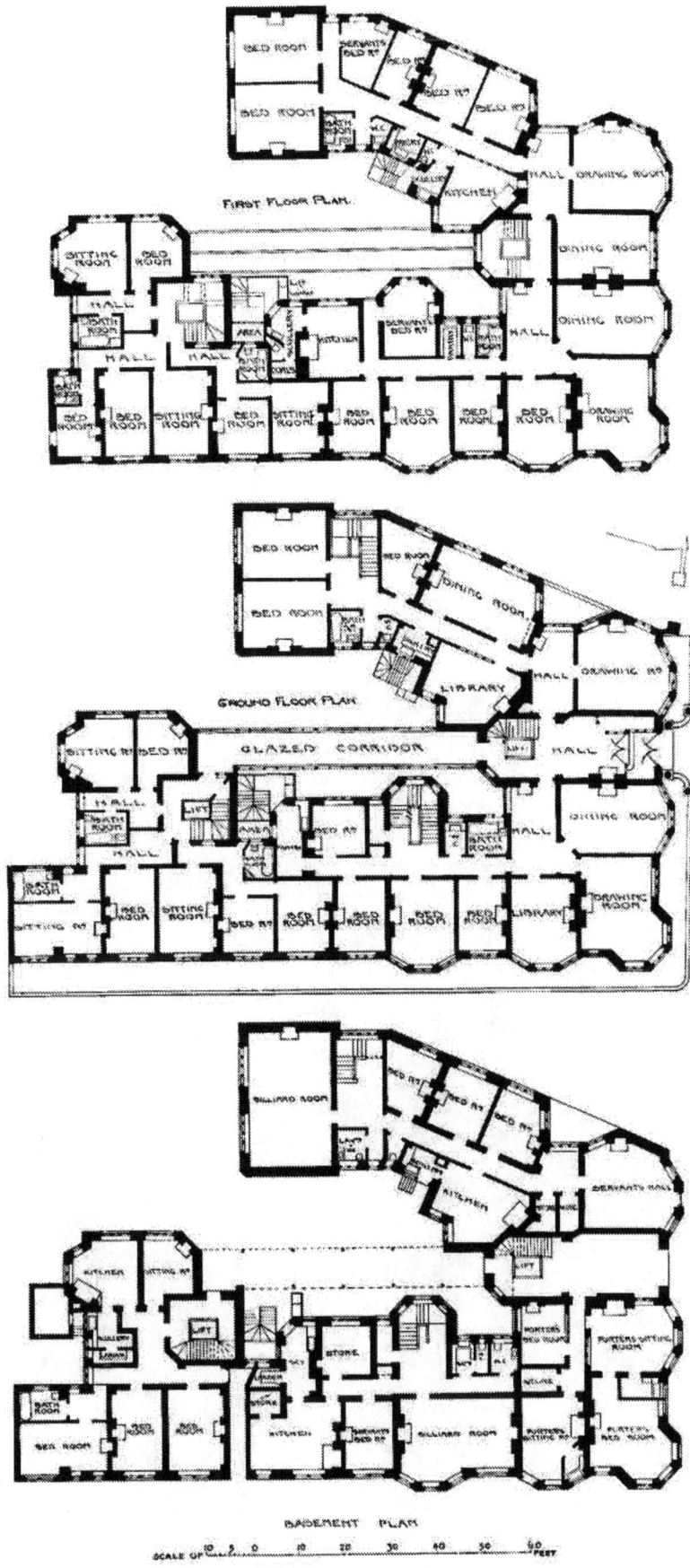

FIRST FLOOR PLAN.

GROUND FLOOR PLAN.

BASEMENT PLAN.

SCALE OF 10 5 0 10 20 30 40 50 60 FEET

FIG. 100.—CLIVEDEN PLACE, SLOANE SQUARE, S.W.

Read & Macdonald, Architects.

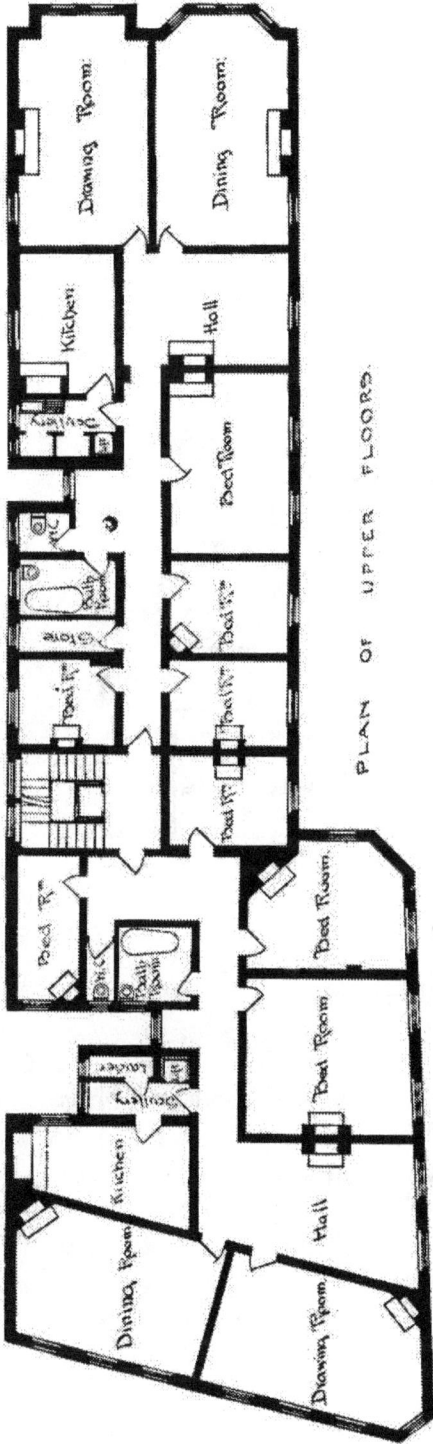

PLAN OF UPPER FLOORS.

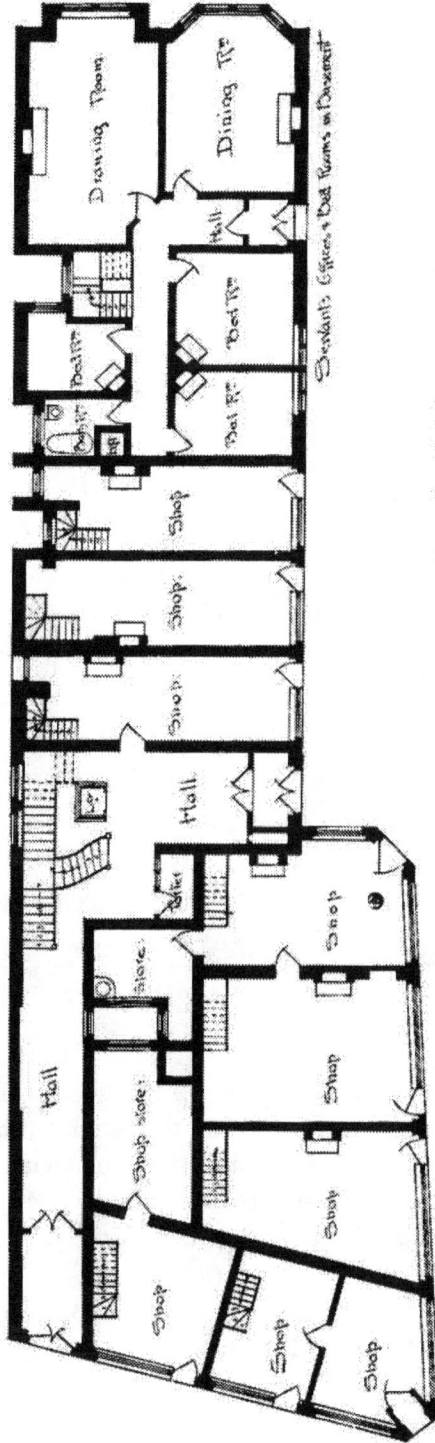

PLAN OF GROUND FLOOR:

SCALE OF FEET.

FIG. 101.—45 ALBERT GATE.

to Knightsbridge, and the narrow end has rooms with a fine view over the Park. There is a narrow foot-passage on one side of the building. The reception rooms have the best positions, and are necessarily far from the entrance to each suite. This building was erected in 1888, and was among the first to have a large hall to each suite; this has

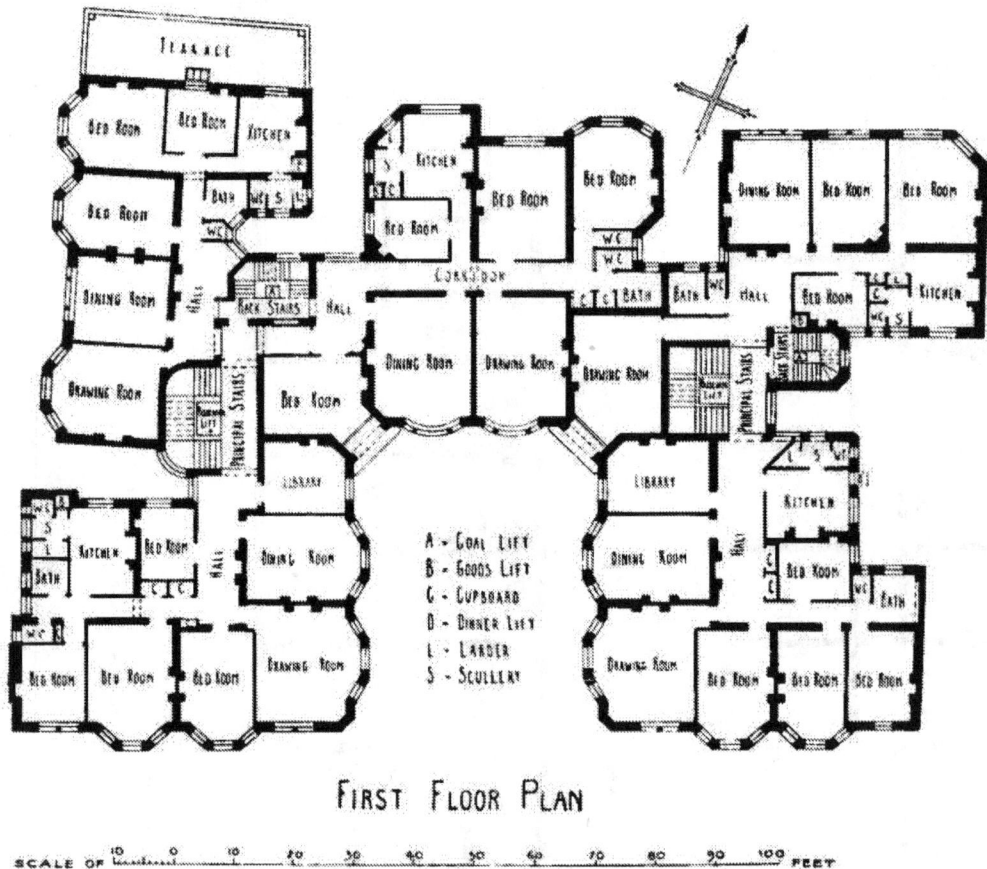

FIRST FLOOR PLAN

SCALE OF ... FEET

FIG. 102.—ASHLEY GARDENS, WESTMINSTER.

E. J. Stubbs, Architect.

been already referred to. The ground floor is partly used for shops, but there is a maisonette at the Park end. This has a private entrance at the side, and no communication with the main entrance staircase, and was the first suite to let. The lift is approached by two entrances; one in the main thoroughfare, and one from the public passage into the Park.

Ashley Gardens (Figs. 102, 103, and 104).—These are plans of a portion of the large estate known as Ashley Gardens. There are two and three suites on each floor served by one lift. One suite on Fig. 106 has an exceptionally large hall. This has proved a great attraction; it is larger than any room in the suite. The bay of the drawing-room in two of the suites should be noticed on Fig. 103.

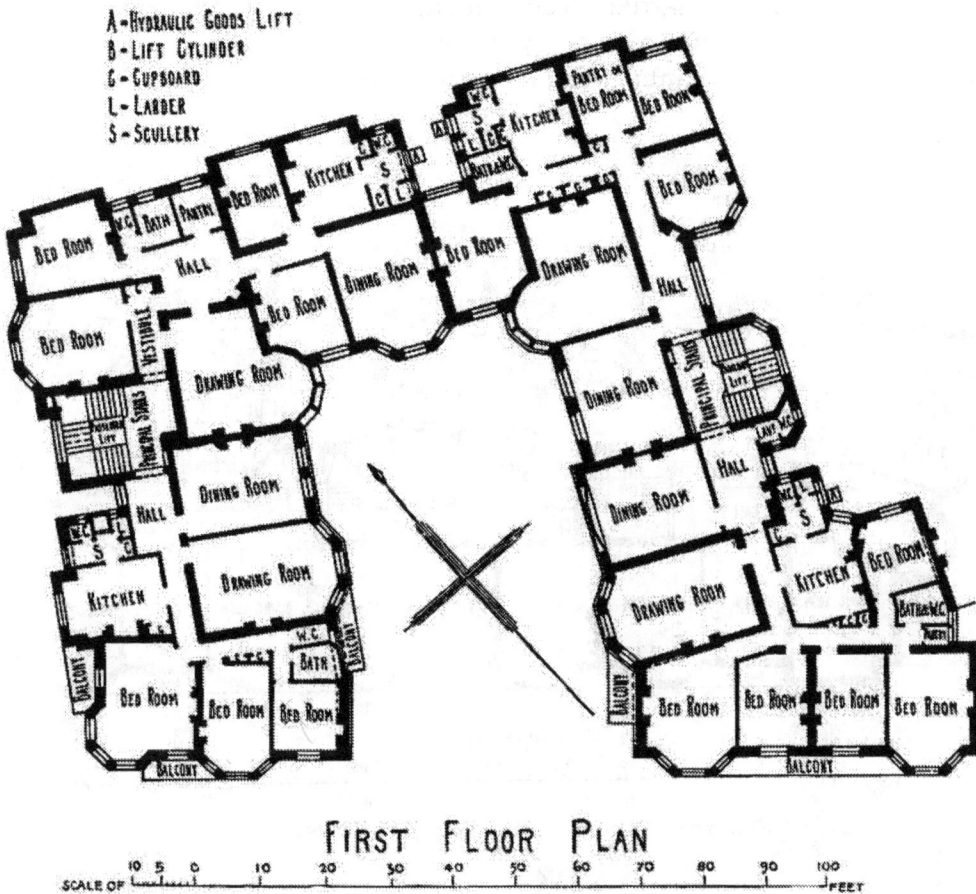

FIRST FLOOR PLAN

FIG. 103.—ASHLEY GARDENS, WESTMINSTER.

E. J. Stubbs, Architect.

Bentinck Street (Fig. 105).—A good example of a recently constructed building. It has one large area. The bedroom with two bays in the right hand suite would be a great attraction to many people. It is exceptionally large for a flat, and could easily be made into two rooms. The left hand suite has the advantage of two bedrooms for

servants. In each case the entrance to the kitchen is through the
scullery—a good arrangement. The entrance to the servants' offices
is kept as far from the main rooms as possible, and a serving hatch is
built into a side corridor. The kitchens are very large, and there is
good wine, coal, and larder accommodation. In Paris there would
probably have been only one servants' W.C. to each floor, entered off
the staircase. A servants' W.C. for two flats might be arranged in
England.

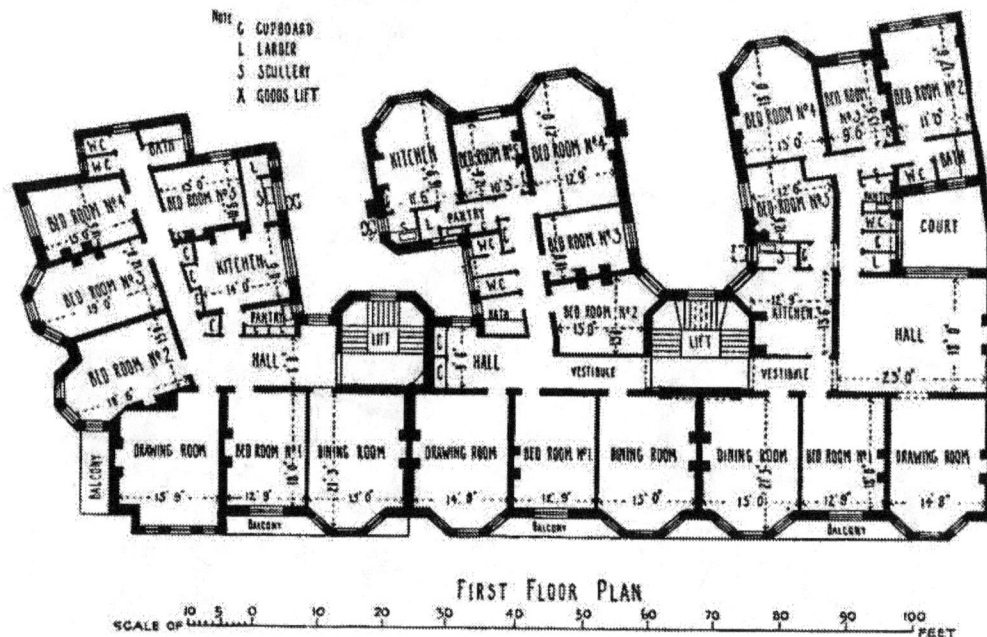

FIG. 104.—ASHLEY GARDENS, WESTMINSTER.

E. J. Stubbs, Architect.

Cleveland Row, St James's Street (Fig. 106).—This building
has just been commenced, and is opposite to St James's Palace—an
exceptional site. There are two large suites to each floor. There
are three sitting-rooms, and a second bath-room is provided for the
servants, a luxury possessed by few other flats.

Albert Hall Mansions (Figs. 107, 108, and 108A).—These buildings have been described in the chapter on planning (page 49). The
staircase occupies a space about 18 ft. by 22 ft. ; this is much more than
would now be reckoned. The stairs are very easy in going, but are not

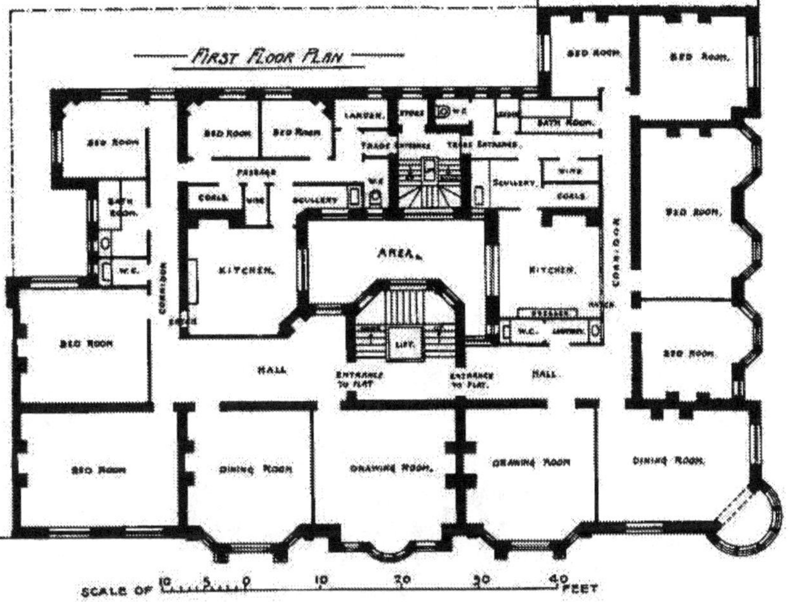

BED ROOM

BED ROOM

BED ROOM BED ROOM

LARDER STORE W.C.

BATH ROOM.

BED ROOM

BATH ROOM

PASSAGE

TRADE ENTRANCE TRADE ENTRANCE

WINE

BED ROOM

COALS WINE SCULLERY

SCULLERY WINE COALS

CORRIDOR

CORRIDOR

BATH ROOM

W.C.

W.C.

KITCHEN

AREA

KITCHEN

W.C.

DRESSER

W.C. LARDER

BED ROOM

BED ROOM

LIFT

BED ROOM

HALL

ENTRANCE TO FLAT

ENTRANCE TO FLAT

HALL

BED ROOM

DINING ROOM

DRAWING ROOM

DRAWING ROOM

DINING ROOM

SCALE OF 10 5 0 10 20 30 40 FEET

FIG. 105.—BENTINCK STREET.

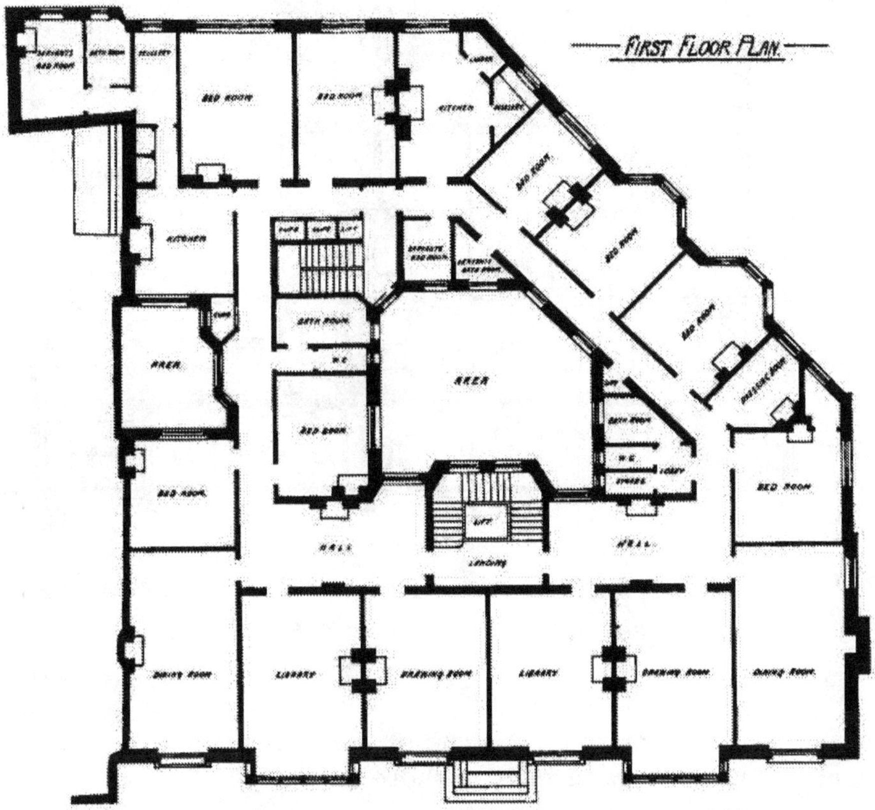

SERVANTS BED ROOM BATH ROOM SCULLERY

BED ROOM

BED ROOM

KITCHEN

NURSERY

LARDER

BED ROOM

KITCHEN

PIPES PIPES LIFT

SERVANTS BED ROOM

SERVANTS BATH ROOM

BED ROOM

CUPBD

BATH ROOM

W.C.

AREA

BED ROOM

AREA

BATH ROOM

DRESSING ROOM

BED ROOM

BED ROOM

W.C. STORES LOBBY

BED ROOM

HALL

LIFT

HALL

LANDING

DINING ROOM

LIBRARY

DRAWING ROOM

LIBRARY

DRAWING ROOM

DINING ROOM

FIG. 106.—CLEVELAND ROW, ST JAMES'S STREET, S.W.

Wm. Woodward, Architect.

often used, as the lift is always handy.   The principal rooms are much larger than those in most modern flats, and being exceptionally high are unequalled in London.   These flats were built about thirty years

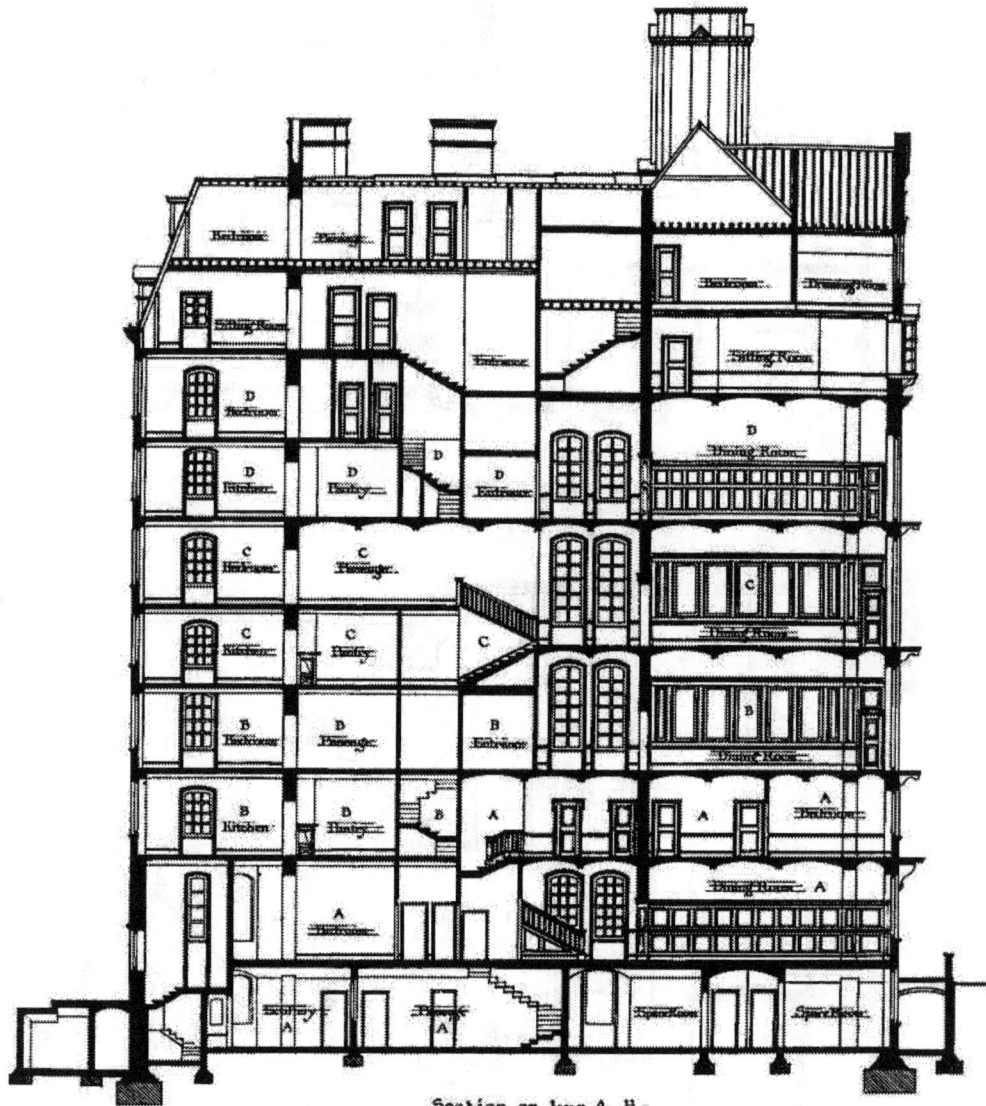

Section on line A.B:

SCALE OF 10   6   0   10   20   30   40   50 FEET

FIG. 107.—ALBERT HALL MANSIONS (SECTION).

R. Norman Shaw, R.A., Architect.

ago, and are still considered some of the best that have been erected. The letters in the section refer to those on the plans, all rooms with the

Mezzanine Floor Plan.

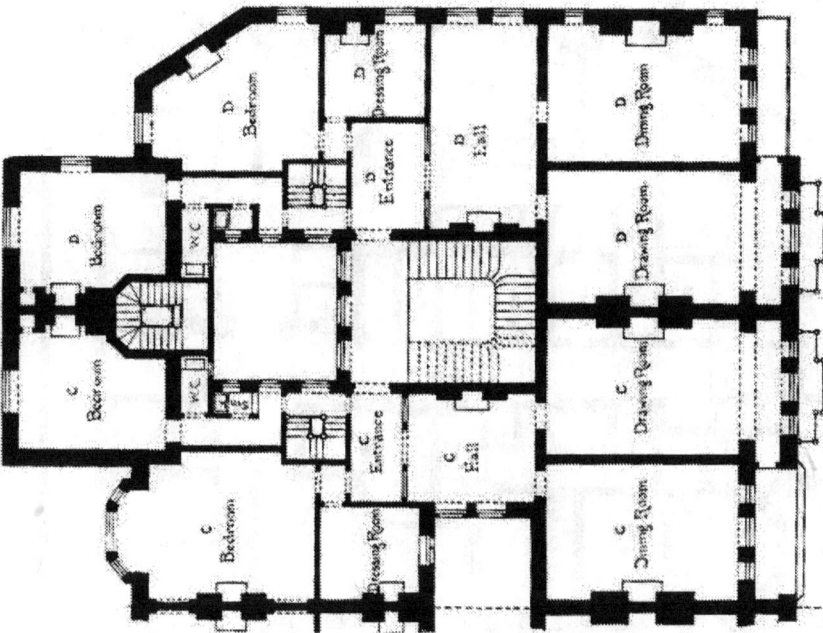

First Floor Plan

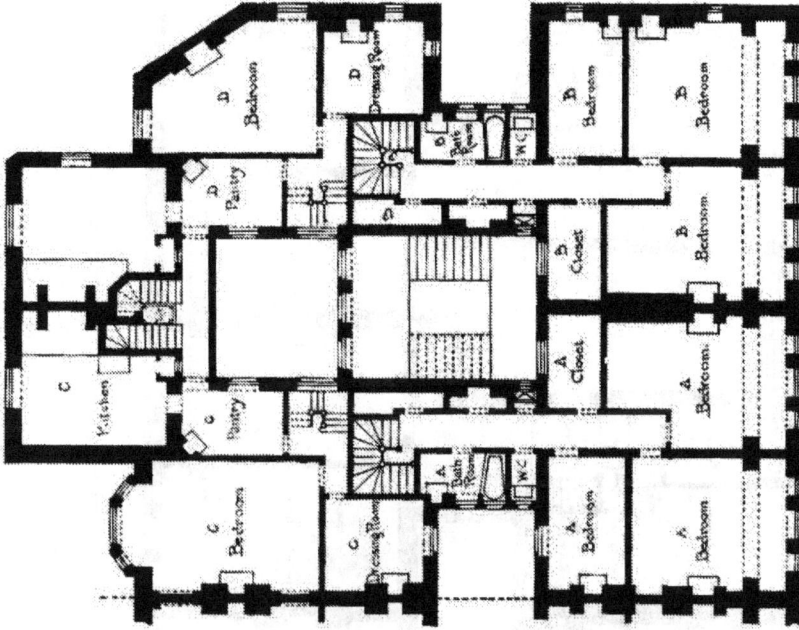

Basement Plan.

B Cellar

D
Cellar

C
Cellar

A
Cellar

D
Cellar

Cellar

Cellar

Cellar

Open Court

B
Kitchen

Bedroom

Area

Spare Rooms

Area

Passage

Porters Living Room

Scullery

b

Passage

B
Scullery

Cellar

Passage

D
Cellar

Cellar

D
Cellar

Cellar

Spare Rooms

D

Spare Rooms

Spare Rooms

Area

Larder

A
Larder

A
Scullery

A
Cellar

Cellar

Cellar

C

Cellar

Corridor

Lobby

Spare Rooms

Spare Room

Bedroom

Kitchen

A
Bedroom

C
Spare Room

Spare Room

Spare Room

Spare Room

Basement Plan. SCALE OF 10 0   FEET

Ground Plan.

D
Bedroom

D
Bed or Dressing Room

A
Bath Room

Vestibule

Porch

Entrance Lobby

B
Bedroom

Entrance

Entrance Hall

Lobby

Bedroom

A

Entrance Hall

Principal Staircase

Wine Cellar

Back Stair

B
Hall

A
Bedroom

A
Bedroom

A
Bed or Dressing Room

A
Entrance

A
Hall

A
Drawing Room

A
Drawing Room

B
Drawing Room

B
Drawing Room

B
Dining Room

Ground Plan

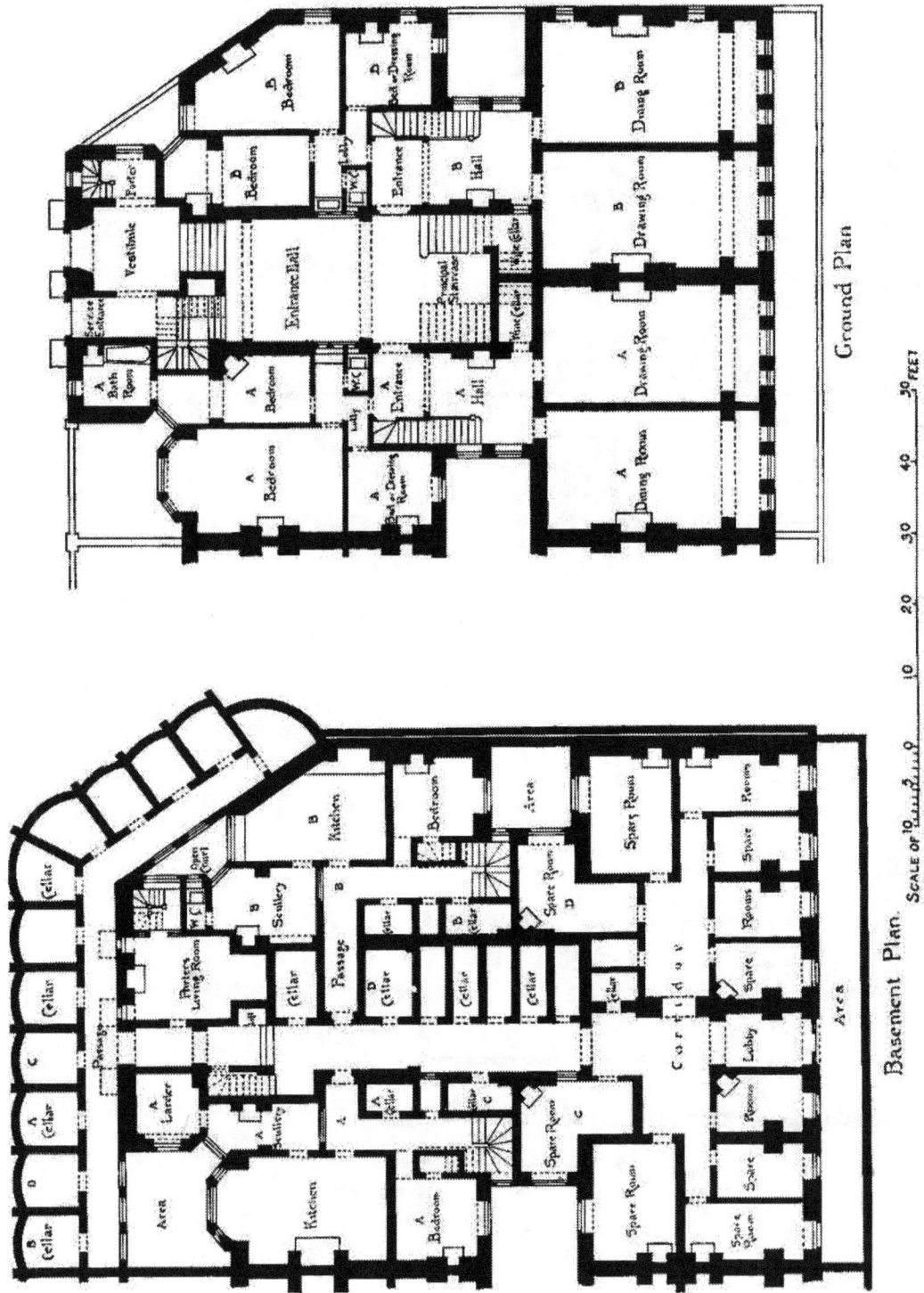

FIG. 108.—ALBERT HALL MANSIONS.   R. Norman Shaw, R.A., Architect.

FIG. 108A.—ALBERT HALL MANSIONS, S.W.

R. Norman Shaw, R.A., Architect.

FIG. 108B.—ST JAMES' STREET, W.

R. Norman Shaw. R.A., Architect.

same letter belong to the same suite. Fig. 108A is a view of this building, and 108B shows a fine block of flats over offices at the bottom of St James's Street, S.W.

Albert Hall Mansions (Fig. 109).—These flats are near those last described. Three suites are served by one lift. They are partially shown on the left side of the view in Fig. 111A.

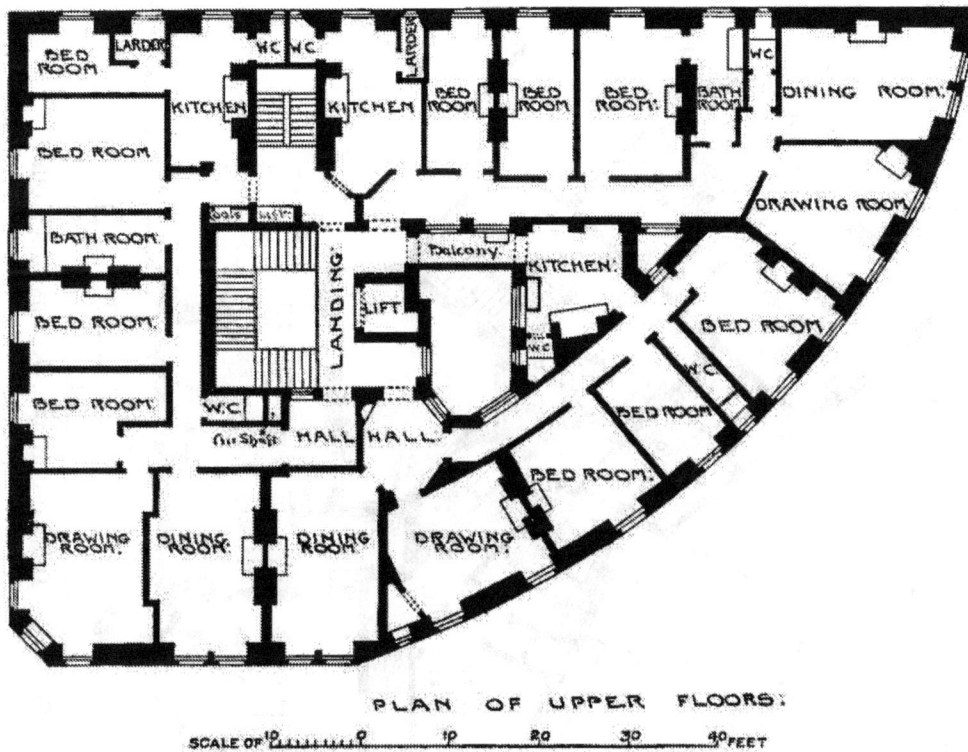

PLAN OF UPPER FLOORS.

SCALE OF 10 0   10   20   30   40 FEET

FIG. 109.—ALBERT HALL MANSIONS.

R. Norman Shaw, R.A., Architect.

Durward House, Kensington Court (Fig. 110).—The site of this building has a peculiar shape. One large area is formed, but no living-rooms are lighted by it. Each hall is large, and a door shuts off each passage, consequently it becomes a third sitting-room. With the exception of a short length the building has light on each of the three sides.

Albert Court (Fig. 111).—This is another example of the arrangement of certain rooms of less height than the main rooms, with a small internal staircase connecting them. The kitchen offices and

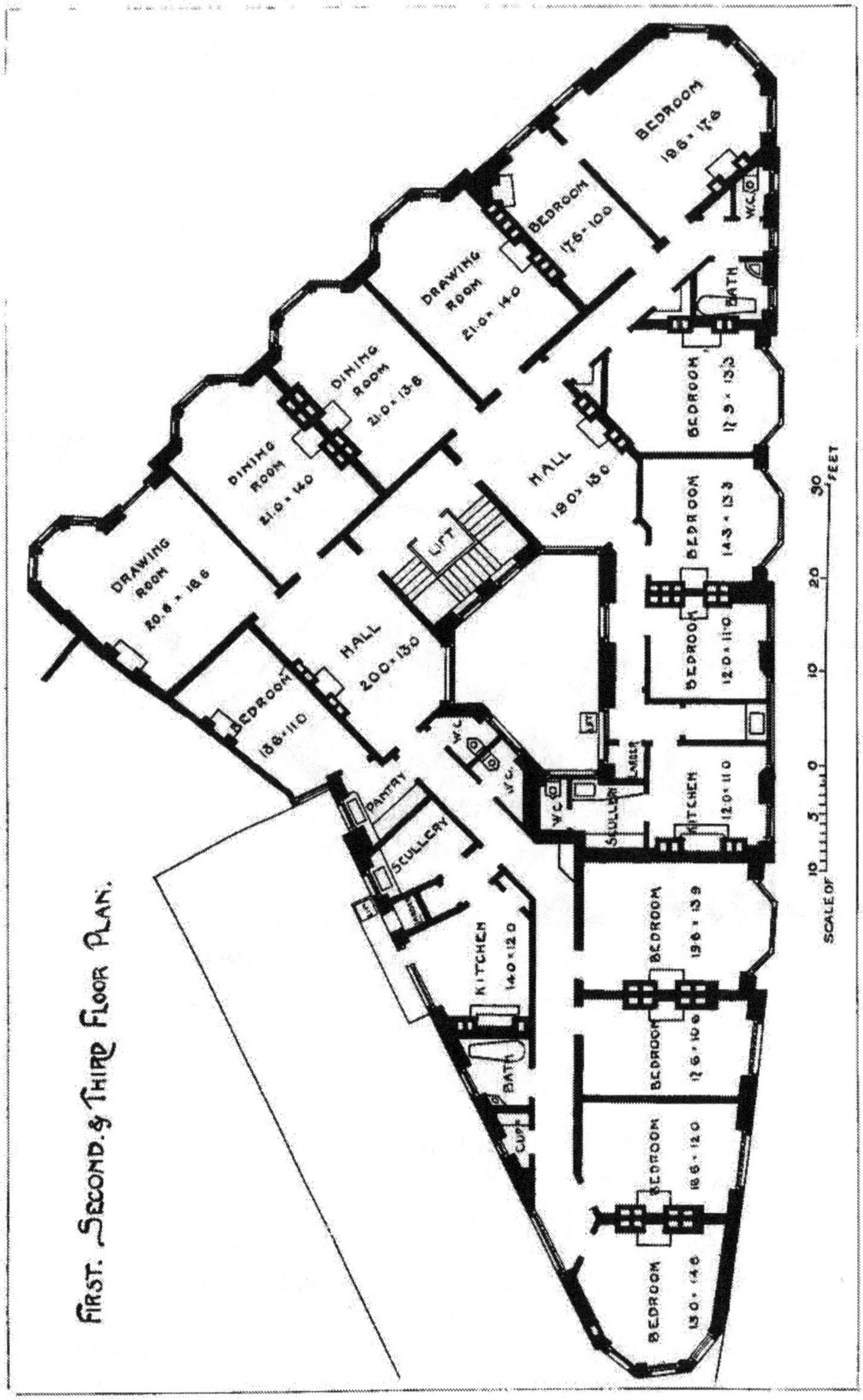

FIRST. SECOND & THIRD FLOOR PLAN.

DRAWING ROOM
20.6 × 18.6

DINING ROOM
21.0 × 14.0

DINING ROOM
21.0 × 13.6

DRAWING ROOM
21.0 × 14.0

BEDROOM
18.6 × 17.6

BEDROOM
17.6 × 10.0

BEDROOM
18.6 × 11.0

HALL
20.0 × 13.0

HALL
19.0 × 13.0

LIFT

W.C.

W.C.

V.C.

V.C.

PANTRY

SCULLERY

SCULLERY

KITCHEN
14.0 × 12.0

BATH

CUP.

BATH

BATH

BEDROOM
13.0 × 14.0

BEDROOM
18.6 × 12.0

BEDROOM
17.6 × 14.0

BEDROOM
13.0 × 13.9

BEDROOM
12.0 × 11.0

KITCHEN
12.0 × 11.0

BEDROOM
12.0 × 11.0

BEDROOM
14.3 × 13.3

BEDROOM
12.3 × 13.3

SCALE OF
FEET

FIG. 110.—DURWARD HOUSE, KENSINGTON COURT.

Durward Brown, Architect.

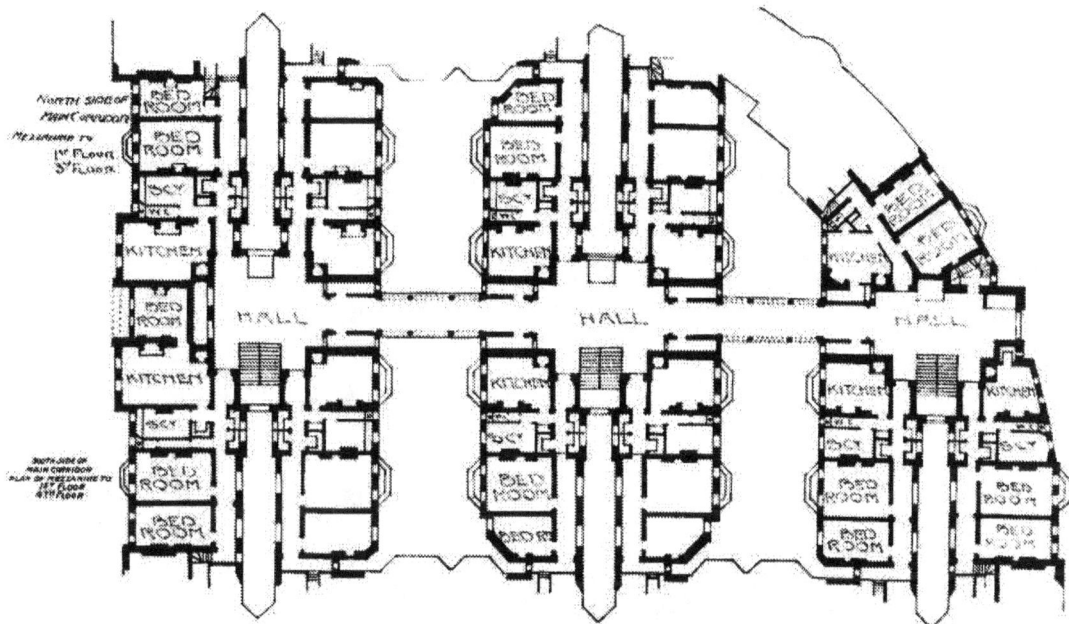

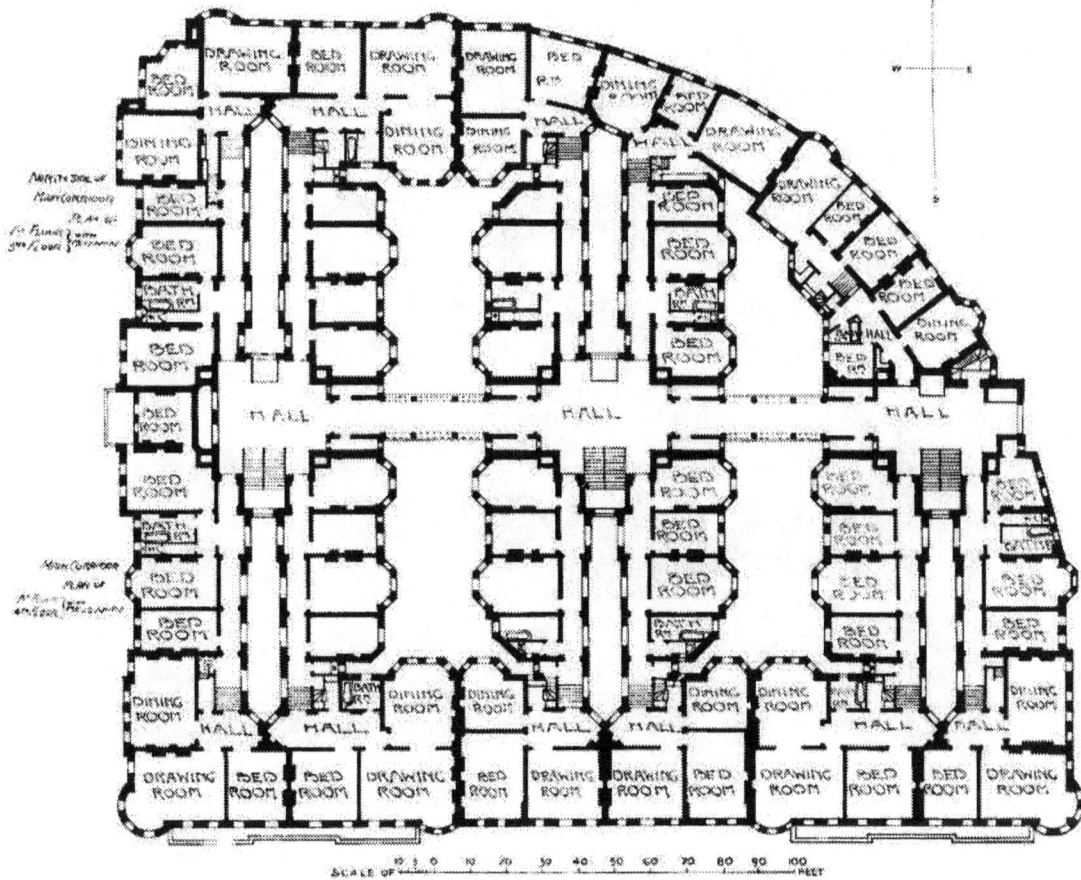

FIG. 111.—ALBERT COURT, KENSINGTON, S.W.

R. J. Worley, Architect.

Fig. 111A.—Albert Court, Kensington, S.W.

R. J. Worley, Architect.

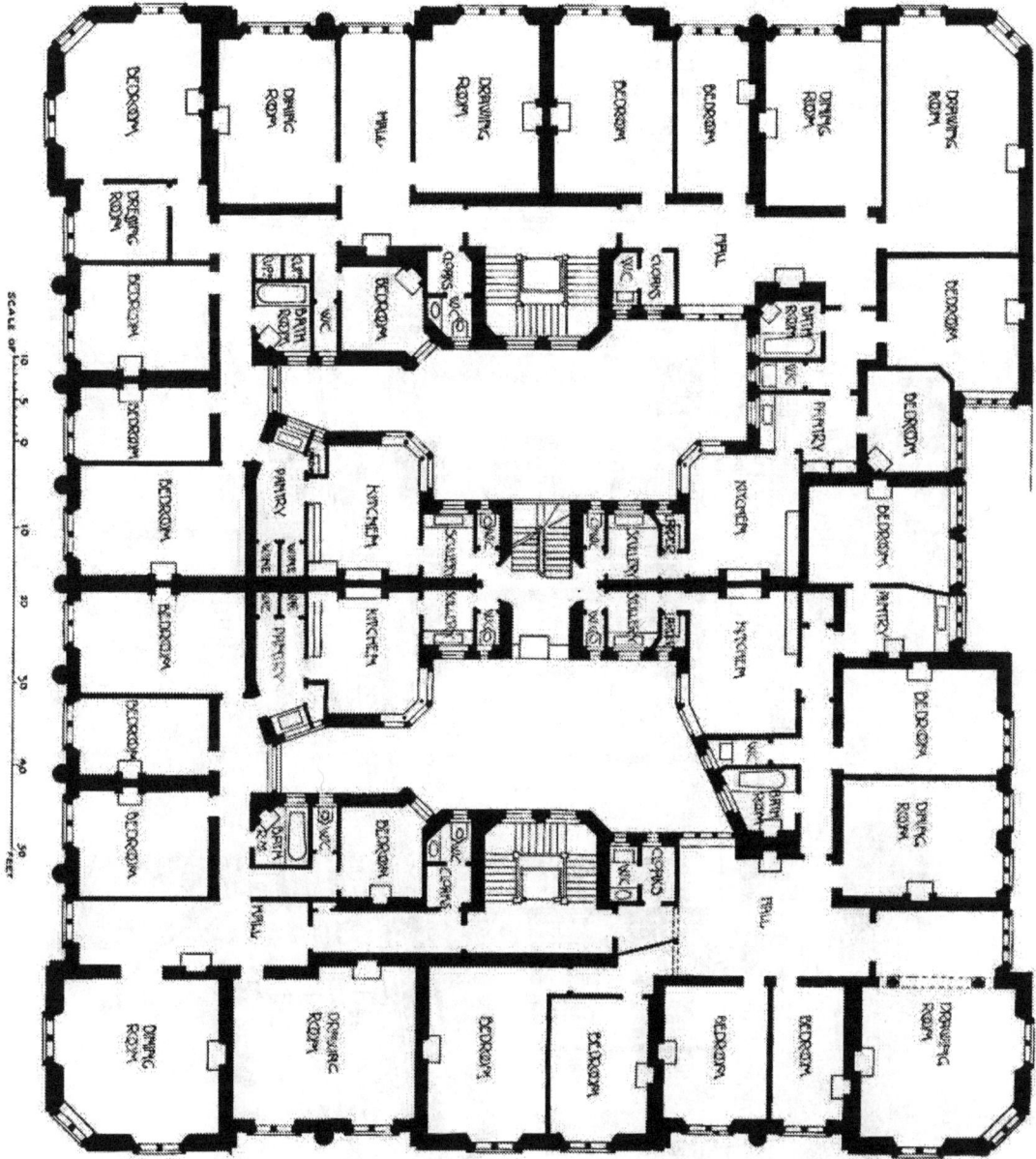

Fig. 112.—SLOAN SQUARE.

Amos F. Faulkner, Architect.

FIG. 112.—RESIDENTIAL FLATS, SLOANE SQUARE, S.W.

E. W. Mountford, Architect.

FIG. 113A.—NO. 22 NORTH AUDLEY STREET, W. (CORNER OF OXFORD STREET).

Read & Macdonald, Architects.

two servants' rooms are on a different level to the remainder of the flat. The maisonette principle is applied to the whole building. A view of the exterior is shown in Fig. 111A.

Sloane Square (Fig. 112). — There are four suites to each floor, two main staircases, and only one trade staircase and stair lift for the four flats; a carefully arranged plan, that somewhat suggests American influence. A cloak-room and lavatory are placed immediately inside the entrance to each suite, following the usual plan of a country house. In flats the lavatory is rarely in this, the best position, perhaps, because a second W.C. becomes necessary in addition to the servants' W.C. Each of these suites has three W.C.'s. A view of the exterior is shown in Fig. 112A. This was made for the original plan, which has since been altered, and the second plan is given; consequently elevation and plan do not quite agree.

No. 22 North Audley Street (Fig. 113).— This is the first floor plan over some shops; part of the floor area is occupied

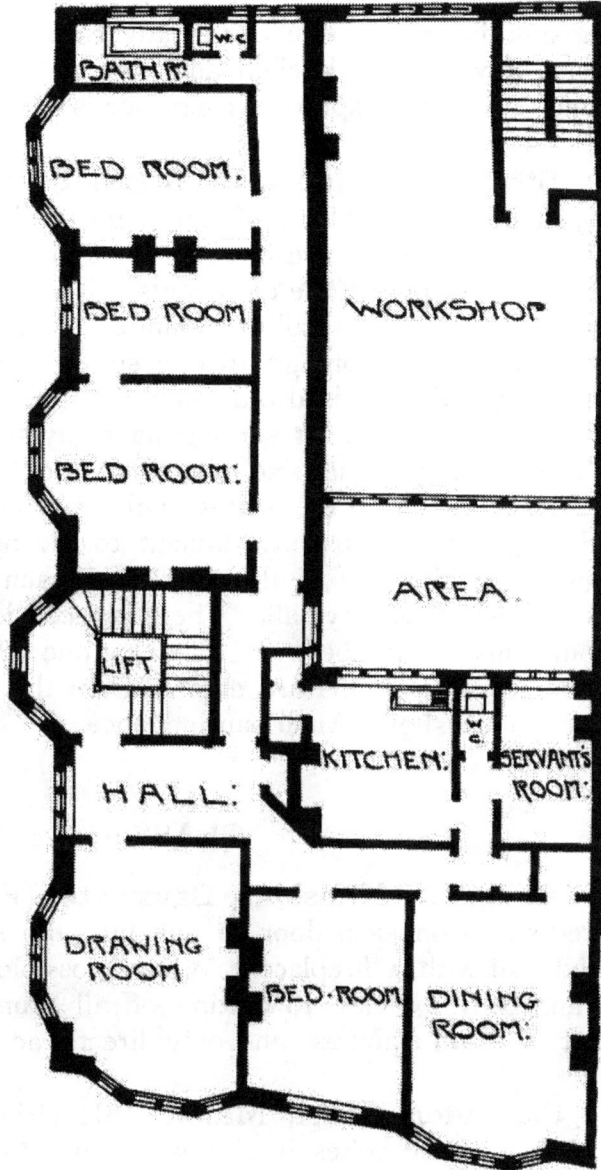

FIRST FLOOR PLAN.

SCALE OF 10 5 0 10 20 FEET

FIG. 113.—No. 22 NORTH AUDLEY STREET.

Read & Macdonald, Architects.

by a workshop entered only from the ground floor by a staircase, and quite cut off from the flat. The servants' W.C. is well placed between the kitchen and the servants' bedroom; there is no scullery, the sink is in the kitchen as advocated elsewhere; there are two doors between the kitchen and the hall to stop the penetration of sound. A photograph of the exterior is given in Fig. 113A.

Strathcona Mansions, Marylebone Road (Figs. 114 and 115).—This large block of buildings is planned upon the courtyard principle. There is a restaurant, a smoking and a billiard room on the ground floor for the use of tenants. This is one of very few buildings with a large entrance hall and lounge. The suites on the ground floor are small. The frontage to one street is used for shops and trade entrances, and there is also a small entrance to the main building. The upper floors have a lift serving as many as six suites on each floor. These suites vary in size, some have only three bedrooms. It is an advantage to have suites with varying accommodation in one building, but it is usually difficult to arrange. The halls are large considering the size of the flats, and each has a fireplace. Small suites rarely have any hall. There is a considerable amount of passage room; this cannot be avoided when one lift serves so many suites. Some servants' rooms are entered from the kitchen. The plan of the ground floor shows American influence.

CLASS No. 2.

Chepstow Mansions, Bayswater (Fig. 116).—Here there are three suites on each floor to one lift; the suites are small, one has a good hall with a fireplace. Where possible the kitchens have been arranged with a view to cutting off all sound: the trade staircase is next the main staircase, and only directly accessible to one suite.

Clarendon Court, Maida Vale (Figs. 117, 118, and 119).—There are some suites in the basement. On the ground floor part of the frontage has been used for a public restaurant, with kitchens, &c., below. There is a private entrance from the flats so that the tenants may have the advantage of self-contained suites combined with some of the advantages of flats where the catering is done by the manager. The lift serves five suites on each floor; the two front reception rooms of each suite have suffered for the benefit of the hall; here the

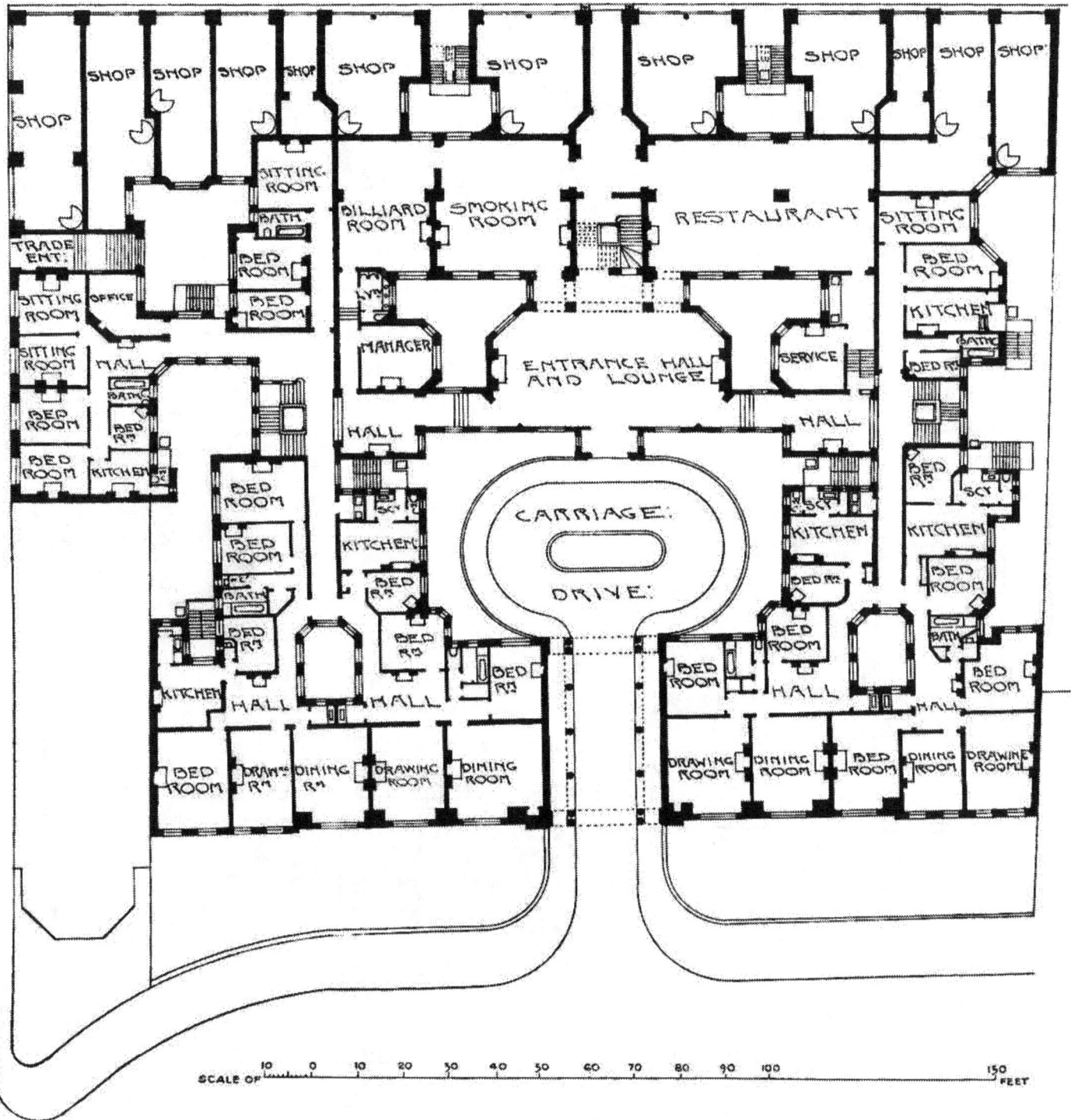

FIG. 114.—STRATHCONA MANSIONS, MARYLEBONE ROAD.

E. Runtz, } Joint
Boehmer & Gibbs, } Architects.

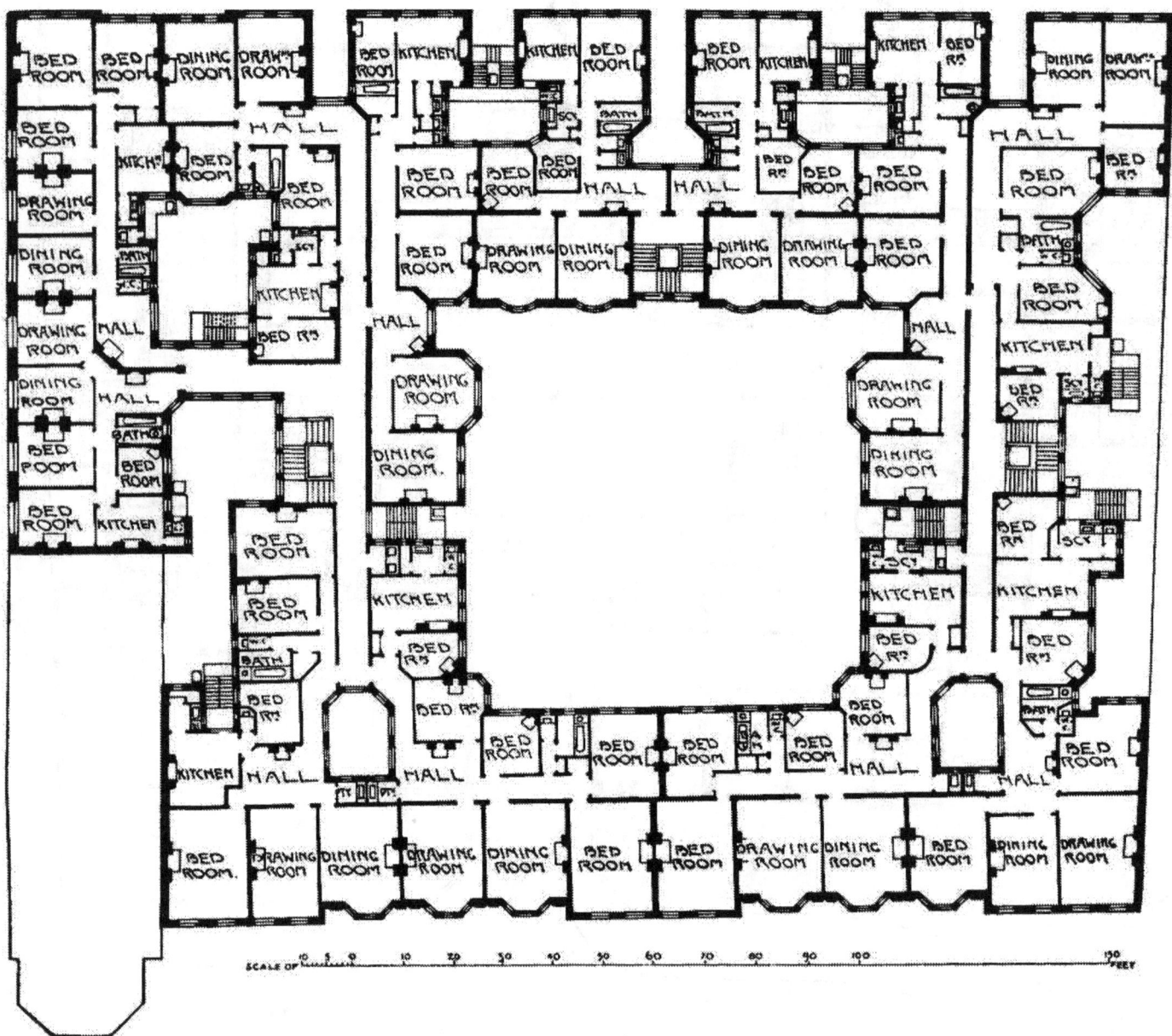

FIG. 115.—STRATHCONA MANSIONS, MARYLEBONE ROAD.

E. Runtz, } Joint
Boehmer & Gibbs, } Architects.

SCALE OF 10 5 0 10 20 30 40 50 FEET

FIRST FLOOR PLAN

FIG. 116.—CHEPSTOW MANSIONS, BAYSWATER, W.

Edwin J. Stubbs, Architect.

extra width was given to allow room for a table to be placed in the hall, which is often used as a dining-room. There is a pantry in addition to a scullery ; the kitchen is also larger than usual for flats of this class.

Blomfield Court, Maida Vale (Fig. 120).—Five suites on each floor are served by one lift. These flats are small and compact, but the passage room is necessarily considerable.

Oxford Street and South Molton Street, W. (Fig. 121). — This building has the awkward street corner site so difficult to deal with. There are two suites on each floor. In the upper suite the dining-room has been placed next the kitchen, a much better position than next to the drawing-room.

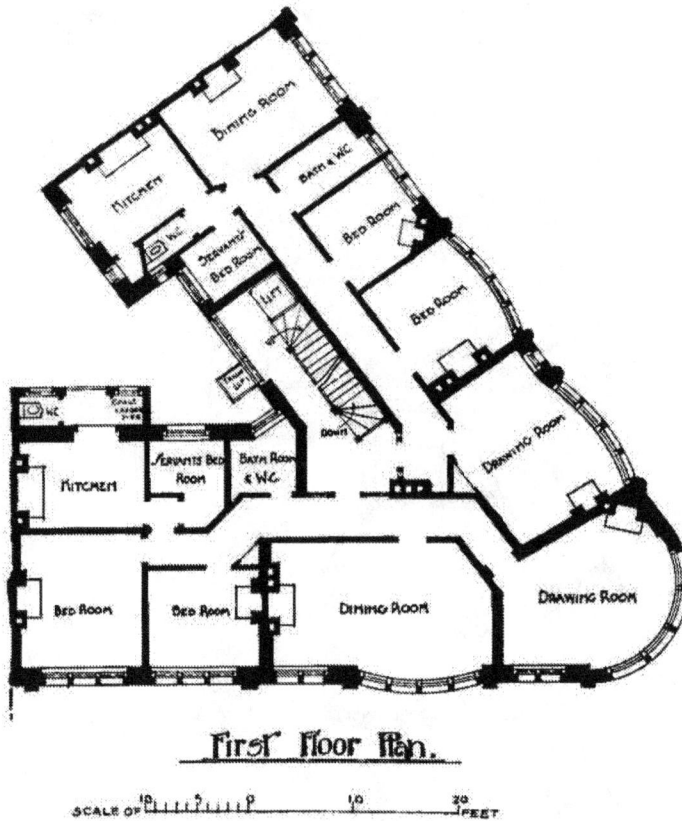

First Floor Plan.

SCALE OF FEET

FIG. 121.—OXFORD STREET AND SOUTH MOLTON STREET, W.

E. Keynes Purchase, Architect.

King's Gardens Estate, West End Lane, N.W. (Fig. 122).— This is a large block built on a radiating plan around a court where some fine old trees have been preserved. The central blocks have two suites to each lift, and the wing blocks have three suites to a lift. The principle of the plan is the cause of some rooms having an awkward shape. The central blocks have the servants' bedroom opening off the kitchen.

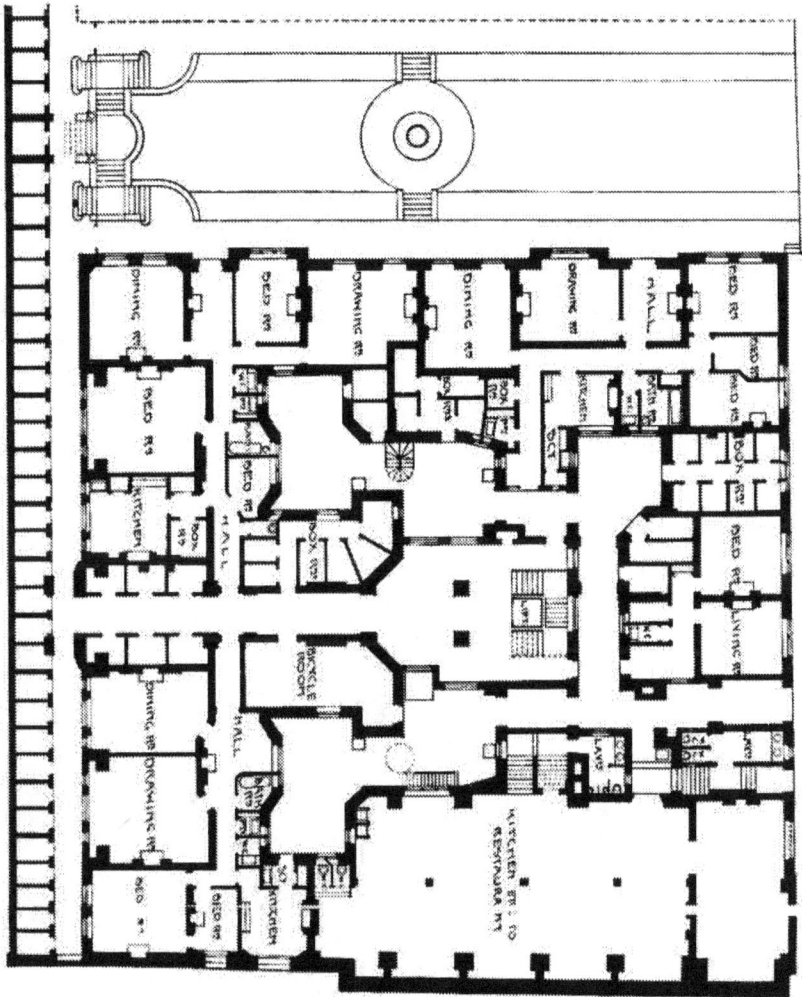

BASEMENT PLAN

GROUND FLOOR PLAN

SCALE OF

FIGS. 117, 118.—CLARENDON COURT, MAIDA VALE.

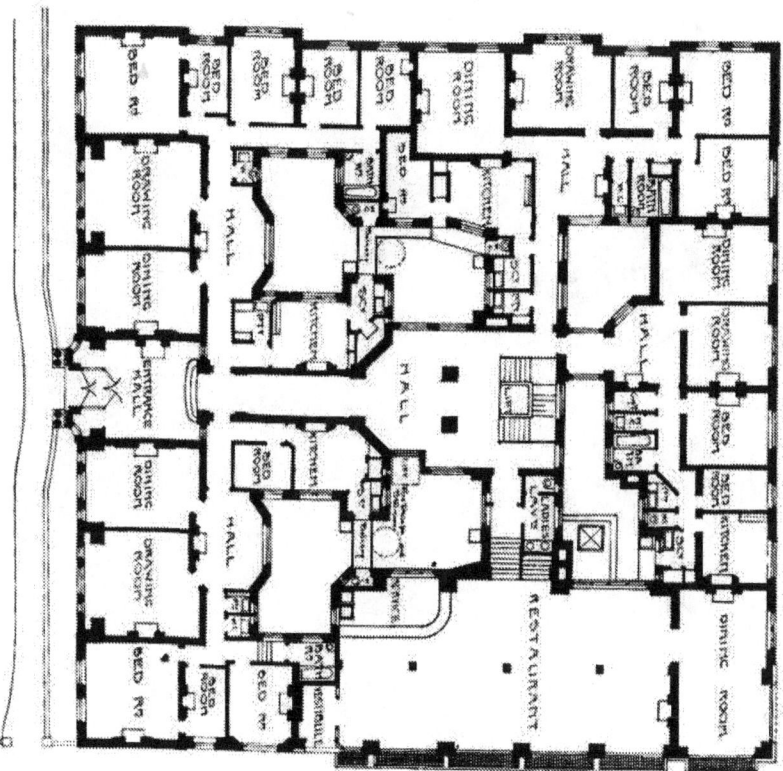

Belcher & Gibbs, Architects.

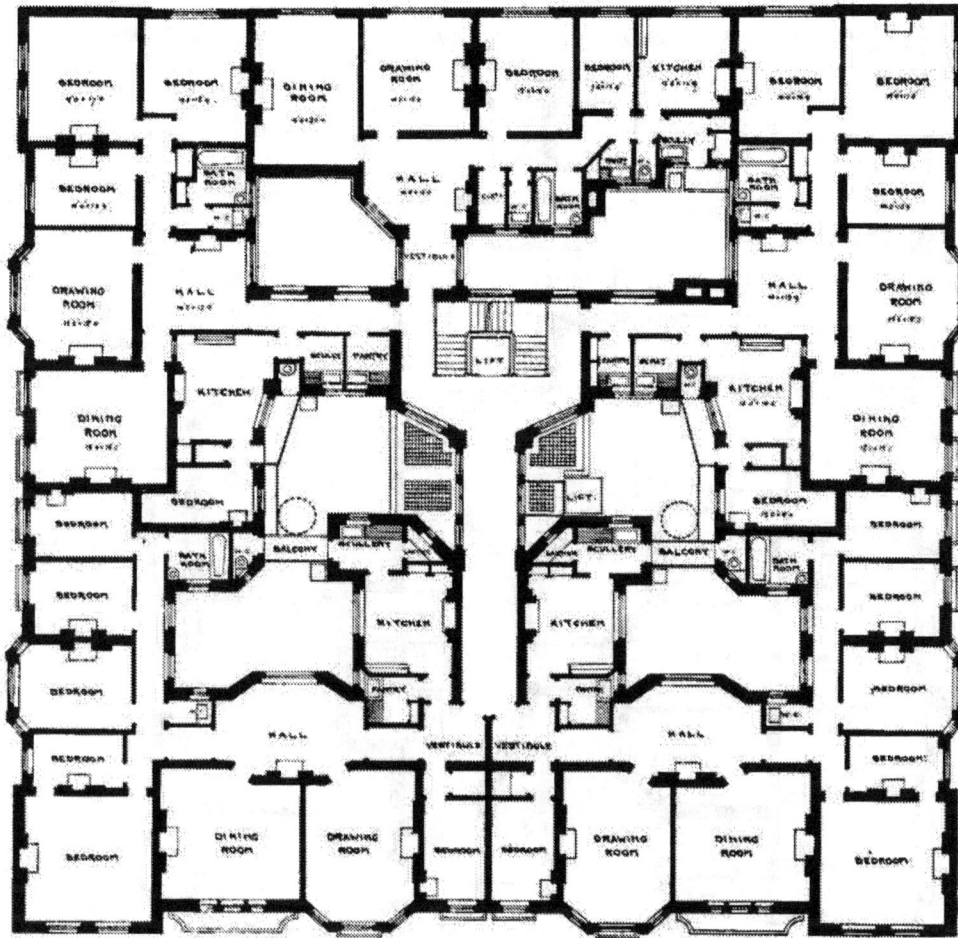

PLAN OF FIRST FLOOR FLATS

SCALE OF 10 5 0 10 20 30 40 50 FEET

FIG. 119.—CLARENDON COURT, MAIDA VALE.

Boehmer & Gibbs, Architects.

Priory Court, Mazenod Avenue, West Hampstead (Fig.

123).—The suites are small, and there are no lifts. Some of them have four bedrooms as in the illustration in Fig. 122, but some have only three. The passages, as usual in low-rented flats, are dependent upon borrowed light. There is no scullery. The lobby of the kitchen in some of the suites is a good arrangement, as the slops do not pass through the kitchen. For small suites it is rare to find two W.C.'s. No bath-room has a W.C. apparatus. When planning cheap flats it

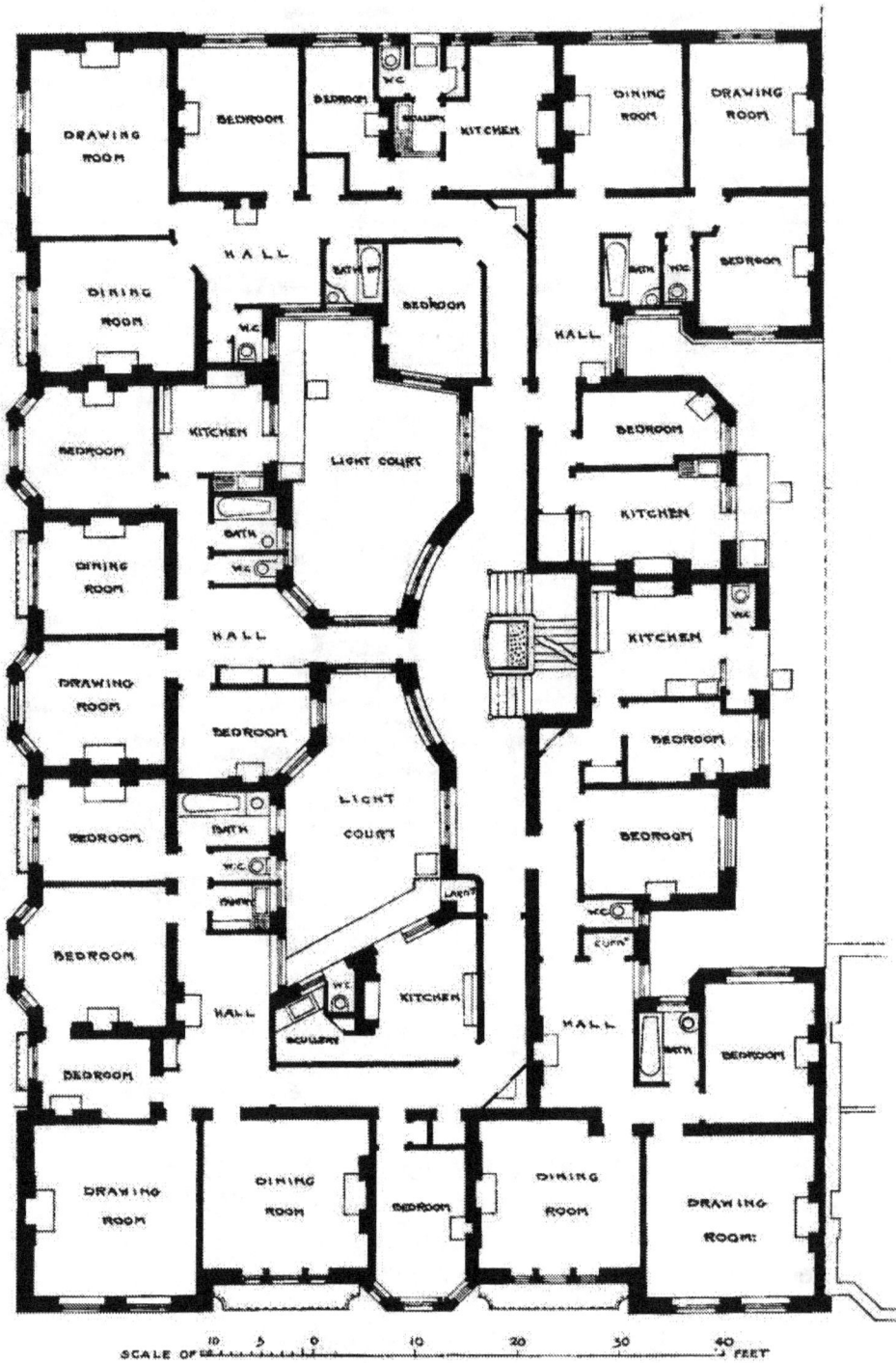

SCALE OF FEET

FIG. 120.—BLOMFIELD COURT, MAIDA VALE.

Boehmer & Gibbs, Architects.

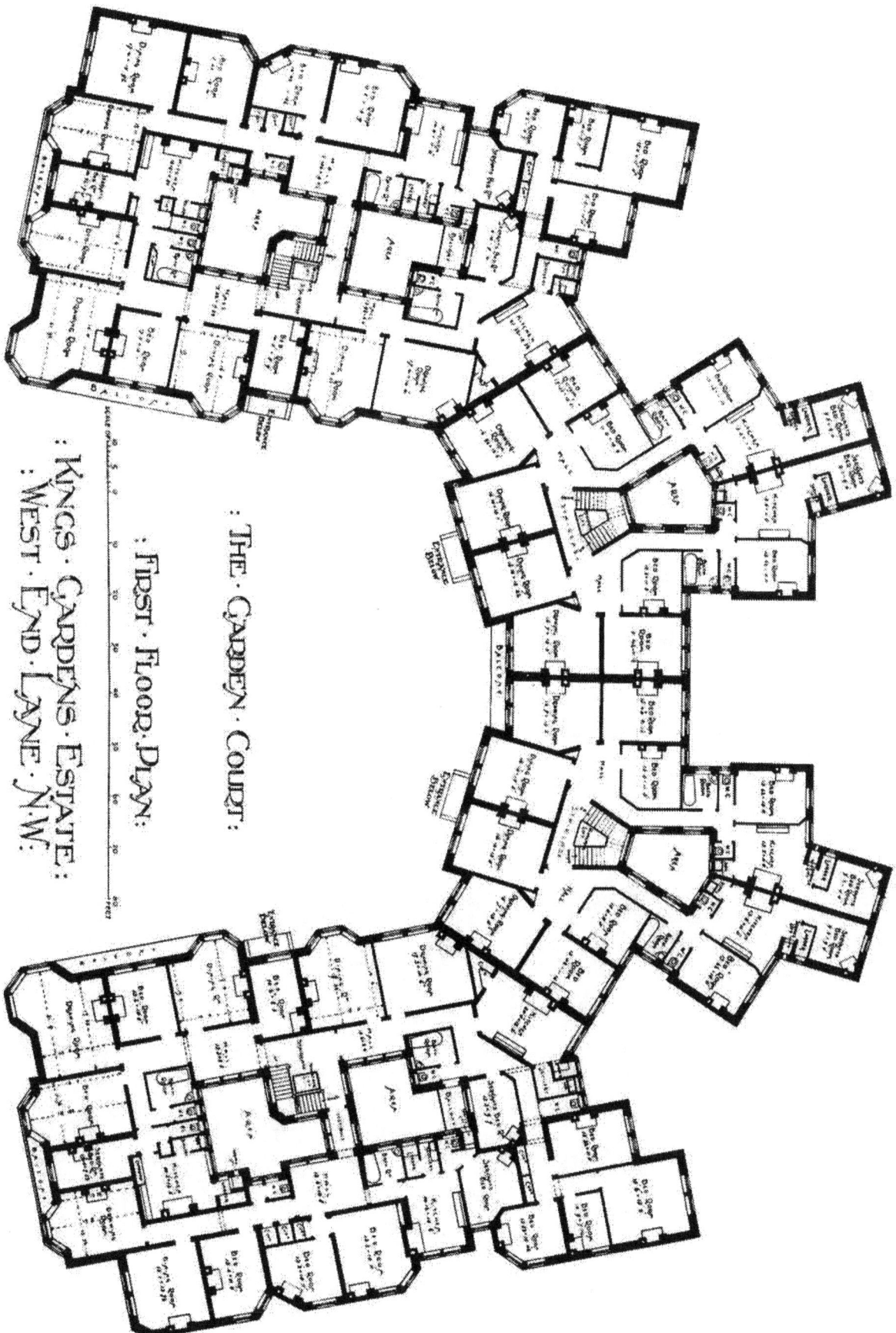

: THE · GARDEN · COURT :

: FIRST · FLOOR · PLAN :

: KINGS · GARDENS · ESTATE :
: WEST · END · LANE · NW :

FIG. 22.

Palgrave & Co., Architects.

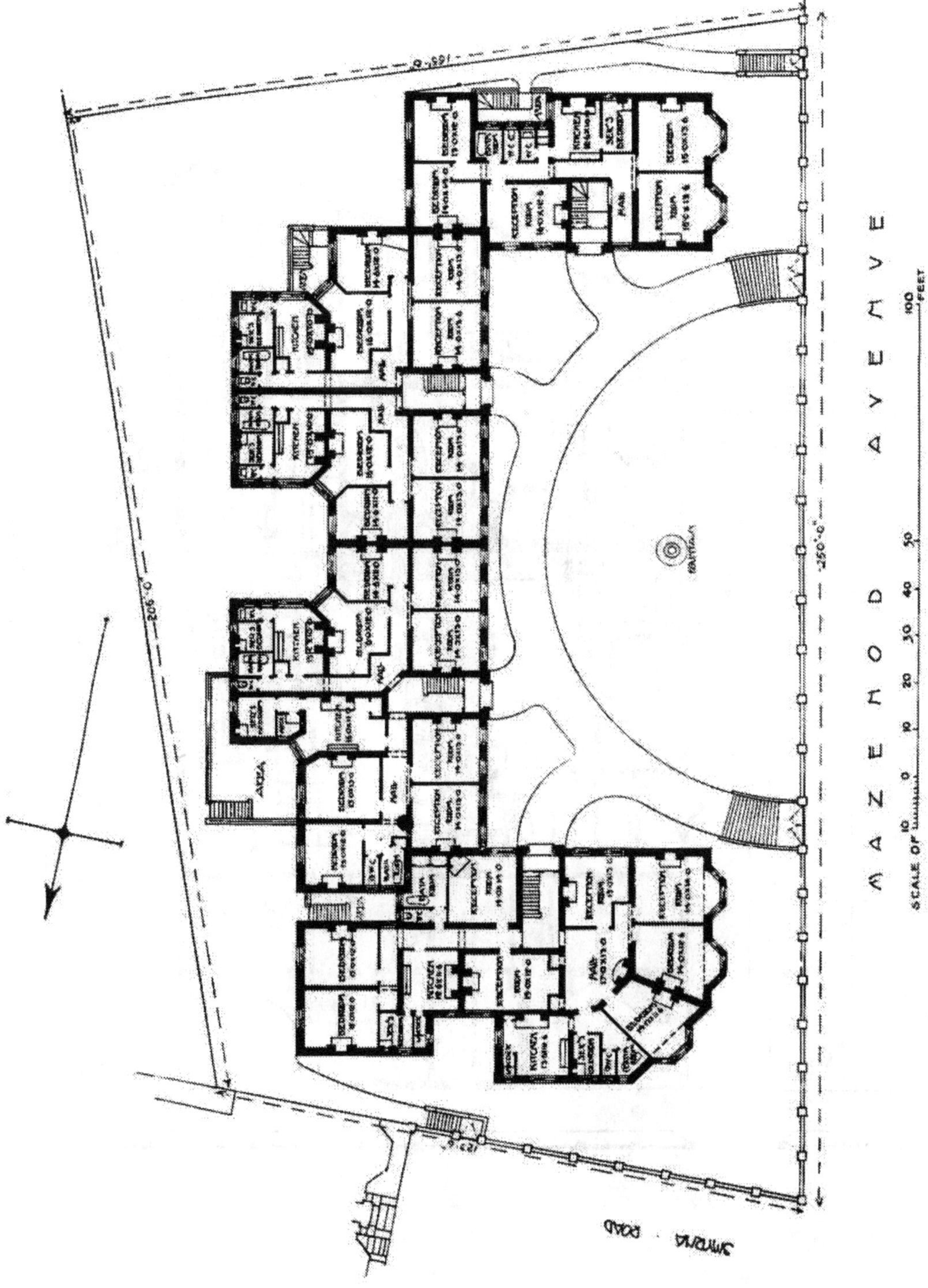

MAZENOD AVENUE

SCALE OF FEET

FIG. 123.—PRIORY COURT, MAZENOD AVENUE, WEST HAMPSTEAD.

Palgrave & Co., Architects.

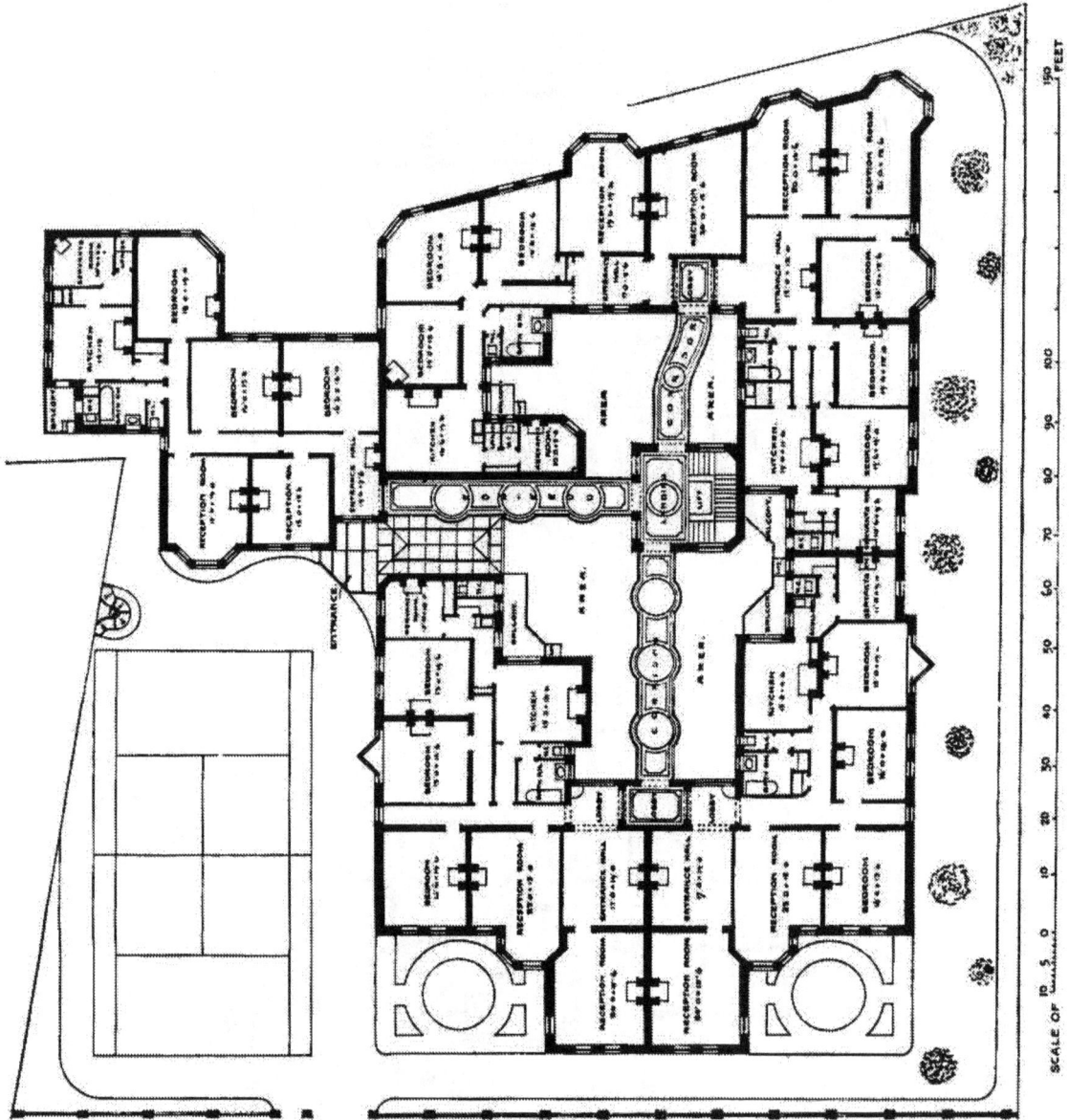

FIG. 124.—FROGNAL, HAMPSTEAD.

Palgrave & Co., Architects.

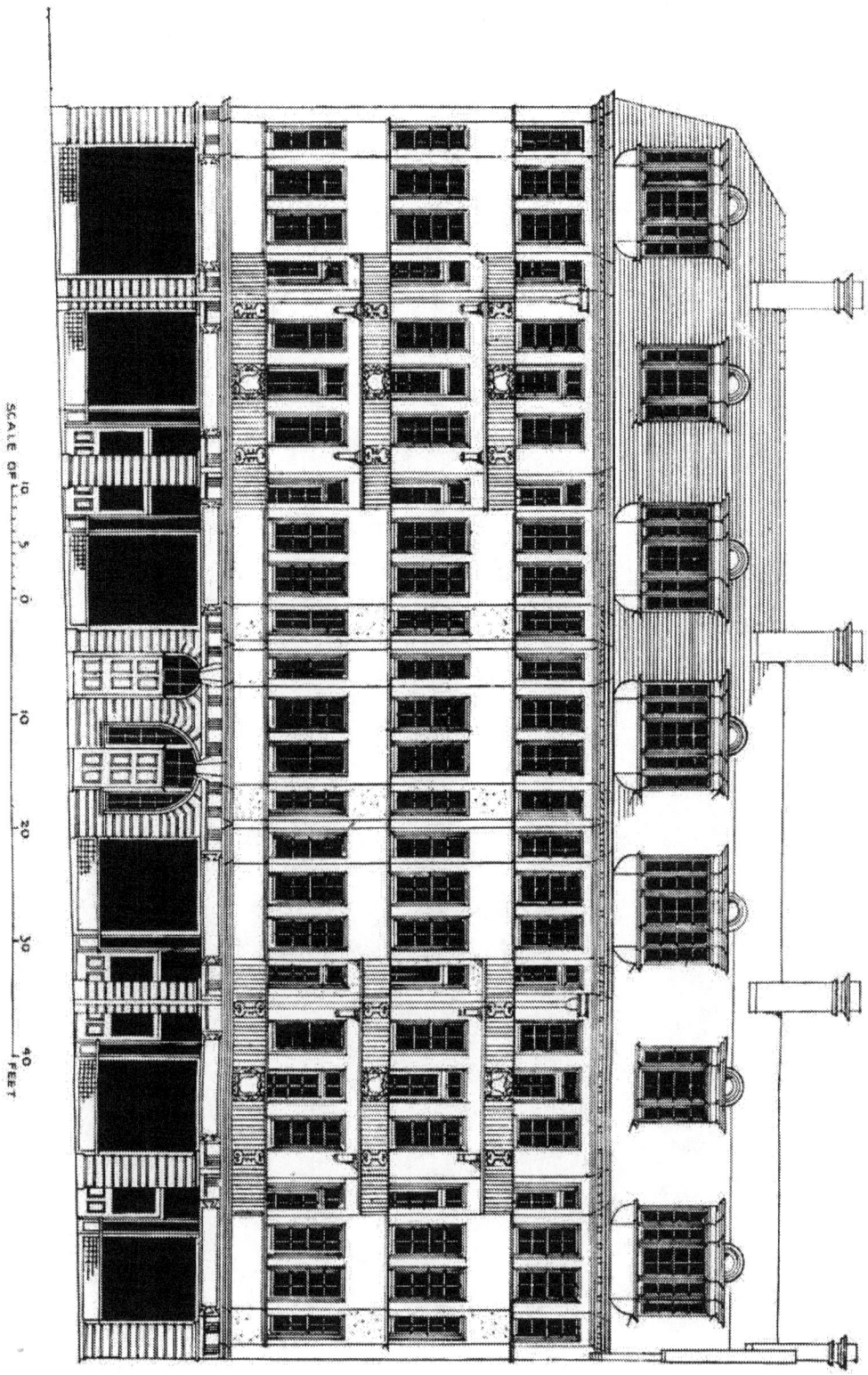

FIG. 124.—RESIDENTIAL FLATS, BENHILL.

SCALE OF 10 5 0 10 20 30 40 FEET

R. A. Briggs, Architect.

is difficult to avoid the servants' bedroom opening off the kitchen, as expense has to be so carefully considered.

Frognal, Hampstead (Fig. 124).—This is a more ambitious building. There is a lift to serve five suites on each floor, necessitating long corridors. In some flats the servants' W.C. is entered from a balcony. The servants' rooms are well planned, and the passages well lighted. The bays to the reception rooms on the left side of the plan have been carefully arranged ; see also those on plan Fig. 105.

Flats at Bexhill (Fig. 125).—This is an example showing a block of flats by the sea. Not many

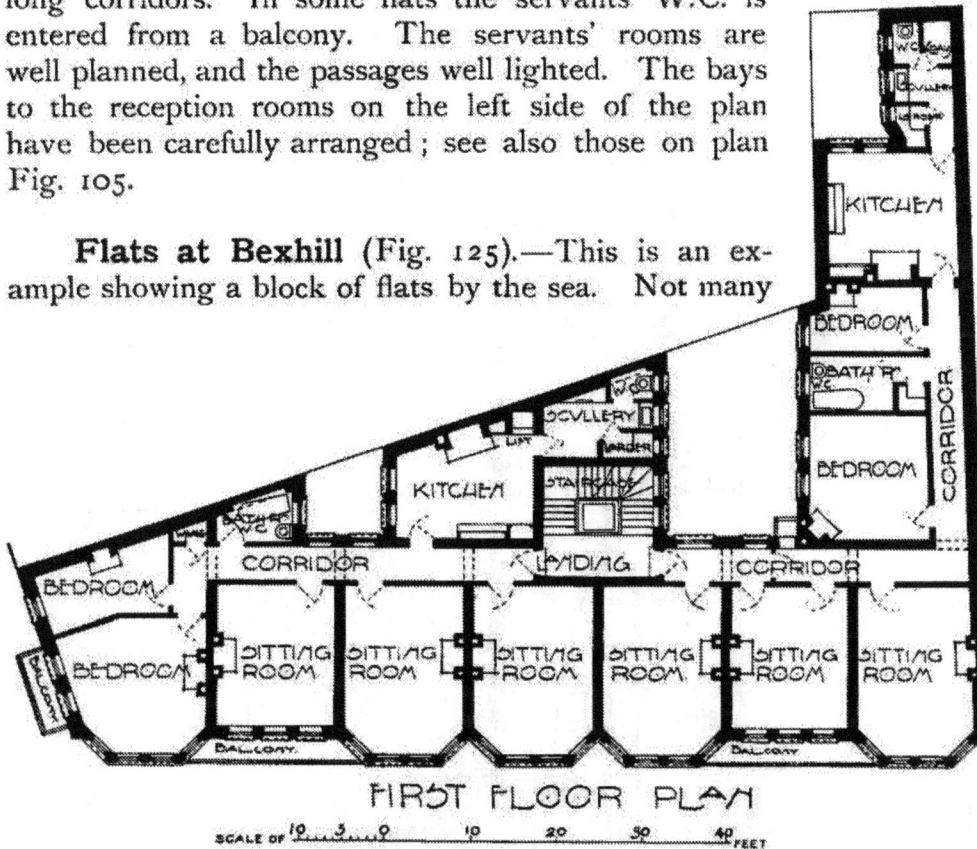

FIRST FLOOR PLAN

SCALE OF 10 3 0 10 20 30 40 FEET

FIG. 125.—RESIDENTIAL FLATS, BEXHILL.

R. A. Briggs, Architect.

have been built. One suite has three sitting-rooms and two bedrooms ; one sitting-room would no doubt be used as a bedroom. Neither suite has a hall. Each flat has two W.C.'s. The offices are good. Fig. 124A shows the elevation.

Proposed Flats, Hampstead (Fig. 126).—Two suites are served by one lift. The servants' bedroom is entered from the kitchen, and the plan is not as good as Fig. 123, by the same architects. The rooms and hall are large for this class of building. The lighting of the

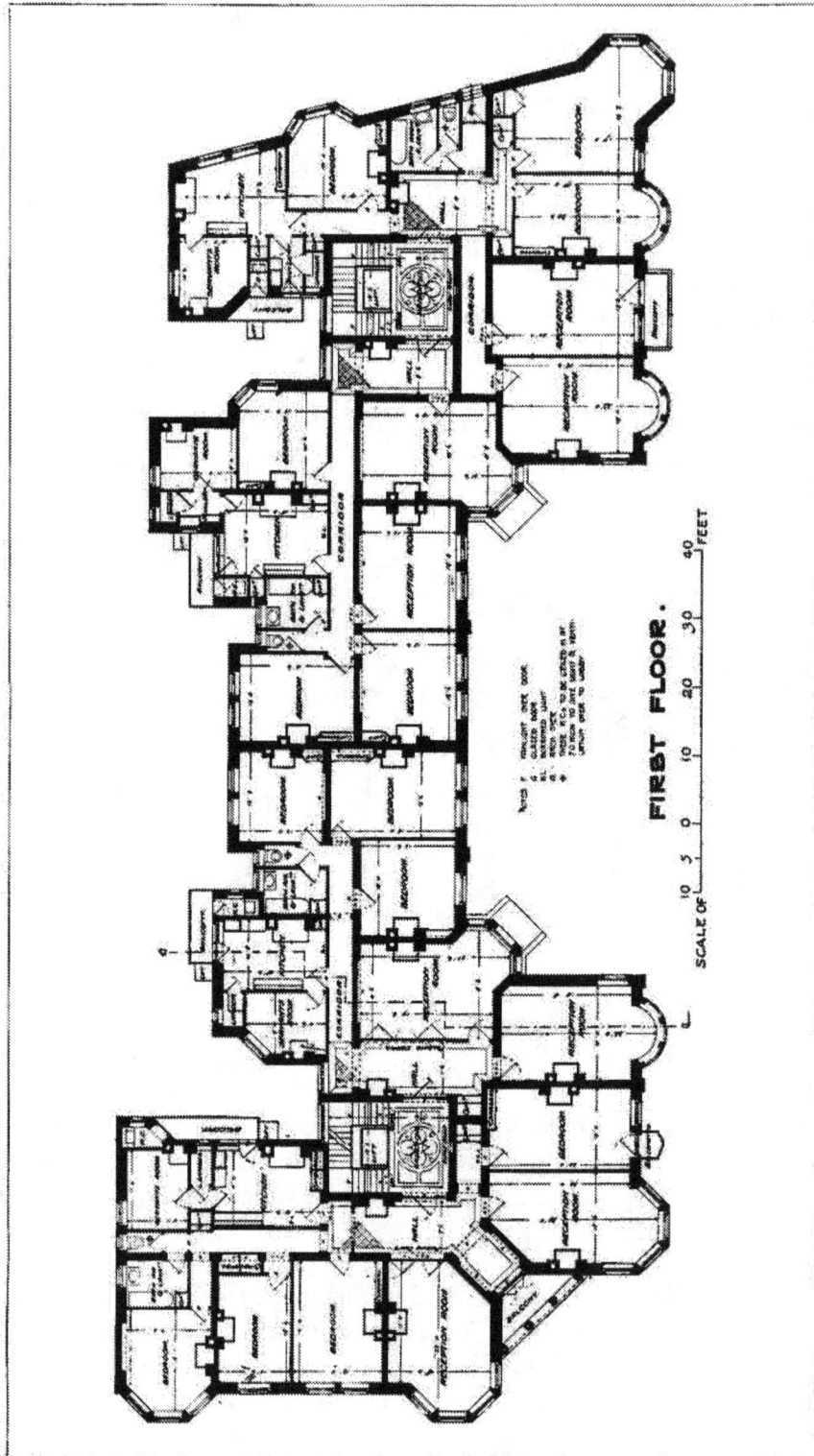

FIG. 126.—Proposed Flats, Hampstead.

Palgrave & Co., Architects.

FIRST FLOOR.

SCALE OF FEET

Fig. 126a.—EARL'S COURT SQUARE, S.W.

R. A. Briggs, Architect.

hall of each end suite has been difficult to arrange; in one case the two reception rooms suffer considerably in consequence.

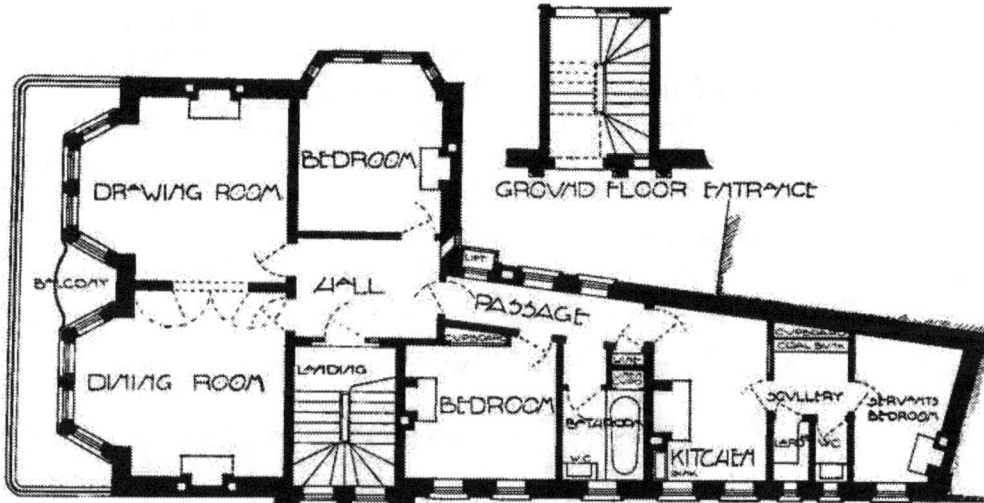

Fig. 127.—Flats at Earl's Court Square.

R. A. Briggs, Architect.

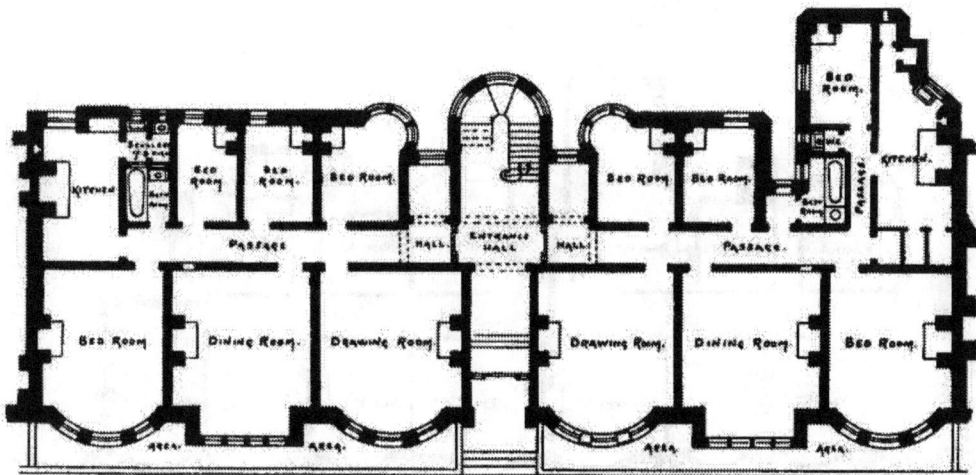

Fig. 128.—Residential Suites, Marylebone, W.

T. E. Eales, Architect.

Earl's Court Square (Fig. 127).—This building has only one suite to a floor.   There are folding doors between the reception-rooms ; often a great advantage to tenants, and too rarely found in English flats.   A larger window to the hall might have been an advantage, even at the expense of the bedroom, but there is good borrowed light from the staircase.   A fireplace might have been planned in the corner of the hall.   These fireplaces are, after all, more for ornament than use, but tenants like them.   In a small hall they are rarely used. The arrangement of the servants' rooms is excellent, and the length of passage is very small.   A perspective view is given in Fig. 126A.

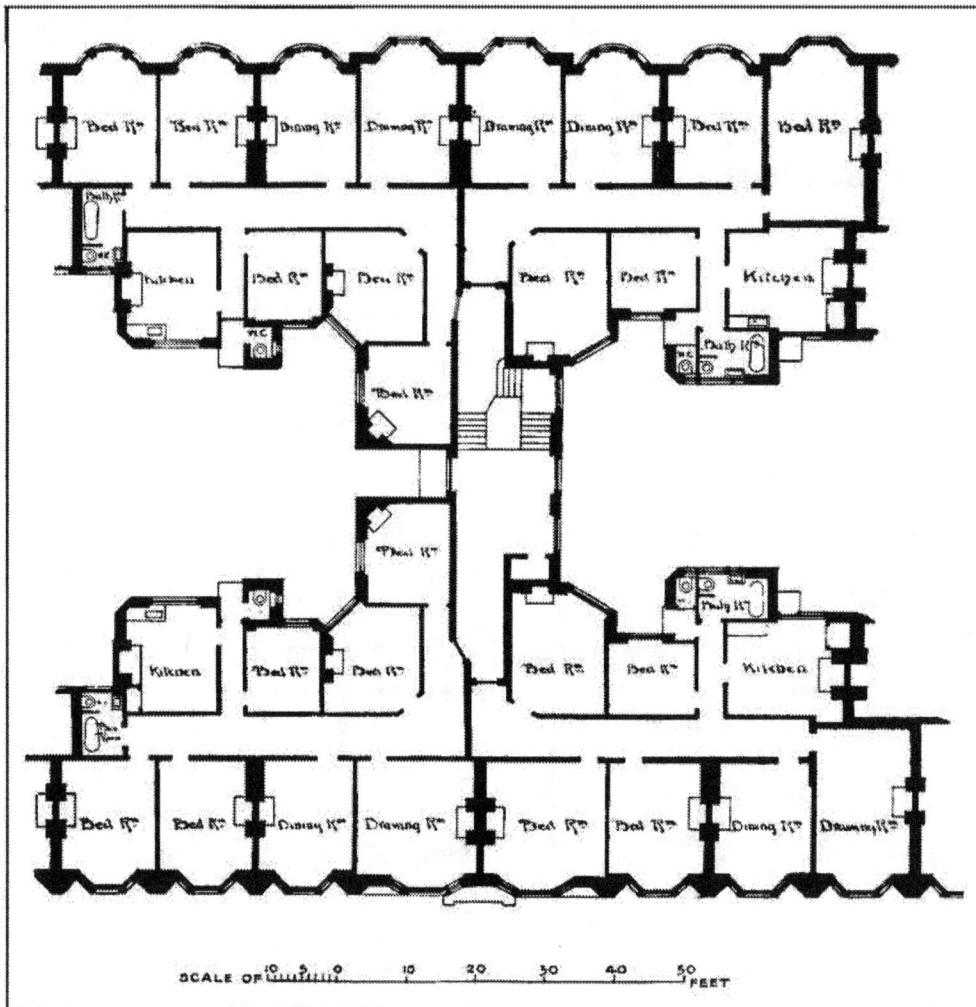

FIG. 129.—HUNTWORTH MANSIONS.

W. A. Scrymgour, Architect

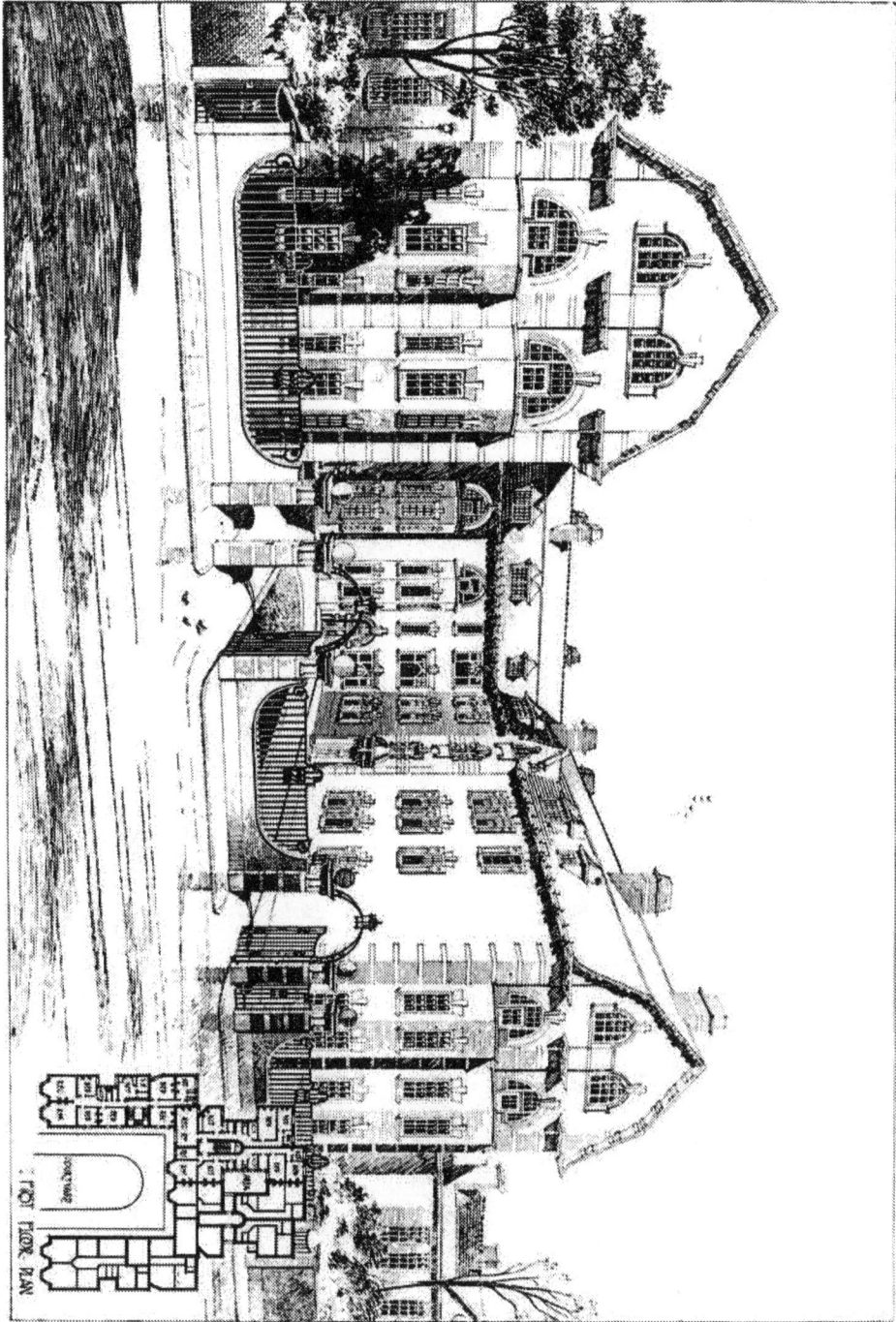

FIG. 129A.—RESIDENTIAL SUITES, SHEPHERD'S BUSH, W.

John D. Clarke,
Septimus Warwick, } *Architects.*

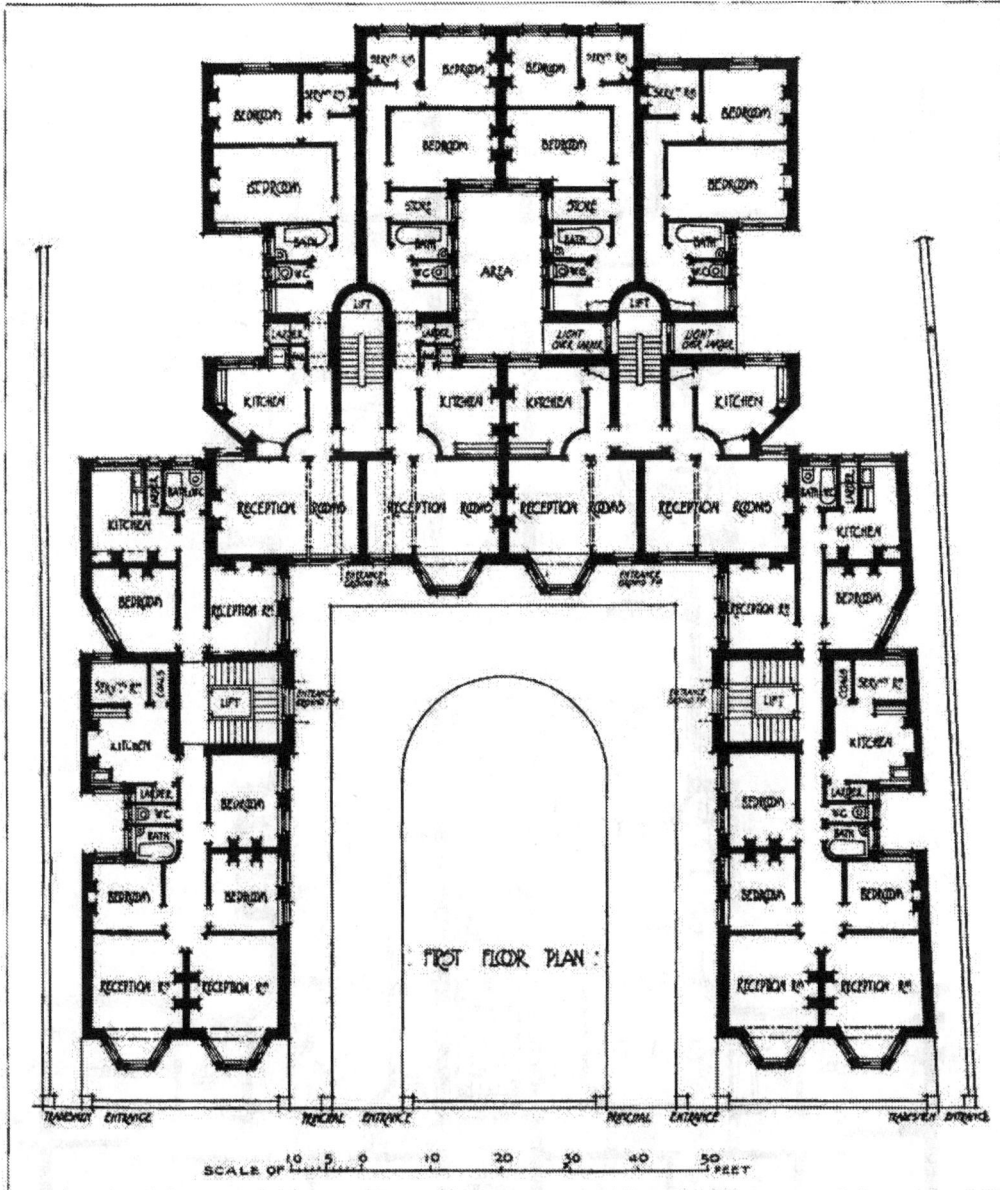

FIG. 130.—RESIDENTIAL SUITES, SHEPHERD'S BUSH, W.

John D. Clarke & Septimus Warwick, Architects.

Marylebone (Fig. 128).—These buildings form part of a large estate that has been a great success. Each suite has a frontage available for three rooms, consequently the planning is simplified.

Huntworth Mansions (Fig. 129).—Four suites on a flat are served by one lift. Each kitchen is large and has a sink, and there is

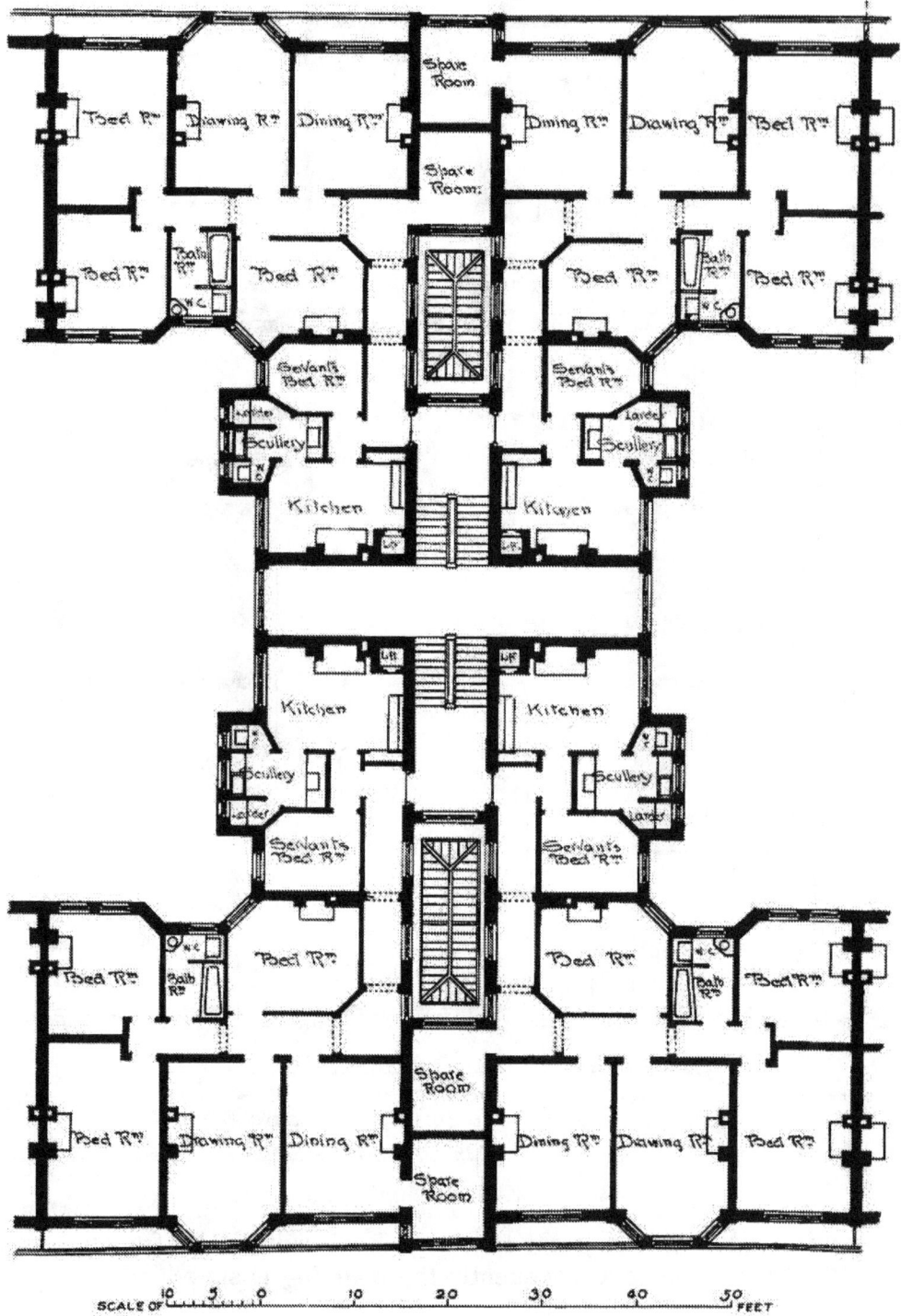

SCALE OF

FIG. 131.—ARGYLL MANSIONS, HAMMERSMITH ROAD.

Turner & Withers, Owners and Builders.

no scullery. The bedroom near the kitchen is often used as a pantry. There is practically no hall, and the passage depends entirely upon borrowed light.

Shepherd's Bush (Fig. 130).—The principal point of interest is the arrangement for lighting the staircase so as to comply with the Building Act, and yet place it at a distance from an external wall. The larder is made of less height than the remainder of the flat, and ventilation is obtained over it on each floor. A perspective is given on Fig. 129A.

Argyll Mansions, Hammersmith Road (Fig. 131). — The central public corridor was left with a view to other blocks of buildings being erected, and passages being continued to them. There is, however, a large amount of public passage space. The servants' rooms are well cut off from the remainder of each suite.

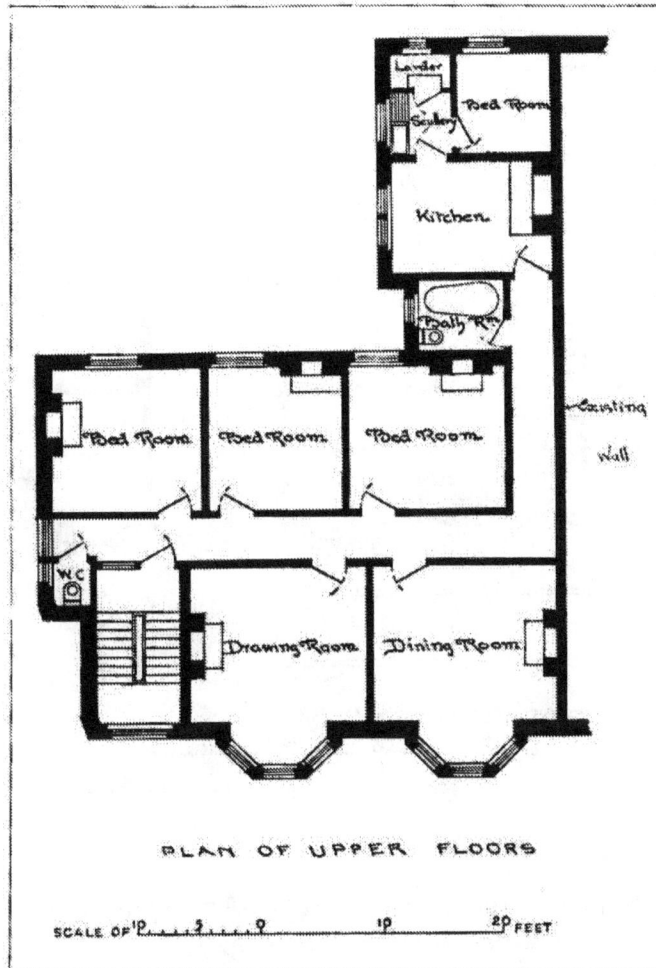

FIG. 132.—WARWICK MANSIONS.

Warwick Mansions (Fig. 132).—These flats were planned as an end block to a terrace of flats with less accommodation shown on Fig. 139. As the kitchen is so large the scullery might have been omitted. There is a W.C. near the entrance, and a second apparatus in the bath-room.

Alexandra House, St Mary's Terrace, W. (Fig. 133).—By setting back slightly in one part, light has been obtained on all four sides of the building. The scullery has been dispensed with. There is room in the bath-room for an additional W.C. apparatus.

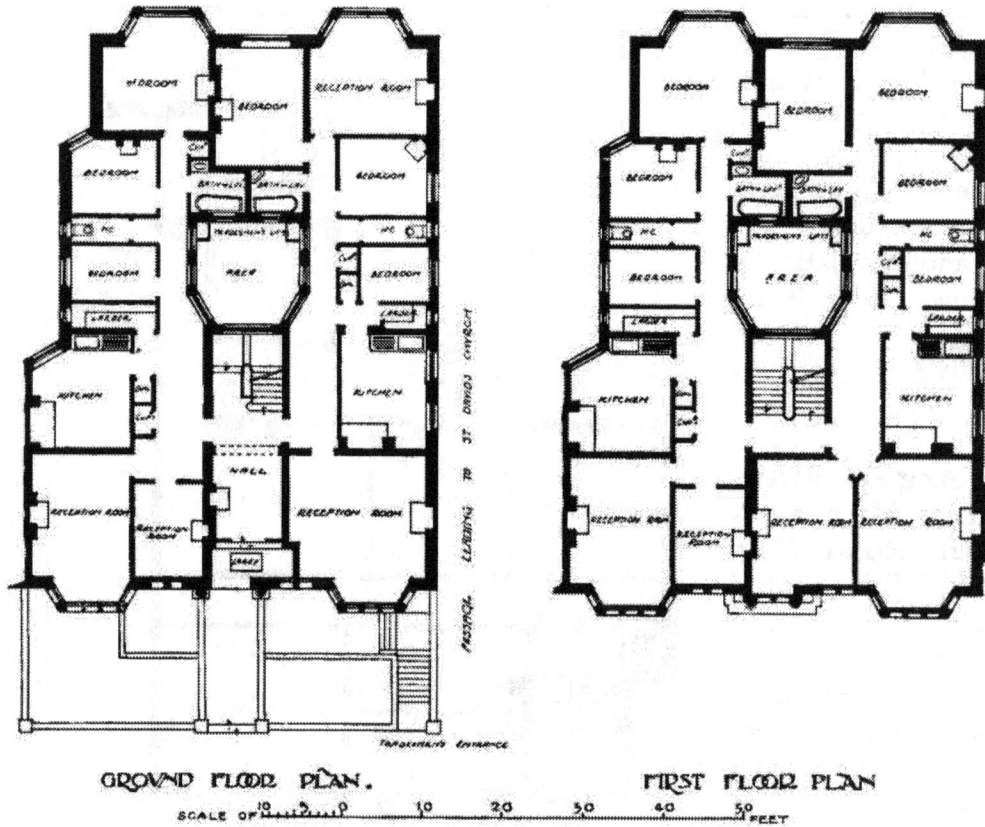

GROUND FLOOR PLAN.   FIRST FLOOR PLAN

SCALE OF FEET

FIG. 133.—ALEXANDRA HOUSE, ST MARY'S TERRACE, W.

Hart & Waterhouse, Architects.

Studio Flats (Fig. 134).—An example of small studio flats, the elevation of which is shown on Fig. 134A.

South Bruntsfield Place, Edinburgh (Fig. 135).—This is an example of an Edinburgh building. The drawing-room is exceptionally large, the extreme dimensions being 20 by 27 ft.; the dining-room is also larger than is usual in a similar London suite. There is no scullery. The parlour would probably be used as a bedroom in London; a flat of this class rarely has three reception rooms. The cupboard accommodation is considerable, and the two drawing-rooms suffer in

FRONT ELEVATION

SCALE OF ½ 0 5 10 15 20 FEET.

FIG. 134A.—STUDIO FLATS.

R. A. Briggs, Architect.

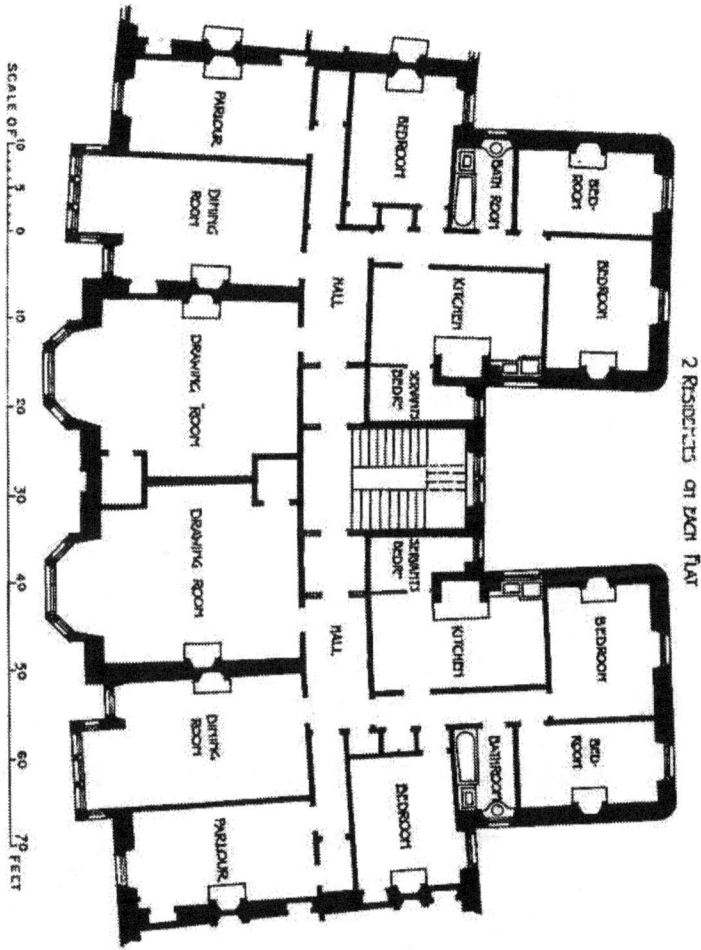

SCALE OF ... 10 5 0 10 20 30 40 50 60 70 FEET

2 RESIDENCES ON EACH FLAT

PARLOUR

DINING ROOM

BEDROOM

BATH ROOM

BED ROOM

KITCHEN

SERVANTS BEDR

SERVANTS BEDR

DRAWING ROOM

DRAWING ROOM

HALL

HALL

DINING ROOM

PARLOUR

BEDROOM

KITCHEN

BEDROOM

BED ROOM

BATHROOM

FIG. 135.—SOUTH BRUNTSFIELD PLACE, EDINBURGH.

Hippolyte J. Blanc, Architect.

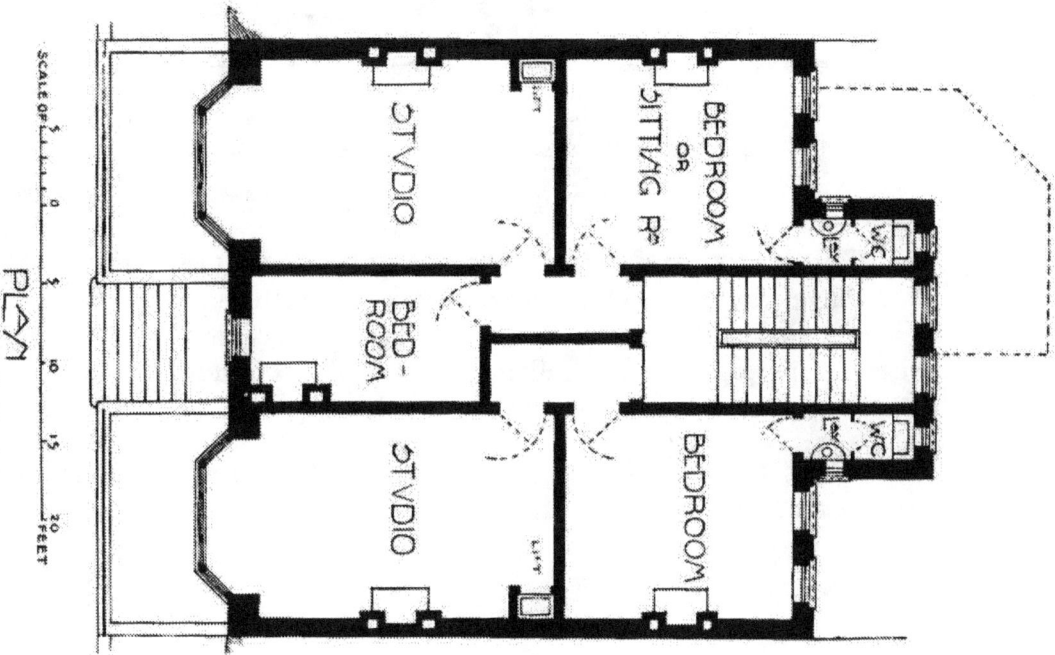

SCALE OF ... 5 0 5 10 15 20 FEET

STUDIO

STUDIO

BEDROOM OR SITTING RM

BED-ROOM

BEDROOM

WC

WC

PLAN

FIG. 134.—STUDIO FLATS.

R. A. Briggs, Architect.

a way that seems hardly necessary. An outer and also an inner hall is shown to each suite. This is rarely done in London, and when the main hall is entirely dependent upon borrowed light, the partition only makes it darker. The rooms of the artisans' dwellings in Edinburgh are also larger than is the rule in England (see Chapter III.).

CLASS No. 3.

The illustrations under this section are of flats not so expensive as those in Class No. 2 ; some of them are just better than artisans' dwellings, and let as low as £45 per annum. Most of the tenants would keep one servant. In some cases no servant is engaged ; lads are sent from different brigades to clean the boots and take down the dust, &c., each morning ; they work at 4d. an hour. Most of the suites have three or four bedrooms.

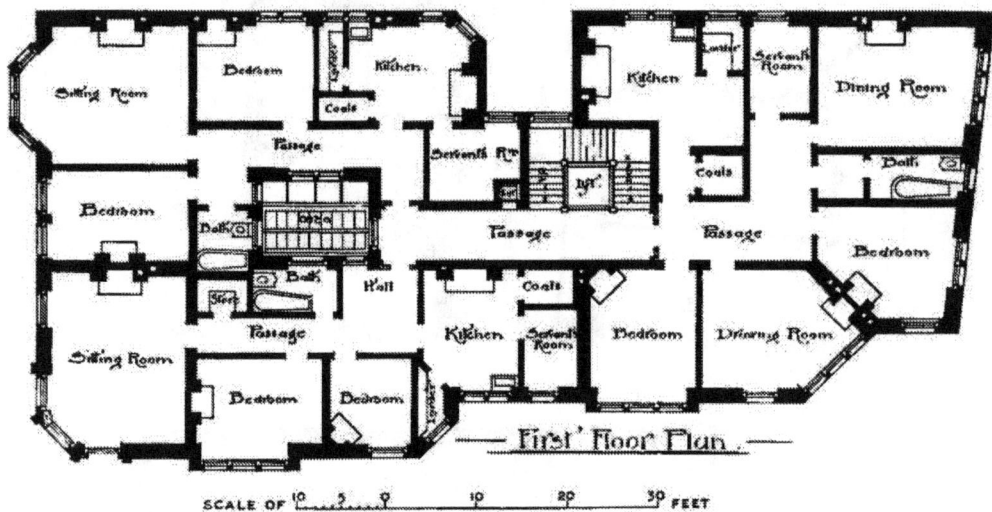

Fig. 136.—Goldhawk and Shepherd's Bush Road.

E. Keynes Purchase, Architect.

Goldhawk and Shepherd's Bush Road (Fig. 136).—These flats have a lift, serving three suites on each floor. The passage space is included with the suites as far as possible. This is a plan where a passage is not called a hall. The kitchens are large, and contain sinks, and good larders are provided.

Flats at Bexhill (Figs. 137 and 138).—Seaside flats at present are not a success, and few have been built. These are a good example

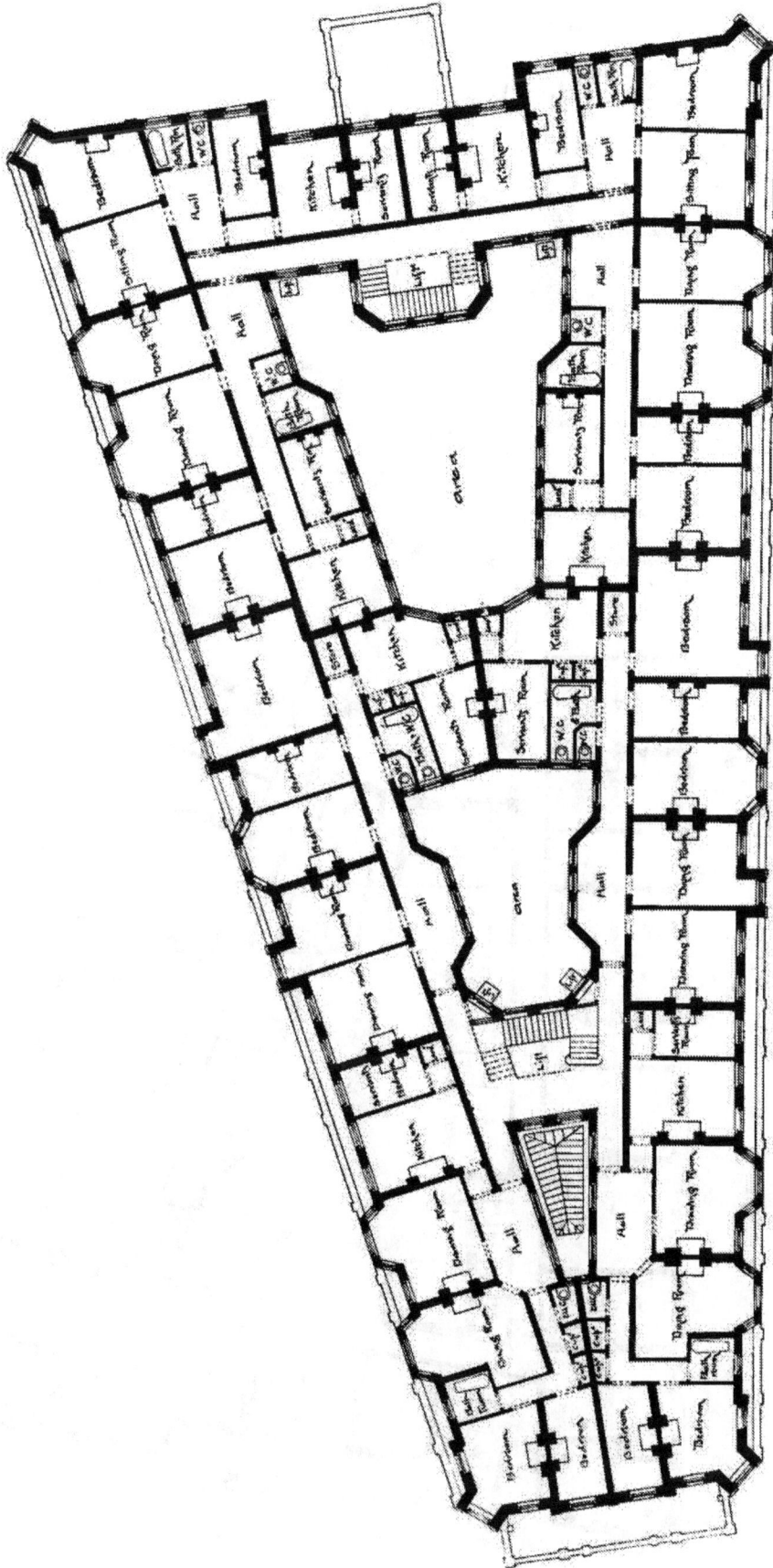

First Floor Plan

SCALE OF 10   0   10   20   30   40   50   60   70   80   90   100 FEET

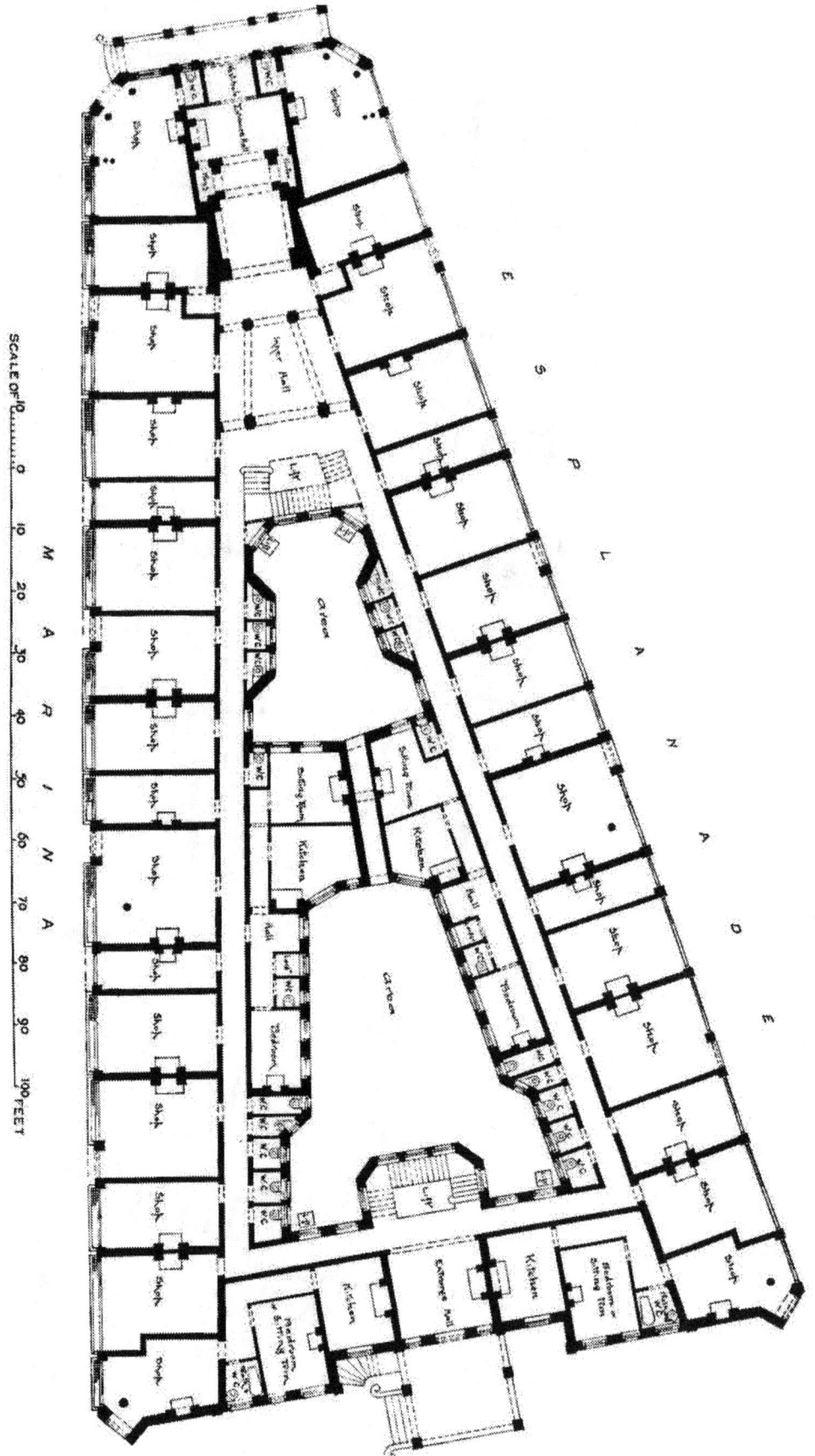

Ground Floor Plan

FIGS. 137 AND 138.—BEXHILL.

Paul Hoffmann, Architect.

SCALE OF
0   10   20   30   40   50   60   70   80   90   100 FEET

of suites over shops, and are some of the few flats in this section that have lifts. Each serves four suites, and there are the consequent long passages. These buildings have also the advantage of two W.C.'s to two of the suites on each upper floor.

St John's Park Mansions, Tufnell Park (Fig. 139).—The frontispiece of this book shows the exterior of these buildings ; several blocks were erected. In all suites except the one at the end, the

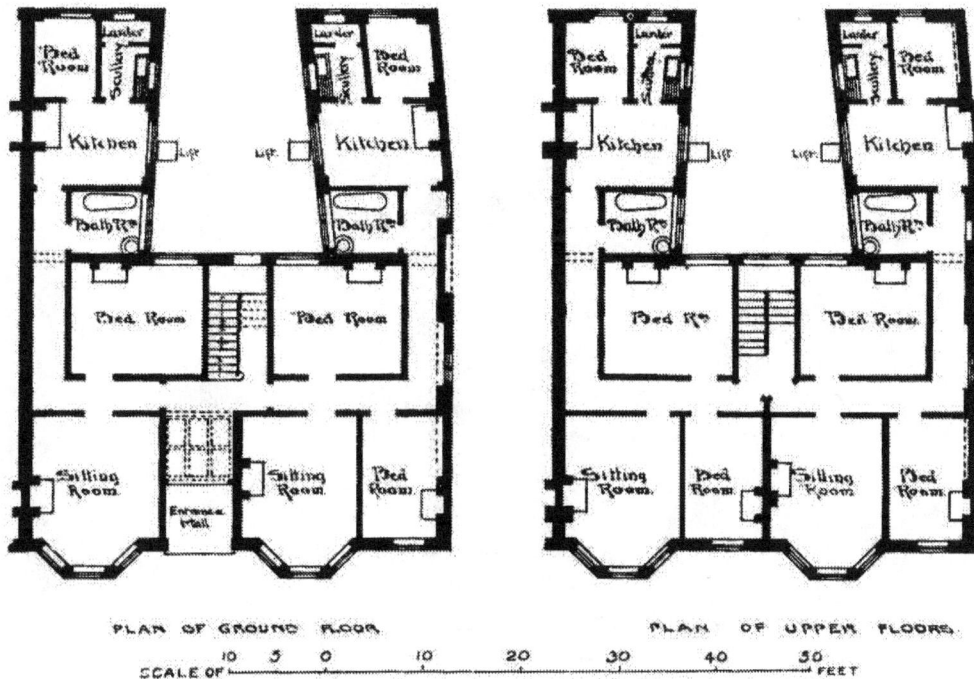

FIG. 139.—St John's Park Mansions, Tufnell Park.

passages are dependent upon borrowed light. The side of the bathroom is entirely glazed, and it is ample. The width of the front bedroom was fixed by the frontage available ; some tenants use it as a sitting-room. Another 2 ft. would have been a great improvement, but it was impossible to manage it. There are coal and bicycle sheds at the rear, and there is an external door under the stairs to give access to the trade lifts. If these buildings could have been built with a top-lighted staircase, the saving would have been considerable, and the tenants would have had larger rooms and better dwellings. One porter looks after several buildings. There are electric bell pushes outside the main entrance doors. These are, of course, closed at night.

Each tenant has a pass key to open his door and the main entrance door.   The cost of these buildings is referred to in Chapter VII.

Paddington Street and Northumberland Street (Fig. 140). —A building by Professor Beresford Pite.   There are two W.C.'s, one in the bath-room.   There is no scullery, but a small pantry is provided. Fig. 140A is the elevation; an excellent example of the good work that can be done at small expense.   Fig. 56 shows the plan of a block with fewer rooms to each suite by the same architect, and Fig. 140B a view of the front of another block by him.

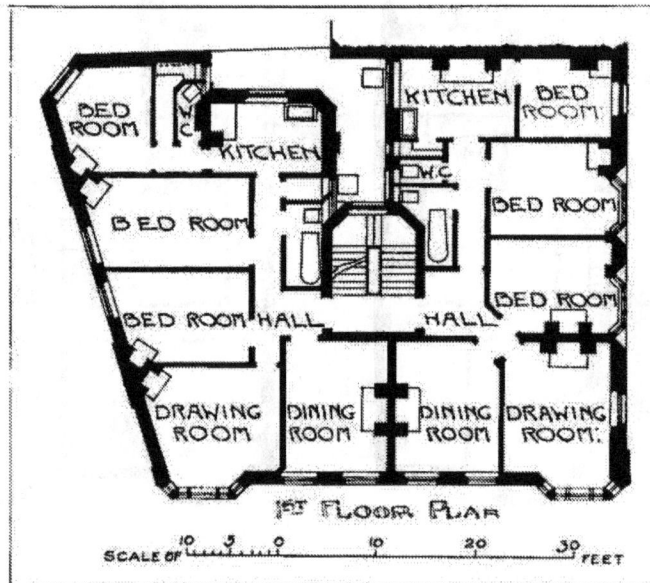

FIG. 140.—PADDINGTON STREET AND NORTHUMBERLAND STREET.

Professor Beresford Pite, Architect.

"Roseberry," 203 Anerley Road, London, S.E. (Figs. 141 and 142).—Now that the suburbs of London are deteriorating so rapidly, it is impossible to let many of the large houses that commanded good rents a few years ago.   If the garden is large the house can be pulled down, and buildings erected on the whole site.   Often this is not possible, and the house has either to be let at a very low rental or altered into flats.   These drawings are illustrations of what may be done, and plans are given before and after the alterations.   The important point to bear in mind is to plan the staircase close to the main entrance.   Alterations such as these are always very expensive, especially to old suburban houses, usually badly built.

FIG. 140A.—PADDINGTON STREET AND NORTHUMBERLAND STREET, MARYLEBONE, W.

Professor Beresford Pite, Architect.

FIG. 140B.—NOS. 18, 19, AND 20 FOLEY STREET, W.

Professor Beresford Pite, Architect.

SUB GROUND FLOOR / OLD PLAN

- BUTLERS PANTRY
- WINE CELLAR
- Cupboard
- BILLIARD ROOM
- LARDER
- stairs up
- LOWER HALL
- KITCHEN
- SCULLERY
- LOBBY
- CELLAR

GROUND FLOOR / OLD PLAN

- MORNING ROOM
- DRAWING ROOM
- W.C.
- HALL
- LIBRARY
- DINING ROOM

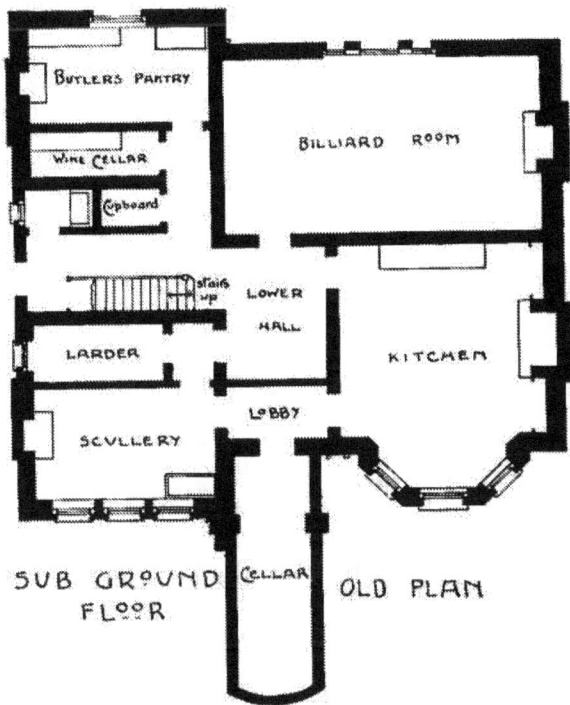

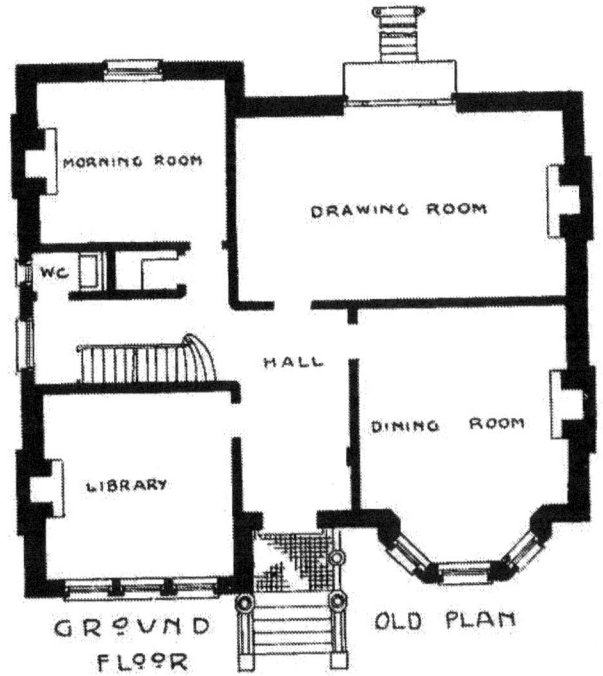

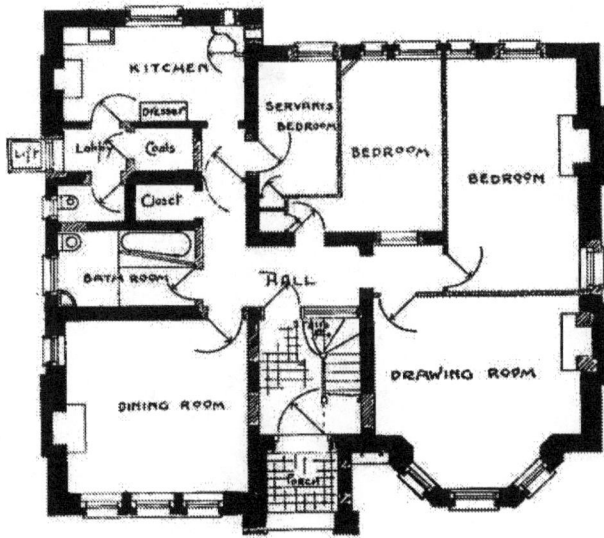

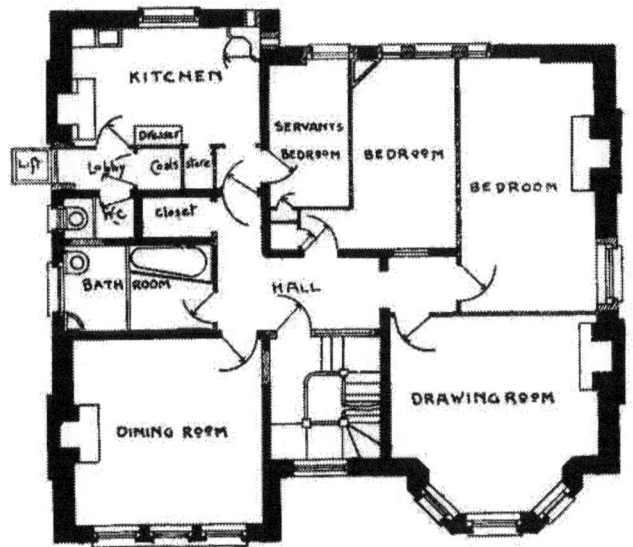

SUB GROUND FLOOR / NEW PLAN

- KITCHEN
- Dresser
- SERVANTS BEDROOM
- BEDROOM
- BEDROOM
- L.F.
- Lobby
- Coals
- Closet
- BATH ROOM
- HALL
- DRAWING ROOM
- DINING ROOM
- PORCH

GROUND FLOOR / NEW PLAN

- KITCHEN
- Dresser
- SERVANTS BEDROOM
- BEDROOM
- BEDROOM
- L.F.
- Lobby
- Coals
- store
- W.C.
- closet
- BATH ROOM
- HALL
- DRAWING ROOM
- DINING ROOM

SCALE OF 10 5 0 10 20 30 FEET

SCALE OF 10 5 0 10 20 30 FEET

FIGS. 141, 142.—"ROSEBERRY" 203 ANERLEY ROAD, LONDON, S.E.

John W. Rhodes, Architect.

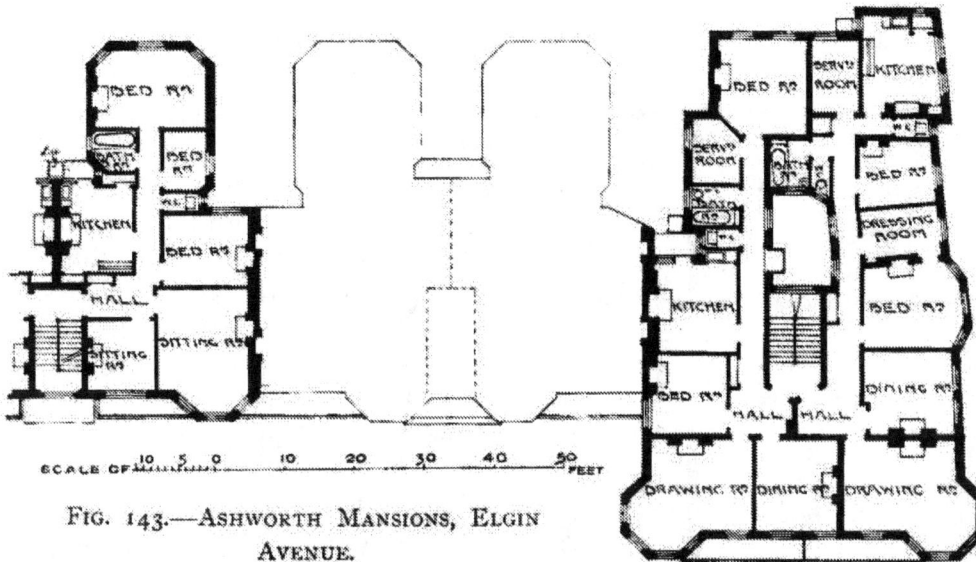

FIG. 143.—ASHWORTH MANSIONS, ELGIN
AVENUE.

Boehmer & Gibbs, Architects.

Ashworth Mansions, Elgin Avenue (Fig. 143).—These suites
have three or four bedrooms and two sitting-rooms. The smaller blocks
have similar accommodation to Fig. 144. The best bedroom is at the
rear, on account of the
view. The passage is in
the centre of each suite,
and consequently there is
a large amount of external
wall. The kitchens are
large, and there are no
sculleries.

**Grantully Man-
sions** (Fig. 144).—These
suites have one more room
than Fig. 139. The stair-
case is in the front, and
the frontage of each block
is greater. The trade
entrances are at the back
of the building off a side
street, the usual arrangement. The servants' room

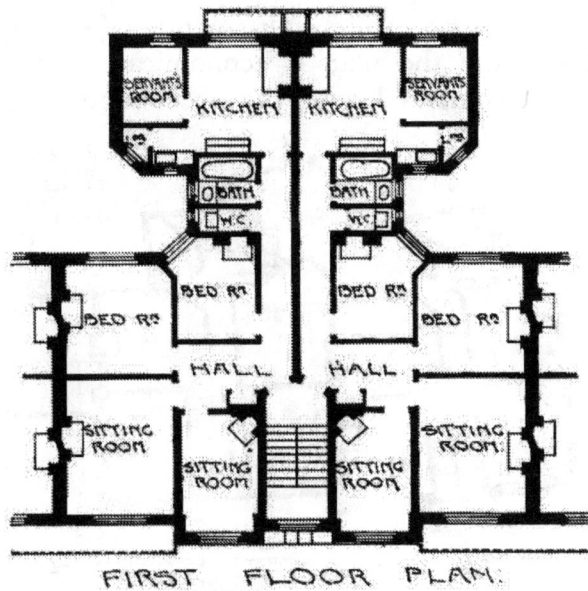

FIRST FLOOR PLAN.

FIG. 144.—GRANTULLY MANSIONS.
Boehmer & Gibbs, Architects.

is entered from the kitchen, and there is no scullery, a sink in a well-planned recess being all that is required.

An attempt has been made to give each of these small flats a good hall, but it is dependent on borrowed light. It may be said generally for all plans under this section that the one point the architect has to consider before all others is the cost of the building, and it is impossible to get an ideal plan with about five rooms in a second-class neighbourhood, and make the scheme a financial success.

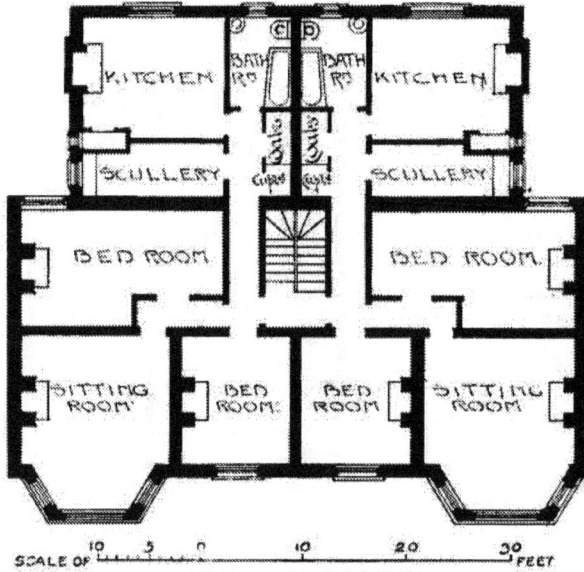

FIG. 145.—A BUILDER'S PLAN.

A Builder's Plan (Fig. 145).—This is an example of a plan upon which a large number of suburban flats were built some few years ago. The staircase has a top light, and the plan is economical. The amount of external wall is small compared with the accommodation, and the less external wall

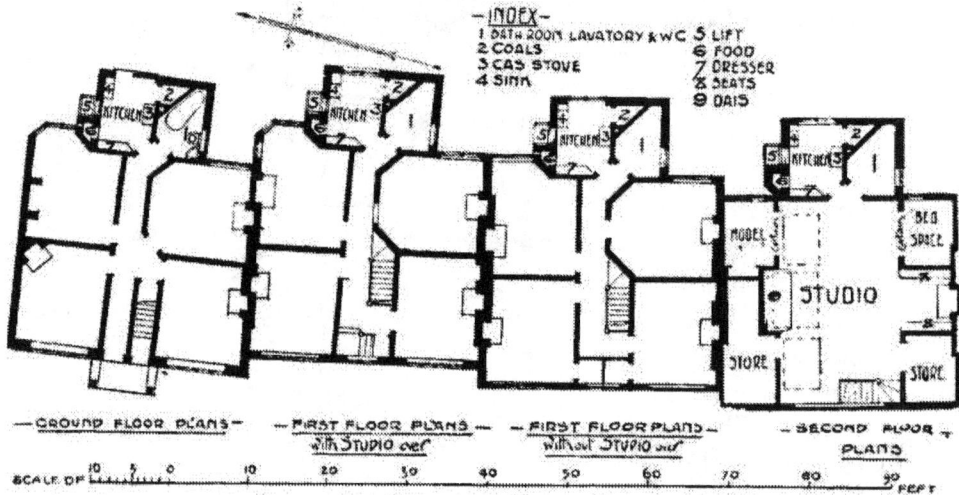

FIG. 146.—PROPOSED FLATS, DULWICH.

John W. Rhodes, Architect.

there is the cheaper and indeed more comfortable is the building. A saving might have been made by omitting the scullery and making the kitchen a little larger. The back bedroom should be better lighted and the bath-room might have been between the kitchen and the bedroom, and the kitchen built across the end of the block. This is not given as an example of a good plan, but as a specimen of a very successful builder's plan.

Proposed Flats, Dulwich (Fig. 146).—These are plans of some two-story buildings, each with a separate entrance to the upper floor. An optional plan for a studio is given.

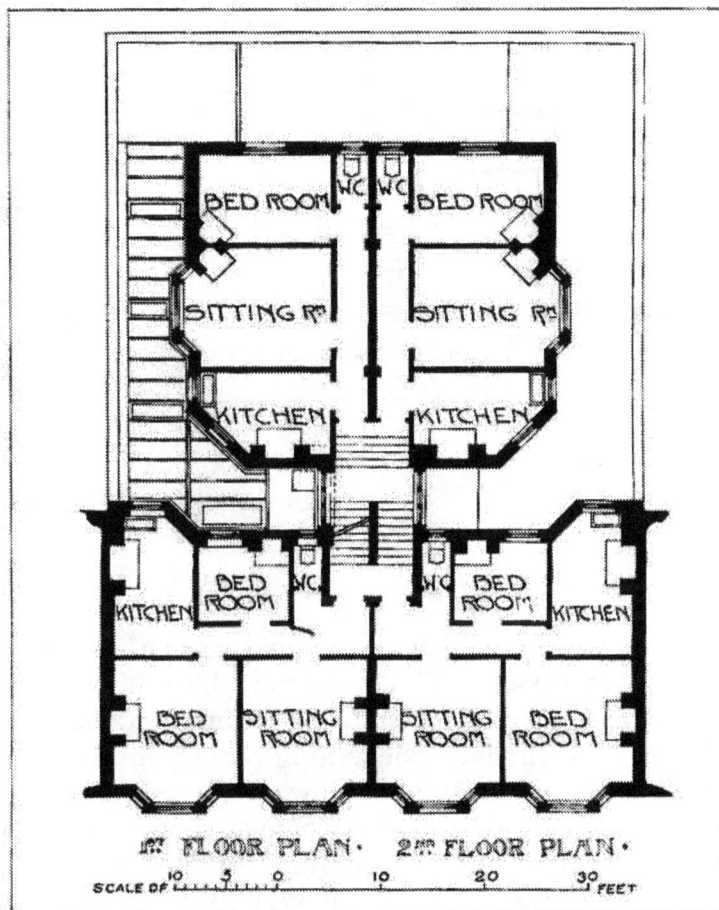

FIG. 147.—38 AND 40 CASTLE STREET.
Professor Beresford Pite, Architect.

Nos. 38 and 40 Castle Street (Fig. 147).—These suites are smaller than those shown on page 150. There is no bath-room. The exterior treatment is of similar style to Figs. 140A and 140B.

Nos. 15, 16, and 17 Saville Street (Fig. 148).—This is a simple plan of a recent building.   There is no scullery.

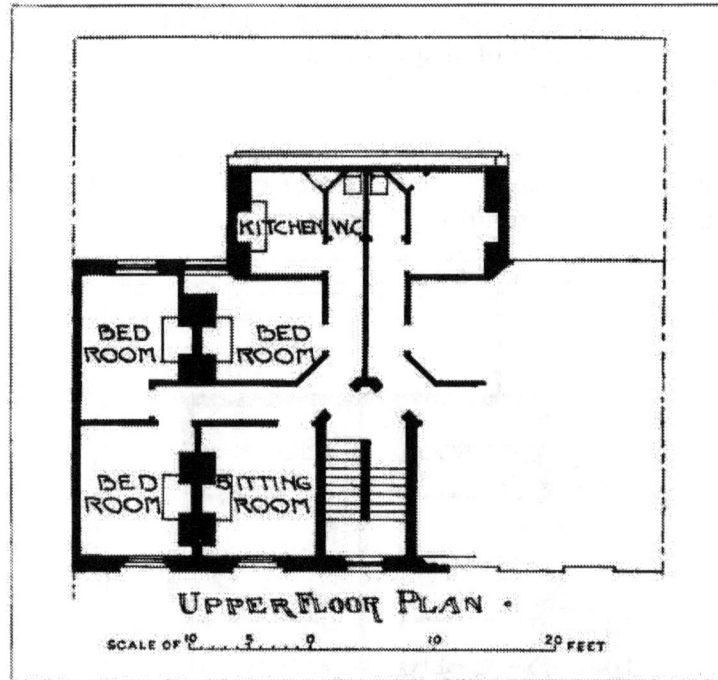

FIG. 148.—NOS. 15, 16, AND 17 SAVILLE STREET, W.
Professor Beresford Pite, Architect.

CLASS No. 4.

The plans of bachelors' flats do not vary much, consequently only a few examples are given.   The same may be said of catering flats. The tenant has a self-contained suite of rooms without any servants' offices, and usually with only one sitting-room, similar to the suites found in most hotels.   As stated elsewhere, these catering flats are often conducted on the same lines as hotels, single meals are served, and a room may be taken for one night.   If possible, a small pantry should be included in the suite ; this is very useful for tea cups, vases, &c.   In ordinary blocks of these flats, if the catering is only done for the residents, the profit is small ; a public restaurant should be arranged if possible, as in Fig. 118.

Mount Street (Fig. 149).—These buildings have three suites on the first and third floors, and two suites on the second floor, the latter

THIRD FLOOR PLAN

Bed Room | Sitting Room | Bed Room | Bath & W.C

Bath Room | Passage | | Lift

Bath Room | | Open Well

Passage

Bed Room | Sitting Room | Sitting Room

Cupboard | Cupboard | Cupboard

THIRD FLOOR PLAN

SECOND FLOOR PLAN

Bed Room | Bed Room | Bed Room

Bath and W.C. | Passage | Cups

| | Open Well | Lift

Passage

Bed Room | Sitting Room | Sitting Room

SECOND FLOOR PLAN.

FIRST FLOOR PLAN

Bed Room | Sitting Room. | Bed Room.

Bath Room | | Bath & W.C.

Bath Room | | Passage

Open Well. | Lift

Passage.

Bed Room | Sitting Room. | Sitting Room

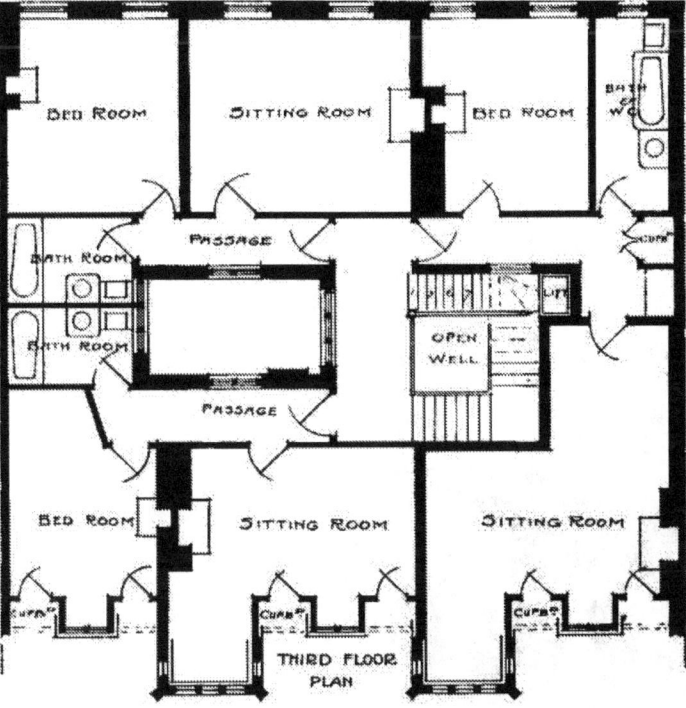

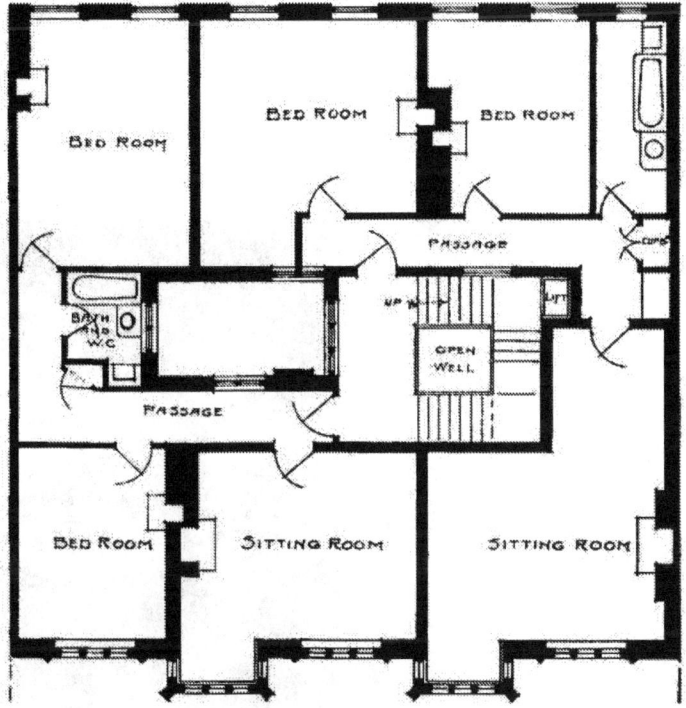

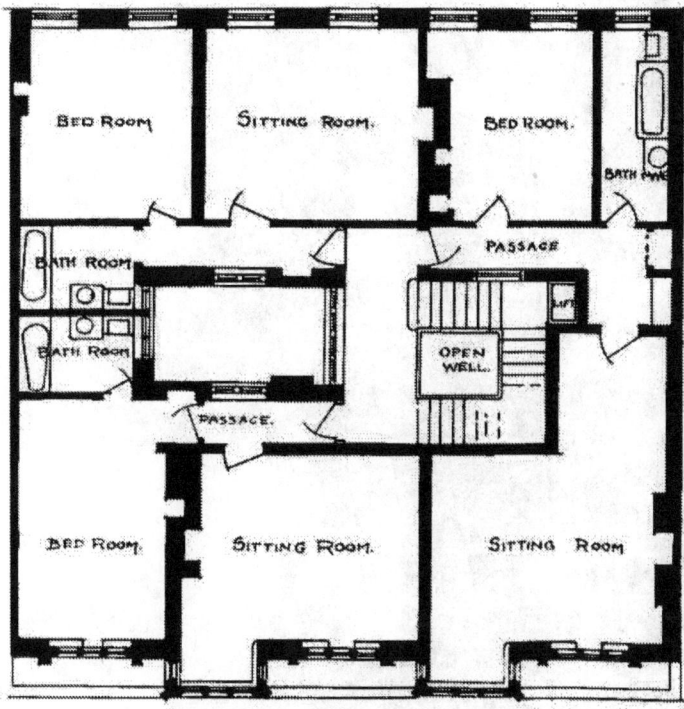

SCALE OF | 10 5 0 10 20 30 FEET

FIRST FLOOR PLAN

FIG. 149.——MOUNT STREET.

Ernest George & Yeates, Architects.

FIG. 149A.—MOUNT STREET, W.

Ernest George & Peto, Architects.

having more than the one usual bedroom.   The bath-room has a W.C.
apparatus ; this is the general rule for bachelors' flats.

Nos. 104-112 Mount Street (Fig. 150).—These suites have the
usual accommodation of sitting-room, bedroom, and bath-room.   The
caretaker's rooms are on the fourth floor.   A view of these buildings
is given opposite.

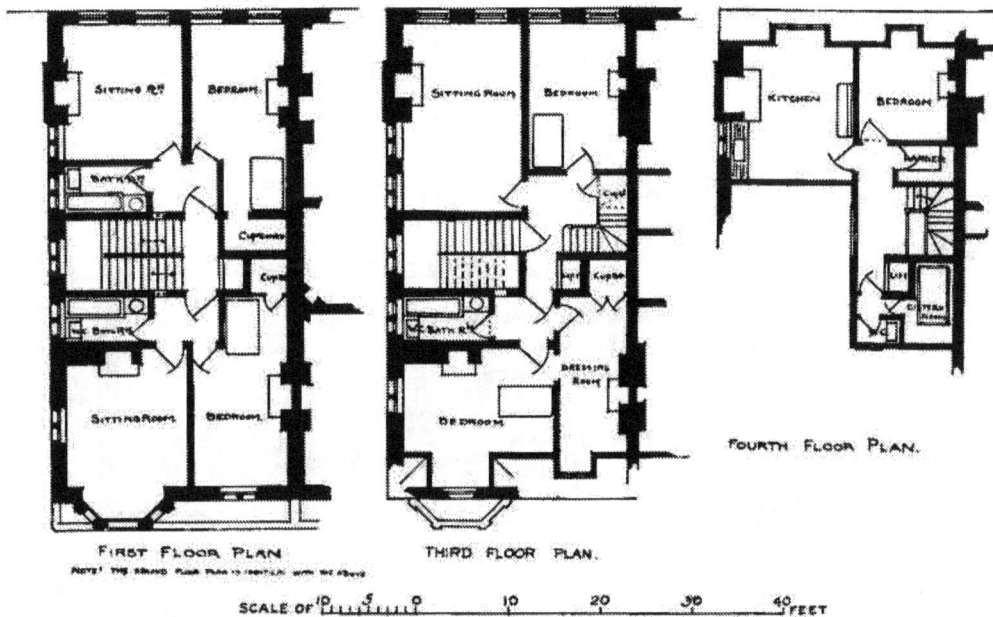

FIG. 150.—NOS. 104 TO 112 MOUNT STREET, W.

Ernest George & Peto, Architects.

Bachelors' Chambers, Park Lane, W. (Figs. 151 and 152).
—In each of these suites there is a long passage between the rooms.
This is much appreciated by the tenants, who have accommodation for
extra bookcases, pictures, &c.   The store-rooms have also proved
useful.   The W.C. is in some instances divided from the lavatory ; this
is unusual.   The caretaker occupies the basement.   The staircase has
a top light ; it was erected before the restriction in the present Building
Act came into force.   A view of the front is given in Fig. 151A.

Marlborough Chambers, Jermyn Street, W. (Fig. 153).—
These are some of the best and most expensive suites in London.

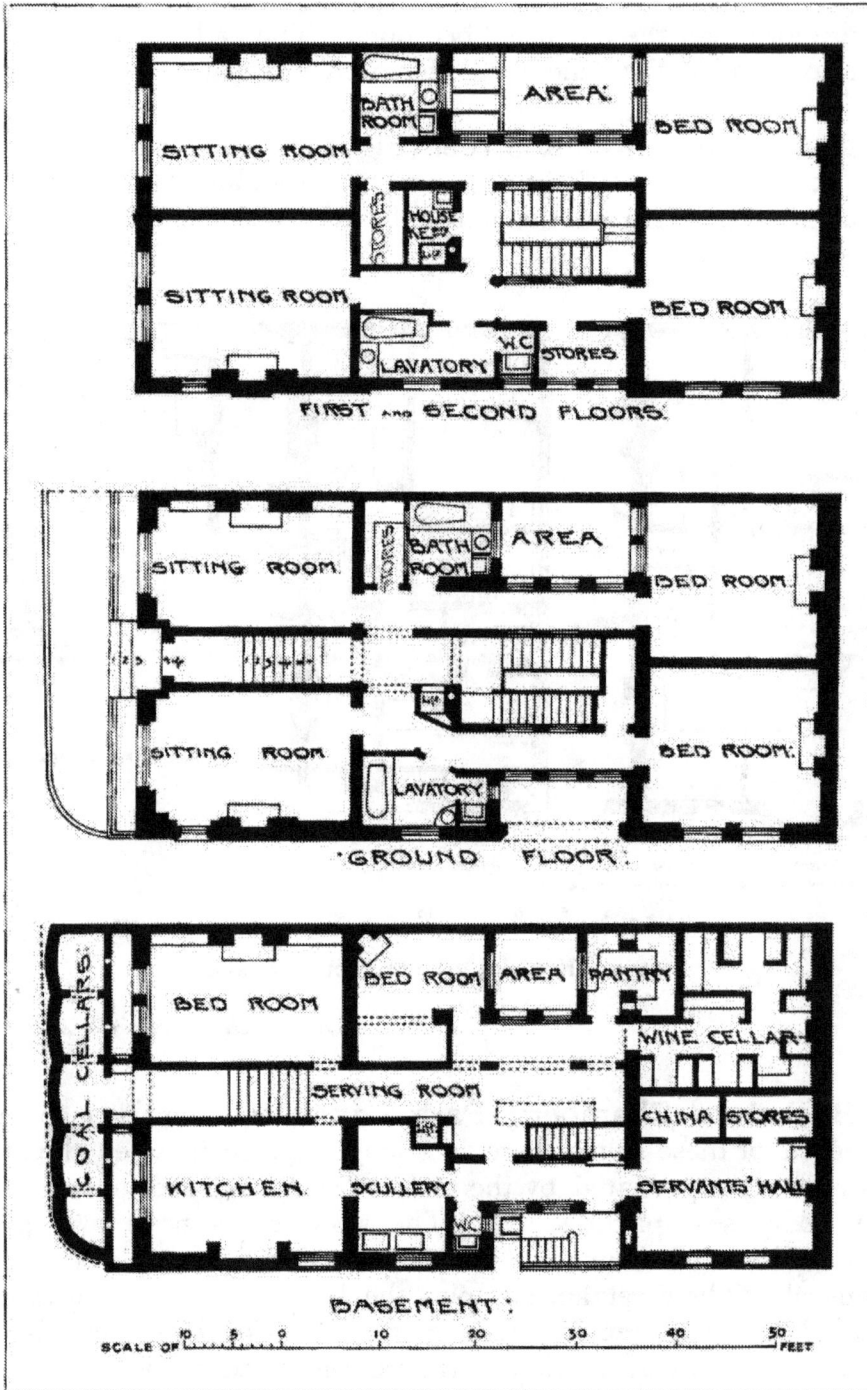

FIG. 151.—BACHELORS' CHAMBERS, PARK LANE, W.

A. Waterhouse, R.A., Architect.

FIG. 151A.—BACHELORS' CHAMBERS, PARK LANE, W.

A. Waterhouse, R.A., Architect.

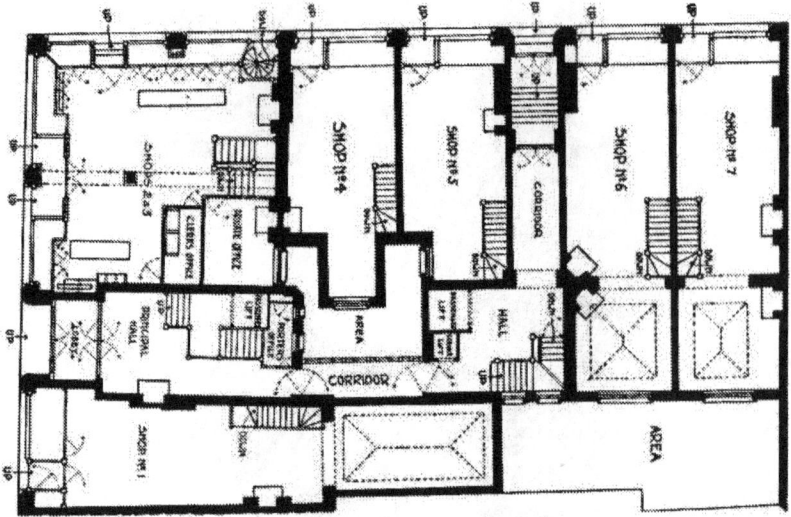

GROUND FLOOR PLAN.

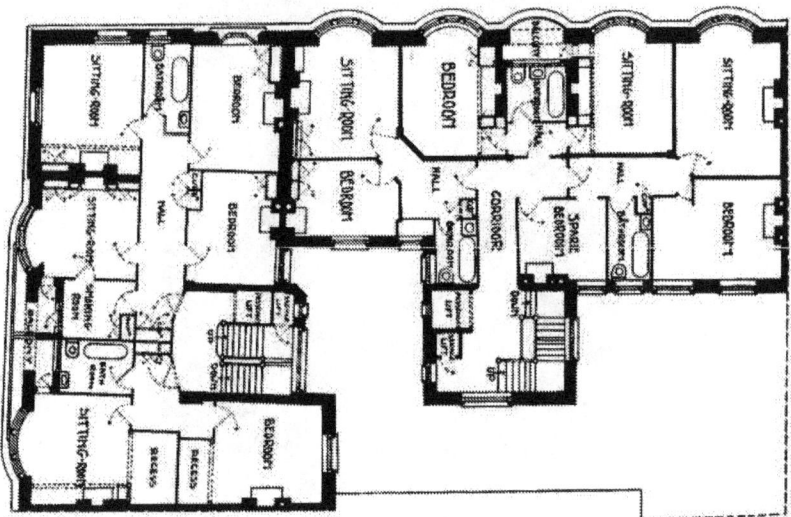

FIRST FLOOR PLAN.

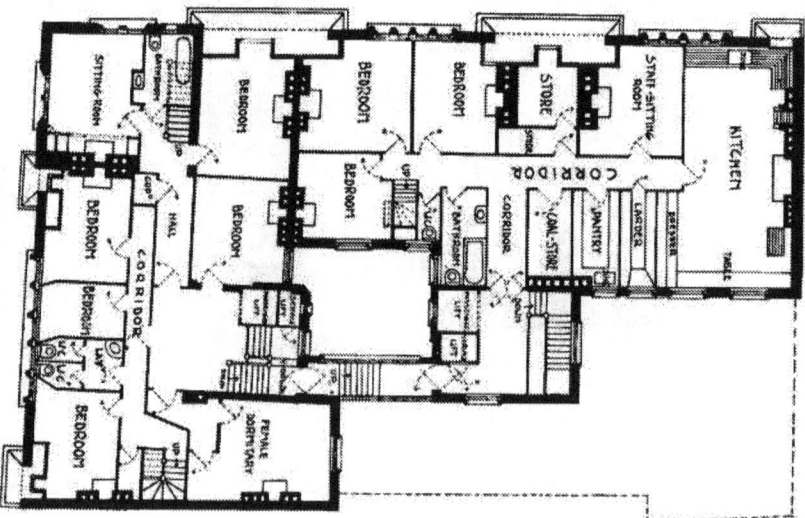

FIFTH FLOOR PLAN.

Fig. 153.—MARLBOROUGH CHAMBERS, JERMYN STREET, W.

Reginald Morphew, Architect.

SCALE OF

FIG. 153A.—MARLBOROUGH CHAMBERS, JERMYN STREET, W.

Reginald Morphew, Architect.

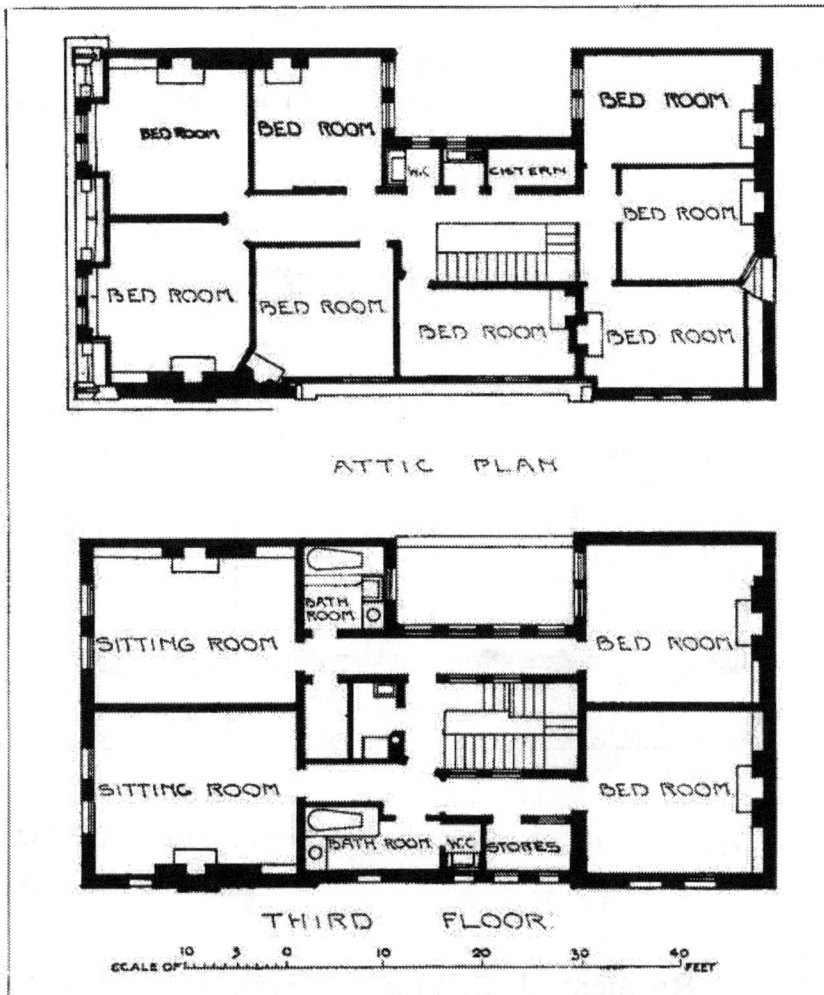

FIG. 152.—CHAMBERS, PARK LANE, W.

Alfred Waterhouse, R.A., Architect.

The recess in the sitting-room is formed to take a small table. The lighting of the private halls is by borrowed light; it is ample, and has been referred to in a previous chapter, which also describes the height of rooms and passages. This building has a sub-basement, so general in Vienna and so rare in England. The top floor shows the accommodation for the staff. In many bachelors' suites the breakfast only is served; in this building provision has been made for serving all meals. Some suites have two sitting-rooms and two bedrooms. A view of this block is given on the opposite page.

Nos. 18, 19, and 20 Jermyn Street, Piccadilly, S.W. (Fig. 154).—A small building with three suites on each floor. On one there is a combined bed and sitting-room, which is sure to let easily in a good neighbourhood.

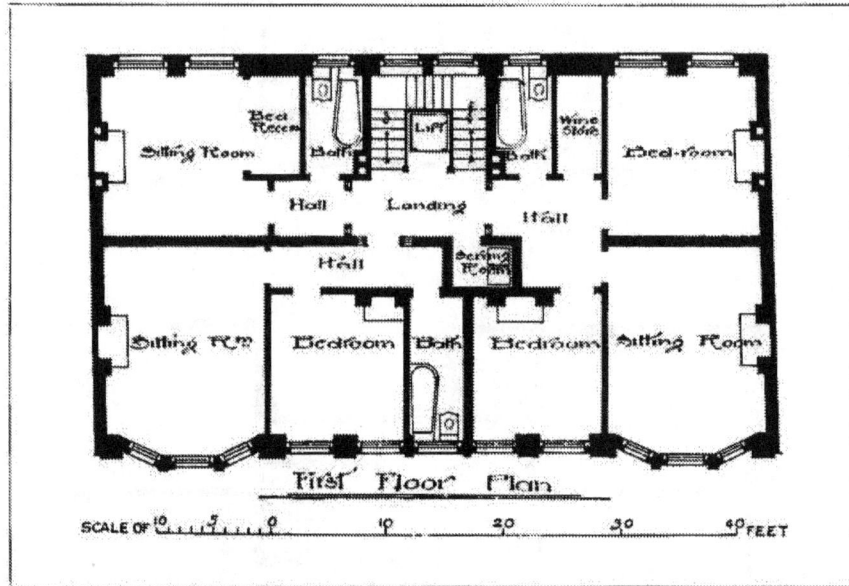

FIG. 154.—NOS. 18, 19, AND 20 JERMYN STREET, PICCADILLY, S.W.

E. Keynes Purchase, Architect.

Ladies' Residential Chambers (Figs. 155 and 156).—The tenants are principally artists, authors, nurses, and other workers. There is a joint pantry and W.C. for each two suites, which are planned on a different principle to bachelors' flats. There is a common dining-room, and it will be noticed that there is only one bath-room for the two floors shown, containing thirteen suites. A view of the building is given on the opposite page.

Campden House Chambers (Figs. 157 and 158).—A block of catering flats, the suites having two, three, or four rooms. The pantry should be noted; this is necessary when meals are served in the suite, and useful in all cases as stated above. The basement plan shows the common dining-room, kitchen, accommodation for the staff, &c. There is a small furnace room under a part of the basement.

Fig. 154A.—Ladies' Residential Chambers, York Street, W.

Balfour & Turner, Architects.

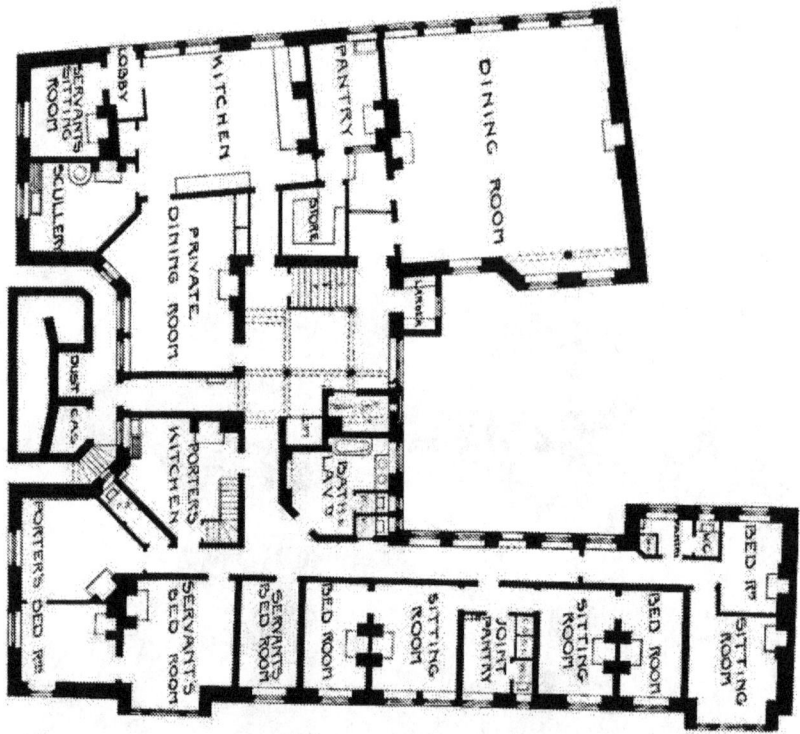

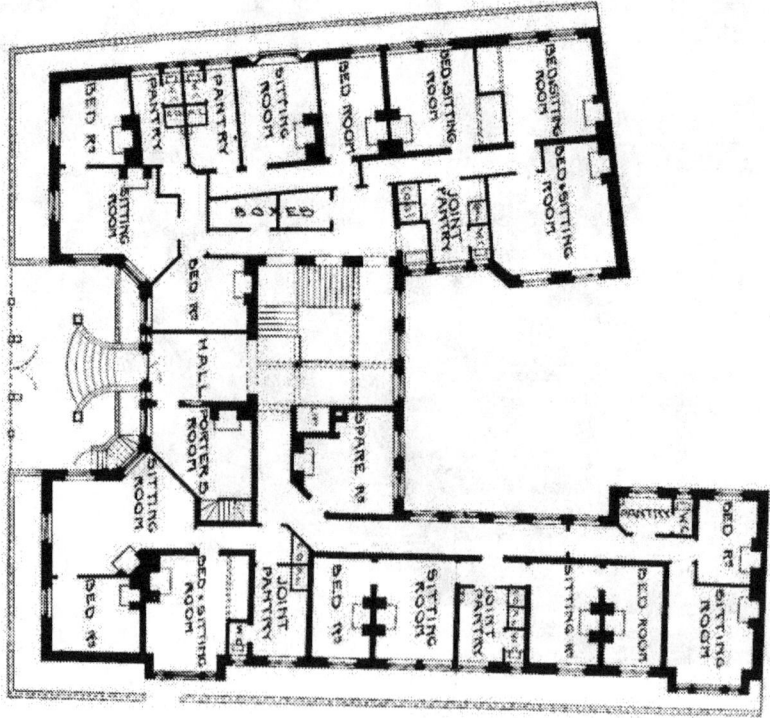

FIGS. 155, 156.—LADIES' RESIDENTIAL CHAMBERS, YORK STREET, W.

Balfour & Turner, Architects.

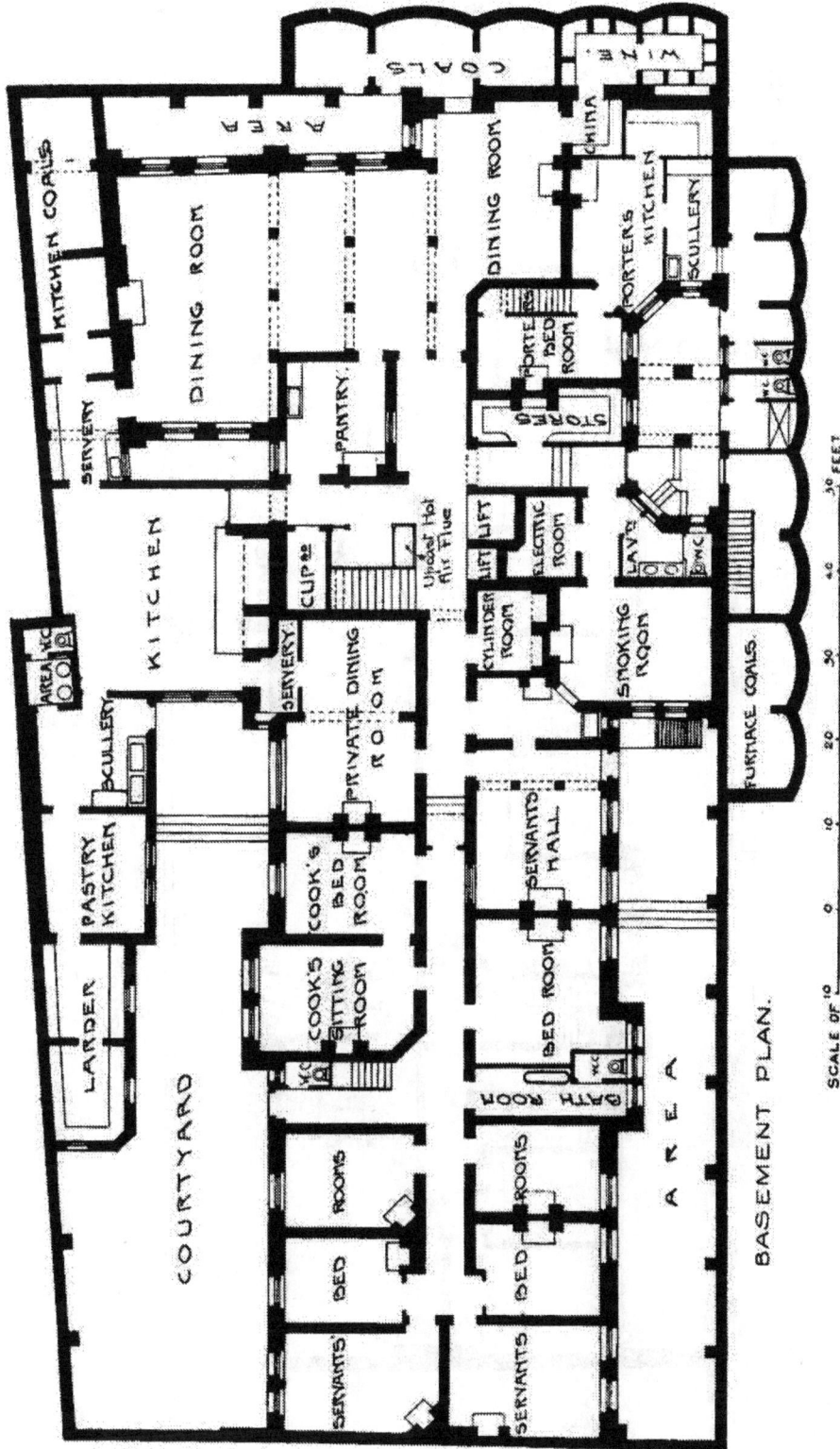

FIG. 157.—CAMPDEN HOUSE CHAMBERS.

Balfour & Turner, Architects.

BASEMENT PLAN.

SCALE OF
0   10   20   30   40   50 FEET

BICYCLE HOUSE

HALL

PORTER'S ROOM

LIFT

LIFT ATTENDT

WAITING ROOM

OFFICE

Balfour & Turner, Architects.

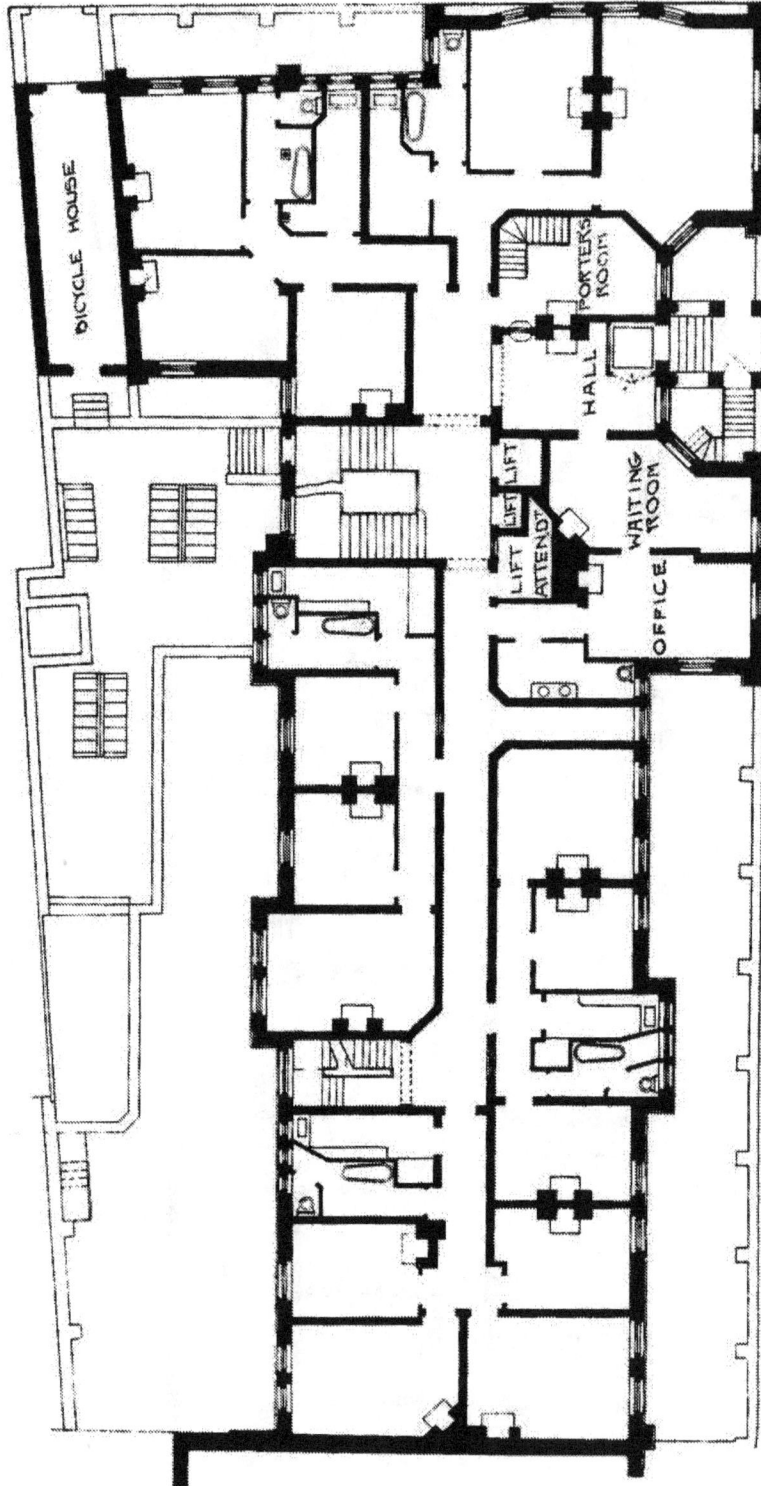

SCALE OF 10   0   10   20   30   40   50 FEET

FIG 158.—CAMPDEN HOUSE CHAMBERS.

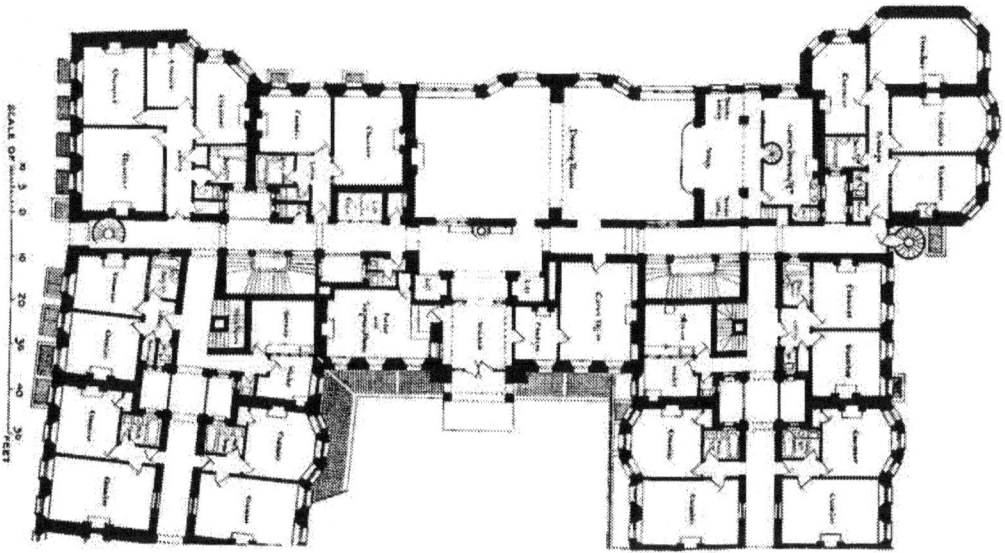

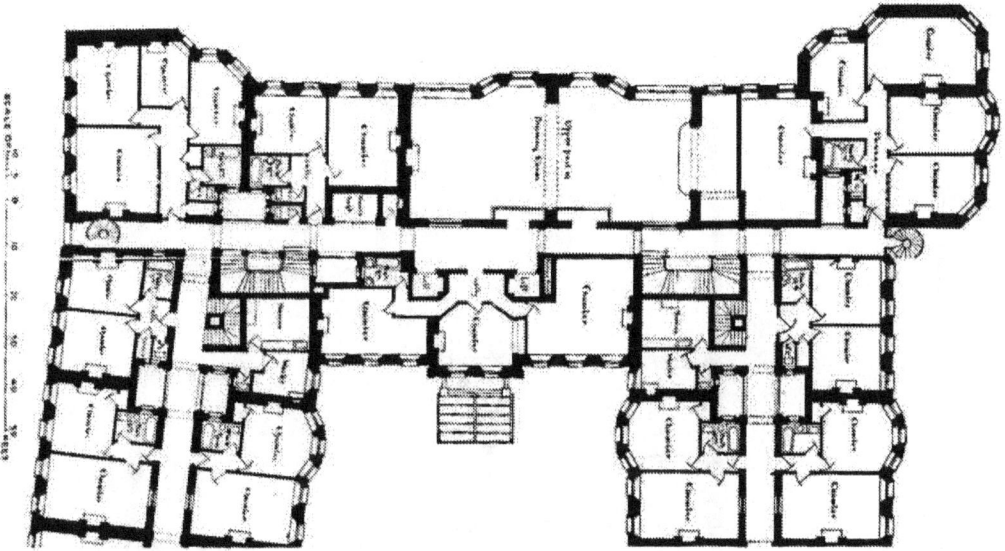

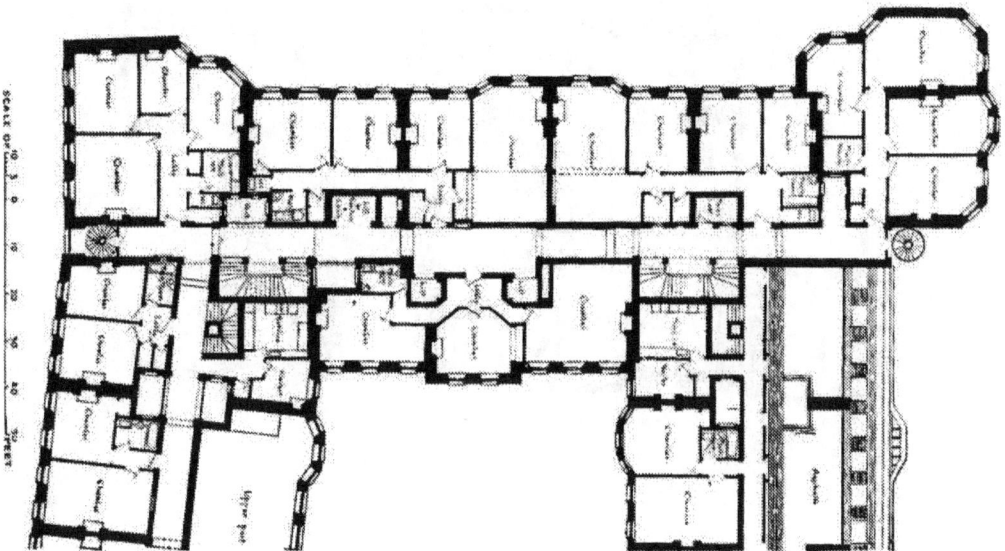

FIG. 159.—QUEEN ANNE'S MANSIONS, WESTMINSTER.

E. R. Robson (Present) Architect.

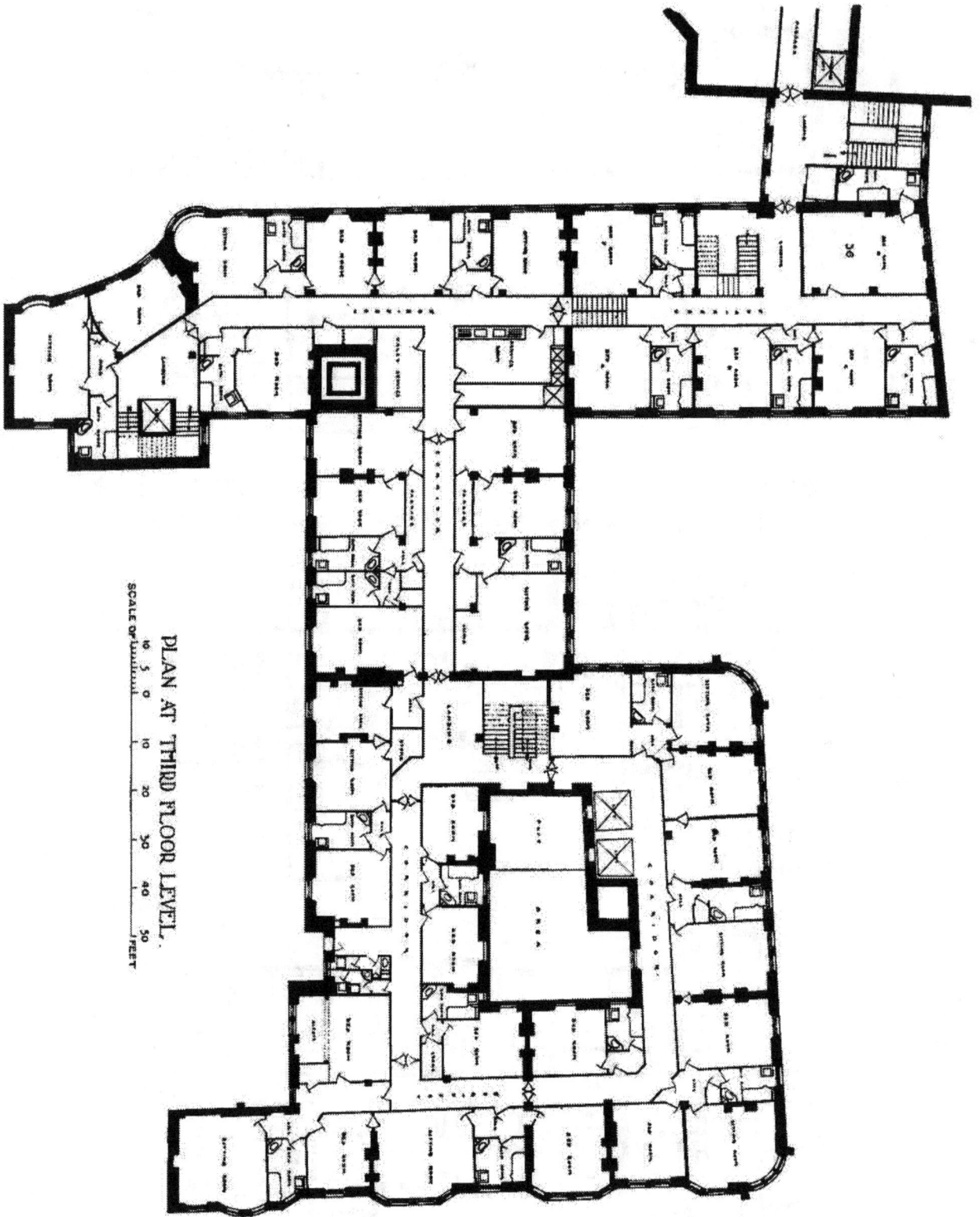

PLAN AT THIRD FLOOR LEVEL.

SCALE OF FEET

10 5 0   10   20   30   40   50
                                                FEET

PLAN AT GROUND FLOOR LEVEL.

SCALE OF 10 5 0 10 20 30 40 FEET

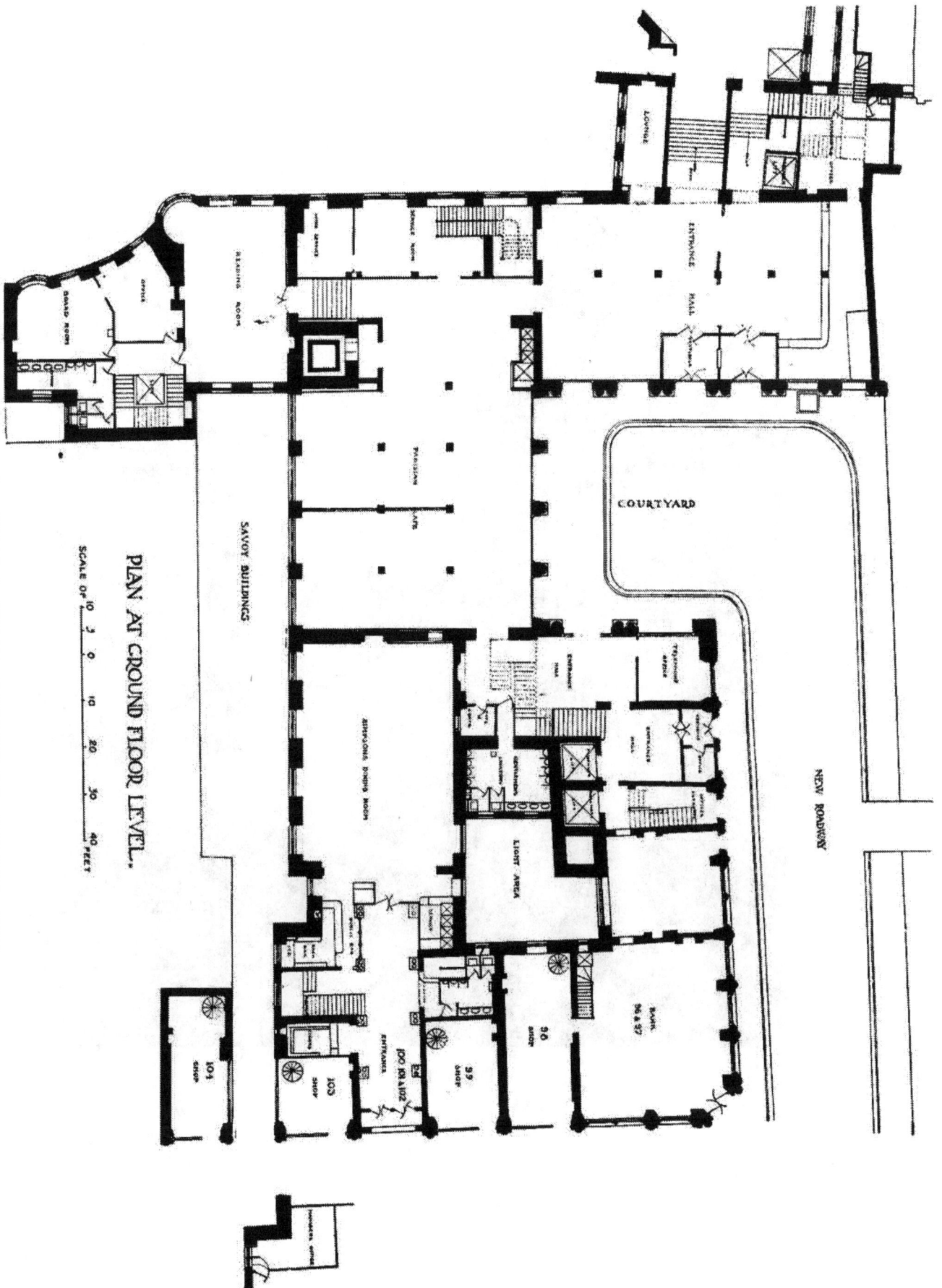

FIGS. 160 AND 161.—SAVOY HOTEL EXTENSION, STRAND, W.C.

T. E. Collcutt,} Joint
Stanley Hamp,} Architects.

COURTYARD

NEW ROADWAY

SAVOY BUILDINGS

ENTRANCE HALL

READING ROOM

BOARD ROOM

OFFICE

RESTAURANT DINING ROOM

LIGHT AREA

SHOP

101 SHOP

103 SHOP

100 STRAND ENTRANCE

99 SHOP

98 SHOP

96 & 97

160A. SAVOY HOTEL EXTENSION.

T. E. Collcutt,
Stanley H. Hamp, } Architects.

Queen Anne's Mansions, Westminster (Fig. 159).—A small portion is shown of this building, the largest block of catering flats in England. The suites have varying numbers of rooms, and there are general dining-rooms, drawing-rooms, &c., making the whole similar to a residential hotel.

Savoy Hotel.—Figs. 160 and 161 show the recent extension, where are suites with varying numbers of rooms. The meals are served either in the private rooms or in the public rooms of the hotel. For some years past the managers of catering flats have been doing an ordinary hotel business. This is the first instance of a large hotel letting off suites of rooms at a yearly rental in every way similar to catering flats, and the advantages over the ordinary catering flat are considerable. Fig. 160A shows a photographic view of the block.

Chapter V.

PRACTICAL NOTES.

The construction of a block of flats is exactly similar to any other building, but certain special requirements exist, and the architect must attempt to meet them.

Penetration of Sound.—For instance it is annoying in an ordinary private house for noise in one room to be heard in another, but the annoyance becomes greater in a block of flats, for what may be suffered in patience in the former case will not be tolerated in the latter buildings.

Floors and Ceilings.—Where expense is considered it is usual to form the fireproof floor with I iron or steel joists, each about 7 in. by 3 in. and about 3 ft. to 4 ft. apart; concrete is filled in between, and small wood bearers are laid on the concrete and the floor boards are nailed to them, being kept clear of the steel joists so as not to transmit sound. Coke breeze is sometimes filled in dry between the wood bearers. Wire lathing is frequently fixed under the flange of the joist to prevent the plaster cracking. The wood bearers are usually about 4 by 3 in. and should not be fixed into the concrete on account of the sound being transmitted. It has been suggested that these bearers might rest on felt; they should never rest on the iron joists.

The ceiling often cracks along the line of joist, and a builder of large experience considers the cause is that the centring for the concrete is removed too soon; he has never known a ceiling crack when time has been allowed for the concrete to set thoroughly.

If the wood bearers are bedded in the concrete and the floor is covered with linoleum, dry rot is likely to take place. If the centring for the concrete is covered with some coarse ashes, the concrete will have a rough surface, and form a much better key than is usual for the plaster.

Sometimes an air space is formed between the concrete floor and the ceiling ; this is, however, rarely done, for should such an expense be contemplated it would be cheaper to have one of the patent floors constructed with cavities.

In some flats the concrete is finished with a smooth cement face, no wood flooring is fixed, but the floors are entirely covered with linoleum or cork carpet. This is a good system to adopt for basements even if it is not used on the upper floors. On account of appearance the linoleum or cork carpet should be laid down before attempting to let the suites ; people who view the flats are informed the rent includes the linoleum.

The idea of a hollow space in the floor is of course to prevent the penetration of sound. Most of the patent floors contain this air space, and there are many good systems in the market. In some cases terracotta is used for floors and also partitions ; a key is formed in the material, and only one coat of plaster is necessary.

In basements a wood block system is the best, and should be fixed in the best suites ; cement covered with linoleum is cold to the feet.

Asphalte Floors.—If a concrete floor is finished with asphalte it is much warmer than it would be with an ordinary cement face.

Linoleum laid on a wood floor is useless to prevent sound, and should never be allowed on account of the chance of its causing dry rot.

Wires and Pipes.—No wires or pipes should be placed under a floor except where absolutely necessary.

Carpets.—Much can be done by carpets to deaden sound. If thick felt and thick carpets are laid not only in all rooms but also in the passages, the result will be found most satisfactory. If managers would insist on this it would be a great benefit to the tenants.

Partitions.—The plaster slabs for partitions now made by many firms are very convenient ; the finished thickness is less than a quarter partition, and there are other advantages. If it is desirable to take special precautions to prevent sound penetrating from one room to the next, two of these partitions can be built with a small hollow space between.

Some of these patent partitions are constructed on the same system as the fireproof floors, having a hollow space. Many are well known ; some finish 2½ in. with a face ready to be painted or papered. The terra-cotta blocks are very light, and have large hollow spaces as stated above.

Division of Rooms.—If it is decided to leave a space that may if required be divided into two or more rooms, the building can be finished so as to be in a complete state to attract tenants. Any partition can rest on the floor boards; the patents referred to are easy and clean to construct, and are soon erected.

Walls.—The steel construction of external walls in America has attracted much attention here. Little advantage is gained by adopting the system in London on account of the present Building Act; the walls would have to be as thick for filling in the framing as if it did not exist. A new Building Act is contemplated, and no doubt this special form of construction will be provided for. Under the present Act a wall of an area a few feet long is as thick as a main wall. If the reader will refer to some of the French plans, such as Figs. 165, 167, or 171, he will see how thin the walls of the areas are, and the great gain of light and air to the rooms and passages of the buildings, which are more healthy in consequence.

Dust Shoots.—Although some architects prefer dust shoots for artisans' dwellings, they are practically unknown in better class dwellings. The dust pail system is universal; the pail is taken down every morning by the porter, who also fills the coal scuttles. The manager of one block of moderate-sized buildings spends a shilling each week on tips for dustmen, otherwise they will not take away the refuse—not always dust—that tenants will put in the bins. The dust is collected twice a week.

Flues.—To prevent a flue smoking, great care should be used at each bend. A 9 in. by 9 in. flue often becomes much larger than that size, and this is a frequent cause of the trouble. The flue should be carefully constructed exactly the same size for the entire length. If the stove is not well bricked in between the top and the arch the air space will also cause the flue to smoke. There should also be an angle formed above the fireplace, taking care that it projects far enough to cover the openings below, as in Fig. 162.

Staircases.—Attention has been called to the circular and oval staircases so general on the Continent, but so rare in England. The shape is pleasing, and "dancing stairs" are easy going, but the great objection is the difficulty of laying carpets on any form of winders. Where carpets are fixed, ordinary flyers and landings are the most convenient.

Trade Staircases.—These are provided more particularly as a means of escape in case of fire. The gate or door at the street level should be fitted with a night latch, so that it cannot be used without a key for entrance at night time. As pointed out elsewhere, these trade staircases allow the servants to leave the flat at any time—the mistress cannot tell when they come and go. Formerly, when there was only one entrance to the flats, she could note any exits or entrances, but that is all changed. Again, these trade staircases open up a fresh field for the enterprising burglar, and precautions should be taken. In most French blocks there is one entrance only from the street; all visitors and tradespeople must pass the concierge, and then proceed either to the main staircase or the trade staircase (see Figs. 164 and 172). This system has obvious advantages, but tenants might object

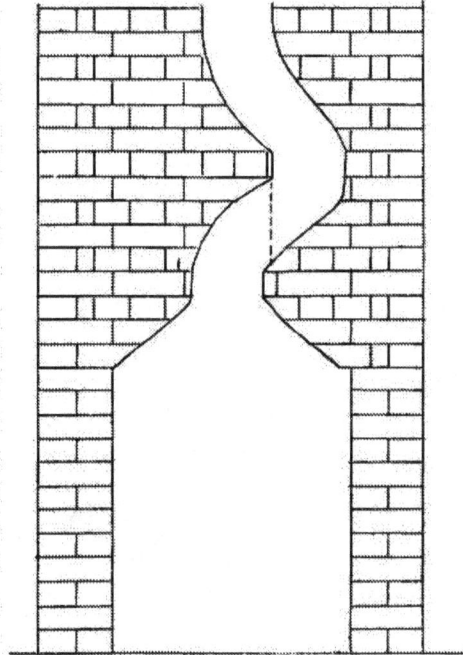

FIG. 162.

to it in England. The two exits would certainly be better in the case of a fire.

Balconies.—If a balcony is carried across the windows of two adjacent suites with a low division between, it would often be a useful means of escape in case of fire. Another idea is to fix a stone sill, projecting about 18 in., and having a high railing extending the whole length of two adjacent windows. The kitchen windows of suites are often close together, and this can be done at small expense, and form a ready means of escape. It is unlikely that a fire will occur at the same time in two adjoining flats. A fire spreads upwards, and some such simple means of escape might save many lives.

Baths and other Fittings.—Tenants are often attracted by the appearance of sanitary and other fittings, and money is well spent on good lavatory basins, and porcelain baths always look clean and bright.

The light and appearance of the kitchen, scullery, and bath-room are improved if the walls are tiled. Cupboard accommodation is much valued. At Marlborough Chambers (Fig. 153) each sitting-room has a bookcase, with drawers, cellarette, and coal cabinet under. These bachelor suites are exceptionally well designed, and these fittings are all suitable for the rooms. The bedrooms have fixed wardrobes, but it is doubtful if this expense should be incurred. Most tenants have their own furniture, and want to use it, and the extra cost for the owner is considerable.

At the residential suites in connection with the Savoy Hotel (Figs. 160 and 161), there are many attractive features. Every bath-room has a shower bath, electro-plated steam-heated towel rails are fixed, similar to those mentioned above, telephones are provided for each tenant, and letters can be posted on every floor. In expensive suites the owners must try to give the tenants some convenience or luxury they cannot get elsewhere.

Speaking tubes should be fixed from the hall to each suite.

Gas and Electric Light.—Gas pipes should be fixed throughout each suite and a meter fixed near the entrance. In many buildings the pipes are connected to each stove ready for a gas fire, and to a position for a gas stove in the kitchen or scullery. The cost is not heavy in the first instance, but if floors and walls have to be cut away after the building is finished the expense is increased considerably.

Every suite should be wired throughout for electric light; each tenant usually has his own meter.

No pipes and wires for a suite should pass through any other suite, the main supplies should be up the staircase, and branches taken to each flat. This is a great convenience if any alterations have to be made, or in the case of a burst pipe or a leakage.

Lifts.—As stated in the chapter on planning, the most convenient arrangement is to have a lift serving not more than two suites on each floor. It is a mistake to serve a large number of suites on one floor. The cost of the lift is not of great importance in a large building, and a boy can work one. In the old blocks of flats most of the lifts are hydraulic, but electric lifts are preferred by most architects. One manager works his lift by the London Hydraulic Power Company. It costs £15 per annum for sixty elevations each day; each elevation is registered and an average is taken. The lift cost £150.

In "The Ansonia" buildings, New York (Figs. 202 and 203), the "Plunger elevators" are used; these are hydraulic. They are said to be perfectly safe and to keep in good repair. The company guarantees to keep them in order for ten years for £4 a year.

The question of hydraulic or electric power for the lifts is one point the architect has to decide. Electric lifts are of more recent date, and the public have been, as usual, somewhat slow to accept a new idea; then again the first of these lifts were not altogether satisfactory, but no complaint can be justified against those of to-day. A few years ago there was trouble in working a lift on an alternating current, but that difficulty has been successfully overcome.

The cost of an electric lift is greater for the first outlay than for an hydraulic elevator, the former costing about 30 per cent. more, but this is an unimportant fact when the annual outlay for working a lift is considered. Electric power costs about one-fifth of hydraulic power. In one large building the annual expenditure for working two passenger and four service lifts by hydraulic power is £84; by electric power it would be about £16.

With regard to repairs, one large firm that makes both classes of lifts charges the same amount per annum for keeping them in order, about five or six pounds in each case.

In Germany there is often no lift attendant, and the passenger works it by means of what is known as the "push button system." This is very simple, and has been used in England, but it is expensive, and as there must be attendants for other duties, there is little advantage in using the system for flats.

In addition to the trade lift a little lift for parcels is sometimes made. This costs little, and is a great convenience to servants, as the heavy trade lift is not used for every little packet.

Water for Baths and Drinking.—In the Ansonia, New York, the water that is supplied to the bath-rooms is four times filtered, and all the water that goes to the butlers' pantries for drinking purposes is delivered there just above freezing-point, and is hygeia-condensed water. Every suite has a refrigerator.

Roofs.—If the top floor is let as a suite, roofing felt or some other substance should always be used to keep the rooms as cool as possible. If the roof is a flat and used by the other tenants, the noise is likely to be a nuisance to the people below. If it should be decided to have a roof garden, it is usually constructed of vulcanite or some similar patent. One of the claims of this substance is that the temperature in the rooms on the top story is less affected than under an ordinary roof. This point should be carefully considered, for in summer the heat in the top floor of some blocks of flats is almost unbearable.

Blinds.—The rent sometimes includes the use of blinds to the front windows; this is done with a view to obtaining a uniform appearance for the building. The owner renews when required, and at the same time for all the suites.

Width of Stairs, Doors, &c.—The entrance door to each suite and the doors of the rooms should be of sufficient width to allow furniture to be moved in and out without damaging the building. Awkward angles should be avoided. This same care should be exercised with reference to the staircase, particularly in flats where there is no lift.

Windows.—As a rule sash windows are better than casements for a town house; they are more convenient for ventilating bedrooms, and a building such as that shown in the frontispiece is effective and cheap.

Objection is sometimes made to casements because they are awkward to clean; but this only happens if odd numbers are fixed. If a single casement is hung, or if there are three, five, or seven, and so on, then one casement will have to be cleaned from the outside. On the other hand if there are two, four, six, or eight, or any even number, and they are hung folding or to alternate mullions, they can all be cleaned, provided none are fixed.

Cisterns.—Each flat should have a cold-water cistern in case the supply is cut off. This is preferable to one large cistern for all the suites. Everything should be done to make each dwelling self-contained, so that in case of complaint the public authorities can be communicated with by the tenants. The owner should avoid any responsibility he possibly can.

Hot-Water Supply.—This also applies to the supply of hot water to all the suites from a furnace and apparatus in the basement. In the case of bachelor or catering suites this is of course necessary, but it is not advisable in the ordinary self-contained flats. If the owner thinks that he can attract tenants by the fact that hot water can be obtained at any time, night and day, or that he will get higher rents in consequence, let him of course do so, but it is very doubtful if he will, and many managers say that this hot-water supply is a constant cause of trouble and annoyance. Two tenants will complain at the same time, one saying that the water is too hot, and the other that it is too cold. Then again the owner contracts to do something that he is dependent upon a servant to have properly performed. The less he undertakes to do, the fewer excuses there will be for complaints, and the tenants of the flats do not hesitate to complain upon the slightest cause. Generally the advice of the managers and owners is, Do not do it. It is not a new idea, but was tried in flats quite twenty-five years ago. In the case of one of the largest estates of flats extending over several streets in London, the first block was built with hot-water supply, and the architect was instructed to omit the system in all subsequent buildings. It is not advisable to have the same system of hot water to supply baths and also radiators throughout a large building. In the summer the radiators are not in use and the heating surface scales off; the result is that bath valves become damaged, and after a short time require renewing. The owner of one block of flats had to spend £57 in one year upon new valves in consequence of his only having one hot-water system.

If hot water is supplied to each tenant, there should be radiators in the public and private passages and halls. A radiator is often fixed in the entrance hall of each suite. If the hot-water pipe in a bath-room is fixed so as to project a few inches, it makes a cheap towel rail. For better class flats the fixed hollow towel rails are much used, hot water circulating through them.

Although there may be a storage cistern of, say, 75 gallons in each flat, there should be a draw-off direct from the rising main; this is advisable for drinking purposes.

On account of height of rooms in flats the cylinder is frequently placed in a horizontal position, and acts equally well.

Exteriors.—Some blocks of flats are as objectionable in appearance as any buildings in London, for builders' ideas of architecture are, to say the least, remarkable. Fortunately an architect has been employed in many cases, and some illustrations, mostly from photographs, are given in Chapter IV. of selected examples of various classes.

Even if one regards flats purely from a business point of view the

question of the exterior must be considered. In the case of one
building in which no attempt at architecture had been made, which was
simply what is usually called "bricks and mortar," the manager said
that the appearance of the flats often drove away a likely applicant.
It is clear that certain outlay and thought expended upon the exterior
will repay the owner.

The design of a block of flats presents certain difficulties not
usually met with in other domestic buildings. The block is generally
higher than a private house, and each floor is the same height, whereas
in the case of ordinary domestic work the first floor is usually higher
than the floors above, which helps an elevation out. If balconies are
required to each floor, the difficulties of a satisfactory appearance are
increased. Lastly, the cost must always be kept down as much as
possible.

In the case of a very high building two stories can be treated as
one, a main dividing line such as a string course being built to alternate
floors, and perhaps pilasters having the full height of the two stories
can be added. A heavy balcony of stone may be built to one floor
and a light iron balcony fixed to the floor above. The lower stories
of the Ansonia, New York (Fig. 203) indicate the principle; the
balconies are used as main horizontal lines on alternate floors.

CHAPTER VI.

FOREIGN FLATS.

UNFORTUNATELY, it was only possible to reproduce a very few of the plans and photographs obtained. Those selected have been chosen after careful consideration ; nearly every plan has been redrawn, and has the English scale. The names of the rooms of those redrawn are in English. On account of the great reduction of some of the plans, many lines have been omitted, such as those showing ceiling decoration, doors, construction, &c. ; this was done to make the plan as clear as possible. Each is given solely to show the arrangement of the rooms.

HEIGHT OF BUILDINGS.

The regulation of the height of buildings is general on the Continent. In Paris, according to the decree of 13th August 1902, the limit for the widest streets is about 65 ft. In Vienna in the central positions the limit is five stories, the level of the floor of the top story to be about 65 ft. above the pavement; in the outlying districts not more than four stories are allowed. In Berlin, under the regulations of 1897, the limit is about 72 ft. for the widest streets. In Budapest the limit is four stories, maximum height about 82 ft. for the widest streets.

Paris.—"The magnificence of modern Parisian streets is almost entirely due to the flat system ; the apparent meanness of English towns is due to our separate houses," so wrote the late Mr P. G. Hamerton, who was no lover of flats, in his recent book on Paris. Although we may not be inclined to entirely agree with him, it is universally acknowledged that Paris is one of the finest cities in the world, and practically all the private residences are flats. But there are other reasons for our admiration, such as the width of the streets, and the universal use of a beautiful building stone. A visitor is struck with the uniformity of the buildings, due to the regulations which limit the height and also the projections. The dimensions of the courtyards are also fixed so that the rooms at the rear may be properly lighted and ventilated.

In the early days of the flat movement, when English and American architects were struggling with the difficulties of planning, charming buildings were being erected in Paris, showing the result of long experience ; and going further back it is astonishing to see the date of the buildings in Calliat's books * when we think of the suites, with dark rooms and cramped passages, that were built at a much later date in England, and still more recently in America.

After examining many French plans, the general impression conveyed is a certain sense of luxury, quite irrespective of the class of buildings. Everything is done on a broader-minded principle than with us. A flat is supposed to be a house, but the sizes of some English rooms and passages seem rather to suggest a ship. No one can say that of French buildings. We are struck with the space given to the entrances ; the areas and recesses are ample, the rooms are large, and the principal passages become corridors.

We all know the difficulties of a site with an acute angle at the corner of two streets, and to see the French architect at his best we should examine the plans of some of these corner buildings. He seems to revel in the defect, and seizes upon it to transform it into the most attractive feature of the plan. This, indeed, happens with many eminent architects of all countries. We admire some feature in a building, usually with reference to the plan, and upon inquiry we find it is due to some great difficulty the architect had to surmount ; not only has he done so, but he has turned his difficulty to such account that it has become the most attractive feature of his building.

The skilful treatment of rooms with a shape that is irregular upon a skeleton plan has already been referred to. It is an art in which the French architect excels, and as so many sites are irregular, an examination of almost any plan will furnish an example.

There seems little doubt that the popular idea with English people is that all bedrooms in a Paris flat communicate, and so passages are avoided. It is true that some such arrangement does exist, but for the purpose of this book a very large number of plans of modern buildings were obtained from Paris, and in every case the rooms were found to have doors into a passage as in England ; doors between the rooms were also provided, a useful provision in flats, for a room adjoining a bedroom may be used as a dressing-room or boudoir, or two rooms may be used as day and night nurseries, and should

* "Parallèle des Maisons de Paris," 2 vols., folio. Paris, 1857-64.

communicate. When planning a private house, the use for each room is decided by the owner before erection, but flats are different. The architect has to provide a certain number of rooms for an unknown occupant, who will use them as he decides. It is no uncommon thing for a dining-room in one suite to become a bedroom in the suite above.

Perhaps the greatest contrast between English and French plans is the staircase. In Paris it is an important feature; the plan is usually oval, circular, or curved in some other way. "Dancing stairs" are the rule abroad and the exception here. The main entrance also receives much attention; it is carefully planned, and much money is spent upon decoration. Mr Hamerton wrote: "The French habit of living in flats makes one doorway the entrance to many buildings, so that an amount of ornament may be lavished upon it which would be extravagant and impossible for a single tenant."

The lift is not usually placed in the well hole of the stairs; it is kept apart, and seems to be considered an undesirable object. Often a recess is formed in the walls of the staircase, and the door alone is visible. The staircase is always a central and important feature. With us the use of the lift became general about the time that flats began to flourish. Not so in Paris: the beauty of the staircase as well as its importance was a tradition; the lift was an innovation, ugly and undesirable; it was disliked, and kept in the background. The result is peculiar; a fine staircase is provided, but people do not use it, as they travel by the lift. Bearing this in mind, would it not be better for us in England to spend as little as possible on the staircase, making the width no more than is absolutely necessary, but to make an attractive feature of each landing, and of course to spend money on the entrance hall? Expense saved upon the stairs might be spent upon the main entrance and the landings.

The plan that appears to be most favoured, when the site permits, is one with two suites to each floor, a large courtyard in the centre, the two suites meeting at the front of the block and at the other side of the courtyard.

A peculiar feature of French plans is the "toilette" opening off each bedroom. Such an arrangement makes the bedroom appear tidy, but the space devoted to two bedrooms and two toilettes is often sufficient for three bedrooms, and seems to us, with our ideas regulated by rent, a waste of space. The bath-room is frequently sandwiched between two bedrooms, with entrances from each and also from the passage—a good arrangement, as it will also serve as a dressing-room. This is also the general custom in America.

It is to be regretted that many English people still think that it is the general practice for French architects to build the W.C. without any ventilation to the outer air. An examination of modern plans of first class architects will show that such an arrangement is extremely rare. As a rule the French plan, from a sanitary point of view, is good, and much resembles English plans. The bath-room is rarely provided with a W.C. apparatus, and the system of ventilating into the small air shafts, so common in America, seems unknown. With regard to a W.C. apparatus in the bath-room, French people seem to object to such an arrangement.

The trade staircase is always enclosed, and we do not see the iron erection so general in London : this staircase is allowed to be top-lighted as ours should be, and the servants' W.C. often opens off this staircase. This is constantly done in offices in London, and there seems no objection to having one servants' W.C. for two suites ; each tenant would have a key. Such an arrangement might be useful for small flats, or where the site was limited, or in some way peculiar. It is better than entering from a scullery, and such an arrangement is well worth consideration. A French writer, recently describing Paris flats, states : " In many instances there are two water-closets for the use of the family, and always one for the servants." The W.C. in Paris is often unnecessarily large, and the same may be said of the bath-room. In some English flats the latter is reduced to a minimum size, and the end of the bath will even be let into an adjoining room ; if our French friends go to one extreme, we certainly go to the other.

In Paris the servants sleep on the top floor of a block of flats, consequently, the planning of a suite is much simplified, for no servants' room is provided. An examination of the plans in this book will show that the position of the servants' bedroom is as hard a feature to properly arrange as any in the suite. The kitchen is often entered through the "office" or pantry ; there is no door from the kitchen to the passage, consequently the pantry acts as a "buffer" room and prevents noise in the kitchen being heard elsewhere in the flat. This plan has been spoken of elsewhere as excellent. There is also a door from the kitchen to the trade staircase. There is no scullery, but when comparing the plans of London and Paris, the place of the scullery of the former flats is occupied by the pantry of the latter. A few years ago a pantry was not often provided here, but it is become general to build one in the best flats (see Figs. 84, 86, 87, 91, 100, &c.). In some cases in Paris when the suite is small there is no "office" ; the kitchen is increased in size, as suggested for English flats when the space is limited

PLAN OF UPPER FLOORS.

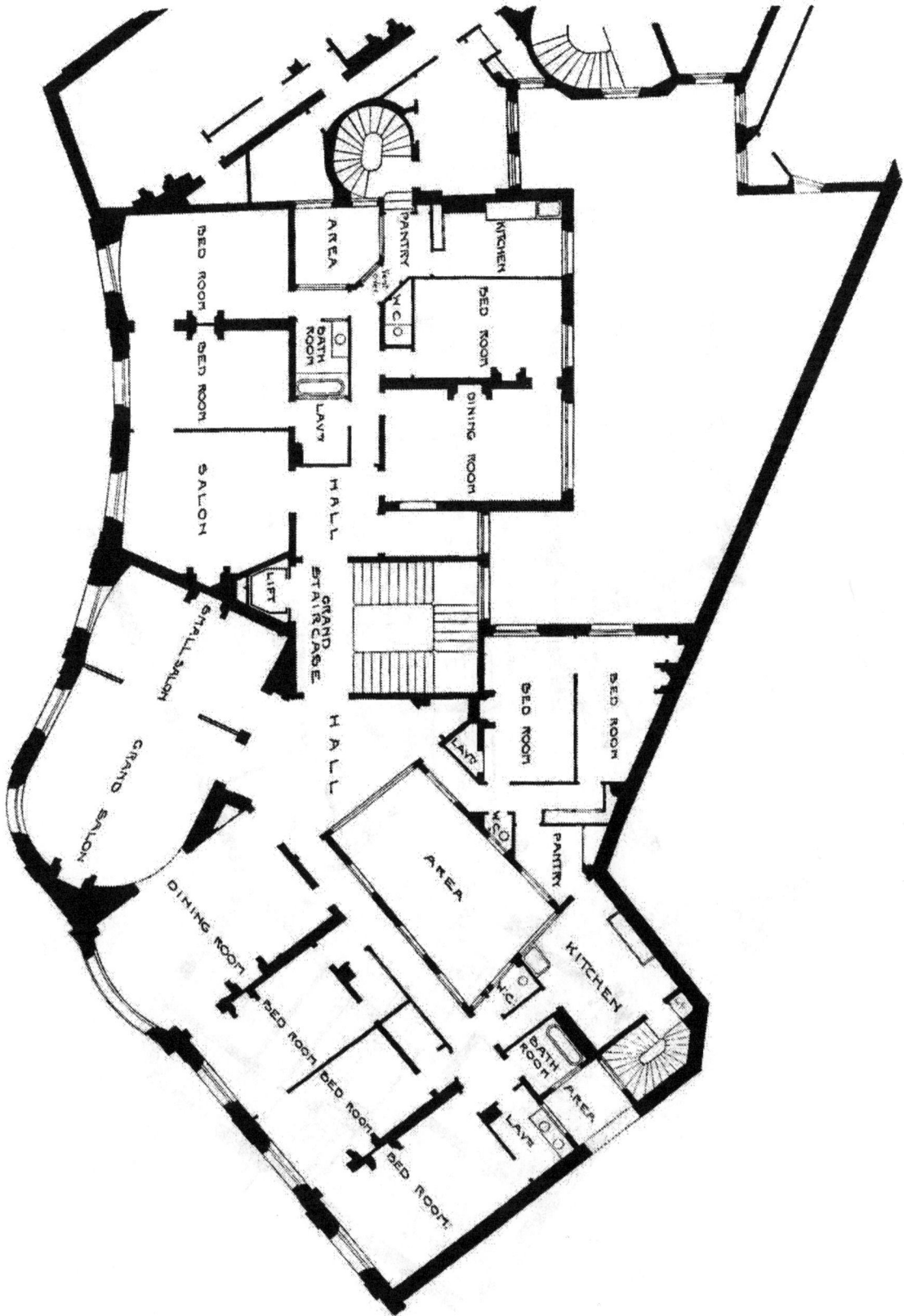

BED ROOM

BED ROOM

SALON

AREA

PANTRY

W.C.

BATH ROOM

LAV'Y

KITCHEN

BED ROOM

DINING ROOM

HALL

LIFT

SMALL SALON

GRAND STAIRCASE

HALL

GRAND SALON

DINING ROOM

BED ROOM

BED ROOM

BED ROOM

BED ROOM

AREA

LAV'Y

W.C.

PANTRY

W.C.

BATH ROOM

LAV'Y

AREA

KITCHEN

BED ROOM

BED ROOM

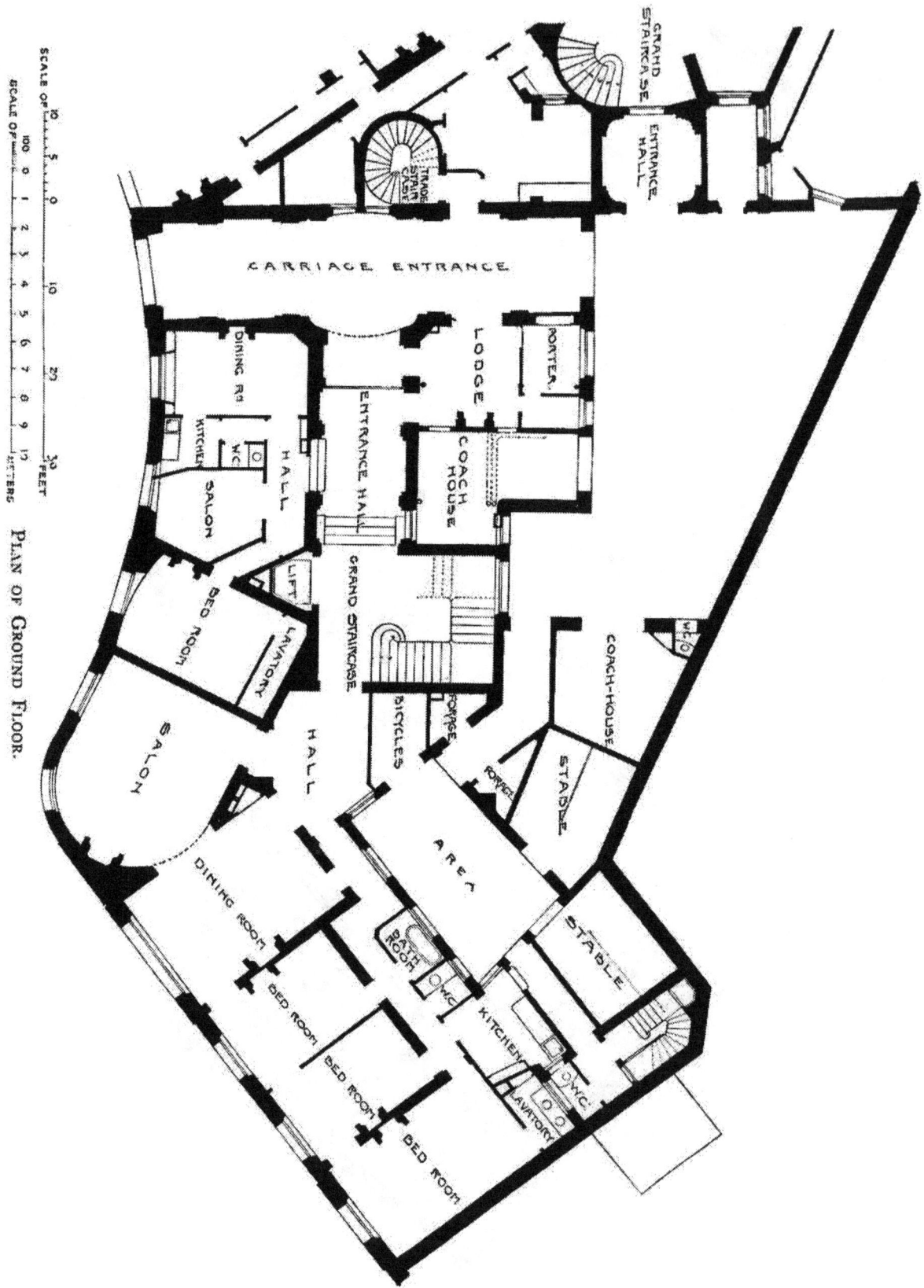

FIG. 163.—RUE SPONTINI, No. 1, PARIS.

PLAN OF GROUND FLOOR.

Gabriel Morice, Architect.

SCALE OF FEET
SCALE OF METERS

and a good-sized scullery is impossible. In large suites where the dining-room is some distance from the kitchen there is sometimes a small second pantry near the dining-room; this is very handy for service (see Figs. 165, 170).

The "maisonette" principle is not much in favour in France, but a self-contained house sometimes occupies the back portion of the site. It is entered from the courtyard, and the front portion of the block is occupied by ordinary flats.

The ground floor is sometimes partly used for stables (see Fig. 163), and in the best modern flats provision is made for the storage of motor cars (see Fig. 164). In England stabling on the ground floor would be impossible; we should object to the noise, and prefer the higher rents obtained from a suite. In Paris the courtyard is often covered with indiarubber, which of course deadens the sound considerably. Basements have also been used in Paris for stabling. The custom is old and dies hard, but it seems strange, now that the telephone is universal, that the stables are not built in a less expensive locality, not too far away from the suites, as in London.

If the site is an awkward shape, it is advisable to let the defect appear in one room only; never mind how irregular it may be, do not try and ease it off gradually, making several rooms slightly irregular. Living in a room with two walls a little out of parallel is as uncomfortable as living in a room very irregular, perhaps more so.

In Paris it is a rule to provide communication between the reception rooms; sometimes the doors are hung folding, and sometimes sliding doors are used. It is a practice we might more frequently follow here; it is often convenient, and rarely inconvenient.

Steel construction is possible in Paris, and the benefit is apparent in the areas; a wall about 8 in. thick is used instead of one perhaps 2 ft. 3 in. The passages are consequently much lighter than in England (see Figs. 163, 165, 168, 171, &c.).

It will be seen that a staircase can be lighted by a lantern, and the unnecessary windows on each floor are not required (see Figs. 163, 168).

We have a general rule to place the dining-room in the front of the building, irrespective of the position of the kitchen. That is done on account of the outlook, but the view from a dining-room is of less importance than from other sitting-rooms. This is recognised in Paris, and the windows often overlook an internal court, and a bedroom is placed in the better position. The benefit is that the dining-room is near the kitchen—the dishes are not carried from one end of the flat to the other—and after dinner the family moves to the drawing-room, far away from any smell of cooking. A good example is shown on Fig. 171.

More cupboards are built in Paris than in England. The usual practice is to have a range of them at one side of a passage or corridor (see Fig. 173).

We always try and arrange that the trade entrance shall be at some distance from the main entrance. In Paris the main entrance is often used for both visitors and servants.

The love for a curve on a plan is great with French architects, who not only make the staircase circular or oval on plan, but also the walls of sitting-rooms, the end walls of corridors, &c., and the effect is charming, but it increases the cost of the building (see Figs. 167, 174, and 176).

As the climate is generally warmer than in England, fireplaces are not provided in the halls. The general arrangement of the flats is to have one or two suites on each floor. The elaborate scheming to make one lift serve several suites on a floor is apparently unknown: the basement or "lower ground floor" suite is also an English idea.

Every plan for a bedroom shows the bed, and if architects made it a rule to do the same here, the building of many badly planned rooms might be prevented.

Flats are more uniform in size in Paris than in London; not more than four or five bedrooms (not including servants' rooms) are provided. Here many suites of eight or more rooms are being built; the tendency with us is to build larger suites than those erected a few years ago.

Now that the mistress has lost control over her servants in consequence of the trade staircases, or fire-escape staircases, there seems no reason why we should not follow the French system of providing servants' bedrooms in some other part of the building. Servants can now leave a flat at any time, unknown to their mistresses, and that being so, why should valuable space be used for a servants' room, when it could better and more profitably be used as a room for the family? Where there is a lift the top floor is too valuable, and in the future we shall no doubt arrange for the servants to sleep in the basement; small suites of rooms could be planned, and common bathrooms arranged. Already it is a practice in large blocks to provide extra rooms in the basement or attics that can be let with the suites. This gives a desirable elasticity to the accommodation a landlord has to offer.

In the recent suites in Paris hot water is supplied to the tenants,

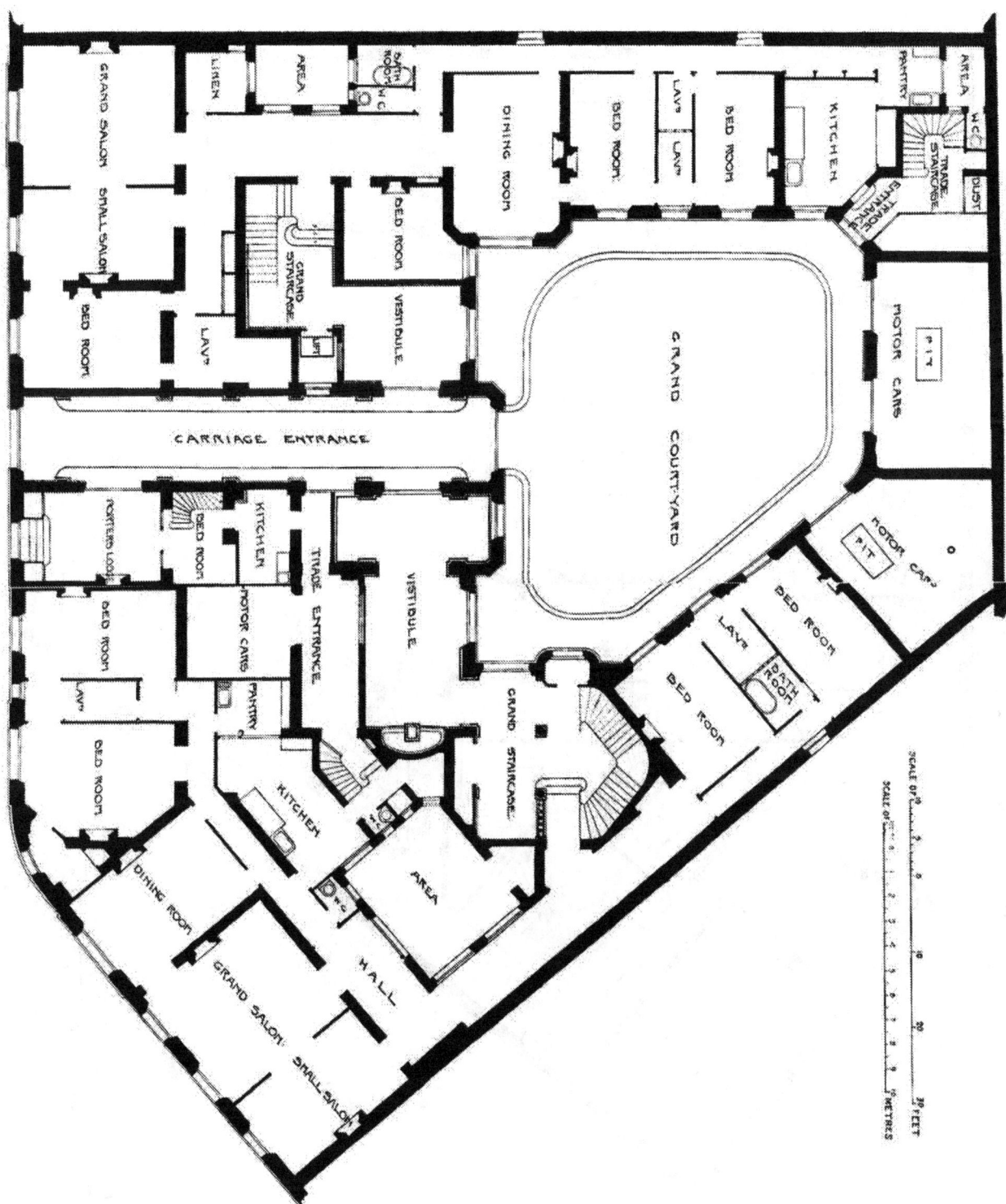

FIG. 164.—RUE DE POMEREU ET RUE DES BELLES FEUILLES, PARIS.

Gabriel Morin, Architect.

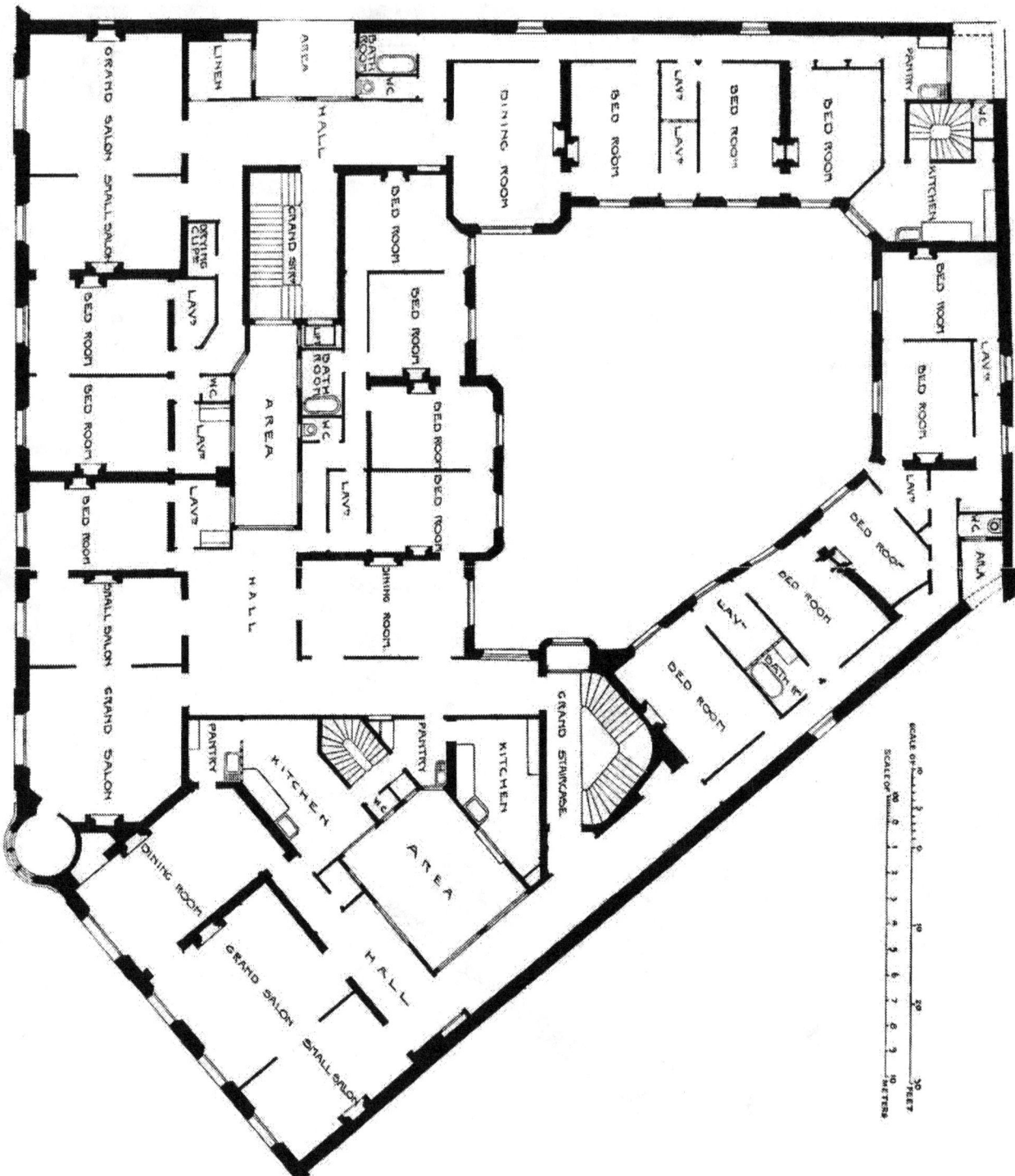

FIG. 165.—RUE DE POMEREU ET RUE DES BELLES FEUILLES, PARIS.

Gabriel Morice, Architect.

not only to the bath-room but also to the "toilette" opening off the bedrooms; these are sometimes almost large enough to be called dressing-rooms.

The question of flats over shops does not seem to trouble French architects, as some of the most expensive suites have shops on at least

Fig. 166.—Maison de Rapport, 49 Rue de Pomereu, Paris.

Gabriel Morice, Architect.

part of the site. Some few examples of exteriors are given, but unfortunately space prevented the reproduction of more.

The authorities in Paris take great interest in the elevations of buildings, and every year as many as five prizes are given for the most successful buildings.

Over seventy plans were obtained from Paris for the purpose

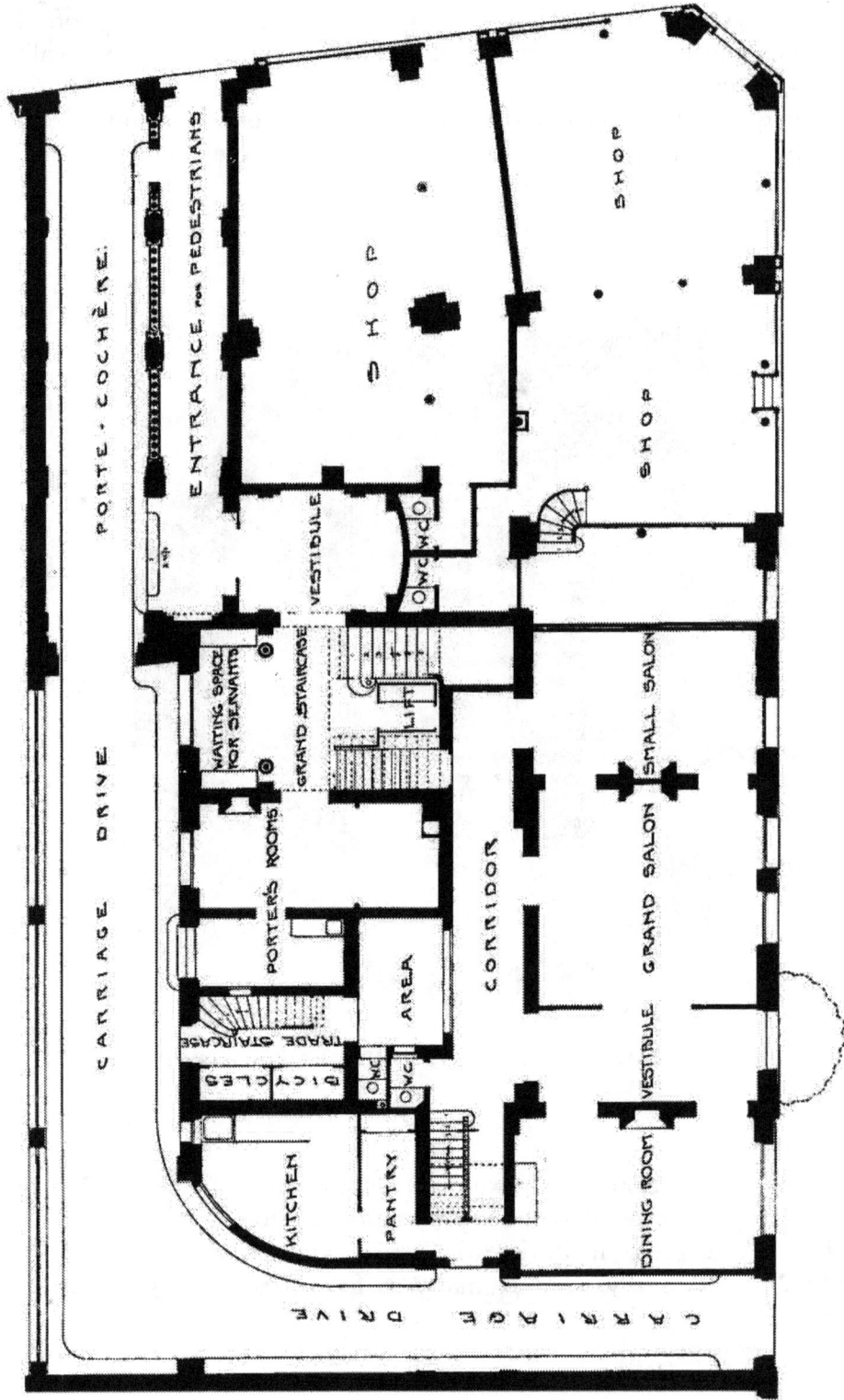

PORTE · COCHÈRE:

ENTRANCE for PEDESTRIANS

SHOP

SHOP

SHOP

VESTIBULE

WC WC

CARRIAGE DRIVE

WAITING SPACE FOR SERVANTS

GRAND STAIRCASE

LIFT

PORTER'S ROOMS

AREA

CORRIDOR

TRADE STAIRCASE

BICYCLES

WC WC

SMALL SALON

GRAND SALON

VESTIBULE

KITCHEN

PANTRY

DINING ROOM

VESTIBULE

CARRIAGE DRIVE

SCALE OF 12 9 6 3 0 10 20 30 FEET

SCALE OF 100 20 0 1 2 3 4 5 6 7 8 9 10 METERS

FIG. 167.—AVENUE DE LA GRANDE ARMÉE No. 16, PARIS.

Gabriel Morice, Architect.

Gabriel Morice, Architect.

GRAND SALON

SMALL SALON

BED ROOM

BED ROOM

LAVy

LAVy

DINING ROOM

HALL

WC

BATH ROOM

AREA

LAVy

LAVy

WC

BED ROOM

BED ROOM

BED ROOM

LIFT

PANTRY

LAVy

KITCHEN

WC WC

AREA

PANTRY

HALL

SMALL SALON

GRAND SALON

BED ROOM

BED ROOM

DINING ROOM

LAVy

BED ROOM

AREA

LAVy

WC

BED ROOM

BATH RM

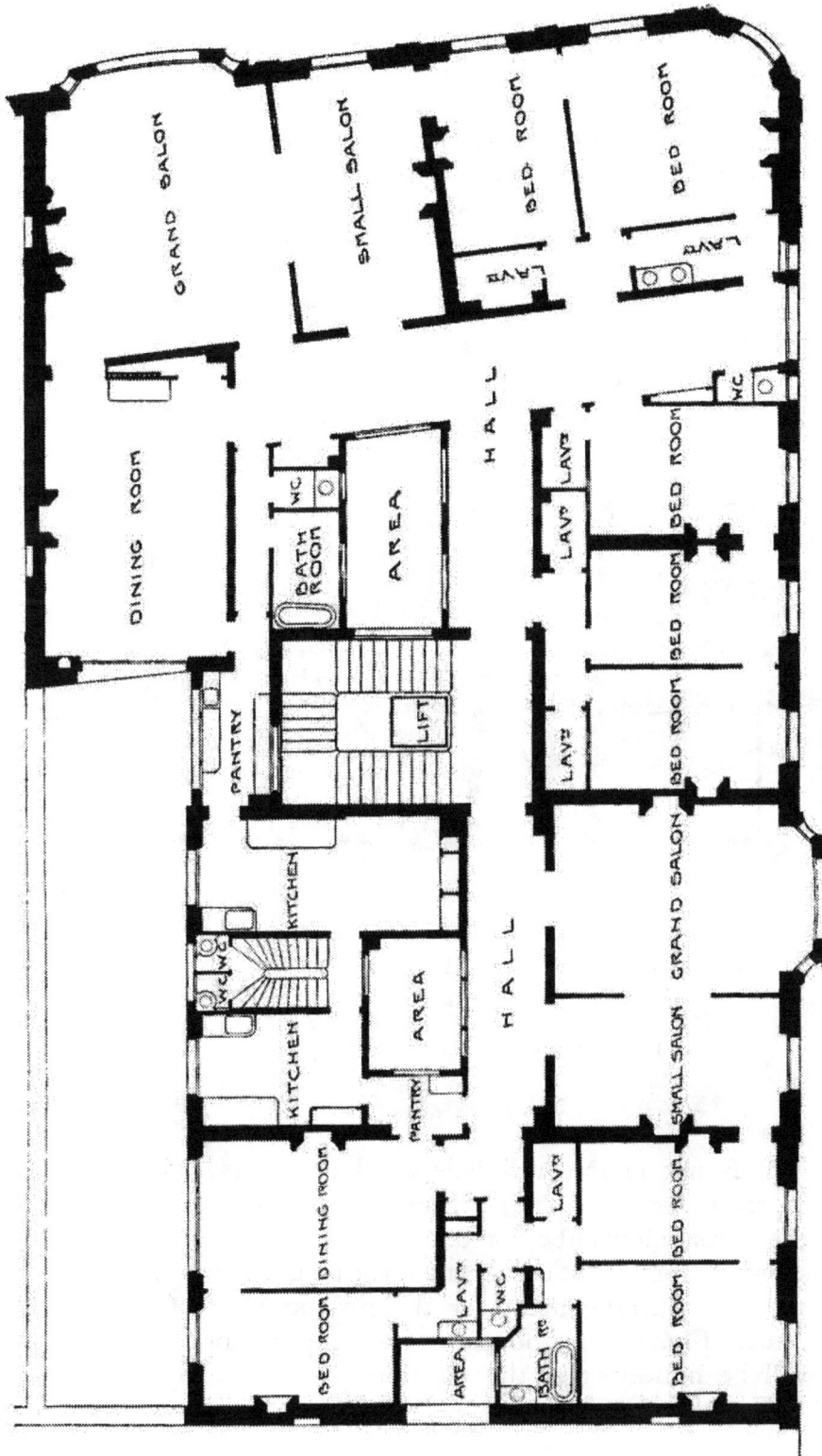

RUE ANATOLE DE LA FORGE.

SCALE OF   10   0   20   30 FEET

SCALE OF 100 50 0   0   1   2   3   4   5   6   7   8   9   10 METERS

FIG. 168.—AVENUE DE LA GRANDE ARMÉE No. 16, PARIS.

of this book, and space alone prevented their reproduction here ; it is much regretted that only so few are included. The reader will note the ventilation to W.C.'s and size of the areas.

Fig. 163 shows the plans of a portion of a large block in the Rue Spontini. The ground floor has stable accommodation, a fine entrance hall and staircase. The salon and bedroom adjoining have been made into symmetrical rooms; top ventilation is provided to one W.C. and

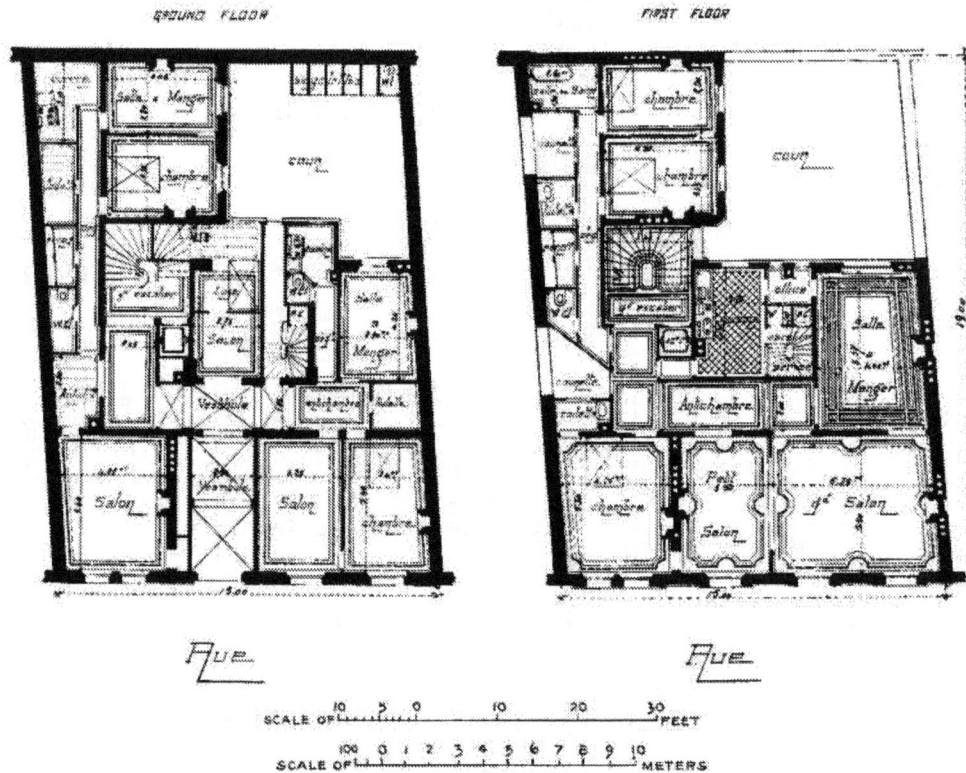

FIG. 169.—RESIDENTIAL FLATS, PARIS.

A. Pregnaud, Architect.

lavatory. The lift is not in the well hole of the staircase, although there was ample room for it in that position. The steel construction of the walls of the areas will also be noted.

Fig. 164 shows accommodation for motor cars ; there is a large vestibule and the usual arrangement for the ground floor of a first class block of flats. Fig. 165 is the plan of an upper floor ; the thin walls of areas will be noticed, also the positions of two dining-rooms overlooking the courtyard. The idea of placing the dining-rooms near the kitchen has also influenced the plan. Fig. 166 is a photograph of the exterior.

Fig. 167 shows another fine hall and staircase, waiting space for servants, accommodation for bicycles, &c. The W.C.'s to shops have top ventilation. Fig. 168 is the plan of an upper floor of the same building. The main staircase has a top light; this much assists the plan, especially with regard to the trade staircase. The W.C.'s for servants, entered from without the flat, will be noticed, also the width and

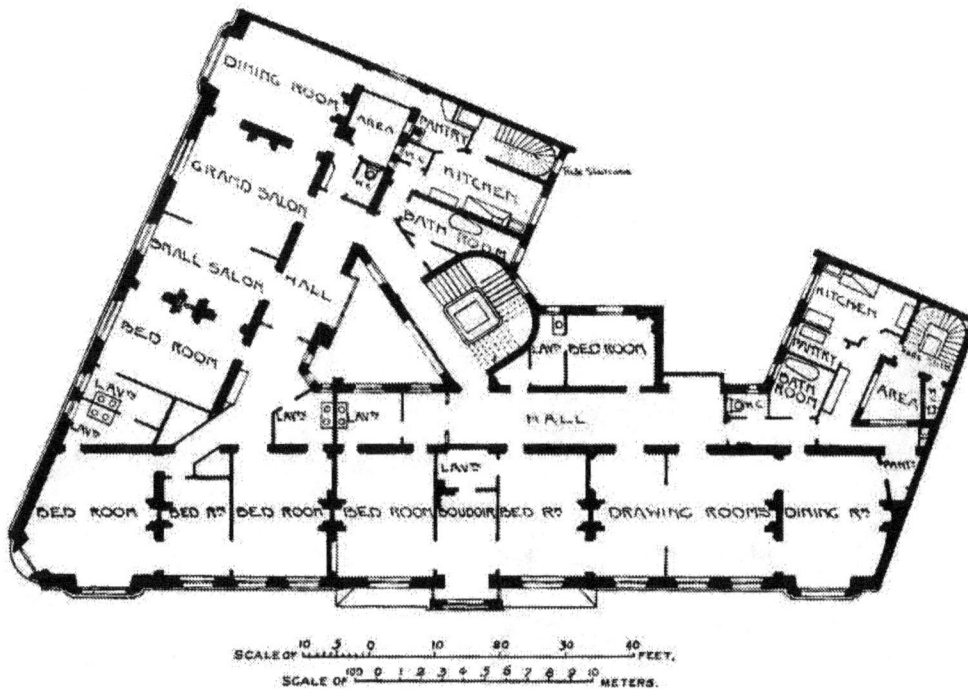

FIG. 170.—66 AVENUE WAGRAM, PARIS.

F. Julien, Architect.

light of corridors. The pantry with two doors on the left-hand suite should be noted.

Fig. 169 is a reproduction of a French drawing, the original of which is but slightly larger than the illustration, and is a splendid example of French work. There is only one suite on the first floor; the kitchen has a central position near the dining-room.

Fig. 170 in some ways suggests an English plan. It will be noticed that one suite has the two pantries referred to elsewhere.

Fig. 171 is another illustration of one suite covering the entire

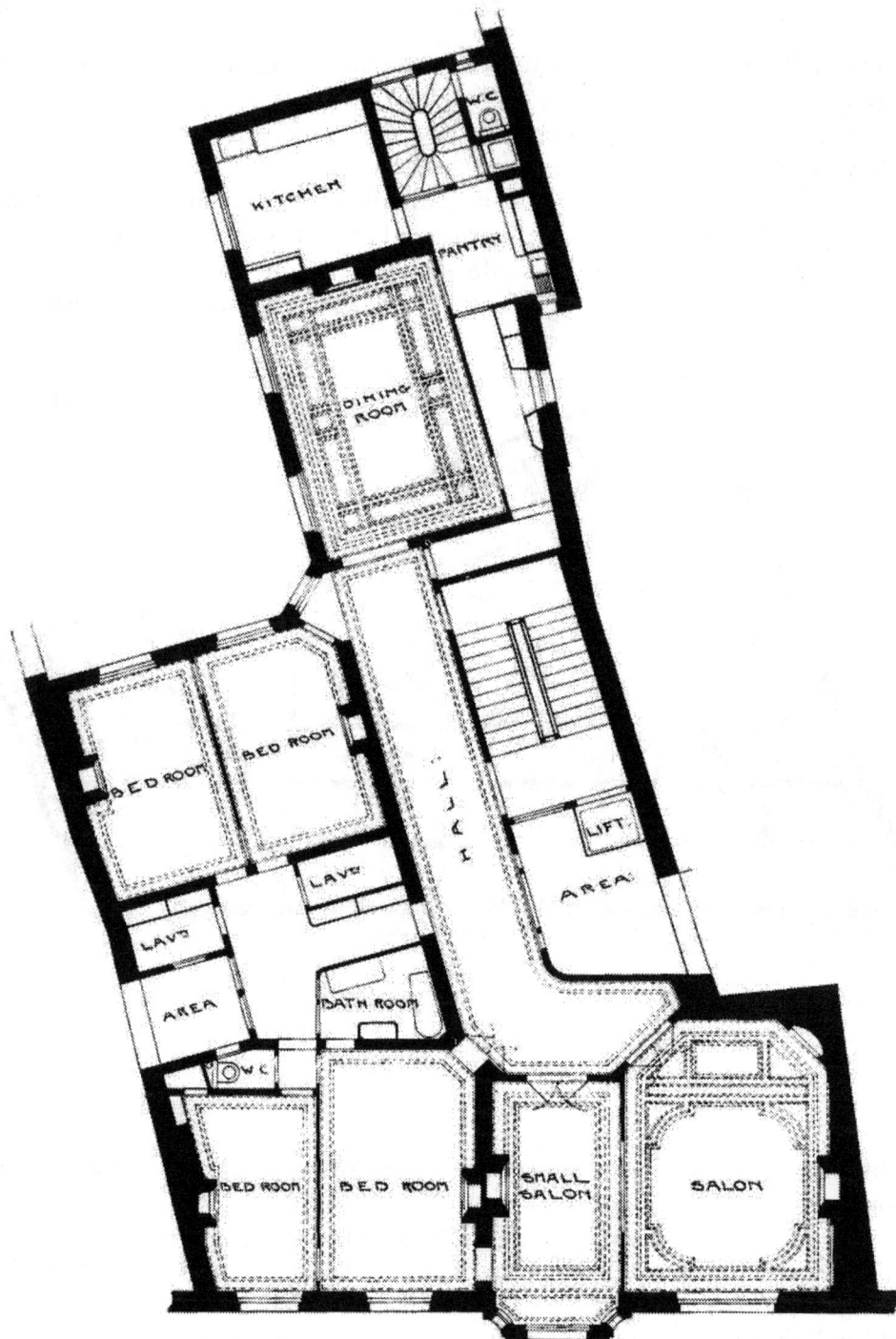

PLAN OF FIRST SECOND THIRD AND FOURTH FLOORS

FIG. 171.—RUE DES FOSSÉS ST JACQUES NO. 20, PARIS.

L. C. Lacau, Architect.

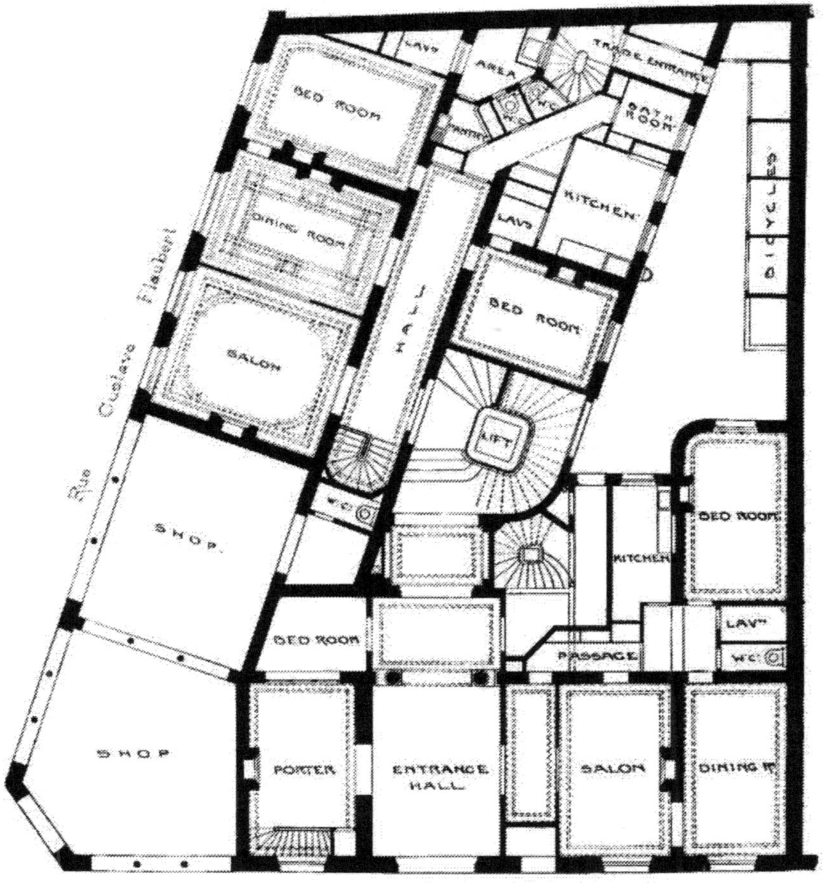

GROUND FLOOR PLAN

Rue Théodore de Banville

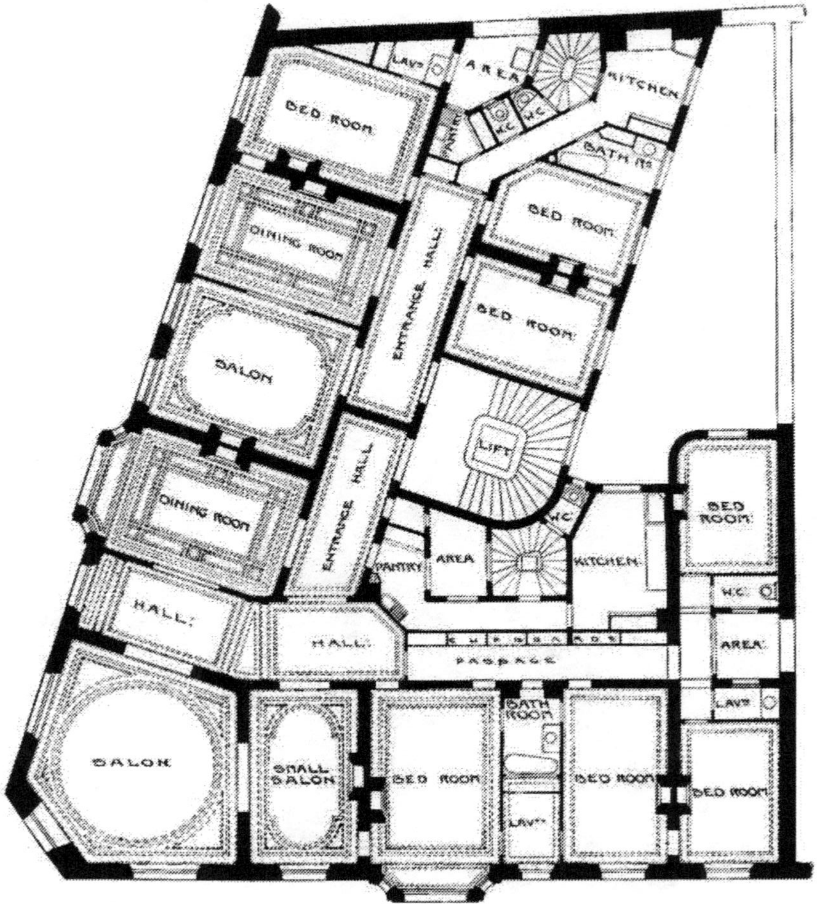

PLAN OF FIRST SECOND THIRD AND FOURTH FLOORS

Rue Gustave Flaubert

SHOP

SHOP

SALON

DINING ROOM

BED ROOM

HALL

BED ROOM

LIFT

KITCHEN

LAV.

AREA

BATH ROOM

TRADE ENTRANCE

PORTER

BED ROOM

ENTRANCE HALL

SALON

PASSAGE

KITCHEN

LAV.

W.C.

BED ROOM

DINING R.

BICYCLES

SALON

SMALL SALON

BED ROOM

LAV.

BATH ROOM

BED ROOM

BED ROOM

HALL

HALL

DINING ROOM

SALON

DINING ROOM

BED ROOM

LAV.

ENTRANCE HALL

ENTRANCE HALL

PANTRY

AREA

W.C.

PASSAGE

KITCHEN

LIFT

BED ROOM

BED ROOM

BATH RM

KITCHEN

W.C.

LAV.

AREA

W.C.

BED ROOM

SCALE OF

SCALE OF

FEET

METRES

FIGS. 172 AND 173.—RUE THÉODORE DE BANVILLE, No. 7, PARIS.

L. C. Laan, Architect.

floor space. Here again the dining-room is placed at the back of the suite facing the courtyard, but close to the kitchen. The thick dividing wall will be noticed, and the wide corridor or hall; the lift is kept apart from the staircase. The bath-room of a French flat is often ventilated into a passage; this happens in cases where external ventilation could easily have been arranged. The symmetrical plan of the salon should be noticed.

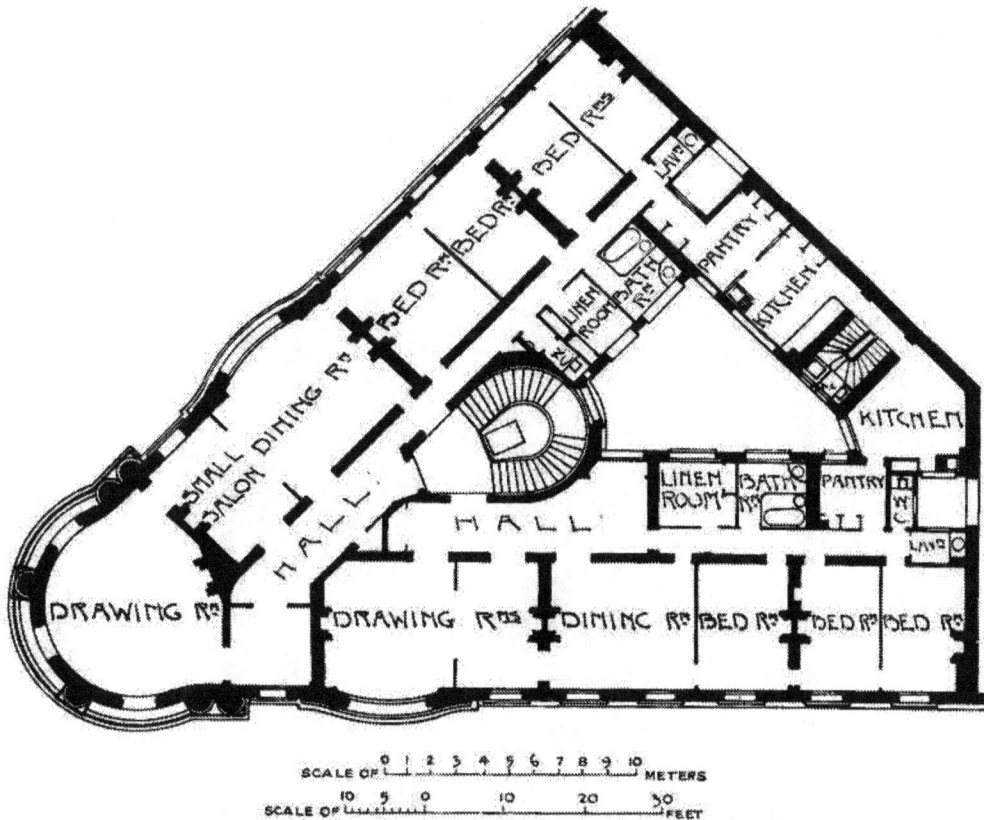

FIG. 174.—AVENUE DE LA GRANDE ARMÉE No. 38ᵇⁱˢ, PARIS.

Gustave Rives, Architect.

Fig. 172 has the usual fine entrance hall and staircase. The servants' W.C. is entered from the trade staircase. The tradespeople must enter through the main hall; this does not seem a good idea to us, but it has an advantage—every one must pass the concierge, and he is able to prevent objectionable characters entering the building by either staircase.

Fig. 173 shows two suites to the floor. In the lower suite, the

FIG. 175.—AVENUE DE LA GRANDE ARMÉE No. 38ᴮᴵˢ, PARIS.

Gustave Rives, Architect.

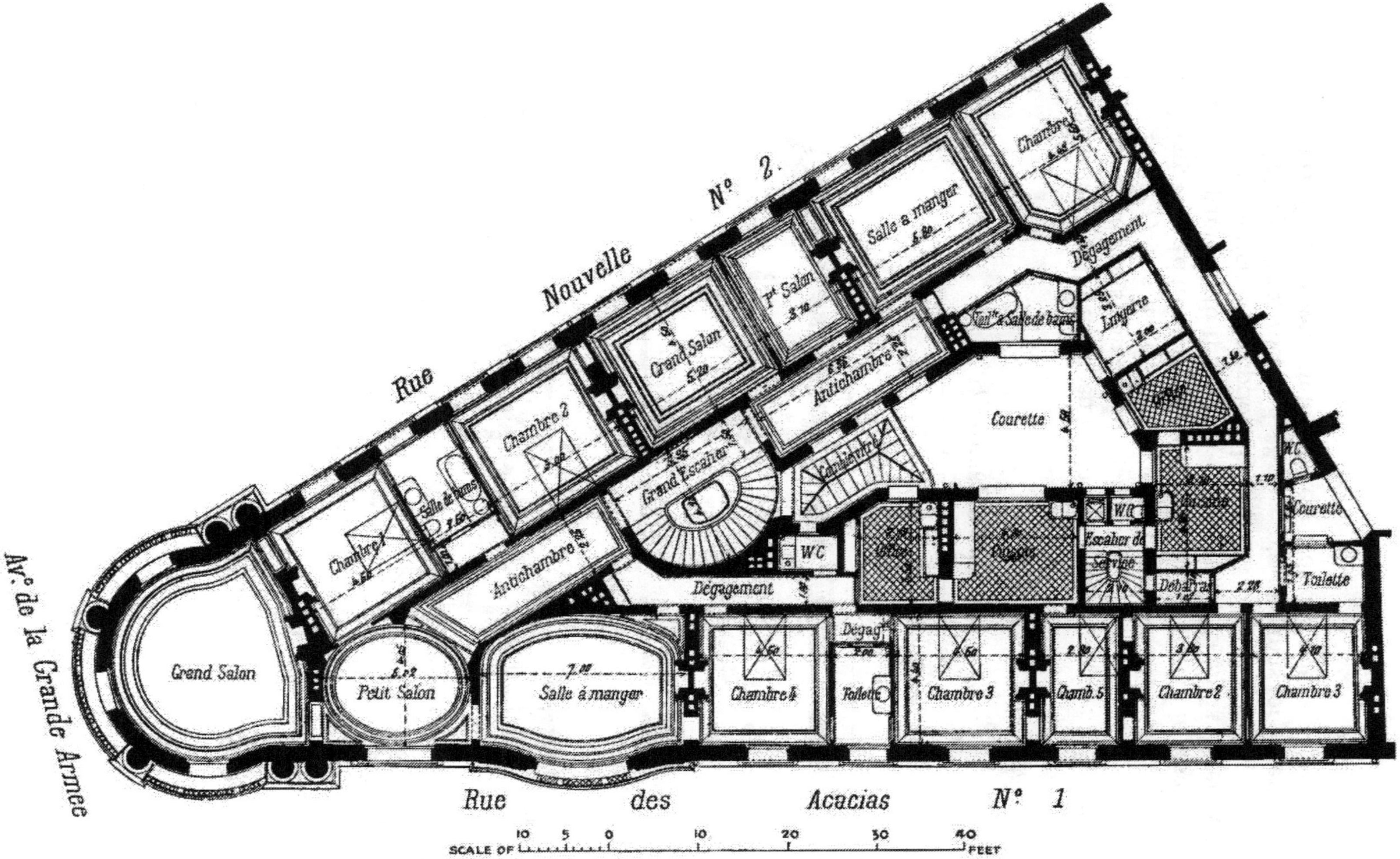

Grand Salon

Petit Salon

Salle à manger

Antichambre

Chambre 1

Salle de bains

Chambre 2

Grand Salon

1er Salon

Antichambre

Salle à manger

Chambre

Dégagement

Lingerie

Courette

Grand Escalier

Vestibule

WC

Dégagement

Chambre 4

Chambre 3

Chambre 5

Chambre 2

Chambre 3

Toilette

Rue Nouvelle   N.o 2.

Rue des Acacias   N.o 1

SCALE OF
10 5 0   10   20   50   40 FEET

FIG. 176.—AVENUE DE LA GRANDE ARMÉE No. 38, PARIS.

Gustave Rives, Architect.

only entrance to the kitchen is through the pantry—a good arrangement, the private passage becomes part of either room. There is much cupboard accommodation for this suite. The servants' W.C. is entered from the trade staircase in each instance.

Fig. 174 is an illustration of a corner building, with a clever plan for the room at the angle. Fig. 175 is a photograph of the exterior, and Fig. 176 is another angle site with two large suites to each floor. The

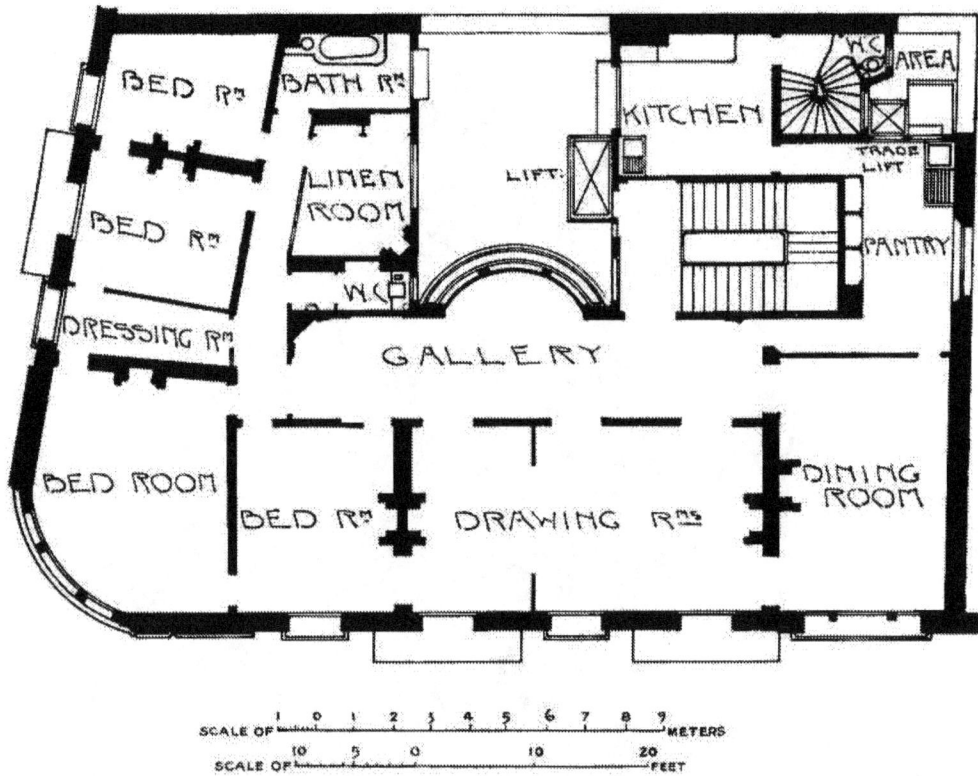

FIG. 177.—RUE BOISSIERE, PARIS.

Gustave Rives, Architect.

kitchens as usual each open on to the trade staircase. There are four good examples of symmetrical rooms.

Fig. 177 has a good hall or gallery; the lift is outside the main building, entered from a corner of the hall. There is a serving hatch from the pantry into the dining-room; the kitchen is entered through the pantry, which is exceptionally large.

Figs. 178, 179, 180, and 181 are photographs of recent buildings, the plans of which were unfortunately crowded out.

FIG. 178.—RUE STE PEACIDE, PARIS.

M. Perronne, Architect.

FIG. 179.—RUE DANTON, PARIS.

M. Perronne, Architect.

FIG. 180.—AVENUE VICTOR HUGO 60, PARIS.

Albert Le Voisvenel, Architect.

FIG. 181.—RUE REMBRANDT, PARIS.

Gustave Rives, Architect.

Vienna. — Like most Austrian and German cities, in Vienna nearly all the private residences are flats. The illustrations given have been selected from about thirty plans. In Vienna flats may be roughly divided into as many as five classes.

The first group comprises buildings in the principal business quarter of the city, where the very high value of the ground necessitates the building plot being used to the utmost advantage. As a rule the ground floor, the basement, and the mezzanine floors are built for business and office purposes, and let at high rentals. The upper floors contain flats of from two to five rooms; these are usually so arranged that if required two suites can be made into one (see Fig. 182). Figs. 183 and 184 are also illustrations of this class of building.

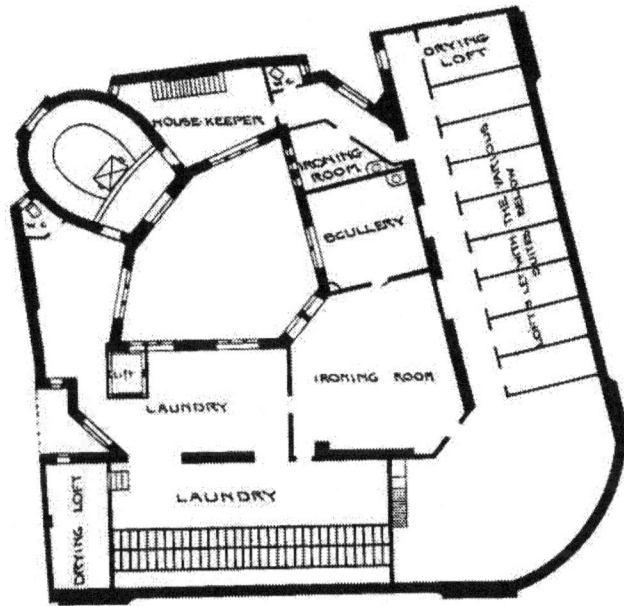

ATTIC   PLAN

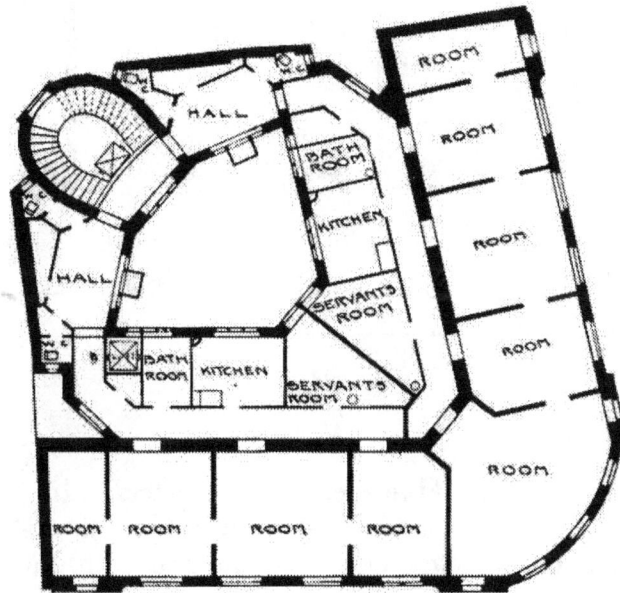

PLAN OF 1ᵀ 2ᴺᴰ 3ᴿᴰ & 4ᵀᴴ FLOORS

SCALE OF ... FEET
SCALE OF ... METERS

FIG. 182.—SEILERGASSE No. 9 & 11, VIENNA.

Julius Mayreder, Architect.

The second group comprises similarly constructed buildings where the value of the ground is less. The third group comprises dwellings and business houses in the more populated quarters of the suburbs, the lower floors being let as offices or shops. In the fourth group may be included those houses in the quieter districts of the town, removed from the business traffic, and which contain exclusively flats of various sizes.

For the fifth group, flats and dwellings of quite modest dimensions, Fig. 185 is selected as an example. It is a building just erected in

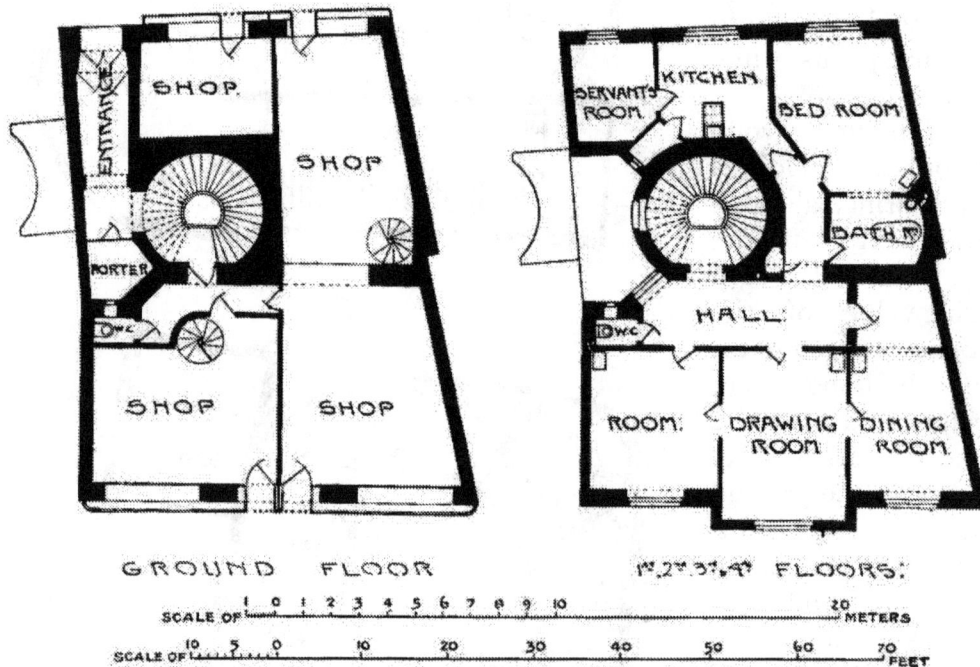

GROUND   FLOOR   1ˢᵗ 2ⁿᵈ 3ʳᵈ, 4ᵗʰ FLOORS.

FIG. 183.—BOGNERGASSE NO. 3, VIENNA.

Krauss & Tölk, Architects.

Krems, on the Danube, North Austria. In this block there are three main floors (ground, first, and second floors) and eighteen suites, of which the smallest comprise one bedroom, kitchen, one servant's room, anteroom, dining-room, and W.C., and the largest, two bedrooms and one study in addition to the above. Each suite has a bath-room and a wash-house in the attics.

In Vienna basements and sub-basements are the rule rather than the exception. The basement is often used as a restaurant with cellars below. The top floor, even in the highest rented buildings, is often

constructed as a laundry (see Fig. 182). The W.C.'s frequently
ventilate into small air-shafts as in America. The circular form of

FIG. 184.—1 BOGNERGASSE NO. 3, VIENNA.

F. F. von Krauss, *}* Architects.
J. Tölk, *}*

staircase is common, and "dancing stairs" seem as general as in
Switzerland; they are so easy "in going," that it seems strange they
are so rarely built in England.

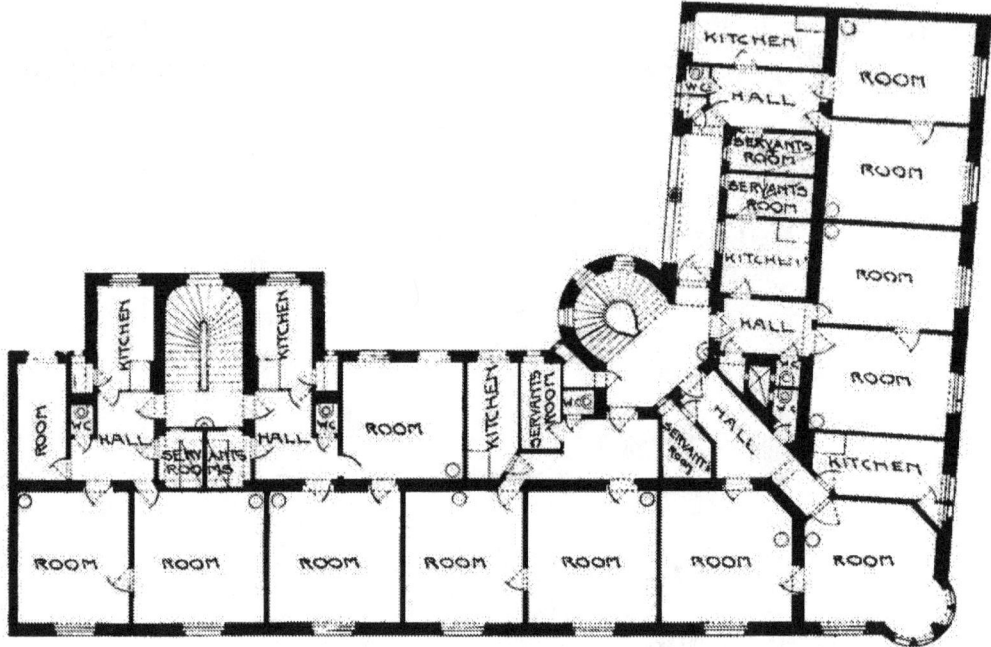

PLAN OF UPPER FLOORS

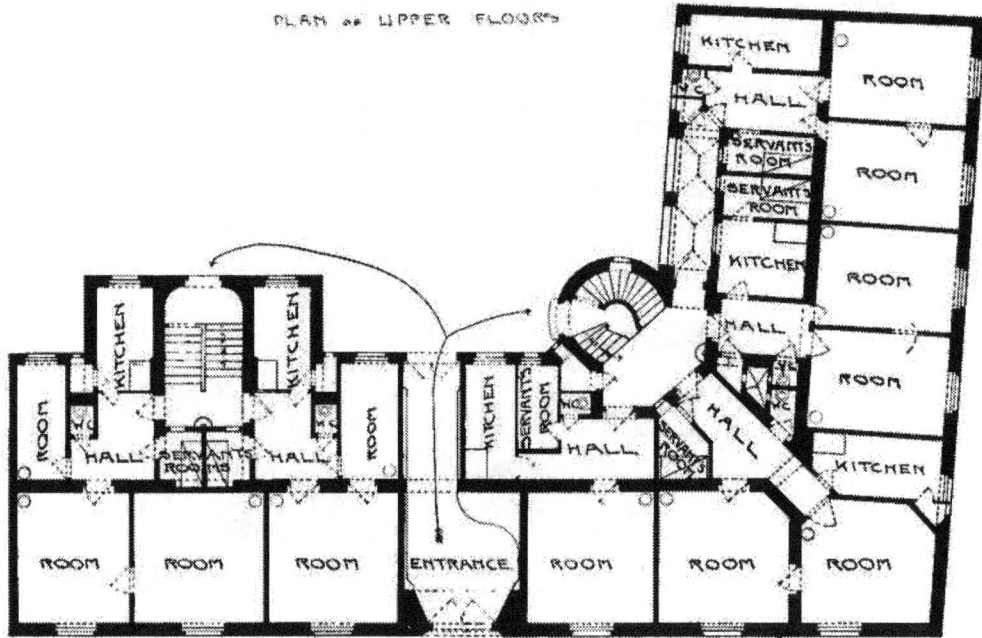

GROUND FLOOR PLAN.

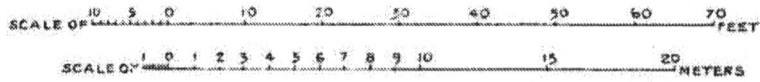

SCALE OF 10 5 0   10   20   30   40   50   60   70 FEET

SCALE OF 10 1 2 3 4 5 6 7 8 9 10   15   20 METERS

FIG. 185.—RESIDENTIAL FLATS, VIENNA.

Professor von Ferstel, Architect.

If a fire occurs it is usually in the laundry, consequently there is a regulation that an iron door must be provided.

FIG. 186.—WOHNHAUS DER GUTSHERRSCHAFT, VIENNA.

(For Plan see Fig. 185.)   *Professor von Ferstel, Architect.*

Madrid.—In the large towns of Spain, most of the houses are flats, as there are only a very few people who can afford the luxury of inhabiting a "hotel," or house for a single family; in the small towns it is different.

Until the middle of the nineteenth century, the construction of houses in Madrid was carried out in an economic manner. The façades had a base about 2 ft. high, of granite from the near hills of Guadarame; the remainder of the building was ordinary brick. The partitions and floors were of wood.

Gradually buildings became more expensive. The stone base became as high as the ground floor, and even went as far as the mezzanine floor. The façades in the principal streets were built with pressed bricks, and some had stone bays. The partitions were brick, and the floors were fireproof. The sanitary arrangements also were much

FIG. 187.—CASA CALLE DE FERN-ANDO EL SANTO, No. 22, MADRID.

E. Adaro, Architect.

improved until there is hardly a house which is not now provided with a supply of water on each floor, a luxury unknown a few years ago.

PLAN OF PRINCIPAL FLOOR

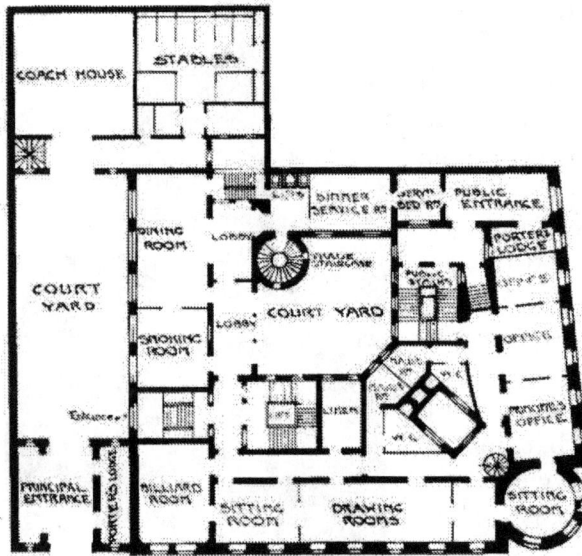

GROUND FLOOR PLAN

SCALE OF [scale in feet]

SCALE OF [scale in meters]

FIG. 188.—CALLE DE FERNANDO EL SANTO,
NO. 22, MADRID.

E. Adaro, Architect.

At the present time it is rare to find a building not lighted by electricity.

In Madrid, Barcelona, Valencia, and other provincial capitals, flats are now very similar to those in Paris. Spanish flats are in many ways interesting. It seems the custom for the owner of the building to occupy the principal floor, which is sometimes the first floor, sometimes the second floor. As he resides on the premises, he is far more likely to direct that a certain care should be bestowed upon the façade of the building than in England, where he has his home elsewhere, and only builds as a speculation or investment, having no interest in the building from an architectural point of view.

An example of a building may, however, be given in London, which at once suggests the Spanish custom. Messrs Willett are erecting a large block of flats at Sloane Square; and will themselves occupy a large portion of the ground floor. Fig. 112A is a view of the exterior of what will certainly be one of the most expensive blocks erected in London, and a glance at the illustrations will show that the money would never be spent solely as a speculation. If this system should develop, it would be a good thing for the architecture of flats.

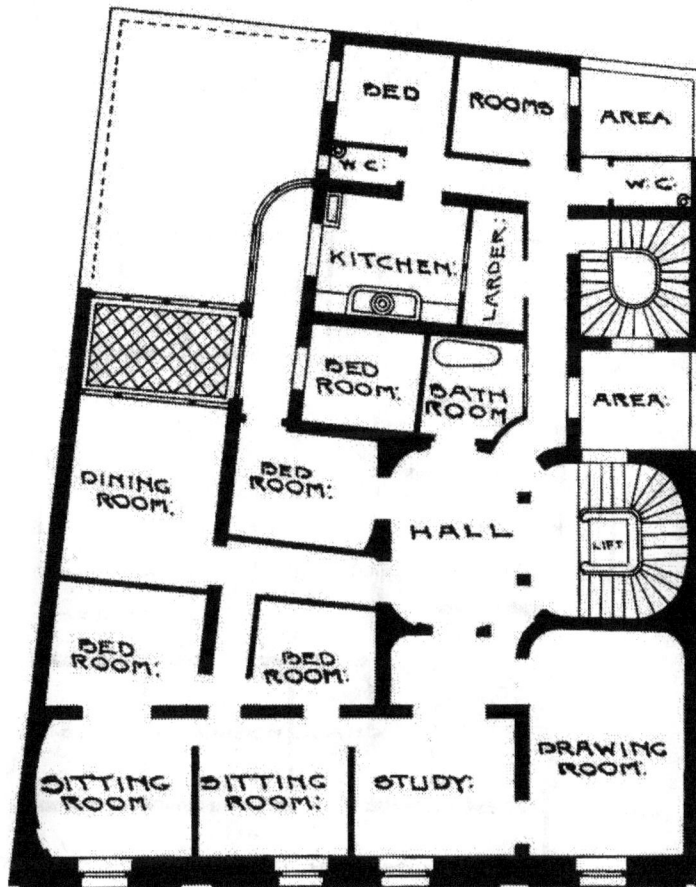

PLAN OF AN UPPER FLOOR

SCALE OF 10 5 0 10 20 FEET

SCALE OF 100 50 0 1 2 3 4 5 METERS

FIG. 189.—No. 20 CALLE DE FERNANDO EL SANTO, MADRID.

E. Adaro, Architect.

There are some other instances, which usually have shops on the ground floor. Perhaps some day we may have the Spanish system in London, the whole building comprising residential suites, and the owner occupying one of them.

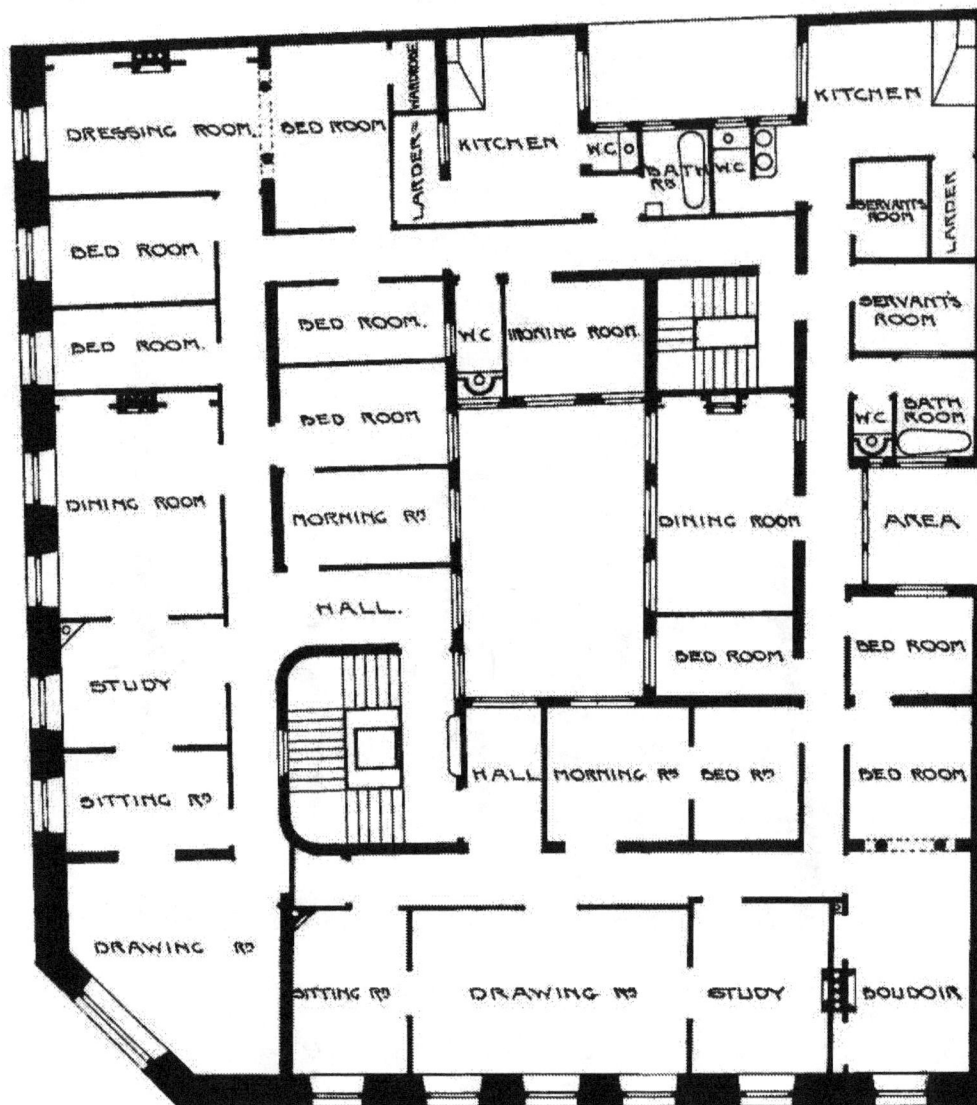

FIRST FLOOR PLAN

SCALE OF ___ 5 ___ 0 ___ 10 ___ 20 FEET

SCALE OF ___ 0 ___ 1 ___ 2 ___ 3 ___ 4 ___ 5 METERS

FIG. 190.—NO. 3 CALLE DE SAN AGUSTIN, MADRID.

Enrique M. Repulles y Vargas, Architect.

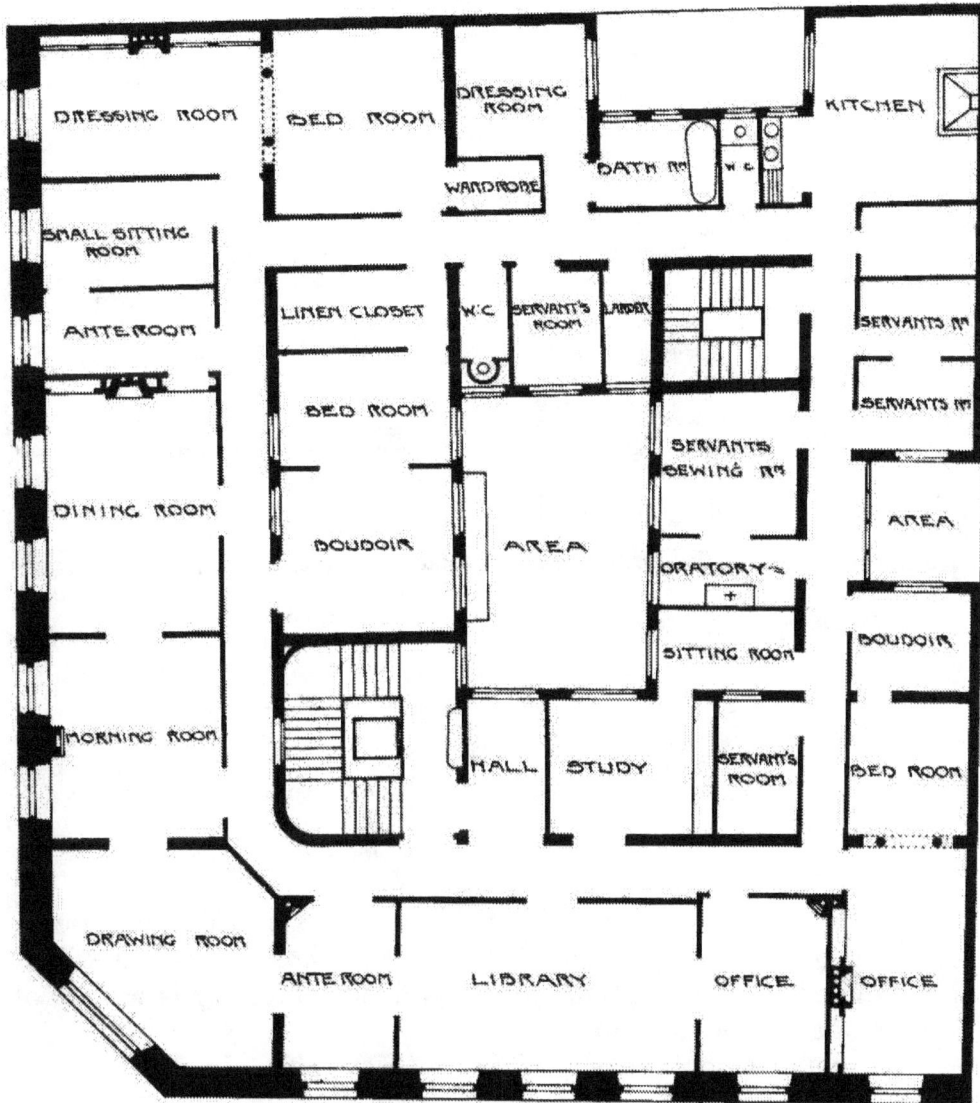

PLAN OF PRINCIPAL FLOOR (2ᵈ)

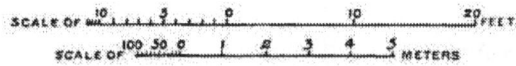

SCALE OF 10 5 0 10 20 FEET
SCALE OF 100 50 0 1 2 3 4 5 METERS

FIG. 191.—NO. 3 CALLE DE SAN AGUSTIN, MADRID.

Enrique M. Repulies y Vargas, Architect.

Fig. 188 shows the "maisonette" principle, part of the ground floor being used as offices; there is a private circular staircase near the principal's office. This plan and Fig. 191 each show an oratory.

The custom of a bed and sitting-room adjoining is general, as shown in Fig. 189; this is sometimes called a boudoir, sometimes a dressing-room (see Fig. 190). An unusually large number of sitting-rooms in a suite is also shown in this example. The W.C.'s have external ventilation, and the kitchen and scullery are combined.

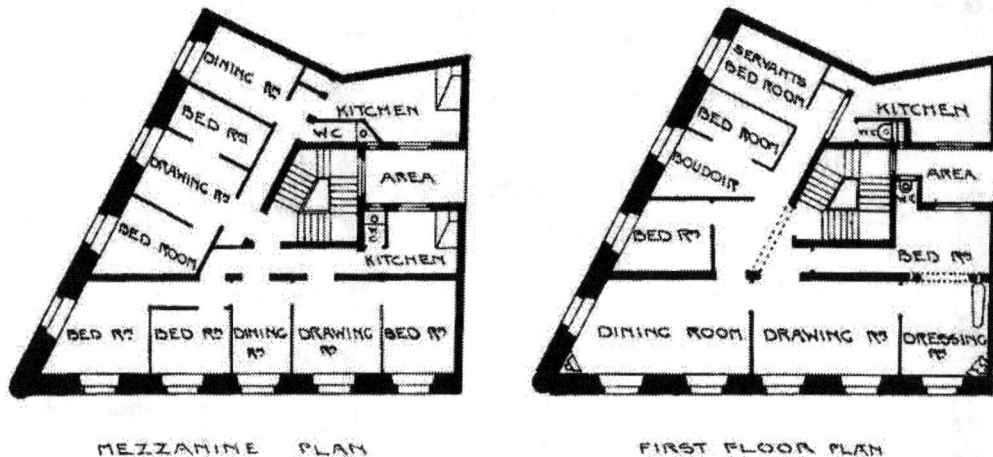

FIG. 192.—CALLE DE S. BERNANDO, MADRID.

Enrique M. Repulles y Vargas, Architect.

No. 22 Calle de Fernando el Santo (Fig. 188).—The proprietor lives on the ground and principal floors. There are coach-houses and stables, and a greenhouse on the principal floor. Fig. 187 is a view of the angle of the building.

No. 20 Calle de Fernando el Santo (Fig. 189).—In this building there is but one set of rooms on each floor.

No. 3 Calle de San Agustin (Figs. 190 and 191).—This is one of the best class flats; the suites let at £100 to £125 per annum. The principal floor, with only one suite, lets at £250 per annum. There are shops on the ground floor with cellars in the basement. There are on most floors two suites, but on the principal floor only one. On the fourth floor are an architect's offices and studios for photographers.

Nos. 30 *and* 32 *Calle de San Bernando* (Fig. 192).—These are low rented flats containing suites for middle-class people. There are shops on the ground floor and cellars in the basement. There are two suites of rooms to each floor except the principal floor, which is wholly given up to one set of rooms for the proprietor.

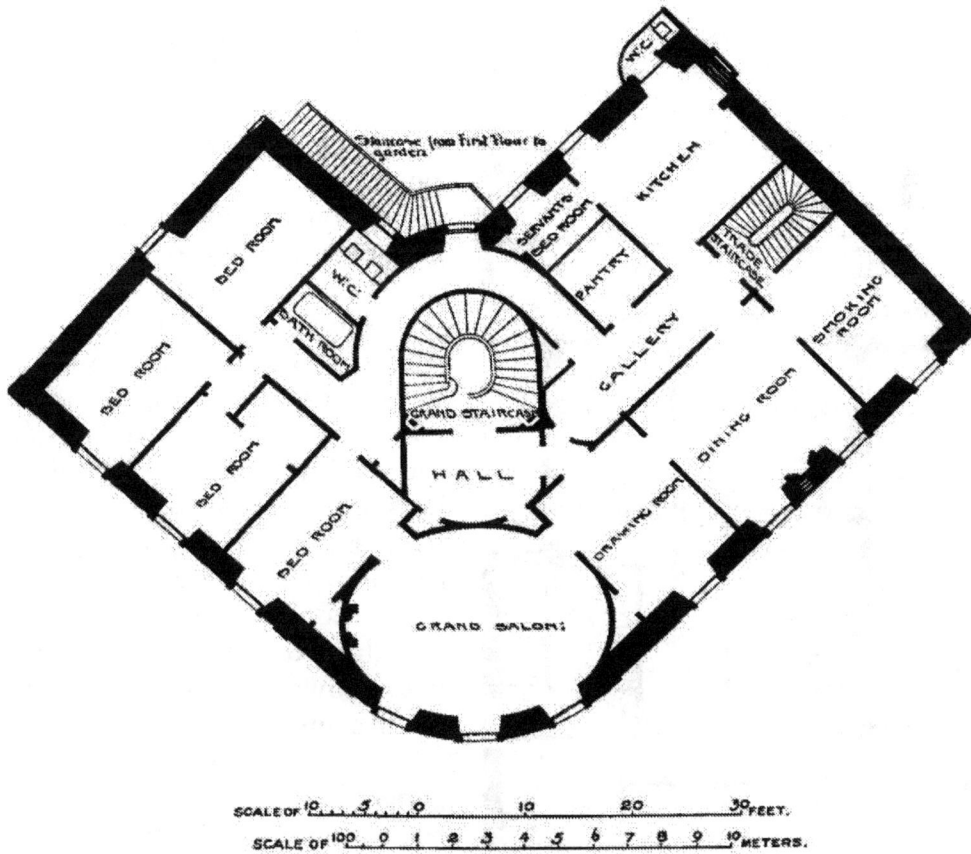

FIG. 193.—LISBON.

L. C. Pedro d'Avila, Architect.

Lisbon.—Two plans of modern buildings in Lisbon have been selected. Fig. 193 is an example of a good class flat. This form of plan with an oval room at the angle seems popular. There is one suite to a floor, and the staircase has a top light; in England we should probably have placed the staircase against the external wall, and made the communication through the hall, which would have been increased by the area of the passage. The shape of the flues is interesting.

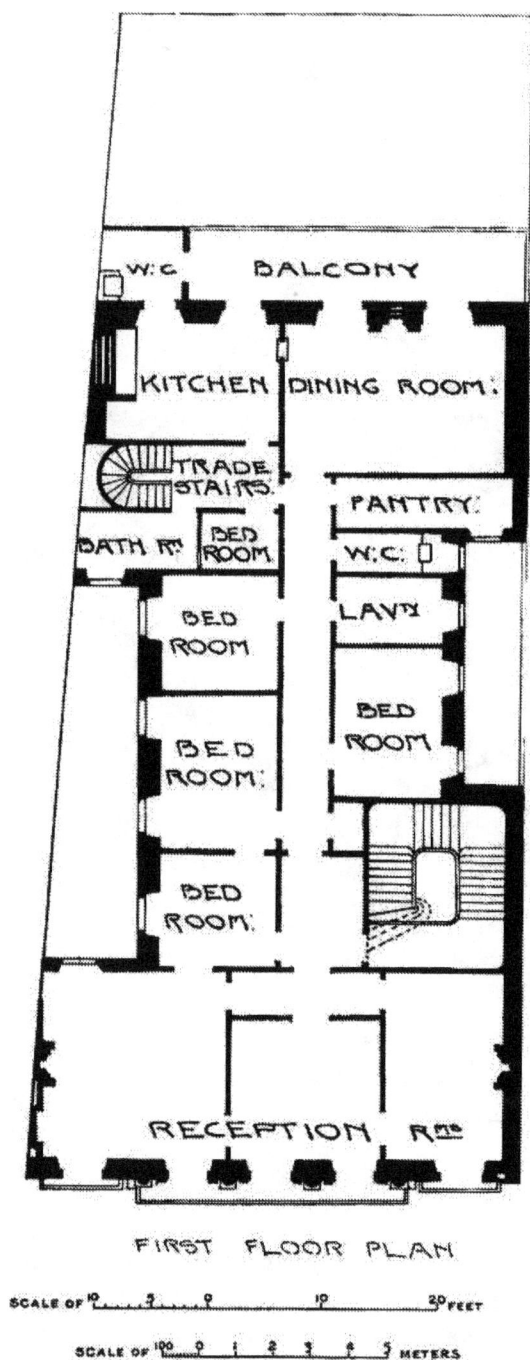

FIRST FLOOR PLAN

SCALE OF

FIG. 194.—LISBON.

L. C. Pedro d'Avila, Architect.

Fig. 194 is a plan showing a large suite. The communication to the trade staircase is at the side of the ground floor. The W.C. is often entered direct from the kitchen, but apart from this the plans generally are not unlike English flats. There is a staircase inside the ground floor suite, no doubt for an optional arrangement, as it does not appear on the plan of the floor above or the floor below.

Budapest is acknowledged to be one of the finest cities in Europe, and it may certainly be described as thoroughly modern. Its buildings are constructed of a good freestone. Elaborate façades are shown in illustrations Nos. 198, 199, and 200,—such a wealth of detail and ornament is unknown in Flat buildings in other countries.

A modern block of flats is generally a building covering a large area, and from three to five stories high. The ground floor is used for shops, cafés, and restaurants. On the outskirts of the city the ground floor is used for residential suites, but this does not happen in the central parts of Budapest. The streets have an average width of 100 ft., but some boulevards are from 250 to 300 ft. wide.

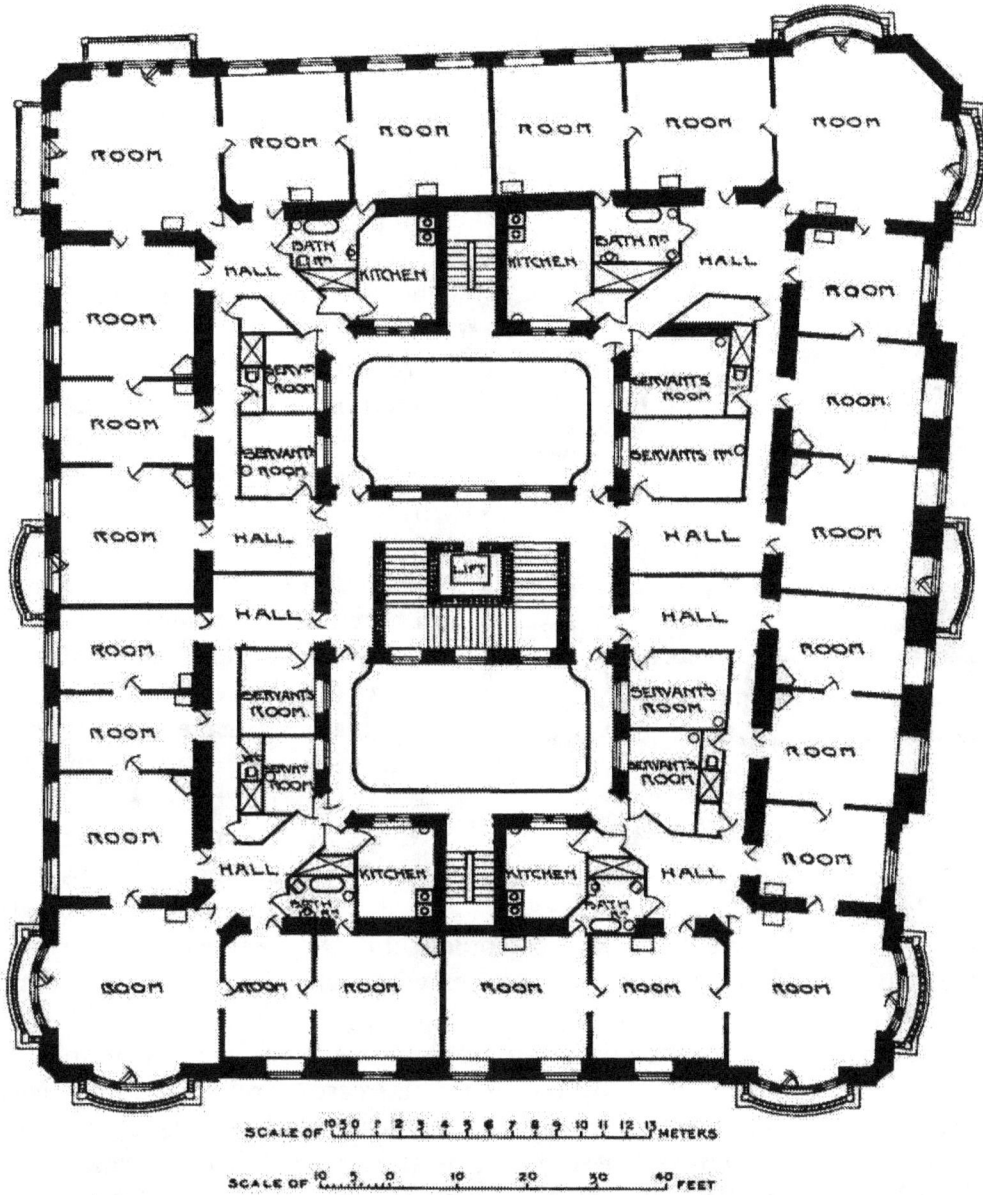

ROOM ROOM ROOM ROOM ROOM ROOM
ROOM
HALL BATH Nº KITCHEN KITCHEN BATH Nº HALL
SERVANT'S ROOM
ROOM
SERVANTS ROOM
HALL HALL
HALL LIFT HALL
ROOM
SERVANTS ROOM
SERVANTS ROOM
ROOM HALL KITCHEN KITCHEN HALL ROOM
BATH Nº BATH Nº
ROOM ROOM ROOM ROOM ROOM ROOM

SCALE OF 10 5 0 1 2 3 4 5 6 7 8 9 10 11 12 13 METERS

SCALE OF 10 5 0 10 20 30 40 FEET

FIG. 195.—BUDAPEST.

Desiderius von Hültl, Architect.

Private houses are unknown in the city; all the inhabitants live in flats, with the exception of the aristocracy, who have palaces. In the suburbs there are a few villas, which are a somewhat modern idea.

The flats are enormous blocks, often built on the balcony system.

The areas and courtyards are large, and consequently the rooms are well lighted. According to the city regulations the courtyards must be 15 per cent. of the whole area for a building three stories high, and 20 per cent. of the total area for a building four stories high. The stairs must be fireproof, and, as in Paris, the main entrance and staircase are the central features of the building, where marble and bronze are the rule rather than the exception, for the best class flats.

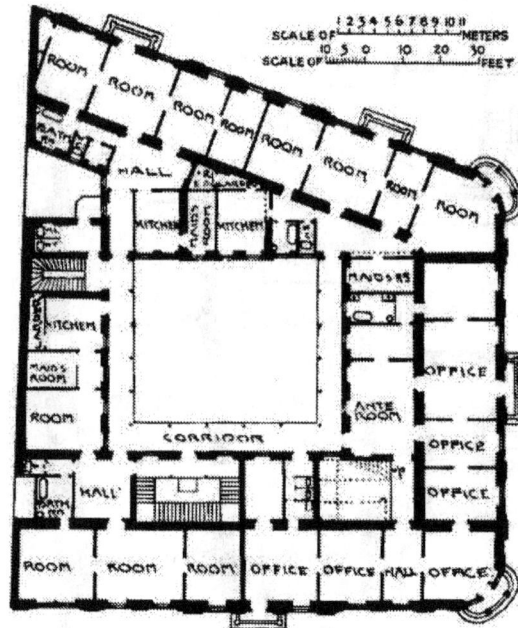

FIG. 196.—BUDAPEST.

Professor Alois Hauszmann, Architect.

Fig. 195 shows a good example of the balcony system. There are eight suites on each floor, four of them being entered from the balcony. There is one main staircase, well lighted and wide, and having the lift as usual in the centre, the whole plan forming an economical arrangement impossible in a cold climate. The offices and servants' rooms front the balconies, and the best rooms overlook the streets. This block has four sides with street frontage, a frequent arrangement, shown also in Figs. 198 and 199.

Fig. 196A is the plan of an upper floor of a very large block, having eight suites served by two main staircases, and trade staircases conveniently placed. The rooms communicate, and passages seem to be avoided as much as possible. The thickness of the internal walls should be noted, also that the W.C.'s ventilate into the small air shafts so strongly objected to in England, but which are still built in parts of America. The suites are small and certainly compact.

Fig. 197 shows another plan by the same architects. In this, part of the block is used as club premises; some of the W.C.'s have ventilation into a large court, and there is a certain amount of passage space. Fig. 198 is a view looking towards the narrow end.

Figs. 199 and 200 are typical examples of the façades of blocks of flats recently erected; the plans are similar in principle

For View of this portion see Fig. 198.

Fig. 197.—FLATS, BUDAPEST.

Korb & Giergl, Architects.

Fig. 196a.—AN UPPER FLOOR PLAN

FIG. 199.—RESIDENTIAL FLATS, BUDAPEST.

Korb & Giergl, Architects.

FIG. 200.—RESIDENTIAL FLATS, BUDAPEST.

Adorjan Gaál, Architect.

to those illustrated, but have unfortunately been crowded out, as have several other plans and elevations.

Holland.—The houses are generally built on what is known as the "top and bottom" system. The entrance doors are side by side at the street level. One tenant has the ground floor and first floor, and the other tenant occupies the second and third floors. The system is very similar to that adopted for artisans' flats around London (see Fig. 58), except that each tenant has two floors instead of one. Flats are, however, built, and Fig. 201 is an example.

The position of the lift is worth consideration. It well fills an odd corner, and even the London Building Act does not require a window on every floor for a lift ; here it is practically inside the suite.

FIG. 198.—MIETHSHÄUSER DER ERZHERZOGIN CLOTHILDE, BUDAPEST.

Korb & Giergl, Architects.

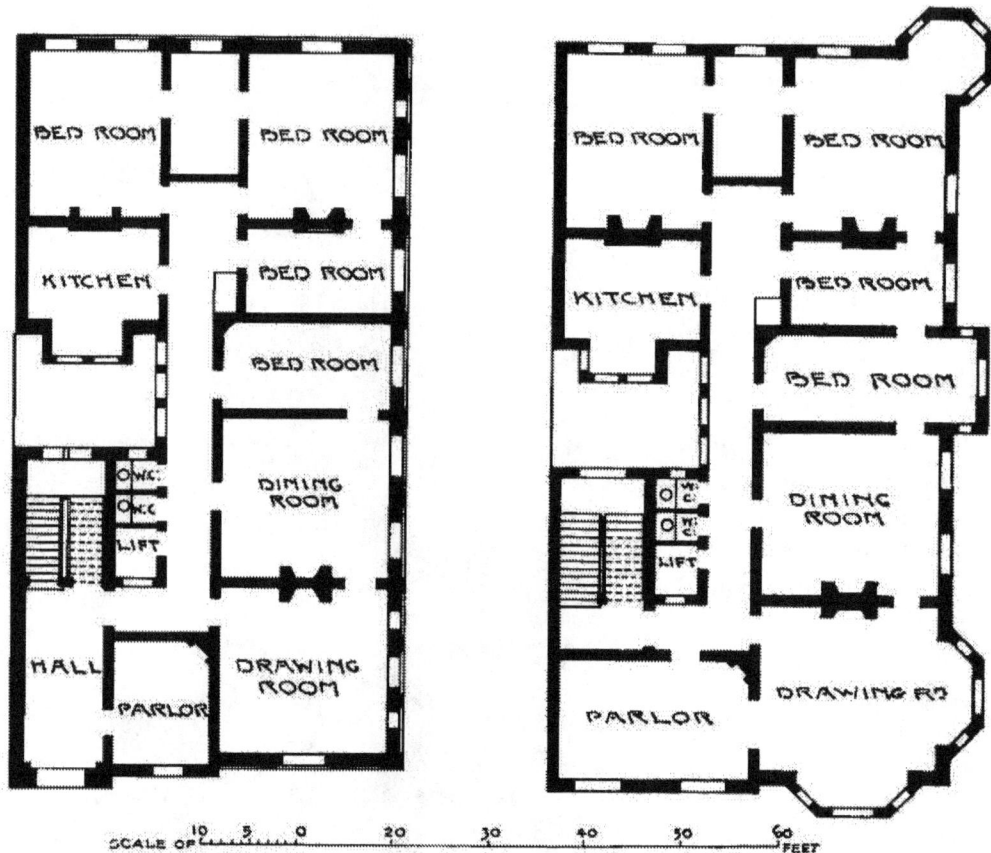

SCALE OF

FIG. 201.—AMSTERDAM.

Dr P. J. H. Cuypers, Architect.

America.—The Ansonia is the largest block of flats in the world. That is typical of America where the expression "sky-scraper" comes from. Yet in the early days the Americans did not take so kindly to the flat movement as we did.

Twenty or thirty years ago architectural students did not go to Paris in such numbers as they do to-day. Had they done so the badly planned buildings would probably have never been built. French plans are admired as much in America as they are in England. In a recent number of the *Architectural Review* (Boston, Mass.), the writer states : "Perhaps no better types for study can be found than those in France." Nearly all the illustrations in the book are French, and no English plans are given.

The early American plans had two defects, each the result of an attempt to build a large block on too narrow frontage—the rooms were badly lighted, and there were long passages. The defect as to light was not so apparent at first, because the blocks usually towered high above adjoining property, but when similar flats were built on each side, the result was that the rooms, with the exception of those with frontages at each end of the site, were quite spoiled.

Architects saw the failure of the early buildings and studied French plans, and the result has been good, and modern blocks have ample frontage to allow a good courtyard or area at the rear. A scullery is not built. There is a sink in the kitchen, and a pantry is planned between the kitchen and the dining-room; this acts as a "buffer" room, as advised in another chapter; sound does not penetrate from the kitchen to the dining-room, and the system saves the servants much work. The ventilation of the W.C. is often arranged in a manner we do not consider satisfactory. In the best class flats the bath-room has a W.C. apparatus, and the only ventilation is into an air shaft about 4 ft. by 4 ft., and when the building is perhaps fifteen stories high, the word ventilation seems an exaggeration.

In many large blocks of flats recently erected, the servants' W.C. is only entered from the bedroom; in fact, it is a slip taken off that room. Such an arrangement would of course be condemned here.

The hall and dining-room often form one room, with an arrangement to shut off the room by screens or curtains if required. This is an excellent method where space is so valuable, and one we might well adopt; passage space is saved and becomes room space.

In an English flat there is rarely more than one bath-room. In a few large suites a bath-room is sometimes provided for the servants, but one bath-room only is the general rule. In America a bath-room is usually built between every two bedrooms; each has a door into it. This room also has a W.C. apparatus, and a flat with five bedrooms will have three bath-rooms and three W.C.'s. In England many people object to a W.C. apparatus in a bath-room; in America it is the universal arrangement. A W.C. as we plan it seems almost unknown, except where a slip is divided off from a bedroom as stated above. In planning from a sanitary point of view, the Americans are not so particular as the French or ourselves.

The "maisonette" principle is not unknown in New York, but it is not so common as it is here. One experiment was tried a few years ago and was not considered a success, but in a large block recently erected, each suite occupies two floors, and it has let well.

With regard to the block plan, Americans are alive to the advantages of a recess over an enclosed area, especially for the large blocks of buildings like the Ansonia (see Figs. 202 and 203). The façade is certainly not improved, and the expense is increased because the architectural features, such as the cornice, &c., must be carried round the recess, while an area would be left perfectly plain. But the advantage for lighting is considerable. The excellence of French flats is so well known in America, that the owner will often refer to his property as "first class French flats."

An examination of American plans shows that a larger number of cupboards are provided than is usual in London. In this feature also the architects follow the French ideas.

In the best buildings there are many little conveniences unknown to us. A writer in the *Architectural Record* (vol. xi.) states : "Here the tenant has provided for him telephones, heat, hot-water service, refrigeration, gas for fuel, storage for his bicycle, filtering plants, indoor laundry and drying apparatus, and frequently a roof garden. Coal and ice bills are to him unknown."

In America there are three classes of flats—(1) self-contained, (2) with a restaurant on the ground floor for optional use, (3) catering flats. We have all these classes of buildings, but in New York flats attached to hotels are very general. The recent extension of the Savoy Hotel (Figs. 160 and 161) is the first attempt on a large scale in England to provide such a building.

In London the address of a block of flats is usually unnecessarily long and often confusing, which titles are so similar, that there seem to be hundreds of "Hyde Court Mansions" and "De Vere Park Gardens," names often given to third and fourth class flats. The result is that the word "Mansion" has long ceased to convey the idea of a mansion, and when "Gardens" are referred to, few people expect to see a garden.

In America the names of flats are less confusing and shorter, and we might well follow the example and name our buildings "The Ansonia," "The Holland," "The Arlington," or "The Hereford."

The law in New York that compels owners to have windows on each floor to ventilate the staircase is strongly objected to by many architects, and the plans given show this harsh regulation does not exist in other American cities (see Figs. 208 and 209).

Many suburban flats have been built in America. The buildings are usually about four stories high, the plan is not so cramped as in the cities, and a certain amount of garden space is frequently found between the blocks.

The servants' room is usually entered from the kitchen only, a defect we are avoiding in the best class flats, but when the W.C. is

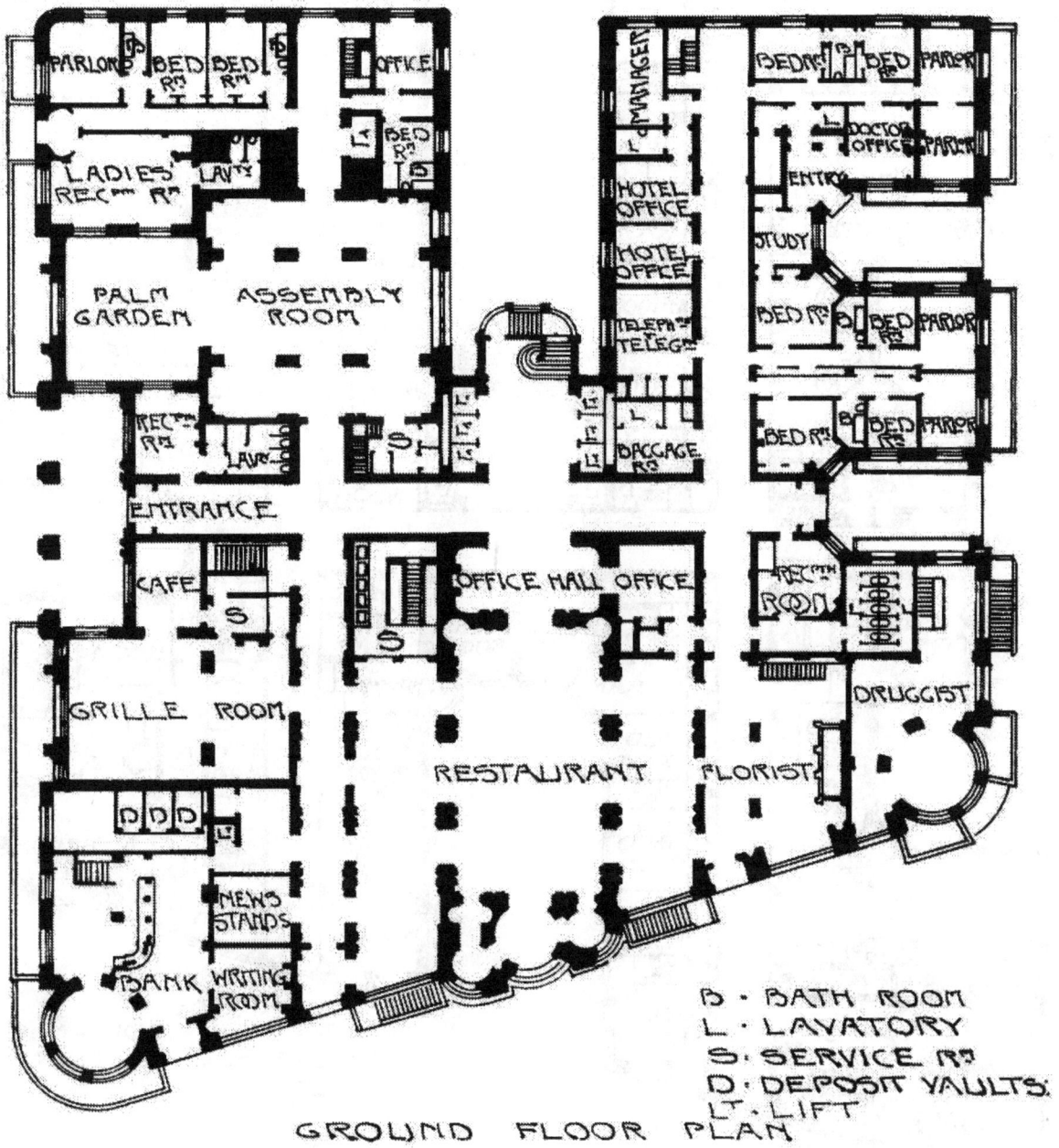

PARLORD | BED | BED | | OFFICE
R^M | R^M

LADIES | LAV^{TY} | | BED
REC^N R^M | | | R^M

PALM | ASSEMBLY
GARDEN | ROOM

REC^N R^M
LAV^Y

ENTRANCE

CAFE | S

GRILLE ROOM

D D D

NEWS STANDS

BANK | WRITING ROOM

MANAGER
BED R^M | BED | PARLOR
HOTEL OFFICE | DOCTOR OFFICE PARLOR
HOTEL OFFICE | ENTRY
TELEPH^N TELEG^M | STUDY
L | BED R^M | BED | PARLOR
R^M
BAGGAGE R^M | BED R^M | BED | PARLOR
R^M

OFFICE HALL OFFICE | REC^N ROOM
S

DRUGGIST

RESTAURANT | FLORIST

B · BATH ROOM
L · LAVATORY
S · SERVICE R^M
D · DEPOSIT VAULTS
LT · LIFT

GROUND FLOOR PLAN

FIG. 202.—THE AN

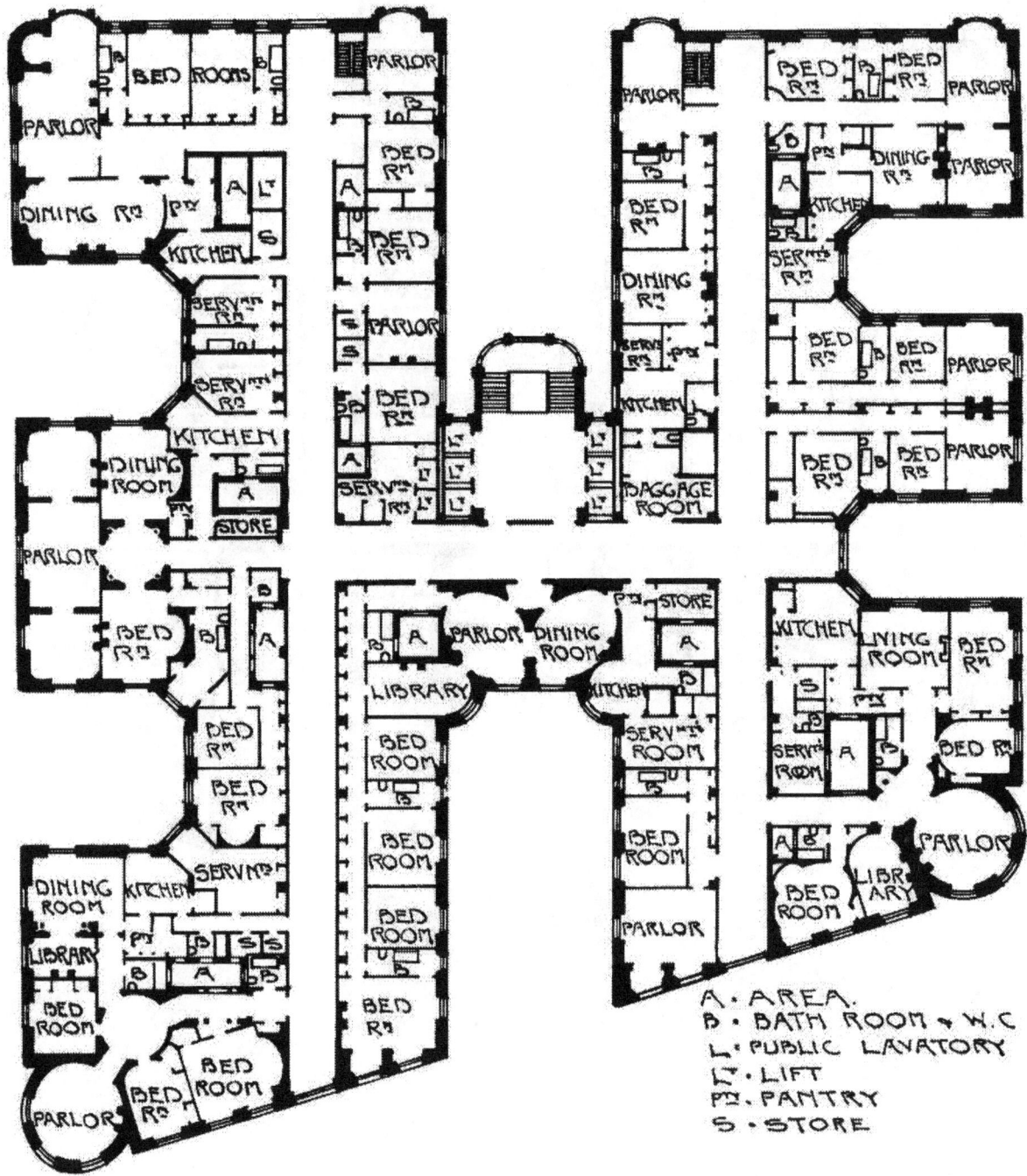

PARLOR

BED ROOMS

DINING RM

KITCHEN

SERVT RM

SERVT RM

KITCHEN

DINING ROOM

PARLOR

BED RM

BED RM

SERVTS

DINING ROOM

KITCHEN

LIBRARY

BED ROOM

PARLOR

BED RM

BED ROOM

PARLOR

BED RM

BED RM

PARLOR

BED RM

PARLOR

LIBRARY

BED ROOM

BED ROOM

BED RM

LIBRARY

PARLOR DINING ROOM

KITCHEN

STORE

SERVTS ROOM

BED ROOM

PARLOR

BED RM

BED RM

DINING RM

PARLOR

PARLOR

BED RM

PARLOR

BED RM

BED RM

PARLOR

SERVTS RM

KITCHEN

BAGGAGE ROOM

KITCHEN

LIVING ROOM

BED RM

SERVT ROOM

BED RM

BED ROOM

LIBRARY

PARLOR

A · AREA·
B · BATH ROOM & W.C
L · PUBLIC LAVATORY
LT · LIFT
PY · PANTRY
S · STORE

PLAN OF UPPER FLOORS

NSONIA, NEW YORK.

Paul Emile Duboy, Architect.

entered only from the bedroom, the slops would of course not pass through the kitchen, but this arrangement is not good. The W.C. should of course be entered from a passage or scullery, or from the open.

Americans are beginning to appreciate the open fireplace, and many blocks are being erected as in England. But the "fake" fireplace, without any flue, and built only for appearance is not unknown.

Sometimes a small lavatory is placed between two bedrooms; this has a fixed basin (no W.C.), and shows again the influence of French plans.

New York is not as smoky or dirty as London, consequently the roof of a block can be used as a garden. A large portion is roofed over, it is open at the sides, and is known as a "sun-parlour."

A bath-room for the servants is as general in America as it is rare here.

There is communication between the sitting-rooms as in Paris, and American plans show the resemblance to French rather than English buildings. The two principal differences from the former are the extra bath-rooms and the servant's bedroom included in the suite. The staircase is rectangular, and the fact that it is little used compared with the lift is recognised. There is often a laundry in the basement.

In America flats are apparently as popular as in London; in New York during 1903, only fifty-six dwelling-houses were built for the occupancy of single families.

In America, blocks of flats not more than three stories high cost 5½d. to 7d. per foot cube; if four or five stories high, part of the building must be fireproof, and a fire-escape staircase must be provided. The cost is 10d. to 1s. per foot cube. If the building is six or more stories high, the cost is 1s. 5d. to 1s. 8d. per foot cube; this includes fireproof construction throughout.

As in England, suburban flats have not proved successful except in a few favourable districts.

Shops on the ground floor are considered undesirable, and basement suites are rare. The space is usually occupied by a laundry, porter's room, furnace chambers, store rooms, &c.

America follows the French example, and the entrance halls and staircases are finer and better decorated than in England.

The Ansonia, New York (Figs. 202 and 203).—An idea of the immensity of this building may be gathered from the fact that it contains 2,710 rooms and domestic offices besides the public rooms. There are more than 179 miles of piping. In the cellar there is an electric plant generating 20,000 sixteen candle-power lamps, and about 400 electric horse-power. There is a large restaurant in connection with the building, and private catering service is supplied to many apartments.

There are 122 suites, known as housekeeping apartments, having kitchens, refrigerator, ice-water, and so on. All the water supplied to the bath-rooms is four times filtered, while the drinking water is delivered to the butlers' pantries at almost freezing point.

There are some 200 bachelor apartments consisting of from one to three rooms and bath-room, so planned that various combinations, such as four rooms and two bath-rooms, may be made as occasion arises. Some of these rooms are let furnished. Tenants can employ either their own servants or those of the house, and this remark also applies to the housekeeping apartments. Any of the tenants can either take their meals in the restaurant, or have them served from their own kitchens in their rooms. A spare room and bath-room is provided on each floor, and may be rented for single nights. The dairy in the basement has a daily turnover of 150 to 200 dollars per day in milk, cream, and eggs alone. Here is also a large laundry where everything is done by machinery. Every particle of clothing is submitted to 650 degrees of steam heat, which is sufficient to ensure the destruction of any possible microbes.

The building has seventeen floors above the street level and two below it, while in some parts there are two additional floors in the roof. There are billiard-rooms and private dining-rooms, while there is a large dining-room on the sixteenth floor seating 450 persons at small tables or 1,000 at large tables. There are twenty-one elevators. The area covered by the building is 50,000 sq. ft. The foundations are of cast-iron columns resting on the solid rock. The floors are fireproof, and consist of a series of arches in a concrete known as the "Roteling." In the basement is a carpenter's shop for repairs, and a fire-hose runs through the building. There is a swimming-bath 100 ft. long. The servants are accommodated on the seventeenth floor.

The architect is a Frenchman.

The Arlington, New York (Fig. 204).—The plan of one floor is given. It will be noted the "first floor" is known in England as the "ground floor." This is a block of catering flats somewhat similar to many in London. One suite on each upper floor has a combined

FIG. 203.—THE ANSONIA, NEW YORK.

Paul Emile Duboy, Architect.

bed and sitting-room, the others have two or three rooms. The exterior is very similar to Fig. 205.

Madison Avenue, New York (Fig. 206).—A compact plan, with useful sliding doors between the drawing-room and library. The

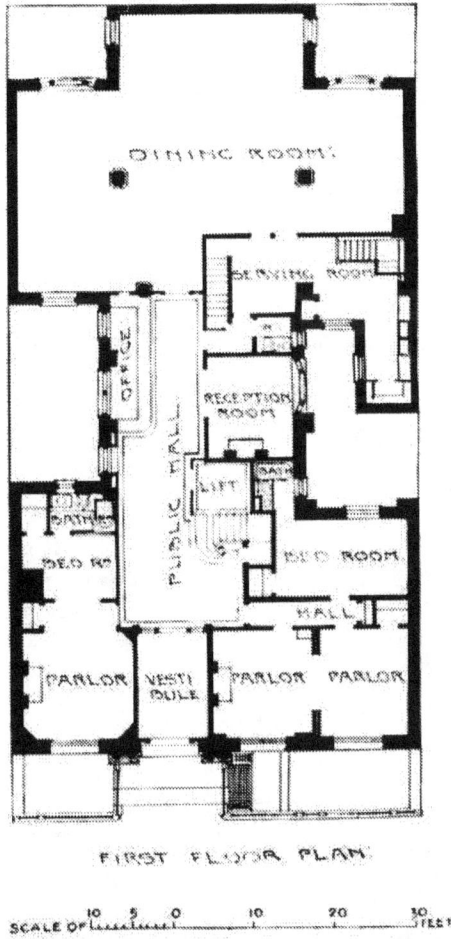

FIG. 204.—THE ARLINGTON, NEW YORK.

FIG. 205.—THE WARRINGTON, MADISON AVENUE, NEW YORK.

Israels & Harder, Architects.

dining-room is near the kitchen with the servants' entrance through the pantry. There is but little passage room considering the size of each suite.

The Alimar, New York (Fig. 207).—This is a typical American plan. The upper ends of the corridors are dependent upon borrowed

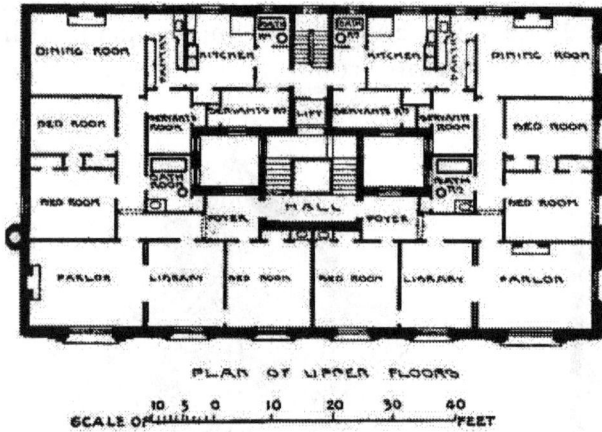

PLAN OF UPPER FLOORS

SCALE OF 10 5 0   10   20   30   40 FEET

FIG. 206.—MADISON AVENUE, NEW YORK.

Buchman & Fox, Architects.

light, but they only lead to bedrooms, and this should not be considered a defect; see the chapter on planning. We should not care for a W.C. to open off a servant's bedroom. The pantry, as usual, is between the dining-room and kitchen.

Brookline, Mass. (Fig. 208).—The arrangement of the hall

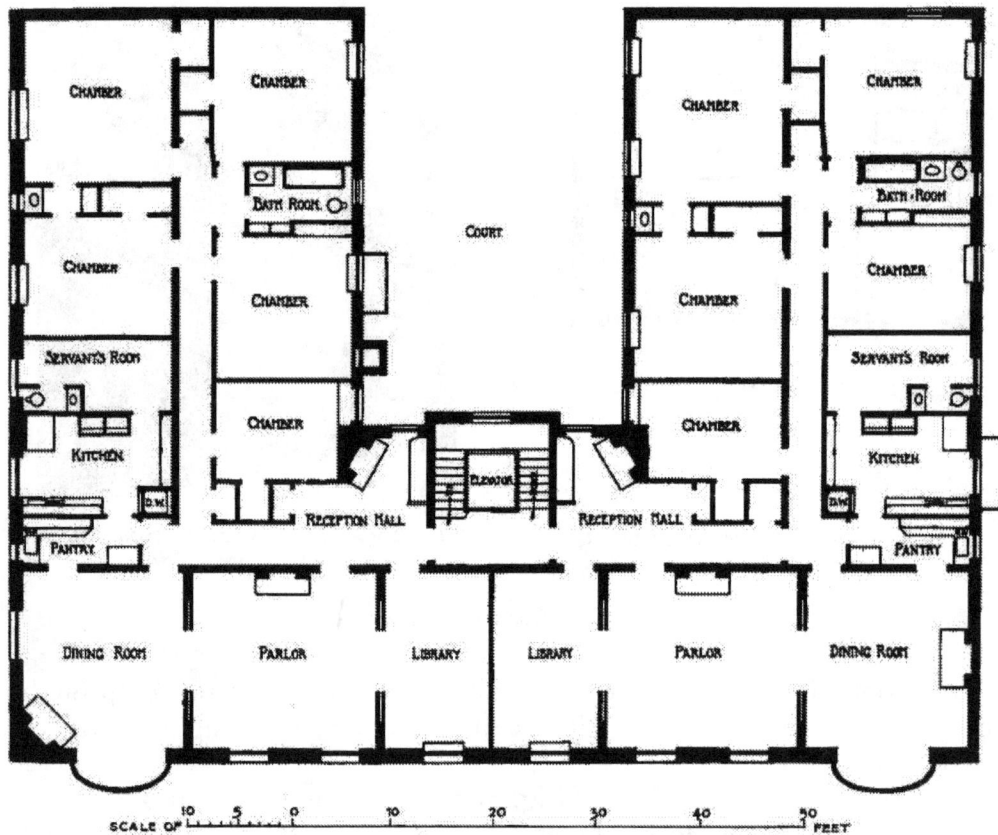

SCALE OF 10 5 0   10   20   30   40   50 FEET

FIG. 207.—THE ALIMAR, NEW YORK.

Janes & Leo, Architects.

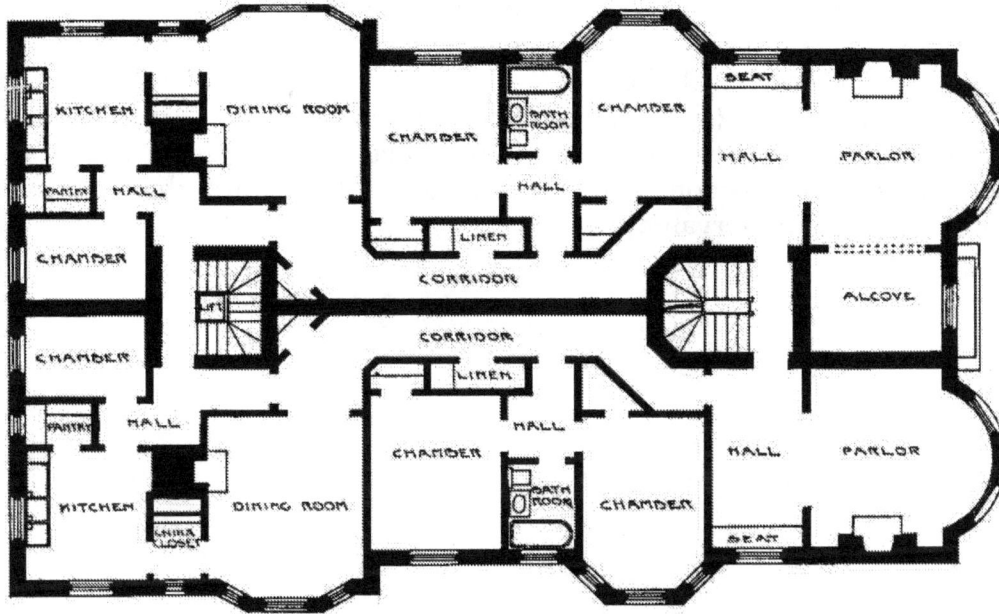

SECOND FLOOR PLAN

SCALE OF 10 5 0 10 20 FEET

FIG. 208.—BROOKLINE, MASS., U.S.A.

Kilham & Hopkins, Architects.

FLATS
BOSTON MASS

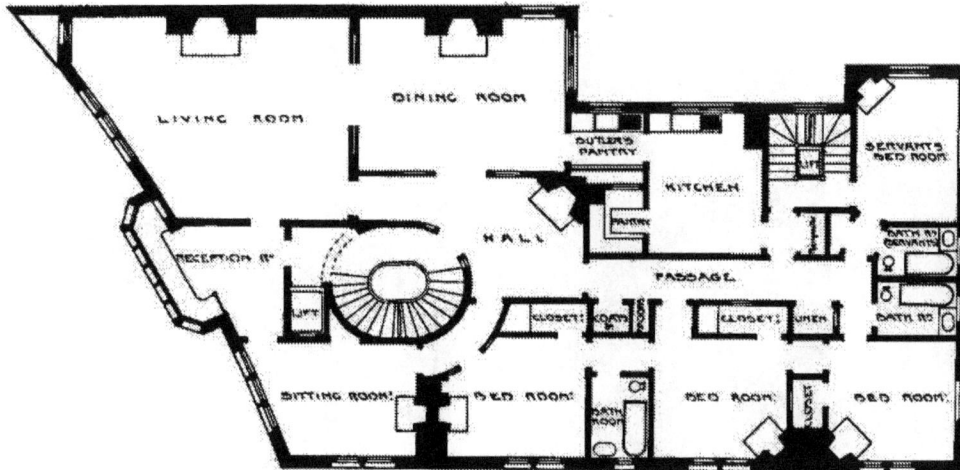

SECOND FLOOR PLAN

SCALE OF 10 5 0 10 20 FEET

FIG. 209.—BOSTON, MASS., U.S.A.

Kilham & Hopkins, Architects.

and parlour should be noted, and the great advantage of having a top-lighted staircase ; the plan is very compact and cheap, but the corridors depend upon borrowed light.

Boston, Mass. (Fig. 209).—Another staircase with a top light. There is one suite to each floor. As usual, the butler's pantry is between the dining-room and the kitchen. There are three bath-rooms, one for the servants.

Chapter VII.

FINANCIAL MATTERS.

The building of flats is a speculation, and like every other building enterprise the result may be satisfactory or a great failure. The risk is considerable, and it is often found that, however healthy the scheme may look on paper, when the buildings are erected, the rents received are less than the estimated figures, while the outgoings are considerably larger.

Profit.—Some builders say they will not entertain a scheme unless they can see a clear 10 per cent. profit. It is doubtful if many flats pay 10 per cent., and if the builder pays 5 per cent. for his capital he cannot make as much. As a private enterprise there should be a return of 7 or 8 per cent., if the scheme is financed upon an honest principle, and if the suites are let at rents over £80 per annum.

Demand and Accommodation.—The demand for flats varies considerably in different districts, and the first point to consider with reference to a site is the likelihood, in that neighbourhood, of easily letting the suites at a fair rent. If there are other flats in the district, they should be visited, and the rents noted, and also the number of empty suites. The architect must arrange to give as good, and if possible, better accommodation for the same rental. This of course applies more particularly to suburban neighbourhoods, where flats are generally let on short tenancies. The result is that the tenants leave the old flats and take suites in the new buildings. This is all very well at first, but in a few years' time other blocks are built, and the recently well-let flats become half empty. The surveyor should bear this in mind when valuing a new block of buildings; the point for him to consider is not so much the rents received and the number of flats let at the time of his visit, but the probable state of affairs a few years later.

Flatland.—Kensington is the old centre for flats ; the movement has spread eastwards gradually and the buildings in the neighbourhood of Piccadilly and the West End generally are of more recent date. There is a large number of these buildings in Chelsea, and the neighbourhood round Kensington, where flats have been built for many years. Southwards from Kensington the movement has spread to Battersea, Clapham, &c., but the great development now is in a north-western direction. The neighbourhood of Baker Street was found to be successful, and many blocks were built in the Marylebone Road. West and South Hampstead followed, and now Maida Vale is much in demand.

Many flats have recently been erected near Piccadilly and St James's Street, several of them for bachelors, and Fig. 106 is the plan of a block being erected on a splendid site opposite St James's Palace. There is no doubt the demand is increasing, for some people want to live in a certain neighbourhood, where they cannot afford a private house, but are willing to pay a greater rent, considering the accommodation they obtain, for a flat ; thus paying something for the locality and the address.

Localities for Flats.—The best neighbourhood for flats, if they are to be a financial success, is one where the rents are high. The site is of course expensive, but that is taken into account. Flats are somewhat different to ordinary dwelling-houses, for a speculation in low-rented property in a poor district will often pay a better return than highly rented houses in a first-class neighbourhood. Flats are different ; they are not a success, generally speaking, away from a fashionable residential quarter. For this reason there is no demand for flats in provincial cities in England ; the fashionable residential neighbourhood in the centre of the town does not exist. There are no good class flats in Manchester, Birmingham, Leeds, or Liverpool. The better class people can get out of the cities in a short time, and naturally people prefer living in the country. That is impossible in London, on account of its size, so it may be said to be the only important city in England that contains a fashionable residential quarter.

Cost of Site.—As a rule the better the site is, the better will be the financial result. The cost of the land is divided between the many suites. The cost of the building is practically the same in a good neighbourhood as in a second-rate locality, but the rents will vary considerably, and in a much greater proportion than the site values.

As an instance compare the value of land in the West End of London and the suburbs, and the rent of a suite, giving the same accommodation in each case.

Rental and Demand.—There is a good demand for suites up to £200 a year, but above that rent the demand decreases. The difference in rents between the best part of London and the suburbs for the same accommodation is quite 50 per cent.; assuming the cost of building to be as much as 10 per cent. less, the difference in the value of the site in a large block of buildings will not make up the balance. Generally it may be said that the risk of a failure in a good residential quarter is much less than in the suburbs. There is one block of flats on the south side of the Thames that cost £9,000, and if bought to-day for £5,000 would only pay 4½ per cent.

Suburban Flats.—These are not, generally speaking, a success at present. The time will no doubt come when the buildings erected will be more in demand. Maida Vale one would hardly call a suburb, and Battersea is part of London. The movement spreads more rapidly towards the north than it does towards the south; the Thames seems to be a boundary. An instance may be given of two blocks, in all respects similar. One was built at Maida Vale, and the suites let readily at £75 per annum; the other was built at Clapham, £65 was asked for the suites, and half of them would not let at that rent. Flats in some parts of Clapham have been a success, and low-rented suites at Brixton have let well. Wimbledon and Putney are not desirable neighbourhoods; flats at Richmond have been a success, but this borough has many advantages, the river, the park, and an exceptional train service. Many large blocks of suburban flats are being built in America, where they seem to be more popular than in England.

Flats near the stations on the "Tube" have increased in value, and in Fulham the rents have improved quite 15 per cent. during the last few years.

Rent per Room.—Kensington flats will let at £30 to £35 a room; in one large block a rent of £40 a room is obtained. A speculator should not entertain a scheme in a good district unless each room, including the kitchen, will let at £20 per annum. Outside London the rents are as low as £10 a room. In the neighbourhood of Earl's Court they average about £15 or £16 a room.

Creating a New Neighbourhood.—Some big schemes have

paid very well in localities where the character of the neighbourhood has been entirely changed by the erection of new buildings. A large area has been bought consisting of several streets of poor property, almost slums, but close to a better neighbourhood, and blocks of flats have been built. The owners, by carrying out a large enterprise like this, are able to avoid difficulties of light and air, which may wreck a small scheme. The owners widen the roads and generally improve the neighbourhood.

Cost of Building.—In London the cost of building is so heavy that flats let at a low rental rarely pay a good percentage upon the outlay. A block of buildings with suites at less than £70 a year is seldom a financial success. As a rule, the higher the rentals are the better the result; as soon as the rents are over £100 the enterprise will look more healthy. Many firms will not entertain a speculation if the estimated rents are below £80 per annum. Good class flats will let on a repairing lease for seven, fourteen, or twenty-one years, but flats at about £60 per annum will only let on a three years' agreement; the result is, that at the end of every period, about £20 has to be spent on decoration.

Profit.—Flats should pay a better profit than other buildings because they are certainly not as desirable as other property. It is impossible to make any rule as to the proportion of empty suites, but a manager with considerable experience stated that with low-rented flats he found as a rule that one quarter were empty; that was an average over a large number of properties.

Objections.—One great objection to building flats is the difficulty in selling a block, even when well let. The average investor prefers other property. So many buildings have failed to pay the profits anticipated, and have fallen into the hands of mortgagees, on account of the trouble of management and the difficulty of selling.

Management.—Although a block of flats has been compared to a terrace of houses piled one above the other, there is, as it were, a portion of the street included; in a terrace it is a public way, repairable by the authorities; in a block of flats it is a staircase, repairable by the owner. This business element is always present with flats—a man may let all his houses in a terrace, and he has parted with all his property—not so with flats, he is still responsible for staircase, external repairs, lift, servants, &c.; he cannot get rid of this liability, and a mortgagee in possession finds he is responsible for something very different to a row of houses : he owns a business.

Speculation.—Flats are erected either by private owners or by speculating builders. In the former case the owners cannot expect to make the profit of the latter class, as the employer has to pay the builder a profit on the prime cost of the work, and apart from that, a builder naturally works in a more economical manner when building for himself, and builders who tender for work under architects are usually picked men, who do work in a manner superior to the speculating builder.

Cost per foot cube.—The cost of buildings erected by tender varies in accordance with the class of flat. Flats let at about £50 per annum will cost from about 9d. to 1s. per foot cube, and the best class flats from about 1s. 2d. to 1s. 9d. Some particulars of the cost of artisans' dwellings are given in the chapter on that subject (p. 56), also on pp. 220-223.

The flats at Tufnell Park (Fig. 139) cost 8½d. per foot cube, excluding the foundations, which were of a peculiar and unusual description.

Small Rooms.—One complaint constantly made about flats is that the rooms are too small. The size is of course regulated by the site, the cost of the building, and the probable return by way of rent, but it is well to remember that increasing the size of rooms does not increase the cost of building at the same rate per foot cube.

Increased Cost for Larger Rooms.—The larger the rooms are, the lower the rate for the whole building, for the expensive parts, the main walls, sanitary work, &c., will remain practically the same. As an instance, if the kitchens at Tufnell Park (Fig. 139) had been 5 ft. longer, the extra cost per block, according to the priced quantities, would have been £68. 19s. 5d., or nearly 3d. per foot cube. As stated above, the cost of the whole was 8½d. per foot cube. The example is perhaps an extreme one, as no cross walls, or thicker joists are taken; a slice, 5 ft. long, is inserted in the middle of the kitchen. Larger rooms as a rule necessitate all the joists being thicker, &c., but the example illustrates the principle, and the architect should not be afraid of larger rooms, and the large number of suites unlet in many well-situated blocks of buildings shows it is false economy to be too careful when building; to remedy the defect afterwards is always very costly, and frequently impossible. It is also a mistake to build five poor bedrooms instead of four good rooms—do not try and crowd too much on the site.

The Speculating Architect.—When the great development of the London suburbs took place some years ago, many speculating builders made large fortunes. Since then the demand for suburban property has fallen off, and the builders have turned their attention to flats, many again most successfully. When they erected suburban villas, they did not require the services of architects—that is apparent, alas! to all; but when they commenced to build in London, there arose difficulties of light and air, the Building Act, the adjoining owner, and the many little worries unknown to a man when developing an entire suburban estate. The architect became necessary to him. That put the architect in touch with speculation, and he started schemes of his own. The result is the speculating architect of to-day. He looks out for a site, obtains the refusal, prepares plans and a financial statement showing the profit to be made, lays his figures before financial people, and if approved he is instructed to proceed, and the building is erected by tender in the usual way. On the other hand his scheme may not be approved; in that case he has done his work for nothing, and commences looking for a better site. There are several architects who do little business except of this nature; their experience with flats is great, and their planning is usually good. Sometimes flats are erected by a method that makes it difficult to discover where the speculating builder leaves off, and where the speculating architect begins.

Catering Flats.—Great care should be taken by an intending purchaser of any of these buildings, as the figures are sometimes very misleading.

Finance.—A speculating builder in a good financial position has no difficulty in carrying out large works; and a man in a small way with a good reputation can get extensive credit, but the builder generally requires to be financed, and he borrows money usually at 6 per cent. Advances are made upon the certificate of a surveyor, say two-thirds of the prime cost, reckoned at about 10d. per foot cube.   Sometimes he draws advances at stated times according to a schedule, so much when the first floor joists are on, so much when the second floor joists are on, so much when the roof is on, &c. When the building is complete, a permanent mortgage can be obtained, but up to that time the proceeding is not without risk for the financier, as the cost of completing a half-finished building by another firm, in consequence of the failure of the builder, is frequently more than is anticipated, and of course much more than it would have cost the original man, had he not become bankrupt.   The speculating builder usually creates an improved ground rent, which is sold at about twenty-two years' purchase.   This is considered to be saleable when the building is roofed in.   The improved ground rent must not be too heavy, as the value of the leasehold interest is correspondingly diminished.   A ground rent is considered well secured if it is not more than one-fifth of the rack rent.

Sometimes a builder will obtain money by selling the improved ground rent before the building is completed, and before it is properly secured; he will sell at say four years' less purchase than it will eventually be worth.   The purchaser waits till the building is completed, and then sells at the full market value and makes his profit.   If the builder does not sell until the proper time, he usually regards the sale of the improved ground rent as his profit on the whole transaction.

Outgoings.—In preparing a scheme an allowance of 33⅓ of the total rack rents is often made for the "outgoings," but the portion is too small, and 40 per cent. should be deducted; and if valuing for a mortgage, a careful estimate should be made of the cost of repairs to the outside and staircase.   The operator who prepares a financial statement for a scheme, naturally views the enterprise in a favourable manner; he is anxious for it to go through, but managers of flat property, as a rule, reckon their outgoings to be quite 40 per cent.   This bears upon the allowance for rating, and some figures are given further on.

Bad Building.—There is no doubt that some years ago flats were badly built.   The speculating builder relied on selling his property as soon as it was completed, when it looked at its best, and before the defects from bad materials and workmanship had time to appear. This applied mainly to small men, and not to large firms who traded in flats and had a reputation to maintain. Of late years matters have improved considerably, and of course the flats erected under contract by good firms under architects are as well built as many other buildings, but the bad building of former days has had an effect on investors, and flats of all sorts and descriptions are regarded as hardly desirable property, and of course ground rents do not sell at the former prices. Some improved ground rents were sold some years ago at twenty-eight years' purchase ; now they would only sell at about twenty-one.

As an example of the cost of finance, &c., in one case the contract for the flats was £105,000. The fees, interests, cost of carpets and other expenses incurred before the tenants could enter, amounted to no less than £25,000.

Low-rented Suites and Artisans' Dwellings.—Flats at rents below £70 do not pay as a speculation in London. They may be built as an investment and yield a fair profit.

Artisans' dwellings cannot be erected to pay a large percentage, but they also can be built to make a fair return.

Cost of Finance.—An instance of the cost of finance may be given. Application was made to a well-known office for an advance of over £100,000. The surveyor's preliminary fee for considering the plans and scheme generally was £200; if the report were favourable, then an additional £300 had to be paid. Money, if lent, would be at the rate of 6 per cent. to 7 per cent., and in addition to this, the lenders frequently require, as an extra security, some good guarantee society to guarantee the loan, and for which the applicant would have to pay such society's premium, which is generally 1 per cent., and for a term of not less than three years.

If a scheme is a good one, and the builder a man in good position, he can get extensive credit from merchants, and obtain money at 5 per cent. upon the building during erection.

Artisans' Dwellings.—According to the Reports on the Dwellings of the Poor issued by the Mansion House Council for the year ending 1903, these buildings can be and are erected so as to return a fair percentage upon the outlay. The following are some of the instances given :—

COMPANY.	DIVIDENDS PAID.
Artisans', Labourers', and General Dwellings Co. Ltd. - -	4 per cent. on the tenements, 5 per cent. on the cottages.
East End Dwellings Co. Ltd. -	4 per. cent on Preference Share Capital, 5 per cent. on Ordinary Share Capital.
Four per Cent. Industrial Dwellings Co. Ltd. - - -	4 per cent. on Share Capital, 3½ per cent. on the Debenture Capital.
Improved Industrial Dwellings Co. Ltd. - - - -	5 per cent.
Peabody Donation Fund - -	2.4 per cent. on the whole Trust.
Tenement Dwellings Co. Ltd. -	5 per cent. to 6 per cent. nett on capital cost of buildings, after all expenses and depreciation.
Wharncliffe Dwellings Co. Ltd. -	£2. 17s. per cent.

In at least one case 1½ per cent. on the original outlay is put aside annually for the cost of repairs.

The following particulars of some flats let as weekly properties at Clapham may be interesting. The tenements are in a good neighbourhood, fairly well built, and let readily, one floor at 11s. 6d., the other at 12s. per week.

Gross rent for one year - - - - -		£61 2 0
Outgoings :—		
Ground Rent - - - -	£6 11 11	
Water Rate, £2. 6s. ; Rates, £12. 1s. 4d. -	14 7 4	
Repairs - - - - -	8 5 7	
Rent Collector (5 per cent.) - -	3 1 0	
Insurance - - - - -	0 6 0	
		32 11 10
Net Income		£28 10 2

In the case of two other houses, the rents were 11s. 6d. for each of the two floors; one suite was empty for nine weeks and eventually let for 12s.

Gross Rent for One Year - - - -		£114 16 6
Outgoings :—		
Ground Rent - - - -	£13 3 8	
Water Rate, £4. 12s.; Rates, £24. 2s. 5d.	28 14 5	
Repairs - - - - -	18 7 10	
Rent Collector (5 per cent.) - -	5 14 10	
Insurance - - - -	0 12 0	
		66 12 9
Net Income		£48 3 9

The following are the figures with reference to the Pott Street and Chester Street tenements, Manchester, giving the cost and income and expenditure for the four years, 1900-1903, inclusive :—

Year.	Receipts for Rents.			Rates, Repairs, and other Outgoings (exclusive of chief Rents and Debt Charges).			Net Rentals.			Cost of Buildings.			Value of Land at 10s. per sq. yd. (Price fixed by Sanitary Committee, 10th April 1899).			Total Estimated Cost (taking Land at Committee's Valuation).			Percentage of Net Rentals (Column 4) on Total Estimated Cost (Column 7).		
	£	s.	d.	£	s.	d.	£	s.	d.	£	s.	d.	£	s.	d.	£	s.	d.	£	s.	d.
								POTT	STREET.												
1900	700	8	2	289	8	2	411	0	0	18,091	7	9	1,957	0	0	20,048	7	9	2	1	0
1901	952	18	6	411	2	6	541	16	0	17,941	19	2	1,957	0	0	19,898	19	2	2	14	5
1902	878	7	11	716	2	11	162	5	0	17,941	19	2	1,957	0	0	19,898	19	2	0	16	4
1903	977	15	10	484	9	0	493	6	10	17,941	19	2	1,957	0	0	19,898	19	2	2	9	7
								CHESTER	STREET.												
1900	910	17	5	395	0	11	515	16	6	14,041	19	10	2,277	0	0	16,318	19	10	3	3	3
1901	981	13	0	393	2	2	588	10	10	14,598	10	9	2,277	0	0	16,875	10	9	3	9	9
1902	998	15	0	527	15	5	470	19	7	14,598	10	9	2,277	0	0	16,875	10	9	2	15	9
1903	1,033	1	3	471	11	4	561	9	11	14,598	10	9	2,277	0	0	16,875	10	9	3	6	7

Some artisans' dwellings were erected in the south-western district of London; the site was exceptionally favourable, as the excavations yielded good sand and gravel. The buildings were erected at less than 6d. per foot cube, and cost £8,600. The suites are let at 10s. 6d. to 12s. 6d., and the gross income is £1,201. 4s.; the outgoings total £680, and include ground rent £170, insurance £60, rates, taxes, &c. £400, and caretaker (proportion) £50. An outlay of £8,600, and a clear profit of £521. 4s. All the conditions are exceptional; there is rarely a vacant tenement. The plan is economical; the flats are well built, and have fireproof floors.

A few figures may be interesting with reference to buildings for the working classes. The East End Dwellings Company pays 4 per cent. on Preference Share Capital, and 5 per cent. on Ordinary Share Capital. A sinking fund is provided for a term of 100 years for freehold property, and for the length of the lease in the case of leasehold property. The following figures are from the property account made up to the 31st December 1903.

Six Freehold Estates.

Actual Cost—Land, £24,472. 18s. 5d.; Buildings, £84,265. 3s.;
Total, £108,738. 1s. 5d.

Buildings—Actual Cost - - - -		£84,265	3 0
Depreciation—			
To 30th December 1902 - £2,038 0 0			
In 1903, Charged to Profit and			
Loss Account - - 264 0 0			
Total		2,302	0 0
Amount on 31st December 1903 - -		£81,963	3 0

Eight Leasehold Estates.

Actual Cost - - - - -		£219,659	7 5
Depreciation—			
To 31st December 1902 - £2,572 0 0			
In 1903, Charged in Profit			
and Loss Account - 530 0 0			
Total - - -		3,102	0 0
Amount on 31st December 1903 - -		£216,557	7 5

The following are the details of rents and expenses for the year 1903. The estate is a large one, and the outgoings being given in such detail are valuable :—

RENTS.

Buildings	Amounts Received.	Amounts Due and Arrears.	Bad Debts.	Unlets.	Gross Rentals.
	£ s. d.	£ s. d.	£ s. d.	£ s. d.	£ s. d.
Katharine Buildings	2,120 12 9	0 15 6	9 18 10	22 14 11	2,154 2 0
Lolesworth "	1,873 0 2	0 3 2	1 4 6	4 9 1	1,878 16 6
Museum "	897 0 4	1 7 6	4 7 6	7 2 0	909 17 4
Gordon Dwellings	806 4 0	7 15 6	3 3 0	7 1 6	824 4 0
Strafford Houses	1,302 19 3			0 18 9	1,303 18 0
Cromer Street Estate	6,782 6 0	6 11 9	12 1 9	43 2 6	6,844 2 0
Meadows Dwellings	1,489 5 0		2 12 6	27 3 6	1,519 1 0
Cressy Houses	1,782 15 3	3 2 6	1 3 9	7 11 6	1,794 13 0
King's Cross Estate	2,648 2 6	0 12 0	0 16 6	30 8 0	2,679 19 0
Ravenscroft Tenements	3,292 6 4	1 5 6	11 6 0	47 3 2	3,352 5 0
" Shops	690 7 5	27 11 6	11 15 0	31 14 1	761 8 0
Dunstan Houses	1,635 4 3	4 2 0		35 1 9	1,674 8 0
Mendip and Shepton Houses	1,815 10 6	6 12 9	6 13 0	329 5 9	2,158 2 0
Victoria Park Square Estate	2,737 3 0	28 0 0	7 4 0	2,248 5 0	5,020 2 0
Thornhill Houses	2,338 8 6	4 6 6	2 5 0	160 2 0	2,505 2 0
	32,211 5 3	92 6 2	74 10 11	3,002 3 6	35,380 5 10

EXPENSES.

Buildings	Cost of Collection and Caretakers' Salaries.	Rates.	Taxes.	Insurance.	Water.	Gas.	Repairs and Incidental Expenses.	Ground Rent.	Total Expenses.
	£ s. d.	£ s. d.	£ s. d.	£ s. d.	£ s. d.	£ s. d.	£ s. d.	£ s. d.	£ s. d.
Katharine Buildings	207 2 0	321 16 8	67 19 7	7 19 6	42 8 11	62 5 0	194 19 2		904 10 10
Lolesworth "	127 11 8	267 19 8	75 17 2	6 19 0	43 17 9	30 5 6	209 13 9		762 5 3
Museum	82 5 2	173 4 6	34 2 9	5 10 0	22 12 7	14 5 4	100 1 9	0 1 0	432 3 1
Gordon Dwellings	38 5 0	147 0 1	33 1 4	4 16 0	20 5 0	17 8 1	180 4 10	0 1 0	441 1 4
Strafford Houses	81 19 9	239 1 7	43 2 5	7 9 6	23 16 6	7 5 5	114 1 7		516 16 3
Cromer Street Estate	271 0 5	1,102 10 3	211 16 8	32 17 9	33 5 8	103 16 11	773 3 1	400 18 0	3,029 17 7
Meadows Dwellings	130 6 10	275 16 6	48 2 2	6 17 7	54 5 6	25 18 4	171 12 9	131 5 0	844 7 9
Cressy Houses	149 6 2	319 6 4	51 10 0	9 14 3	58 16 6	30 15 0	174 0 6	146 12 6	940 3 3
King's Cross Estate	91 0 0	437 9 8	88 12 1	12 2 0	57 18 10	25 2 1	123 3 8		835 8 4
Ravenscroft (including Shops)	170 3 1	711 19 1	99 3 10	23 10 0	82 12 11	34 14 11	494 11 3	403 14 11	2,020 10 0
Dunstan Houses	129 1 0	288 0 2	42 6 4	8 7 0	44 15 5	14 11 10	155 0 0	161 17 10	844 8 10
Mendip and Shepton Houses	98 6 0	402 16 2	47 17 3	15 18 6	48 19 8	39 4 8	172 16 11	196 17 6	1,022 15 6
Victoria Park Square Estate	136 13 0	644 17 0	24 17 2	30 19 6	65 9 3	72 19 8	233 8 3	636 9 11	1,845 14 3
Thornhill Houses	81 5 0	418 10 6	74 17 6	14 12 6	47 19 1	54 12 4	70 14 2	228 0 0	990 11 1
	1,794 14 2	5,750 17 5	943 7 0	187 13 1	747 4 9	533 5 7	3,167 11 8	2,305 17 8	15,430 11 4

The total rents received amount to £32,211. 5s. 3d., and the total expenses, after deducting ground rents of the leasehold estates, are £13,124. 13s. 8d. This is 40.7 per cent. It will be seen that the dwellings on two estates have let badly; if these estates are omitted from the total, the expenses (exclusive of ground rent) are 40.1 per cent. of the rent received. The outgoings are always large in proportion to the receipts for weekly properties, and many surveyors advocate a rough allowance of 50 per cent.

When considering better-class flat property, an allowance of 31 per cent. is sometimes made for outgoings, excluding repairs, cost of collection, and losses from bad debts.

Outgoings for Good Class Flats.—If a block of flats were erected in Kensington, and let at a gross rental of £2,000 per annum, the allowance by the rating authorities would be 33⅓ per cent. if the premises had a lift, and the staircase were carpeted, &c., and the class of building were good. This would work out thus :—

Gross Rental	-	-	-	-	-	£2,000 0 0	
Less ⅓ (33⅓ per cent.)	-	-	-	-	666 6 8	
					£1,333 13 4	
A further reduction of ⅛ (16⅔ per cent.) in accordance with the Third Schedule of the Valuation Metropolis Act, 1869	-	-	-	222 5 6	
					£1,111 7 10	

This the owner would probably reckon as roughly £1,200 : rates would be paid at 6s. 5d. in the pound, and inhabited house duty at 9d. in the pound, a total of 7s. 2d. on £1,200 = £430.

The allowance of one-third is about correct if the following outgoings are considered :—

Rates and Taxes, as stated above	-	-	-	£430 0 0
Porter (provided with rooms)	-	-	-	52 10 0
Porter's Livery	-	-	-	8 0 0
Electric Light, Hall, and Staircase	-	-	-	30 0 0
Water for Lift	-	-	-	40 0 0
Insurance and Repairs to do.	-	-	-	20 0 0
Insurance on Building	-	-	-	12 0 0
Water Rate, if paid by Lessor	-	-	-	60 0 0
Repairs, exterior and staircase	-	-	-	40 0 0
Total	-	-	-	£692 10 0

Roughly £700, a little over one-third of the gross rental of £2,000. But in the above details no allowance is made for cost of collection, or rooms occupied by the caretaker, which are assessed in addition to the above. Again, no sum is included for allowance for empties, commission to agents for letting, or for decoration of flats, in consequence of bad tenants. Consequently it will be seen that the reduction of 33⅓ per cent. is hardly sufficient. It is, as stated above, safer to allow 40 per cent. when making a valuation.

The following are particulars of flats let at various rentals. There is nothing peculiar about the buildings, which were erected under well-known architects :—

BLOCK OF TWELVE FLATS AND FIVE SHOPS AT NOTTING HILL GATE.

Rents received	£655 0 0	(Empties £20).	
Shops all let, total	285 0 0	Tenants pay Rates and Taxes.	
Total Rents received	£940 0 0		

Average Rental of each Suite, £56. 10s.

Outgoings—

Rates and Taxes	£168 0 0	25.6 p. c. on Rents of Flats.			
Water and Gas, Public Lights, and Caretaker's Rooms	44 0 0	6.7	„	„	„
Housekeeper's Account	55 0 0	8.4	„	„	„
Insurance	5 4 0	.8	„	„	„
Sundry Expenses, including Commission on Letting, &c.	15 0 0	2.3	„	„	„
Decorations and Repairs	60 0 0	9.2	„	„	„
	£347 4 0	53.0 p. c. on Rents of Flats.			
Ground Rent	128 16 0				
Balance — Profit Rental being equivalent to 10.3 per cent. on Capital Outlay, £4,500	464 0 0				
	£940 0 0				

BLOCK OF TWELVE FLATS AT CHELSEA.

Rents received   -   - £787 7 8 (Empties, £24. 2s. 4d.)
          Average Rental of each Suite, £67.

Outgoings—

Rates and Taxes - -	£190 0 0	24.0 per cent. on Rents.		
Water and Electricity, Public Lights and Caretaker's Quarters - - -	50 0 0	6.4	,,	,,
Housekeeper's Account -	60 0 0	7.6	,,	,,
Insurance - - -	4 10 0	.6	,,	,,
Sundry Expenses, including Commission on Letting -	40 0 0	5.1	,,	,,
Decorations and Repairs -	50 0 0	6.4	,,	,,

                £394 10 0   50.1 per cent. on Rents.

Profit—Balance, being equivalent to 5.6 per cent. on
  Capital Outlay of £7,000   392 17 8

                £787 7 8

BLOCK OF SEVENTEEN FLATS AND FIVE SHOPS AT SHEPHERD'S BUSH.

Rents received -   - £1,126 18 7 (Empties, £173. 1s. 5d.)
Shops all let, Total   - 245 0 0 Tenants pay Rates and Taxes.

Total Rents received - £1,371 18 7
          Average Rental of each Suite, £76.

Outgoings—

Rates and Taxes -	£300 0 0	26.6 per cent. on Rents of Flats.			
Electricity for lighting Staircase, Landings, &c., Caretaker's Quarters and Working Lift, Water Rate and Gas -	90 0 0	8.0	,,	,,	,,
Housekeeper's Wages and Expenses, including Lift Attendant -	120 0 0	10.6	,,	,,	,,
Insurance - -	29 0 0	2.5	,,	,,	,,
Sundry Expenses, including Commissions on Letting, Gardener's Account, &c. -	50 0 0	4.7	,,	,,	,,
Decoration and Repairs	80 0 0	7.1	,,	,,	,,

              £669 0 0   59.5 per cent. on Rents of Flats.

Balance—Net Profit, being
  equivalent to £4. 7s. 10d.
  per cent. on the Capital
  Outlay, £16,000   -   702 18 7

              £1,371 18 7

The following figures show the outgoings for a block of high-class flats in the West End of London; there are eleven suites, and the building has been very successful. When fully let, the rents amount to £5,957. 13s. Average rental of each suite, £542.

Outgoings—

Rates and Taxes, including					
Water Rate - -	£1,080	0	0	18.2 per cent. on Rentals.	
Manager's Salary - -	50	0	0	.8 ,,	,,
Petty Cash - -	208	0	0	3.4 ,,	,,
Electric Light -	44	0	0	.7 ,,	,,
Gas - - -	24	0	0	.4 ,,	,,
Fire Insurance - -	28	15	0	.5 ,,	,,
Insurance Rent - -	7	11	0	.2 ,,	,,
Lift Insurance - -	12	10	0	.2 ,,	,,
Hydraulic Water Company	40	0	0	.6 ,,	,,
Coals - - -	10	0	0	.2 ,,	,,
Telephone - -	5	10	0	.1 ,,	,,
Totals -	£1,509	15	0	25.3 per cent. on Rents.	

In the above instance of first-class suites it will be seen that the percentage of the outgoings is lower than the other examples. The owners allow an average of 10 per cent. for repairs to exteriors and staircase, renewals of carpets, &c.

If half the building should be empty the outgoings with the exception of rates and taxes would vary only slightly, and the total would be considerably over 40 per cent.

In Kensington the outgoings for a block of flats with an average rent of £200 are as follows :—

House Duty - - -	2½ per cent. on gross Rent.		
Parochial Rates - - -	17	,,	,,
Insurance - - - -	1	,,	,,
Hydraulic Power - -	1	,,	,,
Electric Light and Gas - -	1	,,	,,
Porters - - - -	5	,,	,,
Water Rate - - -	2½	,,	,,

A total of 30 per cent. not including repairs, cost of management, and rent collection, or allowance for porter's rooms.

Rating.—With regard to rating, most flats come under Class 3 of the third schedule of the Valuation Metropolis Act, 1869. This states that the maximum reduction from the gross value to obtain the rateable value is 16⅔ per cent. or ⅙th. This applies to private dwellings, but in the case of flats there are sundry additional outgoings which reduce the profits and must be considered.

There are many flats of all classes in Kensington, and the authorities make deductions of the following percentages according to the character of the buildings :—25 per cent. for flats of which the landlord pays rates and taxes only, and in buildings where there are no lifts ; 27½ per cent. where the landlord pays rates and taxes, and where there are trade lifts and where perhaps hot water is supplied by the landlord ; 30 per cent. where the landlord pays rates and taxes, and also water rate, and where there is a lift and porter ; 33⅓ per cent. where the landlord pays all as last but for buildings of a better class.

In one instance 40 per cent. is allowed. In that case the landlord pays rates and taxes, and pays if suites are let or empty. Service is included, and there is a common dining-room ; all catering is done for the tenants.

In Kensington the rates are low, only 6s. 5d. in the pound. For porter's rooms a nominal sum of £6 to £8 is taken as the rateable value. At the next Quinquennial Assessment a further slight reduction may be made ; where 30 per cent. is allowed, this may be increased to 31 per cent.

In all cases each suite is assessed separately and the tenants are liable ; their names are on the papers, and as a matter of courtesy they are sent to the landlord, but if he failed they could be made to pay.

Chelsea is another district where there are many flats of all descriptions ; the Council's Valuation Committee divide the buildings into four classes, and the allowances are greater than in Kensington, being as follows :—

For First Class Flats	-	-	-	35	per cent.
„ Second „ „	-	-	-	33⅓	„
„ Third „ „	-	-	-	30	„
„ Fourth „ „	-	-	-	25	„

In Hammersmith there are not the high-class buildings of Kensington, and there is not the great variety. A reduction of 33⅓ per cent. is made upon all, but if the passages and stairs are carpeted, a further reduction of 5 per cent. is made. These reductions are more than in Kensington, but the rates are higher, 6s. 10d. in the pound.

In Westminster there is an allowance of about 33⅙ per cent., and the rates in the flat districts of the city of Westminster average 7s. in the pound.

The Marylebone authorities make an allowance of 33⅓ per cent. upon all classes of flats including artisans' dwellings. If there is a lift, the allowance is increased to 40 per cent. for all flats above the second floor. In cases of the best class buildings, where hot water is supplied to the tenants, and the passages, halls, and lounges are particularly well carpeted or furnished, an allowance of 45 per cent. may be made, but each case is specially considered and no hard and fast rule is made.

Increase of Rates.—Flat owners are not always anxious to let on a long lease; if they do so, they run the risk of a heavy increase in the rates, and they of course cannot raise the rent. It is true there is a chance that the rates may decrease and they might get an unexpected profit, but experience has proved that rates do not decrease. The following are a few figures showing the increase in flat districts of London during the last few years :—

				s.	d.	
Battersea, 1896	-	-	-	6	0	in the pound.
,, 1903	-	-	-	8	0	,,
Chelsea, 1899 -	-	-	-	6	0	,,
,, 1903 -	-	-	-	7	0	,,
Fulham, 1899 -	-	-	-	6	6	,,
,, 1903 -	-	-	-	7	4	,,
Hampstead, 1899	-	-	-	5	9	,,
,, 1903	-	-	-	6	10	,,
Kensington, 1899	-	-	-	5	7	,,
,, 1904	-	-	-	6	5	,,
Marylebone, 1898	-	-	-	5	8½	,,
,, 1903	-	-	-	6	9½	,,

With regard to weekly and monthly tenancies the following scale was issued by the London County Council as the result of the Assessment Conference in 1899, and has been adopted by many boroughs. The resolution was as follows :—

WEEKLY AND MONTHLY TENANCIES.

That in converting weekly and monthly tenancies into hypothetical yearly tenancies for the purpose of arriving at the gross value, the annual payments for rates (including water) and house duty (if any) shall be deducted from the annual amount receivable by weekly or monthly payments, which deductions are estimated at from one-fourth to one-third, according to the amount of the rate in the pound, and that the following scale of deductions be approved:—

Weekly rent.		Amount per Annum.		Rates at 4s. 6d. in £.		Rates at 5s. in £.		Rates at 5s. 6d. in £.		Rates at 6s. in £.		Rates at 6s. 6d. in £.		Rates at 7s. in £.		Rates at 7s. 6d. in £.		Rates at 8s. in £.		Rates at 8s. 6d. in £.	
s.	d.	£	s.	*G.V.	†R.V.	G.V.	R.V.	G.V.	R.V.	G.V.	R.V.	G.V.	R.V.	G.V	R.V.	G.V.	R.V.	G.V.	R.V.	G.V.	R.V.
1	0	2	12	2	2	2	2	2	2	2	2	2	2	2	2	2	2	2	2	2	2
1	6	3	18	3	3	3	3	3	3	3	3	3	3	3	3	3	3	3	3	3	3
2	0	5	4	4	3	4	3	4	3	4	3	4	3	4	3	4	3	3	3	3	3
2	6	6	10	5	4	5	4	5	4	5	4	5	4	5	4	4	3	4	3	4	3
3	0	7	16	6	5	6	5	6	5	6	5	5	4	5	4	5	4	5	4	5	4
3	6	9	2	7	6	7	6	7	6	6	5	6	5	6	5	6	5	6	5	6	5
4	0	10	8	8	6	8	6	8	6	7	6	7	6	7	6	7	6	7	6	7	6
4	6	11	14	9	7	9	7	8	6	8	6	8	6	8	6	8	6	8	6	8	6
5	0	13	0	10	8	10	8	9	7	9	7	9	7	9	7	9	7	9	7	9	7
5	6	14	6	11	9	11	9	10	8	10	8	10	8	10	8	10	8	10	8	10	8
6	0	15	12	12	9	11	9	11	9	11	9	11	9	11	9	10	8	10	8	10	8
6	6	16	18	13	10	12	9	12	9	12	9	12	9	12	9	11	9	11	9	11	9
7	0	18	4	14	11	13	10	13	10	13	10	13	10	13	10	12	9	12	9	12	9
7	6	19	10	14	11	14	11	14	11	14	11	14	11	14	11	13	10	13	10	13	10
8	0	20	16	15	12	15	12	15	12	15	12	15	12	14	11	14	11	14	11	14	11
8	6	22	2	16	12	16	12	16	12	16	12	16	12	15	12	15	12	15	12	15	12
9	0	23	8	17	13	17	13	17	13	17	13	17	13	16	12	16	12	16	12	16	12
9	6	24	14	18	14	18	14	18	14	18	14	17	13	17	13	17	13	17	13	17	13
10	0	26	0	19	15	19	15	19	15	19	15	18	14	18	14	18	14	17	13	17	13
10	6	27	6	20	16	20	16	19	15	19	15	19	15	19	15	19	15	18	14	18	14
11	0	28	12	21	17	21	17	20	16	20	16	20	16	20	16	20	16	19	15	19	15
11	6	29	18	22	18	21	17	21	17	21	17	21	17	20	16	20	16	20	16	20	16
12	0	31	4	23	19	22	18	22	18	22	18	21	17	21	17	21	17	20	16	20	16
12	6	32	10	24	20	23	19	23	19	23	19	22	18	22	18	22	18	21	17	21	17
13	0	33	16	25	20	24	20	24	20	23	19	23	19	23	19	22	18	22	18	22	18
13	6	35	2	26	21	25	20	25	20	24	20	24	20	24	20	23	19	23	19	23	19
14	0	36	8	27	22	26	21	26	21	25	20	25	20	25	20	24	20	24	20	23	19
14	6	37	14	28	23	27	22	27	22	26	21	26	21	26	21	25	20	25	20	24	20
15	0	39	0	28	23	28	23	28	23	27	22	27	22	26	21	26	21	26	21	25	20
15	6	40	6	29	24	29	24	28	23	28	23	28	23	27	22	27	22	26	21	26	21
16	0	41	12	30	24	30	24	29	24	29	24	28	23	28	23	28	23	27	22	27	22
16	6	42	18	31	25	31	25	30	24	30	24	29	24	29	24	28	23	28	23	28	23
17	0	44	4	32	26	32	26	31	25	31	25	30	24	30	24	29	24	29	24	28	23
17	6	45	10	33	27	33	27	32	26	32	26	31	25	31	25	30	24	30	24	29	24
18	0	46	16	34	28	34	28	33	27	33	27	32	26	32	26	31	25	31	25	30	24
18	6	48	2	35	28	35	28	34	28	33	27	33	27	32	26	32	26	32	26	31	25
19	0	49	8	36	29	36	29	35	28	34	28	34	28	33	27	33	27	32	26	32	26
19	6	50	14	37	30	36	29	36	29	35	28	35	28	34	28	34	28	33	27	33	27
20	0	52	0	38	31	37	30	37	30	36	29	36	29	35	28	35	28	34	28	34	28

* Gross value.   † Rateable value.

Vacant Suites.—It is impossible for the flat owner to make a proper allowance for empty flats : this may be done with a certain degree of accuracy for weekly properties or poor class flats, but when you have suites let at £500 a year or even more, the question is different. Rates are not paid upon an empty flat, but the loss is all so much profit gone, the cost to the owner of maintenance, external repairs, and lighting and lifts is practically the same.

In good class properties it often happens that a flat is sub-let or the lease is sold. When the original tenant leaves, the rooms are usually redecorated, and it is often six months before the new tenant takes possession. As soon as the suite is vacant, the landlord should give notice to the authorities, and a saving may be made upon the rates ; as the full rent is being paid during the period, the saving of the rates is a little extra profit.

Cost of Building.—An American writer has stated that "a given accommodation can be obtained in the form of a flat for less than one-half the outlay required to obtain it in the form of an independent dwelling built on the same land." His figures are carefully worked out, and are given in the *American Architect* of 4th January 1890. There are a large number of suites in the building, which has common dining-rooms, &c. These calculations would not be correct for an ordinary block of flats in England. It is true that the foundations and roof for one building cover several suites, but the area is greater than in a private house let at the same rent, and the cost of additional pipes, thicker walls, lifts, fireproof floors, &c. &c., is considerable. The subject is hardly worth considering in detail, for competition is so great that rents have been reduced to the lowest possible figures, and in many cases, buildings that are well let return but a poor percentage upon the outlay. Materials and wages have increased in cost enormously during the last few years, rates have also increased, and rents must follow in the same direction.

Lighting Staircase, &c.—In some agreements and leases the tenant pays a small sum, say about £1 per annum, towards the cost of lighting the staircase ; this is of course in addition to the rent. The lessor can often obtain this without any trouble ; sometimes he pays a fixed sum towards the cost of rates, taxes, lighting the staircase, and general maintenance. A sum may also be charged when hot water is supplied by the landlord. Sometimes tenants pay £10 a year for water rate and hot water, if the same are not included in the rent ; it is an advantage when the rateable value is considered.

Attendance.—Less attendance is necessary for a block of first class flats than for second class buildings. In the former case the tenants are often away for long periods, and give much less trouble than tenants who pay less, and who seem always on the look-out for something to complain about. In one of the highest rented buildings in the West End there are ten suites, and two porters and one boy are found quite sufficient attendants.

Servants.—In a chapter dealing with money matters generally, the servant question may be referred to. Although the rent of flats may seem high, there is much less work than in a private house, and a family can manage with one servant less. In one block of suites let at about £75 many tenants commenced by keeping two servants, and subsequently found that only one was necessary, and this saving also applies to better class buildings, two servants being ample for a family that kept three in a private house. In flats with rents as high as £100 one servant has been found sufficient, and if the cost of a servant is reckoned at about £50, the saving is well worth considering. Servants are supposed to have objected to flats in days gone by, but many now advertise for a situation in one, they prefer them to private houses.

Porter.—The cost of a license for a porter is 15s. a year, and he is paid about £1 a week and usually allowed two rooms. He is often allowed light and coals, otherwise there may be complaints from the tenants; he works the lift, and looks after the dust and coals. No license is necessary for a caretaker, provided he does not perform any of the duties of an ordinary man-servant; if he works the lift, or is in attendance for a regular number of hours a day, the license is necessary. The question has been one of difficulty for the authorities, who decide each case on its merits. Some flat owners try to avoid paying the tax, contending the man is only a caretaker.

The porter is an important person, and great care should be exercised to select a suitable man. So much depends upon him that it is advisable he should be well paid, and allowed a chance of making a little money by doing sundry odd jobs for the tenants. It is a mistake to bind him down so as to prevent this. He is luckily a very different person to the concierge in Paris, usually a terror to the tenants; but he represents the owner, and pleasant relations between him and the tenants should be maintained.

Dilapidations.—A fixed sum is often stated in the lease to be paid for any dilapidations at the end of the term ; the amount is usually equal to one quarter's rent.   This is a good arrangement, and prevents trouble and perhaps litigation.   The sum paid covers any claim that might be made for ordinary decorative repairs, but does not include compensation for any wilful or structural damage.

In the case of some small flats, an arrangement is made that if the tenant leaves at the end of three years £30 is to be paid for dilapidations, if at the end of five years a sum of £20, and if at the end of seven years only £15.   This reduction is often an inducement for a tenant to remain longer than he otherwise would.

Sometimes a tenant takes possession and redecorates the premises himself, on entry, and it is agreed the flat be left in a bad state of repair at the end of the term.   He pays his money at the commencement instead of at the end, and this system has many advantages ; it saves discussion as to price of papers, &c., and the tenant can decorate as he likes.

A builder who owns many flats, has stated that the prime cost of labour only to redecorate a suite let at about £50 per annum, was roughly £8.

One good system adopted for suites usually let for three or five years, is to let for seven years, and allow the tenant to leave at the end of three years upon payment of a fine of half a quarter's rent. The landlord does not object to sub-letting.   The result is that the tenant tries hard to sub-let and so avoid the fine, and the owner has all his suites let for seven years.

Fire Insurance.—The question of danger from fire in high blocks of flats has received attention for many years.   Seneca complained that the poor tenant perched up in the top stories of the flats in ancient Rome would have little chance of escape.   To-day many people think that there is more danger from fire in a block of flats than there is in a private dwelling.   In the early days of the movement this was an objection to taking a flat.   But is there greater danger?   One of the largest insurance offices, the Norwich Union, charges exactly the same rate for insuring flats as it does for insuring a private dwelling-house, and this rate, 1s. 6d. per cent., is the lowest there is.   The rate for furniture, 2s. per cent., is also the same in each case.   Facts like these are worth more than any arguments.

A brick building will resist fire longer than one of stone, and iron construction should be, and usually is, protected by concrete.

During the last five years the total number of fires in flats has been thirteen; in most cases the damage was done to furniture or clothing and was very slight; no block of flats has ever been burnt down in London.

When a fire occurs on a lower floor of a building, it is well known that the staircase acts as a flue and the draught drives the flames up the building; this ventilation is always taking place and is the reason for the objection to the restrictions in the London Building Act, 1894, with reference to top lights, made in another chapter.

It is not likely that a fire would break out in more than one suite at a time, and in all buildings the tenants should be able to pass into a neighbouring tenement or down a second staircase. If this is not possible the occupants of a flat on an upper floor of a high building might be in great danger. In London there are many blocks of flats with only one staircase, and communication by means of a balcony or some other method should be arranged between the suites.

Fire Risk.—At a recent interview, Colonel Fox, the Chief Officer of the London Salvage Corps, stated that he did not remember one case of loss of life from fire in a modern block of flats; this should be comforting to many people. At the same time he said that there were very few deaths from fire in good class private houses; the risk is very small. Colonel Fox considers a second staircase of great importance, and is a strong believer in the external iron escapes sometimes used for trade purposes. He made one excellent suggestion for the managers of flats, and that was, that a lift attendant should be on duty all night, with strict injunctions to keep to his post and work the lift as long as possible, and not to bolt at the first alarm of fire. In most large buildings there is a night porter, but so often that means a man who sleeps somewhere near the entrance, dressed and ready to open the door when the bell is rung. The night porter should not be allowed to sleep, and he should visit each floor at stated hours, and his visits should be recorded by clocks in a similar way to the visits paid to different parts of factories, &c. If the night porter rushes out to give the alarm, no one can work the lift, and volumes of smoke soon render the staircase impassable.

If the ground floor is occupied by shops, and they communicate with the remainder of the building, the risk of fire is increased, and the insurance offices require a much higher premium for the flats above, but if the business portion of the house is separated by fireproof floors and walls, the premium is the same for the suites as it is in buildings where there are no shops ; evidently the offices consider the risk is as small in one case as the other.

A flat roof is the best in case of fire ; the access should be easy, and through an ordinary door, and the staircase should be continued to the roof level.

Deterioration of Neighbourhood.—There is one question that should be seriously considered by the owners of large estates in certain parts of London. As private houses have become vacant they have been pulled down and blocks of small flats have been erected, each suite containing only a few rooms. The landowner may obtain a better rent than he would have received had private houses been built, but the class of people who live in these buildings is well known, and the result has been the deterioration of the whole neighbourhood. Estate owners should consider this, for by allowing these buildings to be erected the remainder of their property must suffer considerably in the course of time.

Furnished Flats.—In London there is a regular trade done in furnished flats. In the case of one block of building, illustrated in this book, one lessee has taken the entire building above the ground floor, which is occupied by shops. He works the lift, provides porters, &c., repairs the exterior and staircase, and pays all rates, &c. ; the lease is for a long term. The suites are furnished and sub-let, and the profit, after making all allowances, is considerable.

CHAPTER VIII.

AGREEMENTS.

THERE are several books connected with the law of flats, and it is unnecessary to deal with the subject here. At the same time it is thought that some forms of Agreement might be interesting. Those printed below are in use for well-known buildings in London: the first forms refer to low-rented flats, the latter to better-class suites. Certain rules and regulations for the tenants are given. The question of an agreed sum, a proportion of the rent for dilapidations, has already been mentioned.

FORM No. 1.

AN AGREEMENT made the   day of   One thousand nine hundred   BETWEEN   (hereinafter called "the Landlords") of the one part and   of   (hereinafter called "the Tenant") of the other part WHEREBY in consideration of the rents and covenants on the Tenant's part hereinafter reserved and contained   The Landlords let and the Tenant takes ALL that Flat on the   floor of consisting of   and known as No.   aforesaid TOGETHER with the use in common with other tenants of the Entrance Hall and Stairs leading to the said premises and other passages thereto and therefrom from the   day of   One thousand nine hundred and   for the term of   years at the rent of   payable by four equal quarterly payments on the Twenty-ninth day of September the Twenty-fifth day of December the Twenty-fifth day of March and the Twenty-fourth day of June in each year the first of such quarterly payments to become due on the day of   next and the last of such quarterly payments to become due and payable in advance on the   day of   One thousand nine hundred and   And the Tenant hereby covenants with the Landlords as follows: To pay the said rent on the days and in manner aforesaid. To use the said demised premises for residential purposes only and will not pull down nor alter or in any wise interfere with the construction or arrangement of the premises nor alter nor injure any of the walls timbers or floors of the premises nor without the previous consent in writing of the Landlords affix any board placard or notice upon any external part of the premises or on any of the windows thereof nor permit to be done on the premises anything which may annoy or lead to the annoyance of the other tenants of the premises or prejudice the character thereof as residential chambers nor permit the same to be used for any improper purpose or allow any auction or public sale thereon or keep or allow upon any part of the said premises any dog cat or other domestic animal and will not do or suffer to be done therein anything which shall invalidate the insurance of the building against loss by fire or increase the risks so that the premises shall not be insurable in the office in which the insurance may for the time being be effected at the ordinary rate nor will at any time during the said term transfer demise or underlet the said premises hereby demised or any part thereof to any person or persons whomsoever without the consent in writing of the Landlords And further that the Tenant will allow the Landlords or any person or persons authorised by them at all reasonable times to enter the said rooms and inspect the same and to make searches and take inventories of the fixtures and fittings to be yielded up at the expiration of the said tenancy and to do any repairs that may from time to time be requisite to any other portion of the buildings And also will permit the Landlords or their Agents to exhibit a bill or bills in the windows of the said Flat announcing the said Flat to let at least three months before the expiration of the said tenancy and will allow the Landlords reasonable access to show over intending tenants during that period And will also during the said term keep the interior of the said rooms with the fixtures and appurtenances thereto belonging in good and decorative repair order and condition and particularly will paint paper whitewash colour and decorate such parts of the inside of the said premises as are usually papered whitewashed coloured and decorated once in every three years of the said term and will leave the said premises at the expiration of the tenancy in as good repair and condition as the same are now in damage by fire excepted And it is hereby expressly declared that the Tenant is to be bound by the Memorandum in the Schedule hereinafter written PROVIDED ALWAYS that if at any time the rent hereby reserved or any instalments thereof shall be in arrear or unpaid for Twenty-one days after the days hereinbefore appointed for payment thereof whether the same shall have been legally demanded or not or in case the Tenant shall permit the said premises to be used for any improper purpose or shall become a nuisance to other occupants of the said building or shall fail to keep and observe the covenants herein contained or in the event of any execution being issued against the goods and chattels of the Tenant or if he shall commit any act of bankruptcy or execute any bill of sale or remove the goods and chattels from the premises the whole of the then current quarter's rent and charges shall become due and payable and it shall be lawful for the Landlords to distrain upon the same goods and chattels for the then current quarter's rent and charges as well as for any rents and charges then in arrear and also at any time thereafter it shall be lawful for the Landlords to exclude the Tenant entirely from and to re-enter the said premises hereby demised and the same to hold and enjoy as if this Agreement had never been made And the Landlords do hereby covenant with the Tenant to pay all rates and taxes in respect of the said premises And also that the Landlords will pay for the lighting of the staircase and front entrance of the said   and also will pay the wages of the Hall Porter and also keep the said premises insured against loss or damage by fire to the full value thereof And the Tenant paying the said yearly rent hereby reserved in manner aforesaid and observing and performing all the covenants hereinbefore contained and on his part to be observed and performed shall and may peaceably and quietly hold and enjoy the said premises hereby demised during the said term without any eviction or disturbance by the Landlords or any person or persons lawfully or equitably claiming by from or under them And it is declared that where the context allows the expressions "the Landlords" and "the Tenant" used in these presents include respectively beside the said   their successors and assigns and beside the said   his executors administrators and assigns.

IN WITNESS whereof the said parties to these presents have hereunto set their hands the day and year first above written.

_____

THE SCHEDULE REFERRED TO.

REGULATIONS.

MEMORANDUM OF REGULATIONS.

There are two entrances to the building and the care of such entrances will be in the charge of a Porter appointed and removable by the Landlords.

Tenants have the right to the services of the Porter as hereinafter defined and which are to be performed free of charge and are as follows :—

To be in attendance in the building committed to his charge either by himself or some trustworthy assistant between the hours of 8 A.M. and 11 P.M.

To cleanse the general stairs passages and entrances and to attend to the lighting thereof.

Any special or extra services are to be considered as rendered by him as the servant of the Tenant and for which or the consequence whereof the Landlords will not be responsible.

MEMORANDUM. The premises are taken by the Tenant subject to the regulations made by the Landlords with respect to the duties of the Porter and other matters for the general convenience of the Tenants. The regulations are set forth in the Schedule to this Agreement and are to be considered as forming part thereof. The Landlords however reserve to themselves the right of altering and modifying these regulations from time to time as circumstances may require but not so as to alter the amount to be paid by the respective Tenants or to reduce the services to be rendered by the Porter as aforesaid.

FORM No. 2.

TERMS OF LETTING FLAT LETTER   IN No.   dated
this   day of   190 given by   and
Owners (hereinafter referred to as " the Landlords ") to and accepted by
          (hereinafter referred to as " the Tenant ").

TENANCY   from the   day of   190

RENT   per annum including all rates and taxes payable quarterly
in advance. The first payment to be made on the signing hereof and the next
quarterly payment to be made on   190

CONDITIONS—The tenant hereby agrees with the landlords to pay the rent
regularly.

To keep the premises including the fixtures clean and in good order and
condition and particularly to replace forthwith any cracked or broken window
glass and to deliver up the same clean and in such good order and condition at
the expiration or sooner determination of the tenancy.

To permit the landlords and their agents or servants to enter at all reasonable hours and as often as they may require to view the condition of the premises
or to execute repairs to the premises or other parts of the mansions. To allow
intending tenants to view the premises during the last six weeks of the tenancy
at reasonable hours in the daytime.

To use the premises as a private residence only and not to carry on or
permit to be carried on thereon any trade business or profession and not to use
the same or permit the same to be used for any illegal immoral or improper
purpose and not to make or to do or permit to be made or done in or upon the
said premises any noise or anything to the annoyance nuisance damage or injury
of the landlords or any of their tenants.

Not without the consent of the landlords to underlet the premises or any
part thereof either furnished or unfurnished and not to take any lodgers or
boarders or to drive any nail or nails into the wall or woodwork of the said
premises except into the wood fillet specially provided and fixed for that
purpose.

Not to waste or permit to be wasted any water and not to exhibit or suspend
at or from any window any card ticket notification or article whatsoever and for
the purpose of keeping the uniformity of the exterior of the mansions to use a
kind of blind or flower box approved by the landlords and not to keep or permit
to be kept any dog upon the premises.

Not to allow any person or persons or children to loiter or play in the
passages landings or stairs nor soil the same in the carrying of coals or other
articles and not to use the same in any way except for the purposes of ingress
and egress. The coals to be kept only in the cellar provided for that purpose.

To make good any damage that may be caused to the premises or the
passages landing stairs or walls by the carrying or removing of furniture or in
any other way and generally to conform to the rules that may be laid down by
the landlords for the observance of the tenants of the said mansions.

To give to the landlords three months' written notice prior to the expiration
of the tenancy should the tenant desire to renew his tenancy.

PROVISO—That on non-payment of the rent by the tenant when the same shall become due or on non-performance by   of any of the agreements on   part herein contained it shall be lawful for the landlords without any previous demand or notice by force or otherwise and without any process of law to take possession of the said flat and to break open any doors necessary for that purpose and to retain possession thereof as of their former estate and in the event of any action or suit being brought against the landlords in respect of any such resumption of possession they may plead the license of the tenant in bar thereto and thereupon the tenancy hereby created shall be at an end but without prejudice to any of the legal rights or remedies of the landlords and further that in case on any such resumption of possession any goods or effects shall be found on the premises the landlords may dispose of the same by public auction or private contract and after deducting from the proceeds thereof all rent then in arrear and an apportioned part of the then current   rent calculated and apportioned up to and including the day of the removal of the tenant's goods from the premises and the cost of putting the premises into proper order and all expenses of advertising warehousing and sale the balance thereof shall be held for the use of the tenant when and so soon as but not before   shall apply for the same.

NOTE—Extensive Sanitary Repairs and Improvements have been effected in   and the drainage may be examined by the tenant or his professional advisers but the Landlords do not guarantee or authorise any person on their behalf to guarantee the Drains or other Sanitary Arrangements or give any warranty as to their condition.

FORM No. 3.

MEMORANDUM OF AGREEMENT made the   day of   One thousand nine hundred and   BETWEEN   in the County of   (hereinafter called the Landlords) of the one part and   (hereinafter called the Tenant) of the other part   WHEREBY it is agreed by and between the parties hereto as follows :—

1. The Landlords agree to let and the Tenant agrees to take subject to the rent and covenants rules and regulations hereinafter reserved and contained ALL those several rooms with bath-room and servants' offices situate and being upon the   floor of a mansion erections and buildings called   in the county of   and called or intended to be called No.   Mansions aforesaid AND TOGETHER ALSO with the use of the entrance hall staircases and passages leading to the rooms in common with the

Landlords and the other tenants and occupiers of the said mansion for the term
of   years from the   day of   One thousand nine
hundred and   at the yearly rent of
payable in advance clear of all deductions by four equal quarterly payments
the first of such payments for the quarter ending on the   day
of   next to be made on the execution of these presents
and the subsequent payments to be made in advance for each quarter on the
twenty-fifth day of March the twenty-fourth day of June the twenty-ninth day
of September and the twenty-fifth day of December in every year. The Landlords agree not to demand payment of the said rent in advance as aforesaid
unless (1) the Tenant shall commit a breach of any agreement or condition
herein contained (other than that relating to the payment of the said rent in
advance) or (2) unless the Landlords or their Agents see cause to think that the
Tenant contemplates quitting the said rooms and premises or removing therefrom furniture or effects in order to avoid payment of rent or to otherwise
deprive the Landlords of their right of distress or other lawful remedies in
relation thereto or (3) unless the Tenant from any other cause removes the
furniture or effects from the said rooms and premises or (4) unless the Tenant
ceases to occupy the said premises.

2. THE TENANT agrees to pay the said rent on the days and in manner
hereinbefore mentioned whether formally or legally demanded or not clear of all
deductions whatsoever except any rates taxes charges and impositions (other
than for rent of gas or electric meter and supply of gas electricity or other
illuminant to the said rooms) which the tenant may be lawfully called upon to
pay and shall actually have paid previously to the day on which the rent shall
have fallen due out of which he shall claim to deduct any such payments.

3. THE TENANT will use and occupy the said rooms and premises in a fair
and tenant-like manner and will make good any damage which may be done to
any of the ceilings walls or paperhangings or other parts of the said rooms and
also will keep the drains and water-closets of the said rooms unstopped and in
proper acting order and will reinstate any cracked or broken boiler and will as
often as need or occasion shall require thoroughly sweep and cleanse all chimneys
and flues and clean all the windows and glass and will keep clean and in good
order the kitchen boiler cisterns and hot water connections thereto and will keep
all taps in repair and also will reinstate and repair any broken windows or glass
and will keep all locks and fastenings perfect and generally will keep the said
rooms and premises and all stoves bells cupboards fixtures and things thereto
belonging in as good repair and condition as the same are now respectively in
and so leave the same at the end of the tenancy.

4. THE TENANT agrees that it shall be lawful for the Landlords or Superior
Landlord or Landlords or their agents surveyor workmen and other persons by
their direction to enter into the said premises for the purpose of examining the
state and condition thereof or of the meters or otherwise and to execute such
works therein as they may deem advisable or for them or any of their tenants
of the adjoining premises (such tenants having previously obtained the consent
in writing of the Surveyor for the time being of the Landlords or their Superior

Landlord or Landlords) to enter into the said premises for the purpose of examining the state and condition thereof and of repairing the adjoining premises making reasonable compensation to the Tenant for all damage occasioned thereby ALSO at the request of the Landlords or their agent or representative to permit any intending purchaser or mortgagee or their surveyor or valuer to view the said rooms and premises and during the last three months of the tenancy to permit at all reasonable times in the daytime any intending tenants to view accompanied if desired by the caretaker or hall porter of the mansions.

5. THE TENANT will not at any time during the said term without the licence in writing of the Landlords take in any lodgers or boarders or use or permit the said rooms or any part thereof to be used for the purpose of any trade auction sale exhibition manufactory or school or for any business or profession whatsoever or transact therefrom as an address any trade business or profession or use the address for the issue of circulars or advertisements or as a brothel madhouse or receptacle for lunatics idiots or insane persons nor keep or cause to be kept upon the said premises any dog cat or other animal but shall and will keep and use the said rooms as and for a private residence only and subject to the rules and regulations incorporated in the Schedule hereto AND will not suffer to be erected placed or fixed in or upon any part of the said rooms any steam engine forge or furnace or any bill placard poster or advertisement whatsoever or any blind signboard plate or other contrivance or thing conveying a notification of trade or business or the letting of lodgings or do or suffer to be done in the said rooms or any part thereof any act or thing that may be or grow to be a nuisance annoyance (whether amounting to a nuisance or not) or any injury damage or danger to the Landlords or the ground or Superior Landlord or Landlords or his or their respective tenants in the neighbourhood or other the tenants of the said mansion or any of them nor do or suffer to be done in upon or with respect to the said rooms anything which may injure or tend to injure the character of the said mansion as a private residence or to diminish the quietude amenity privacy or value of the said mansion or any part thereof as a private residence or whereby the rate of insurance premium may be increased beyond ordinary private house risk or the insurance may be invalidated or allow the children of any servant or caretaker to live on the premises.

6. THE TENANT will not waste or permit to be wasted any water on the said premises AND will not use the said passages landings and stairs in any way except for the purposes of ingress and egress nor without such licence as aforesaid cut or maim any of the principal timbers or walls of the said premises or any part thereof or in any way alter the plan height elevation or arrangement of the said rooms or erect any additional building therein and thereon nor without such licence as aforesaid assign under-let or part with the possession of the said rooms or any part thereof (but such licence shall not be unreasonably or arbitrarily withheld in repect of a proposed tenant for the whole of the said rooms and premises who shall be shown to be desirable and eligible as to character and means and in every other respect) and such licence shall not be necessary for the under-letting of the whole of the said rooms furnished to some one tenant only for a period not exceeding three months.

7. AND IT IS HEREBY AGREED that if the said rent or rents or any part thereof shall be in arrear for fourteen days (whether the same shall have been legally demanded or not) or if and whenever there shall be a breach by the Tenant of the agreements and conditions rules and regulations above expressed or any of them or if the Tenant shall become bankrupt or suffer any execution to be levied on   goods then it shall be lawful for the Landlords to forthwith re-enter on the said premises without giving any notice to quit and expel the tenant therefrom without the necessity of bringing an ejectment or other legal or equitable proceedings such re-entry not to prejudice any of the legal rights of the Landlords.

8. THE LANDLORDS shall at all times keep the outside of the said mansion and entrance hall staircases and passages leading to the said rooms in good repair plight and condition and properly lighted and shall provide and maintain a proper supply of water and the Tenant paying   rent or rents hereby reserved the Landlords shall pay all existing and future taxes rates charges assessments and impositions whatsoever whether parliamentary parochial or otherwise charged or to be charged in respect of the said premises whatsoever as part of the said mansion or otherwise with the exception of the rent for hire of gas or electric meter or meters and supply of gas electricity or other illuminant to the said rooms.

9. THE LANDLORDS will at their own expense provide at all times during the said term a man servant to act in the capacity of hall porter such man servant to be from time to time appointed and removed by the Landlords at their own absolute discretion.

10. THE TENANT paying the said rent hereby reserved and observing and performing all and singular the agreements and conditions aforesaid on part to be observed and performed shall during the said tenancy quietly hold and enjoy the said rooms without any interruption by the Landlords or any person or persons claiming under them.

11. IT IS FURTHER AGREED that the sum of Two guineas towards the cost of preparing this Agreement shall be borne and paid by the Tenant on the signing hereof and the Tenant shall also pay the Stamp Duty in respect thereof and if the Tenant sub-lets assigns or parts with the possession of the premises under Clause 6 hereof a like sum shall be paid by the Tenant to the Landlords' Solicitor for approving on behalf of the Landlords of the instrument of assignment or sub-letting taking copy and inquiring into the references of the proposed assignee or sub-lessee.

AS WITNESS the hands of the said parties hereto.

SCHEDULE OF RULES AND REGULATIONS.

1. Entrance doors of Flats shall be kept shut, and no Tenant shall, on any account whatever, leave any perambulators, bicycles or velocipedes, boxes, parcels, refuse or rubbish, in the entrance halls, passages, or landings.

2. Tenants shall each morning, before 8.30 A.M., place in the service lifts of their respective Flats, in a proper and convenient form for removal, the ashes, rubbish, and refuse of the previous day.

3. Tenants shall keep all baths, sinks, cisterns, and waste and other pipes connected with their Flats clean and open and in proper repair, and shall be responsible for all damage occasioned to their own, or other Flats, through any breach of this rule, or through the improper use or negligence of themselves or servants, or through the stopping up or bursting of the said pipes, sinks, baths or cisterns.

4. In the event of any Tenant desiring to have electric light fittings or appliances connected with or fitted in the Flat, the person or firm employed to supply such connections, fittings or appliances, or to make any repairs or alterations, or additions, or to do any work in relation thereto, *shall be nominated or previously approved by the Landlords*, but. no electric light shall be introduced into the Flat (unless already provided) without the previous written consent of the Landlords.

5. Passages inside the Flats shall be *carpeted* by the Tenants to deaden any noise of footsteps in the Flats below.

6. No coals or coke shall be delivered by the staircase, but only by the service lift.

7. So far as possible all goods shall be delivered by tradesmen, and all orders taken by them, by means of the service lifts and speaking tubes respectively provided for these purposes.

8. The Landlords will take every reasonable precaution to employ no one but a competent and trustworthy person (or persons) as Hall-porter (or caretaker), but shall not be held responsible for any act committed by the Hall-porter (or caretaker) or any person acting under him, and complaints of any negligence or incivility shall be made to the Landlords, but the Hall-porter, or caretaker, is under no obligation to furnish attendance or other use of his services to Tenants for their private convenience.

9. The tradesmen's lifts and passenger lifts (if any) shall be under the exclusive control of the Hall-porter (or caretaker), or other person appointed by the Landlords, and if any Tenant or their servants or tradesmen cause any damage thereto, the Tenant shall be responsible for such damage.

10. Complaints of all sorts, and applications with regard to external repairs, &c., outside the Flats shall in the first instance be always made to the Hall-porter (or caretaker); and such complaints, differences between the tenants, or disputes of any kind, shall, in the last resort only, be referred to the Landlords, their agent or representative.

11. The Hall-porter or caretaker is charged with the duty of seeing to the carrying out and observance of these Rules and Regulations, reporting any breaches thereof to the Landlords, their agent or representative; enforcing order among the tradespeople, and removing loiterers, beggars, and disorderly persons from the building.

12. The Landlords shall have the right of altering these Rules and Regulations from time to time, but any alterations made by them shall not be binding on the tenants until notified to them by letter or circular.

FORM No. 4.

AN AGREEMENT under seal made the   day of   One thousand nine hundred   Between   hereinafter called "the Landlord" of the one part and   hereinafter called "the Tenant" of the other part (which respective terms "Landlord" and "Tenant" shall include the executors administrators and assigns of the Landlord and Tenant respectively) as follows :—

THE LANDLORD agrees to let to the Tenant who agrees to take the Suite of Rooms distinguished by the number   on the   Floor of the Building known as   in the County of   comprising   Sitting-rooms Bedrooms Kitchen Servant's Bedroom and Lavatory   Together with the exclusive use of the Coal Cellar marked   in the basement of the said building and the use in common with the Landlord and his other Tenants of the Hall Passages Staircases and Lifts in the said building so far as convenient for access to the said Rooms subject to the General Regulations contained in the Schedule hereto which shall be considered as forming part of this Agreement.

TO HOLD the same from the   day of   One thousand nine hundred   for the term of   years thence next ensuing PAYING THEREFOR to the Landlord the yearly rent of   pounds by equal quarterly payments on the usual quarter days that is to say the Twenty-fifth day of March the Twenty-fourth day of June the Twenty-ninth day of September and the Twenty-fifth day of December in each year The first payment to be made on the   day of   next.

THE TENANT shall have possession of the said premises on the   day of   and shall pay   for a proportion of Rent up to the ensuing quarter-day

THE TENANT agrees with the Landlord as follows :

1. To pay the Rent quarterly as aforesaid and also for any Gas or Electric Lighting which shall at the Tenant's request be supplied to the Premises hereby demised.

2. To keep the interior of the Premises and all fixtures therein in good repair and condition and so to yield them up damage by fire excepted. And also as often as occasion shall require to thoroughly sweep and cleanse all chimneys and flues and clean all the windows (inside and out). In place of the usual covenant to clean scour whiten paint paper etc. to pay to the Landlord a sum of money equal to one quarter's rent at the expiration of the term hereby granted or at any time on the determination of the tenancy whether by the Landlord or the Tenant the said sum of money to be in addition to the rent hereinbefore reserved and to be as and for liquidated damages.

3. It shall be lawful for the Landlord and also the Superior Landlord and all persons appointed by them respectively at all reasonable times to enter and view the condition of the Premises. And also to permit the Landlord and the said Superior Landlord and their respective Surveyors and Workmen at all reasonable times to enter the said Rooms and Premises to repair the outside of

the said Building and to exercise and fulfil all the rights and obligations under or subject to which the said Building is held by the Landlord and not at any time after the Tenant shall have had notice thereof to suffer or do anything in the said Rooms whereby any such rights or obligations shall be infringed or the performance of them prevented.

4. Not to pull down or alter or in any wise interfere with the construction or arrangement of the Premises nor injure any of the walls timbers or floors thereof. Not to use or permit the Premises or any part thereof to be used for the purpose of any trade or business or for any profession or otherwise than as a private dwelling-house nor allow any auction sale or any meeting for any religious political or other purpose to take place therein without the Landlord's consent in writing being first obtained. Not to use or permit the Premises or any part thereof to be used for any improper purpose or as the residence of a kept woman or a lunatic idiot or insane person nor keep any dog cat or other animal on the Premises. Not to affix any board placard sign or notice upon any external part of the Premises or on or in any of the windows thereof nor hang or allow to be hung any clothes or other articles on the outside of the Premises. Not to waste or permit to be wasted any water on the Premises. Not to use the passages landings and stairs of the Premises in any way except for the purpose of ingress and egress. And particularly not to do or suffer to be done on the Premises or any part thereof any act or thing that may be or grow to be a nuisance annoyance injury damage or danger to the Landlord or the Superior Landlord for the time being or their respective Tenants or any of them nor do or suffer to be done in upon or with respect to the Premises anything which may injure or tend to injure the character of the said Building as one for private residences or to diminish the quietude privacy and value of the said Building.

5. Not to assign underlet or to part with the possession of the Premises or any part thereof without the consent in writing of the Landlord first obtained and a copy of the Assignment or other document delivered to the Landlord.

6. In case the rent hereby reserved shall be unpaid for twenty-one days after any of the days whereon the same ought to be paid as aforesaid (although the payment may not have been legally demanded) or in case the Tenant shall remove the furniture and cease to reside in the Premises for a period exceeding two calendar months or shall fail to observe and keep all the agreements on the Tenant's part hereinbefore contained it shall be lawful for the Landlord to exclude the Tenant entirely from and to re-enter on the Premises and to determine the tenancy hereby created and to make such re-entry by force without any process of law and this Agreement may be pleaded in bar to any action for such forcible entry; and in the event of such determination of the tenancy between any two of the said quarter-days a proportion of the said Rent up to the day of the determination of the tenancy shall thereupon be payable.

THE LANDLORD hereby agrees with the Tenant as follows :—

1. To pay all taxes rates and assessments (including water rate) in respect of the premises and to indemnify the Tenant therefrom.

2. To keep the said Building externally and also internally so far as the use thereof in common is hereby let in good tenantable repair and condition and in case of damage by fire to cause the same to be repaired or reinstated as soon as they reasonably can and if the Premises or any part thereof shall be destroyed or damaged by fire to cause the same to be reinstated or repaired with all reasonable speed.

IN WITNESS whereof the said parties hereto have hereunto set their hands and seals the day and year first above written.

THE SCHEDULE ABOVE REFERRED TO.
GENERAL REGULATIONS.

The entrance to the Building and the care of entrance will be in the charge of a Porter appointed and removed by the Landlord.

Tenants have the right to the services of the Porter as hereinafter defined and which are to be performed free of charge and are as follows :—

(a) To be in attendance in the Building or Buildings committed to his charge either by himself or some trustworthy assistant.

(b) To work the passenger lift and convey the Tenants and their friends up and down from 8.30 A.M. till 11 P.M.

(The passenger lift shall not be used for tradespeople or servants or for the conveyance of bicycles or luggage. Whenever requisite the Landlord shall have a reasonable time allowed for repairing and re-adjusting the machinery.)

(c) To cleanse the general stairs passages lifts and entrances attached to the section and attend to the lighting therein.

(d) To receive and deliver to the Tenants parcels and messages.

(e) To deliver coal from the Tenant's coal cellar and to remove dust before 9 A.M.

NOTE.—The above Regulations may be altered or modified by the Landlord from time to time as circumstances may require but not so as to reduce the services to be rendered by the Porter as aforesaid. Neither the Porter or Under Porters are allowed to render any private service to Tenants except as above-mentioned.

Signed sealed and delivered by the
    above-named

    in the presence of

Signed sealed and delivered by the
    above-named

FORM No. 5.

THIS INDENTURE made the   day of   One thousand nine hundred and   BETWEEN   of   in the County of   (hereinafter called the Lessor) of the one part and   of   in the County of   (hereinafter called the Lessee) of the other part WITNESSETH that in consideration of the rent hereinafter reserved and of the covenants and agreements on the part of the Lessee and conditions hereinafter contained THE Lessor DOTH hereby demise unto the Lessee ALL that Flat consisting of Entrance Hall, Drawing Room, Dining Room,   best Bedrooms, Bath Room, best W.C. and Linen Cupboard and also the Servant's Bedroom, Wine Store, Larder, Kitchen, Scullery and W.C. all being situate on the   floor and forming Flat No.   on that floor being part of a messuage situate and being in   in the County of   and known as   and which messuage is hereinafter referred to as "the Mansions." Together with the use by the Lessee his visitors friends and servants and others of the Common Entrance Hall, Passenger Lift and Service Lift, stairs and passage leading to the Rooms, and the Tradesmen's Entrance, in common with the Lessor and his servants and the other tenants and occupiers of the Mansions (except and reserved unto the Lessor and the person or persons for the time being occupying any other part or parts of the Mansions the passage of gas water and other pipes and the electric light wires passing through the demised premises and the free running of gas water soil and other matters and the electric light wires passing through the demised premises and the free running of gas water soil and other matters and the electric light in and through the pipes and wires connected with the demised premises) TO HOLD the same unto the Lessee for the term of Twenty-One years from the   day of   One thousand nine hundred and   YIELDING AND PAYING during the said term the yearly rent of   payable quarterly on the four usual quarter days clear of all deductions whatsoever the first of such quarterly payments to be made on the   day of   One thousand nine hundred and   AND ALSO YIELDING AND PAYING a proportionate part of the said rent for the fraction of the current quarter up to and immediately upon the determination of the said term in case the same shall determine under the proviso for re-entry hereinafter contained AND the Lessee doth hereby covenant with the Lessor in manner following.

1. THAT he the Lessee will during the said term pay the said rent on the days and in manner aforesaid and also will pay for all gas water and electric light consumed upon the demised premises and also will pay monthly for all coal supplied by the Lessor as hereinafter provided And further will provide a small sanitary dust bin for daily use in the Kitchen and will cause such dust bin to be sent daily down the Service lift between the hours of eight and ten A.M., and emptied into the dust bin provided by the Lessor in the basement And the demised premises being now in good decorative repair and condition will at his own expense during the said term repair maintain and keep the demised premises with their appurtenances in as good decorative repair and condition as

they are now in And will also make good any damage done or permitted by the Lessee to the outside Balconies, Railings, Terra Cotta or Brickwork. And will once in every seventh year of the said term paint the whole of the wood and ironwork of or belonging to the demised premises where now or usually painted with two coats at least of good oil colour And also paper grain varnish polish gild colour and whitewash all the parts of the said demised premises now or usually papered grained varnished polished gilded coloured and whitewashed in a workmanlike manner And the last painting papering graining varnishing polishing gilding colouring and whitewashing of the demised premises to be done in the month immediately preceding the determination of this Lease whether by effluxion of time or notice. And will at the end of the tenancy deliver up the demised premises and the landlord's fixtures as enumerated in the Schedule signed by the parties hereto and all other appurtenances to the demised premises belonging in such good state and decorative repair and condition as aforesaid (damage by accidental fire excepted) And will keep all the chimneys and flues thoroughly swept and cause all the windows belonging to the demised premises to be cleaned at least once a month And will keep all sinks cisterns and waste pipes connected with the demised premises clean and open and will be responsible for all damage occasioned through the bursting or stopping up of pipes if caused by his negligence And will not allow any dirt rubbish rags or other refuse on any account to be thrown down any W.C.

2. AND will not use or permit the demised premises or any part thereof to be used for the purpose of any trade or business or carry on therein the profession of a Musician, Teacher of singing or any musical instrument or any other profession whatever without the license in writing of the Lessor or as a brothel private madhouse or receptacle for lunatics or insane persons but will keep and use the same as and for a private residence only And will not keep or permit to be kept on the demised premises any bird dog cat or other animal which occasions annoyance to the other tenants and after the keeping thereof shall have been objected to by the Lessor And will not except when reasonable or necessary allow any tradesman to go up the principal stairs or use the Passenger Lift.

3. AND will not suffer to be erected or placed upon any part of the demised premises any steam engine forge furnace or any placards posters or advertisements whatsoever or any blind signboard plate or other contrivance or thing conveying a notification of trade or business or do or suffer anything which may be or grow to the annoyance of the Lessor or his Tenants or do or suffer to be done anything which may injure or tend to injure the character of the Mansions as a private residence but will as much as lies in his power contribute to the respectability of the Mansions.

4. AND will conform to any reasonable regulations which the Lessor shall at any time make with regard to the management of the Mansions on such regulations being communicated to the Lessee.

5. AND also that he the Lessee will allow the Lessor and his Agents and workmen at all reasonable times in the daytime upon reasonable notice to enter

upon the demised premises to repair the outside of the Mansions and will also allow the Lessor and his Agents with or without workmen at all seasonable times in the daytime to enter and view the condition of the demised premises and of all defects then and there found to give notice in writing on the demised premises for the Lessee to repair and amend the same within the space of three calendar months next after such notice within which time the Lessee will well and sufficiently repair and amend the same accordingly.

6. AND will allow the workmen of the Lessor and his tenants of the adjoining premises (such tenants having previously obtained the consent in writing of the Lessor) at all reasonable times in the daytime to enter into the demised premises for the purpose of repairing the adjoining premises making reasonable compensation to the Lessee for all damage occasioned thereby.

7. AND will not alter the plan height elevation architectural decoration or arrangement of the demised premises or erect any additional building thereon nor assign underlet or part with the possession of the demised premises or any part thereof without the license in writing of the Lessor such License not to be unreasonably or arbitrarily withheld and not to be necessary for the underletting of the demised premises furnished for a period not exceeding six calendar months and will furnish a copy of every such Assignment or Underletting save as aforesaid to the Lessor's Solicitors and pay them a fee of One Guinea for such License and in respect of such copy.

8. PROVIDED ALWAYS And it is hereby agreed that if the said rent hereby reserved or any part thereof shall be in arrear for the space of twenty-one days (whether legally demanded or not) or in case there shall be a breach of the covenants hereinbefore contained on the Lessee's part then it shall be lawful for the Lessor to re-enter upon the demised premises or any part thereof in the name of the whole and thereupon the said term hereby created shall absolutely cease and determine.

9. AND the Lessor doth hereby Covenant with the Lessee that the Lessee paying the said rent hereby reserved and performing and observing the several covenants by the Lessee hereinbefore contained may peaceably hold and enjoy the demised premises during the said term without any interruption by the Lessor or any person or persons lawfully claiming through him AND FURTHER that he the Lessor will during the continuance of the said term keep the outside of the Mansions and the Lifts Common Entrance Hall passage staircases and tradesmen's entrance leading to and from the demised premises clean and in good and substantial repair but the Lessee is not to be entitled to any compensation in respect of any reasonable stoppage in the working of the lifts And will by all means in his power provide and maintain a proper supply of water and will cleanse and keep cleansed and in good order and condition the main soil and main waste pipes outside the demised premises and will provide the Lessee with three latch keys to the front door of the demised premises and with one latch key to the main entrance door to the Mansions and will provide and deliver into the Lessee's Coal Bunkers upon the demised premises in sacks of one hundred and twelve lbs. each kitchen or house coal at the current price of the day for coal delivered at customer's doors And will pay all taxes rates assessments charges and impositions charged upon the demised premises

whether as part of the Mansions or otherwise with the exception of the Water Rate and Gas or Electric Lighting Rate to be charged for Water and Gas or Electric Light consumed or used on the demised premises and that he the Lessor will at his own expense provide at all times during the said term a Man servant who shall act in the capacity of Hall Porter and Lift Attendant and who shall attend to the Passenger Lift from ten A.M. to eleven P.M. and who shall also haul or carry coals to the outside of the demised premises whenever reasonably required by the Lessee between the hours of eight and ten A.M. and keep the Landing immediately leading to or adjoining the demised premises properly washed cleansed whitened and dusted at least once in each week such Man servant to be from time to time appointed and removed by the Lessor at his own absolute discretion and that he the Lessor will at his own expense insure and unless where any Policy or Policies shall be vacated or forfeited by any act of the Lessee keep insured the demised premises (either separately or jointly) with all the other Flats in the Mansions in an adequate sum against loss or damage by fire in some respectable Insurance Office and will produce to the Lessee whenever required the Policy or Policies of such Insurance and the receipts for the then current year's premium or premiums and will lay out all moneys which shall be received under or by virtue of any such Policy or Policies in case the demised premises are insured separately or a due proportion of such moneys in case they are insured jointly with any other premises in rebuilding or repairing such parts of the demised premises as shall have been destroyed or damaged by fire   And also will keep the Entrance Hall Staircase and Passages at all reasonable times sufficiently lighted PROVIDED ALWAYS And it is hereby declared that if during the continuance of the said term the demised premises shall be burnt down or so damaged by fire as to be unfit for occupation and the same shall not be rendered fit for occupation within twelve calendar months from the happening of such fire then and in such case (provided the Lessee shall have done no act whereby the Lessor shall be prevented from receiving the moneys assured to be paid by any Policy of Insurance effected upon the premises) the rent hereby reserved shall from and after the expiry of such twelve calendar months be suspended and the Lessee shall not be liable to pay the same during such time thereafter as the demised premises shall remain unfit for occupation PROVIDED ALSO   And it is hereby lastly agreed and declared that if the Lessee shall be desirous of determining this demise at the end of the first seven or fourteen years and of such his desire shall deliver to the Lessor or leave at his usual or last known place of abode in England or Wales six calendar months next before the expiration of such seven or fourteen years then and in such case at the end of such seven or fourteen years as the case may be the said term hereby granted shall absolutely cease and determine but without prejudice to any right of the Lessor in respect of any breaches of any of the Lessee's covenants herein contained And it is declared that where the context allows the expressions "the Lessor" and "the Lessee" used in these presents include besides the said his executors administrators and assigns and besides the said   his executors administrators and assigns IN WITNESS whereof the said parties to these presents have hereunto set their hands and seals the day and year first above written.

———

THE SCHEDULE ABOVE REFERRED TO.

FORM No. 6.

MEMORANDUM OF AGREEMENT made the   day of   one thousand nine hundred and   BETWEEN   a limited Company whose registered office is at   (hereinafter called "the Landlords") of the one part and   of   (hereinafter called "the Tenant") of the other part whereby it is agreed as follows:

1. The Landlord agrees to Let and the Tenant agrees to take All that Suite of Apartments consisting of   rooms bath-room and   W.C. known or intended to be known as Number   on the   floor of   in the Parish of   in the County of

2. The said tenancy shall be for the term of   years commencing on the   day of   at a rental of £   per annum payable quarterly the first payment to be made on the   day of   next and thereafter the payments to be made on the usual quarter days without any deduction whatsoever.

3. The Tenant will pay all charges for electric light and gas consumed by him on the said premises and will also pay to the Landlord the sum of one guinea per annum payable quarterly together with and in addition to the rent towards the expense of the lighting and cleansing of the entrance and staircase to the said mansions and of one guinea further and payable as aforesaid for the use and keep of the roof-garden.

4. The Tenant will occupy the said rooms only as private dwelling-rooms and will not carry on thereupon any business profession or calling of any kind nor receive boarders (without the previous consent in writing of the Landlord) therein nor store therein any material or thing of a dangerous or inflammable character or do anything or erect or fit any stove which might invalidate or affect or increase the premium on any insurance of the said premises and will not do or suffer to be done on the said premises any act or thing which may be or grow to be a scandal nuisance annoyance or disturbance to the Landlord for the time being or to the other Tenants of the said messuage or of the adjoining premises or which may tend to injure the character of the said messuage.

5. The Tenant will not keep on the said premises any live animals without the written consent of the Landlord first obtained and will not shake or allow to be shaken or beaten any mats or rugs or any other thing or hang or allow to be hung any linen or clothes out of the windows or on the landings or staircases of the said messuages nor expose the same upon the land attached to the said messuage and also will not permit any sale by auction therein nor exhibit any notice on any part of the said premises nor waste any water therein. No pianoforte or other musical instrument shall be played so as to cause annoyance or discomfort to other Tenants.

6. The Tenant will not assign or underlet the said suite of apartments and premises or any room or part thereof without the license in writing of the Landlord first had and obtained which shall not be unreasonably withheld.

7. The Tenant shall not allow any person or persons or children under his

control to loiter or play in the entrance way landings or stairs of the said messuage and shall not suffer the said premises to be soiled by the carrying of coal or other articles (except as hereinafter provided for) and shall not use the same in any way except for the purpose of ingress egress and regress. He shall not put or suffer to be put any boxes or obstacle whatever upon the said landings or staircase. He shall not suffer any coal or other articles which tend to soil the landings and staircase or to block the same to be brought on the premises after eight in the morning of any day.

8. The Tenant shall and will dispose without delay of all dirt and ashes from the premises by throwing the same into the ash shoot or receptacle provided for that purpose but no vegetable corruptible objectionable or obstructive matter must be so disposed of until thoroughly burnt to ashes and once in every two months of the said term properly clean the windows belonging to the said demised premises.

9. On the determination or expiration of the said tenancy the Tenant will deliver up the said premises with all Landlord's fixtures to the Landlord in as good order and condition as the same now are in reasonable use wear and tear in the meantime and damage by fire only excepted.

10. The Landlord may by himself or his Agents at all reasonable times in the day time be at liberty to enter and view the state and condition of the said premises and within one month prior to the determination of the said tenancy the Landlord shall be at liberty to put up a bill on such part of the said premises as he may think fit intimating that the said premises are to be let and the Tenant will not during such period remove or deface the said notice and will permit at all reasonable hours intending Tenants to view the said premises.

11. The Tenant will not cut maim or injure any of the principal timbers or walls of the said suite of apartments and will not make any alteration in the architectural decorations thereof or make any additions thereto without the consent of the Landlord in writing first had and obtained.

12. The Landlord will keep the entrance and staircase properly lighted and in good repair and free from dirt and will pay all rates taxes and charges (including water rate but excluding Tenants' gas and electric rate) payable by Landlord in respect of the said premises.

13. The Landlord will not be responsible for any losses or injuries arising from or alleged to arise from the negligence of any of his tenants or the negligence or misfeasance of any of his servants.

14. PROVIDED ALWAYS that if the said yearly rent hereby reserved or any part thereof shall be behind and unpaid for the space of fourteen days after any of the days whereon the same ought to be paid as aforesaid whenever the same shall be legally demanded or not or if the Tenant shall commit any breach of any of the agreements on the part of the Tenant hereinbefore contained then and in any such case it shall and may be lawful for the Landlord to enter upon the said premises and the Tenant and all occupiers to expel (and by force if necessary) and for such purpose may break open any door or window and this

Agreement shall be deemed a license and authority for such purpose or purposes and so long as the Tenant continues to observe the conditions herein contained he shall be entitled to enjoy peaceable and quiet possession of the said premises during the said term.

15. The Tenant shall pay to the Solicitors of the Landlord the sum of one guinea the costs of this Agreement and five shillings or such sum as may be required for the stamp on the counterpart. As Witness the hands of the parties hereto.

}.. .

....

FORM No. 7.

AGREEMENT made the   day of   One thousand nine hundred
                    BETWEEN   hereinafter called
      "the Landlords" of the one part and
      hereinafter called "the Tenant" of the other part which respective terms
      "Landlords" and "Tenant" shall include the executors administrators
      and assigns of the Landlords and Tenants respectively as follows :—

THE LANDLORDS agree to let to the Tenant who agrees to take the Suite of Rooms distinguished by the Number   on the   Floor of the Building known as   in the County of   comprising   Reception Rooms   Bedrooms Kitchen Servant's Bedroom and Lavatory. Together with the exclusive use of the Coal Cellar marked   in the area of the said Building and the use in common with the Landlords and their other Tenants of the Hall Passages Staircases and Lifts in the said Building so far as convenient for access to the said Rooms subject to the General Regulations contained in the Schedule hereto which shall be considered as forming part of this Agreement.

TO HOLD the same from the   day of   One thousand nine hundred   for the term of   years thence next ensuing

PAYING THEREFOR to the Landlords the yearly rent of   and also as further rent the sum of   towards the cost of Rates Taxes Lighting and cleaning Staircase and general Maintenance by equal quarterly payments on the usual quarter days that is to say the Twenty-fifth day of March the Twenty-fourth day of June the Twenty-ninth day of September and the Twenty-fifth day of December in each year. The first payment to be made on the   day of

THE TENANT shall have possession of the said premises on the   day of   and shall pay   for a proportion of Rent up to the ensuing quarter-day

THE TENANT agrees with the Landlords as follows :—

1. To pay the rent as aforesaid together with the quarterly sum of

for service in general with other Tenants for removing dust and carrying up coal each morning.

2. To keep the interior of the Premises and all fixtures therein in good repair and condition and so to yield them up damage by fire excepted. And also as often as occasion shall require to thoroughly sweep and cleanse all chimneys and flues and clean all the windows. In place of the usual covenant to clean scour whiten paint paper &c. to pay to the Landlords a sum of money equal to one quarter's rent at the expiration of the term hereby granted or at any time on the determination of the tenancy whether by the Landlords or the Tenant the said sum of money to be in addition to the rent hereinbefore reserved and to be as and for liquidated damages.

3. It shall be lawful for the Landlords and also the Superior Landlords and all persons appointed by them respectively at all reasonable times to enter and view the condition of the Premises. And also to permit the Landlords and the said Superior Landlords and their respective Surveyors and Workmen at all reasonable times to enter the said Rooms and Premises to repair the outside of the said Building and to exercise and fulfil all the rights and obligations under or subject to which the said Building is held by the Landlords and not at any time after the Tenant shall have had notice thereof to suffer or do anything in the said Rooms whereby any such rights or obligations shall be infringed or the performance of them prevented.

4. Not to pull down or alter or in any wise interfere with the construction or arrangement of the Premises nor injure any of the walls timbers or floors thereof. Not to use or permit the Premises or any part thereof to be used for the purpose of any trade or business or for any profession or otherwise than as a private dwelling-house nor allow any auction sale or any meeting for any religious political or other purpose to take place therein without the Landlords' consent in writing being first obtained. Not to use or permit the Premises or any part thereof to be used for any improper purpose or as the residence of a kept woman or a lunatic idiot or insane person nor keep any dog cat or other animal on the Premises. Not to affix any board placard sign or notice upon any external part of the Premises or on or in any of the windows thereof nor hang or allow to be hung any clothes or other articles on the outside of the premises. Not to waste or permit to be wasted any water on the Premises. Not to use the passages landings and stairs of the Premises in any way except for the purpose of ingress and egress. And particularly not to do or suffer to be done on the Premises or any part thereof any act or thing that may be or grow to be a nuisance annoyance injury damage or danger to the Landlords or the Superior Landlords for the time being or their respective Tenants or any of them nor do or suffer to be done in upon or with respect to the Premises anything which may injure or tend to injure the character of the said Building as one for private residences or to diminish the quietude privacy or value of the said Building.

5. Not to assign underlet or part with the possession of the Premises or any part thereof without the consent in writing of the Landlords first obtained

such consent not to be unreasonably withheld in the case of a respectable and responsible Tenant.

6. In case the Rent hereby reserved shall be unpaid for twenty-one days after any of the days whereon the same ought to be paid as aforesaid (although the payment may not have been legally demanded) or in case the Tenant shall remove the furniture and cease to reside in the premises for a period exceeding two calendar months or shall fail to observe and keep all the agreements on the Tenant's Part hereinbefore contained it shall be lawful for the Landlords to exclude the Tenant entirely from and to re-enter on the Premises and to determine the tenancy hereby created and to make such re-entry by force without any process of law and this Agreement may be pleaded in bar to any action for such forcible entry: and in the event of such determination of the tenancy between any two of the said quarter-days a proportion of the said Rent up to the day of the determination of the tenancy shall thereupon be payable.

7. That the Landlords shall not be responsible to the Tenant for the acts neglects defaults or misfeazance of any servants or employee of the Landlords either of commission or omission nor for any accidental loss or damage which may at any time during the tenancy be done to the premises or to any of the goods or property of the Tenant thereon by reason of any act neglect or default of any other Tenant in the said messuage or any such servant or employee as aforesaid in breach neglect or non-fulfilment of his duty or arising by reason of the defective working accidental stoppage or breakage of any pipes appliances apparatus or machinery in or connected with or used for the purposes of the said messuage or any other part thereof.

8. And it is hereby agreed and declared that if the tenant should not be desirous of continuing beyond the term hereby granted then six months' notice previous to the expiration of this term shall be given.

9. To pay on the signing hereof the amount of *ad valorem* stamp duty together with the sum of   for copy of this Agreement (if required).

THE LANDLORDS hereby agree with the Tenant as follows :—

1. To pay all taxes rates and assessments (including water rate) in respect of the Premises and to indemnify the Tenant therefrom.

2. To keep the said Building externally and also internally so far as the use thereof in common is hereby let in good tenantable repair and condition and in case of damage by fire to cause the same to be repaired or reinstated as soon as they reasonably can and if the Premises or any part thereof shall be destroyed or damaged by fire to cause the same to be reinstated or repaired with all reasonable speed.

AS WITNESS the hands of the parties hereto the day and year first above written.

THE SCHEDULE ABOVE REFERRED TO

GENERAL REGULATIONS.

The entrance to the building and the care of the entrance will be in the charge of a Porter appointed and removed by the Landlords.

Tenants have the right to the services of the Porter as hereinafter defined.

(a) To be in attendance in the Building or Buildings committed to his charge either by himself or some trustworthy assistant.

(b) To work the passenger lift and convey the Tenants and their friends up and down from 8.30 A.M. to 11 P.M.

[The passenger lift shall not be used for tradespeople or servants or for the conveyance of bicycles or luggage. Whenever requisite the Landlords shall have a reasonable time allowed for repairing and re-adjusting the machinery.]

(c) To cleanse the general stairs passages lifts and entrances attached to the section and attend to the lighting therein.

(d) To receive and deliver to the Tenants parcels and messages.

NOTE—The above Regulations may be altered or modified by the Landlords from time to time as circumstances may require but not so as to reduce the services to be rendered by the Porter as aforesaid. Neither the Porter nor Under-Porters are allowed to render any private service to Tenants except as above-mentioned.

Witness {

FORM No. 8.

AN AGREEMENT made the   day of   One thousand nine hundred   BETWEEN   (hereinafter called "the Landlords") of the one part and   (hereinafter called "the Tenant") of the other part WHEREBY IT IS AGREED AS FOLLOWS:—

1. THE Landlords will before the   day of   One thousand nine hundred and   complete upon the premises hereinafter agreed to be demised so as to render such premises fit for immediate occupation by the Tenant ALL and singular the works decorations and finishings specified in the First Schedule hereunder written and will give to the Tenant possession of the premises so completed on the   day of   One thousand nine hundred and

2. THE Landlords will by Deed immediately after the said   day of   One thousand nine hundred and   grant and the Tenant will accept a Lease of ALL that Suite of Rooms closets and passages in the Residential Chambers known as   and on the   floor   thereof which suite of rooms closets and passages comprise Flat No.   Together with the use of a Coal Cellar in the Basement and of the Entrance Hall and Stairs and Lifts leading to the said premises for a term of   years from the   day of   One thousand nine hundred and   determinable nevertheless by the Tenant at the end of the first   years of the said term at the option of the Tenant at a yearly rent of   Pounds payable on the usual quarter days for payment of rent in the year and without any deduction the first quarterly payment to be made on the   day of   One thousand nine hundred and   and the last to be made in advance one calendar month before the expiration of the said term.

3. THE Lease shall be in the form given in the Second Schedule hereunder written and the Tenant will execute and deliver to the Landlords a counterpart of such Lease.

4. THE Lease and counterpart shall be prepared by the Landlords' Solicitors and such Solicitors' costs charges and expenses attending the preparation execution and stamping thereof (this Agreement and duplicate being included in such costs) shall be paid by the Tenant.

As WITNESS the Common Seal of the Landlords and the hand of the Tenant the day and year first above written.

THE FIRST SCHEDULE.

Clercole and distemper white all ceilings and cornices.

Line the walls of all best rooms and paper same with a paper value 7s. 6d. per piece to the drawing and dining rooms 5s. per piece to the best bedrooms and corridor and a 5s. 6d. per piece varnish tile paper in bathroom.

Prepare and paper walls of pantry with a varnished paper value 3s. 6d. per piece and walls of butler's room with sanitary paper value 1s. 6d. per piece corridor and W.C. with a 3s. 6d. per piece varnished tile paper staircase and servants' bedrooms with a paper at 1s. 6d. per piece.

Prepare and paint all woodwork in best rooms and corridor four oils and flat and enamel and that in servants' quarters knot stop prime and paint four oils.

Distemper out coal hole.

THE SECOND SCHEDULE.

FORM OF A LEASE TO BE GRANTED.

THIS INDENTURE made the   day of   19   BETWEEN   (hereinafter called "the Lessors" which expression shall include their successors and assigns) of the one part and   (hereinafter called "the Lessee" which expression shall include his executors

R

administrators and assigns) of the other part WITNESSETH that in consideration
of the rent hereinafter reserved and of the covenants by the Lessee hereinafter
contained the Lessors do hereby demise unto the Lessee ALL THAT suite of
rooms closets and passages in the residential chambers known as   and
on the   floor thereof which suite of rooms closets and passages compose
Flat No.   and a coal cellar in the basement together with the use in common
with the other Tenants of the Lessors of the apparatus for the supply of hot
water for domestic purposes and for heating the said premises and of the
entrance hall and stairs and lifts leading to the same premises TO HAVE
AND TO HOLD the said premises unto the Lessee for the term of
years (determinable nevertheless as hereinafter mentioned) from the
day of   19   YIELDING AND PAYING unto the Lessors
therefor during the said term the yearly rent of £   by equal
quarterly payments on the usual quarter days the first of such quarterly
payments to be made on the   day of   19
and the last quarterly payment to be made in advance one calendar month
before the expiration of the said term such rent to be paid clear of all deductions. AND the Lessee doth hereby covenant with the Lessors that he the
Lessee will during the said term pay unto the Lessors the said rent on the
days and in manner aforesaid AND shall also pay all charges for gas and
electric lighting for the time being payable in respect of the gas or electricity
consumed on the premises hereby demised and a sum of £   per quarter for
water rate AND will not do or permit to be done during the said term any
damage or waste to the said premises AND will at least once in every two
months during the said term properly clean the windows of and belonging to
the said premises AND will as often as occasion requires during the said term
at his own expense without being thereunto required repair maintain and keep
the said premises in such repair and condition that the same shall at all times
be suitable and ready for the occupation of a tenant AND in particular will in
every seventh year paint in the best manner with two coats of paint all the
inside woodwork of the demised premises which are now painted and colour
paper or whitewash all the walls and ceilings of the rooms and passages where
now coloured and papered and whitewashed and in the same character and of
the same quality as the same now are AND will permit the Lessors and all
persons authorised by them at all reasonable times to enter upon the said
premises for the purpose of viewing the condition of the said premises and
giving or leaving in writing a notice upon the said premises for the Lessee of
all defects and wants of repair and acts of misuser there found AND will within
three calendar months after every such notice well and sufficiently repair and
make good such defects and wants of repair and correct such acts of misuser
whereof notice shall have been so given or left But nevertheless without
prejudice to any other right or remedy of the Lessors in respect of such defect
want of repair or misuser AND will at the expiration of the tenancy leave and
deliver up possession of the premises in good repair to the Lessors or as they
may direct Together with all chimney pieces stoves windows doors fastenings
partitions locks keys and all other fixtures matters and things which at the time
of entry of the Lessee on the premises shall be found there or which at any

time during the tenancy shall be added to the premises and so fastened thereto as to be incapable of removal without injury or damage to such premises AND will not without the written consent of the Lessors pull down or alter or in any manner interfere with the construction or arrangement of the premises or cut alter or injure any of the walls timbers or floors of the said premises or in any manner deface or disfigure the walls or ceilings thereof or use or occupy the premises or any part thereof for any unlawful or immoral purpose or for any purpose other than as a private residence or without the previous consent of the Lessors affix any board placard or notice upon any external part of the premises or on any of the windows thereof or leave or deposit any offensive goods or materials on the said premises. AND will not do or allow to be done or allowed in or upon or with respect to the premises anything which may annoy or tend to the annoyance of the other tenants or occupiers of the said mansions or may injure or tend to injure the character thereof as a place for private residence AND in particular will take subject to observe and perform the Rules contained in the Schedule hereto and the Regulations for the time being in force and to be observed by the Tenants of the said Mansions a copy of which said Rules and Regulations shall at all times be placed in a conspicuous position in the entrance hall thereof AND ALSO will not without the consent in writing of the Lessors assign underlet or part with the possession of the premises or any part thereof or any interest therein (except in the case of letting the premises furnished for a term of one year or less which the Lessee is at liberty to do to a respectable Tenant without obtaining permission of the Lessors) BUT IT IS HEREBY AGREED AND DECLARED that the Lessors' consent shall not be withheld unless there shall be a reasonable objection to the character or solvency of the proposed Assignee or Underlessee PROVIDED ALWAYS AND THESE PRESENTS ARE UPON THIS EXPRESS CONDITION that if and whenever any part of the rent hereby reserved shall be in arrear for twenty-one days whether the same shall have been first demanded or not. Or if and whenever there shall be a breach of any of the covenants by the Lessee hereinbefore contained the Lessors may re-enter upon any part of the said premises in the name of the whole and thereupon the said term of   years shall absolutely determine AND the Lessors do hereby covenant with the Lessee that he paying the rent hereby reserved and performing and observing the several covenants by the Lessee hereinbefore contained may peaceably hold and enjoy the said premises during the said term without any interruption by the Lessors or any person or persons lawfully claiming through them or any of them AND further that they the Lessors will during the continuance of the said term pay all rates taxes (other than the charges for gas electric light and water consumed within the premises hereby demised) assessments or impositions Parliamentary parochial or otherwise howsoever charged or to be charged or to which either Landlord or Lessee may become subject in respect of the said premises AND will at their own expense insure (and unless where any policy or policies shall be vacated or forfeited by any act of the Lessee) keep insured the said demised premises (either separately or jointly with all or any of the other Flats in the same Mansions) in an adequate sum against loss or damage by fire in the Law Fire or other good Insurance Office

AND will when thereunto required produce to the Lessee the policy or policies of insurance and the receipts for the premiums and other sums payable for effecting and keeping on foot the said insurance and will lay out all moneys which shall be received under or by virtue of any such policy or policies (in case the said demised premises are insured separately) or a due proportion of such moneys (in case they are insured jointly with any other premises) in rebuilding or repairing such parts of the said premises as shall have been destroyed or damaged by fire AND will during the continuance of the said term at their own expense cleanse and maintain in a proper condition and state of repair the entrance hall door or doorway stairs and lifts leading to the demised premises AND also the main drains pipes and sewers belonging to the said premises and the hot water service both for domestic and heating purposes the Lessors having full power to enter upon the premises hereby demised for the purpose of doing all such works and for examining repairing and replacing any wires for electric lighting cleansing repairing or unstopping any pipes or drains in upon or under the said premises and whether belonging to the same or to any other parts of the said premises the Lessors using all reasonable despatch and making good all damage done to the demised premises and provide a Resident Porter to take charge of the said entrance and to perform all such services for the Lessee and other the Tenants using the same entrance as are usually performed by porters in like establishments PROVIDED ALWAYS AND IT IS HEREBY AGREED that if the said Lessee shall be desirous to determine this present demise at the end of the first   years of the said term and of his desire shall give six calendar months' notice in writing to the Lessors before the expiration of the said
years then and in such case this Lease and every clause and thing herein contained and the term hereby granted shall at the expiration of the said
years henceforward cease and be void in like manner as if the whole of the said term of years had run out and expired without prejudice to any claim which may have arisen between the said parties hereto.

IN WITNESS whereof the Lessors have caused their common seal to be hereunto affixed and the Lessee hath hereunto set his hand and seal the day and year first above written.

SCHEDULE.

RULES AND REGULATIONS TO BE OBSERVED BY THE TENANTS.

1. The front door will be kept closed between the hours of 8 P.M. and 9 A.M. but each Tenant shall be furnished with a latch key which shall not be transferable and shall be given up to the Landlords at the end of the Tenancy.

2. No Tenant shall on any account whatever leave any boxes parcels refuse or rubbish in the passages or on the landings.

3. Each Tenant shall keep all sinks cisterns and waste pipes connected with his apartments clean and open and shall be responsible for all damage occasioned through the bursting or stopping up of pipes if caused by his negligence.

4. No dirt rubbish rags or other refuse shall on any account be thrown down any W.C.

5. No bird dog or other animal shall be kept in any apartment which shall cause annoyance to the other Tenants or after the keeping thereof shall have been objected to by the Landlords.

6. The Landlords will at their own expense provide a porter whose duties shall be as follows :—

(*a*) In the absence of the Landlords to receive all complaints of the Tenants and to see to the due observance of these Rules and Regulations and to report all breaches thereof to the Landlords.

(*b*) By himself or his representative to be at hand to open the front door or otherwise attend to all persons calling between the hours of 8.30 A.M. and 11 P.M.

(*c*) To superintend and work the passenger lifts between the hours of 10 A.M. and 12 P.M.

(*d*) To clean and keep clean the hall and doorstep the passages staircases and landings and lifts.

(*e*) To light the staircases and passages as soon as it becomes dusk.

(*f*) To remove each morning before 9.30 A.M. the ashes rubbish and refuse which shall be placed in the luggage lift in a convenient form for removal by the Tenants' servants.

(*g*) To hoist up each morning a sufficient supply of coal for the day and to raise all goods left with him at the principal entrance for delivery to the separate Flats or otherwise deliver them to the respective Tenants.

7. All provisions are to be supplied by the tradespeople to the different Tenants by means of a lift provided for that purpose and the porter shall not be required to take in any such at the principal entrance.

8. The Landlords will deliver quarterly accounts of the amounts due from each Tenant in respect of the water electric light and gas and such accounts shall be settled at the same time as the then quarter's rent.

9. The porter will be provided with duplicate keys to the entrance doors to each suite of Apartments, but he will only be allowed to use them in case of emergency.

10. Each Tenant is requested to give immediate notice by letter to the Landlords of any incivility want of attention or excessive exercise of authority on the part of the porter.

11. The Landlords shall not be bound by any act of the porter not falling strictly within the duties hereby assigned to him or be responsible for the loss of any parcel left with or entrusted to the porter or his representative.

12. No tradespeople other than those to whom the porter shall give authority shall be permitted to go up the principal stairs either with or without goods. No repairs except such as will not admit of delay shall be carried out between the months of March and August (inclusive) in any year and no plant or materials for repairs decorations or other similar purposes or large articles shall be taken up or down either the stairs or lifts except by previous arrangement

with the porter and as a general rule only between the hours of 6 o'clock and 7.30 in the morning and such stairs and lifts shall only be used by sweeps or other workmen by previous arrangement as aforesaid and sweeps shall not be allowed to ascend or descend except between the above-mentioned hours.

13. All differences between the Tenants concerning these Regulations are to be referred to the Landlords who shall have full power finally to decide the same and they are to have the right of altering any of the foregoing Regulations but any alteration made by them shall be forthwith communicated to the Tenant in writing and shall not bind him or his under-tenants unless assented to by him or in case of difference respecting the same unless such difference has been settled by arbitration in accordance with the provisions of the Arbitration Act 1889 or any statutory modification thereof at least fourteen days before such alteration shall take effect.

14. Nothing in the above Regulations contained shall be construed as in any way limiting the operations of any of the provisions in the Leases under which the Tenants hold.

INDEX.

*(For Names of Architects whose Work is Illustrated see Separate List at the beginning,
pp.* xiii *and* xiv.)

www.ingramcontent.com/pod-product-compliance
Lightning Source LLC
Chambersburg PA
CBHW081427270326
41932CB00019B/3121